The Mental Corpus

'Linguists have long since lost the paradise of intuitions. John Taylor, a leading cognitive linguist, argues, convincingly and with a lot of intriguing examples (such as the collocational difference between 'total failure' and 'total success'), that linguists, no longer able to afford to sit in an armchair, should turn seriously to corpora in people's minds. *The Mental Corpus*, focusing on usage-based analyses of real-world expressions, covers idioms, constructions, collocations, frequency, polysemy, and blending, and does so in a crystal-clear, highly readable style.'

Ken-ichi Seto, *Bukkyo University*

'A refreshing and thoroughly empirical approach to the linguistic description of English. John Taylor's rich collection of examples drawn from the corpora shows that the traditional parts-of-speech (noun, verb, etc.) and their subclasses (e.g., mass noun, transitive verb, etc.) cannot possibly be defined in any consistent way. Instead, he proposes that speakers rely on a rich linguistic memory containing vast numbers of exemplar patterns. This revolutionary story is told in a very readable style that will interest many laymen as well as linguists, psychologists of language and teachers of English-as-a-second-language. The book serves as a profound attack on some of the most fundamental assumptions of modern linguistics and should be read by all who have an interest in how a language really works.'

Robert Port, *Professor of Linguistic and Cognitive Science, Indiana University*

The Mental Corpus

How Language is Represented in the Mind

JOHN R. TAYLOR

OXFORD
UNIVERSITY PRESS

OXFORD
UNIVERSITY PRESS

Great Clarendon Street, Oxford OX2 6DP
United Kingdom

Oxford University Press is a department of the University of Oxford.
It furthers the University's objective of excellence in research, scholarship,
and education by publishing worldwide. Oxford is a registered trade mark of
Oxford University Press in the UK and in certain other countries

First published 2012
First published in paperback 2014

Impression: 1

Published in the United States of America by Oxford University Press
198 Madison Avenue, New York, NY 10016, United States of America

British Library Cataloguing in Publication Data

Data available

ISBN 978-0-19-929080-2 (Hbk.)
ISBN 978-0-19-929081-9 (Pbk.)

Contents

1

Conceptualizing language

Readers of this book will probably be familiar with the following situation. You are preparing a speech, a paper, or a report. You remember having read something recently which would fit in beautifully with what you are now working on. You would like to quote it, or at least include a reference to it. The trouble is, you didn't bookmark the page or highlight the passage in the margin. And you don't have the time or the inclination to re-read a 200-page book in search of a single quotation.

Fortunately, help may be at hand. Although you cannot remember where in the book the passage occurred, you do have a mental image of where on the page it was located, say, somewhere on the left-hand page, about one-third of the way down, a couple of lines into a new paragraph. You page through the book, scanning the left-hand pages, glancing at the paragraphs beginning about a third of the way from the top. Quite often the strategy works and in a matter of minutes you have located the passage. More often than not, the passage does indeed turn out to be relevant to your current project.

Many people that I have discussed this with report experiences of this kind. Sceptics, to be sure, might wonder whether there is any real effect here. Perhaps we just remember the few successful outcomes of the strategy and suppress the numerous failures. As a matter of fact, the reality of the 'position of text on the page phenomenon' has been confirmed experimentally (Lovelace and Southall 1983; Rothkopf 1971). Not only this, but memory for position on the page correlates with memory for content: readers who remember the content tend also to remember its location, and when we are denied the possibility of remembering location (as when we scroll down a text on a computer screen) our comprehension of the text may be hindered. People who prefer to read documents in hard copy may have a point (O'Hara, Sellen, and Bentley 1999).

Here, though, I want to emphasize some other aspects of the phenomenon. It illustrates, firstly, the importance in our mental life of EPISODIC MEMORY, that is, our ability to recall specific episodes in the past, sometimes with great clarity, as well as our ability to recall INCIDENTAL features of a situation. When you were reading that book several weeks ago, you were not planning the speech or the report that you are now working on; otherwise you would probably have underlined or highlighted the passage in question. But now, focusing on your new project, you recall something you came across earlier and which may not have been central to your interests at the time. Moreover, when you were reading the book, you were almost certainly focusing on its content, not on the page layout. Nevertheless, in order to access the content you had to process the printed words, positioned on the page. It seems that this incidental property of the text is not only remembered, but remembered in association with its content.

When searching for that elusive quotation, you have an EXPLICIT, or conscious memory of its location on the page. Very often, however, we are not able to consciously recall past experiences. Nevertheless, these past experiences must have been recorded, for they influence our behaviour on subsequent tasks. In this case we may speak of IMPLICIT memories (Schacter 1987). As an illustration of this phenomenon, compare the two sentences in (1):

(1)   a. The trip was a total failure.
       b. The trip was a total success.

Both of these are fully acceptable English sentences. The first, however, is likely to be judged 'more idiomatic' than the second: *a total failure* somehow 'sounds better' than *a total success*. Why should this be so? One factor could be that *total failure* has a much higher frequency of occurrence in the language than *total success*.[1] Our intuitions with regard to (1), then, would simply reflect our previous experience with the language. Notice, however, what this account entails. It entails that speakers have been keeping a mental record of the number of times they have heard *total* in association with various nouns. You might not be able to recall a single occasion on which you heard any of these word combinations and you certainly have not been consciously keeping count of them. Nevertheless, intuitions with regard to the sentences in (1) strongly suggest that speakers have implicit memories of their experience of the language pertaining, in this case, to the frequency with which a word combination has been encountered. It is almost as if speakers have been tallying the number of times they have heard the word in association with other words.

Suppose that we generalize from this observation to considering the nature of linguistic knowledge in general. Suppose that our knowledge of a language (English, let us say) is in large part constituted by (mostly implicit) memories of past linguistic experiences. Let us suppose further that learning a language consists in building up this memory store and that our performance on a linguistic task—be it producing language in speaking or writing, comprehending language when listening or reading, or even judging the acceptability of a phrase as in the task presented above—is a function of our accumulated memories. This is the thesis that I want to advance in

---

[1] *Total failure* occurs about four times more often in the language than *total success*. Grounds for making this assertion will be given later in this chapter.

this book. The title—the mental corpus—is intended to capture the idea that language as represented in the brain is analogous to a collection of texts, that is, a corpus, and that knowledge of a language consists in knowledge of the kinds of facts that are recorded in a corpus and that can be extracted from it.

The idea that people go around with collections of texts in their heads might seem preposterous. Even more preposterous is the idea that having a collection of texts in the head is all there is to knowing a language. The notion of the mental corpus should not, of course, be taken too literally. There are, in particular, three ways in which the mental corpus differs from a conventional corpus. These concern its content, its format, and its temporal dynamics.

    a. *Content.* According to the mental corpus thesis, each linguistic encounter lays down a trace in memory. The trace pertains not only to the linguistic signal as such, but also to the context in which it is encountered. The context may include the characteristics of the speaker (her accent and voice quality, for example), and features of the situation in which the utterance is encountered, as well as the presumed semantic intent of the speaker. The mental corpus is therefore vastly more rich in detail than any available text collection, in that each element is indexed for its contextual features. The elements in question may be speech sounds, words, or combinations of words.

    b. *Format.* A text has a linear structure; some things occur before others. While the sequence of events may well be recorded in memory, it may be more useful to think of the mental corpus as having a hypertext format, with each element being linked up with (and providing access to) countless other elements, on the basis of their similarity or in virtue of shared indexing. The format thus permits a degree of generalization to emerge from the myriad impressions laid down in the memory traces.

    c. *Temporal dynamics.* Memory traces do not endure forever. While the mental corpus is constantly being updated with new linguistic experiences, traces laid down long ago may be subject to decay.

In making the case for the mental corpus, I will be appealing above all to the linguistic evidence—the evidence of what people actually say. I make no excuse for focusing primarily on the linguistic evidence. I am, by profession, a linguist, not a psychologist, neurologist, or brain scientist. While other disciplines must obviously have their part to play in a fully worked out theory of language and the mind, I shall be mainly concerned with the kinds of data which any such theory must be able to accommodate. It will be my contention that the linguistic evidence, if properly evaluated, leads to the conclusion that speakers have recorded very specific facts of usage, pertaining to such matters as the frequency with which items have been encountered and the contexts in which they have been used. A further claim is that memory traces, linked by patterns of similarity and related by emergent generalizations, are all there is to knowing a language. How this knowledge might be neurally implemented is not my concern. From my perspective as a linguist, however, the stakes are high. At issue is the nature of linguistic knowledge and its relation to language as we encounter it.

E-language and I-language

When linguists study a language, what exactly are they studying? The question hinges on how we define 'a language'. There are, broadly speaking, two approaches to the matter.[2] On one approach, a language is defined by what people say (and write); a language, in other words, is an 'external' object, a set of utterances (spoken and written). The other approach sees a language as an 'internal' object, that is, as a body of knowledge residing in the brains of its speakers.

The external approach was endorsed by Bloomfield. In his 'Postulates for linguistic analysis', Bloomfield (1957 [1926]: 26) defined a language as "the totality of utterances that can be made in a speech-community".[3] A notable feature of this definition is that it refers to a potential, not to an actual object. A language is not constituted by the totality of utterances that *have* been made in a speech community, but to the totality of utterances that *can* be made. In principle—though obviously not in practice—it might be possible to obtain a record of the totality of utterances that have been made; suppose, for example, that every speaker went around with a permanently switched-on tape recorder.[4] A more realistic objective would be to assemble a representative sample of the utterances that have been made. Many of the available corpora, such as the 100 million word British National Corpus (BNC; Davies 2004-)[5] or the 400 million word Corpus of Contemporary American English (COCA; Davies 2008-)[6] were compiled with this objective in mind. There are, as we shall see, some serious conceptual problems associated with the notion of a representative sample of utterances. Leaving these issues aside, it will be clear that a sampling of actual utterances does not, indeed cannot, address the status of language as a potential object. The fact that some particular combination of words has never been uttered, or is not in the

---

[2] This section elaborates ideas presented in Taylor (2010).

[3] The definition presupposes that we are able to identify 'a speech community'. Since 'a language' is defined by reference to 'a speech community', it would be circular to define a speech community in terms of a shared language. Bloomfield got round this problem by defining a speech community as consisting of individuals who agree that certain utterances are 'the same' as other utterances. Thus, *I'm hungry*, spoken by different people, in different circumstances, would count, for members of the speech community, as 'the same'.

[4] With respect to the linguistic experience of a young child, the aim of recording the totality of utterances, both heard and spoken, may be more easily attainable (at least, over a limited time period); see Tomasello and Stahl (2004).

[5] http://www.natcorp.ox.ac.uk/

[6] http://www.americancorpus.org/

sample, does not rule out the possibility that some day it may be uttered. On the other hand, the non-occurrence of some expression might be an indication that it could not, in principle, occur. Sampling what people have said, or even collecting a complete record of what people have said, would not enable us to decide between these two possibilities.

Considerations such as these led some linguists—Chomsky most notably—to shift the focus of attention from E-LANGUAGE, that is, 'external' language, as encountered in the world, to the study of I-LANGUAGE, or 'internal language', that is, the system of knowledge which resides in speakers' brains and which underlies their linguistic performance.[7] A language thus comes to be seen, not as a set of utterances and their properties, but as a device for generating all (and only) the grammatical sentences of a language, where the grammaticality of a sentence is determined not by reference to its occurrence on the lips of speakers, but by appeal to the intuitions of native speakers:

> ...the study of generative grammar shifted the focus of attention from actual or potential behavior and the product of behavior to the system of knowledge that underlies the use and understanding of language, and more deeply, to the innate endowment that makes it possible for humans to attain such knowledge. The shift in focus was from the study of E-language to the study of I-language, from the study of language regarded as an externalized object to the study of the system of knowledge of language attained and internally represented in the mind/ brain. A generative grammar is not a set of statements about externalized objects constructed in some manner. Rather, it purports to depict exactly what one knows when one knows a language: that is, what has been learned, as supplemented by innate principles.
>
> (Chomsky 1986: 24)

Chomsky motivated this shift, in part, through the observation that E-language is not a well-defined object. Do we include dialectal speech, slang, and specialized jargons in E-language? What about evident mistakes? Speakers do sometimes commit slips of the tongue; they also make false starts, they may change the structure of a sentence in mid-stream, and often leave their sentences incomplete. The crucial issue, however, concerns the 'creativity'[8] of language use. Speakers do not learn sentences; rather, they have learned the principles which can generate any and every grammatical sentence.

The 'cognitive turn' initiated by Chomsky accords, by and large, with the everyday, non-specialist use of the term 'language' and what it means to 'know a language'. If

---

[7] It is important to bear in mind that I-language does not refer to inner speech, that is, the language that we use when silently 'talking to ourselves'. In terms of Chomsky's distinction, inner speech is an example of E-language.

[8] 'Creativity', as used here, is a technical term of Chomskyan linguistics, and refers to the fact that speakers can put words together to form grammatical sentences in ways that they have not previously experienced. For further discussion, see Chapter 11.

we say that a person 'knows English', we certainly do not mean that she knows the totality of English utterances, nor even that she has committed to memory a representative sample of English utterances. In speaking of knowing a language we are referring to the knowledge which enables a person to fully participate in the linguistic life of the community, by producing utterances that others can understand and by understanding the utterances that others have made, even though the utterances in question might not have been previously encountered in exactly the same form. It is this knowledge which, for Chomsky, is the only valid object of linguistic enquiry.

Statements about I-language are, of course, bound to be speculative, given the present state of knowledge about brain states and their relation to facts of language. Nevertheless, Chomsky claims that I-language is a real object, it is an "aspect of the physical world" and a "real element of particular minds/brains" (1986: 26). Somewhat paradoxically, perhaps, he (p. 27) regards the focus on I-language as a "move toward realism", in the sense that statements pertaining to it are, in principle, either true or false. As the above cited passage tells us, an account of I-language is supposed to "depict exactly" what one knows when one knows a language.

E-language, in contrast, is regarded as, at best, "an epiphenomenon", derivative on I-language (Chomsky 1986: 25). Chomsky's dismissive attitude towards E-language is based, first, on the fact that the possible utterances in a language are infinite in number. Consequently, we are unable in principle to grasp E-language in its totality; the most we can do is to record and analyze a tiny and hopefully representative sample. Even this goal may be unattainable, however, since E-language is not a clearly delimited object, being subject to various social, sociopolitical, and psychological factors, such as attention span, prescriptive norms, and errors of various kinds. Moreover, even with respect to sampled utterances, their analysis does not, according to Chomsky, deliver to us true facts about any aspect of a language. How we analyse these samples, how we segment them, and how we classify their parts and their arrangement, is a methodological issue and subject to criteria such as theoretical parsimony, internal coherence, and descriptive adequacy, not, however, to the criterion of truth. "The linguist is free to select the grammar one way or another as long as it correctly identifies the E-language.... Questions of truth and falsity do not arise" (Chomsky 1986: 20).

Nowadays most linguists, I venture to say, will be inclined to endorse Chomsky's views on the priority of I-language. Even those who are highly critical of many aspects of the Chomskyan programme, such as Lakoff, Langacker, and other self-styled Cognitive Linguists, would certainly want to maintain that the goal of linguistics is a description of the mental structures which constitute linguistic knowledge and which underlie linguistic activity. The aim is not to describe the properties of utterances, but to infer the cognitive reality which gave rise to these properties.

Although I-language may be regarded as a 'real' object, its properties cannot be directly observed; they must be inferred on the basis of observed data. The situation, as Chomsky has reminded us, is not all that different from that encountered in many fields of scientific enquiry, where we infer underlying principles on the basis of observations. In principle, there are many kinds of data which might feed into the study of I-language: the course of acquisition by children, language disorders, language change over time, performance on experimental tasks, and, of course, the evidence of E-language itself, that is, what people actually say (and have said).

It may come as a surprise to non-linguists to learn that Chomsky (as well as a great many linguists who would not be keen to classify themselves as Chomskyans) has tended not to appeal to the evidence of what people say. Rather, the principle evidence consists in intuitions about the properties of invented sentences.[9] Such judgements are presented by Chomsky (1986: 36) as mini-experiments. The linguist hypothesizes a certain element of I-language; certain predictions about grammaticality follow and sentences are constructed accordingly; these are then tested for grammaticality on native speaker intuitions. There are, as Chomsky acknowledges, some methodological problems associated with this approach. These have to do with the possibility that intuitions about grammaticality (and hence, about the contents of the I-language) may be contaminated by the intrusion of non-linguistic factors, such as, for example, the plausibility of the semantic content and various performance mechanisms:

In actual practice, linguistics as a discipline is characterized by attention to certain kinds of evidence that are, for the moment, readily accessible and informative: largely, the judgments of native speakers. Each such judgment is, in fact, the result of an experiment, one that is poorly designed but rich in the evidence it provides. In practice, we tend to operate on the assumption, or pretense, that these informant judgments give us "direct evidence" as to the structure of the I-language, but, of course, this is only a tentative and inexact working hypothesis...In general, informant judgments do not reflect the structure of the language directly; judgments of acceptability, for example, may fail to provide direct evidence as to grammatical status because of the intrusion of numerous other factors.... These are, or should be, truisms.   (Chomsky 1986: 36)

The alleged "intrusion of...other factors" is often cited by Chomskyan linguists as a reason for not paying too much attention to the properties of E-language. As Culicover puts it, in his textbook introduction to Chomskyan theory,

This approach to linguistic theory proceeds with the presumption that what people say reflects what they know, but that the relationship between the two is somewhat inexact....What

---

[9] The foundational texts of Cognitive Linguistics, such as Langacker (1987, 1991), Lakoff (1987), and Lakoff and Johnson (1980), also rely heavily on this methodology, in that they are based on the introspective analysis of mostly invented examples. References to attested data are rare.

people actually say does not reflect simply competence, but competence as it is revealed and *distorted through performance.*   (Culicover 1997: 2; my emphasis)

The Chomskyan programme led to a rather specific conception of I-language, which I shall refer to as the DICTIONARY PLUS GRAMMAR BOOK MODEL, or, more generally, as the GENERATIVE MODEL. The model is by no means restricted to Chomskyan linguistics. On the contrary, it constitutes, I suggest, the mainstream view of what it means to know a language. The idea is that knowledge of a language can be partitioned into two components. One component is the dictionary (or lexicon), which lists the basic building blocks of the language (prototypically, the words). The other component is a set of rules (the grammar, or syntax) for combining words into sentences. Some of the rules are recursive, that is, the rules can apply to their own outputs. In virtue of this property the rules are able to generate an infinite set of sentences, thus accounting for the creativity of language use.

This approach, in spite of its very wide acceptance, is unsatisfactory for a number of reasons. A major problem is that I-language, as conceptualized and formalized in terms of the dictionary plus grammar book, fails to generate language as it is encountered. The model both OVERGENERATES—it generates sentences which do not occur—and UNDERGENERATES—it fails to generate things that people do say. This mismatch between E-language and the output of I-language raises a particularly acute problem with respect to acquisition. How can I-language, as conceptualized, be learned on the basis of input whose properties diverge from those of its output? The solution to this paradox—often referred to as the POVERTY OF THE STIMULUS problem (Chomsky 1980)[10]—was to propose that the basic architecture of I-language is not in fact learned at all; it is innate, present in all individuals by genetic inheritance. The trouble with this appeal to innateness is that quite a lot of things that people know about their language—as evidenced by the things that they say—pertain to fine-grain details: matters such as the ways in which individual words are used, the kinds of words that can occur in a certain construction, or the very specific semantic value attaching, idiosyncratically, to certain expressions, and even to the numerous exceptions to otherwise valid generalizations. It is highly implausible that these particular facts can be genetically inherited. They have to be learned on the basis of exposure to actual language data.

The alternative model which I wish to advance proposes a dialectic relation between language as it is encountered and language as mentally represented. A person's I-language—the system of knowledge residing in her brain—is the product of her exposure to a set of E-language events; her I-language is as it is because of the properties of the E-language which triggered its acquisition.

---

[10] For a critical account of the poverty of the stimulus argument, see Pullum and Scholz (2002), Sampson (1999), and Scholz and Pullum (2002).

Conversely, the language that a speaker produces (that is, her contributions to the totality of utterances in the E-language) reflects her current I-language; E-language has the properties that it has in virtue of the I-language of its speakers.

As a working hypothesis, therefore, we will want to align I-language as closely as possible to E-language. On the most radical version of this hypothesis, a person's I-language is simply a record of the E-language that she has encountered and producing language will consist in little more than the regurgitation of previously learned expressions. There are some aspects of language behaviour for which this account might well be valid: highly ritualized exchanges, for example, or formulaic small talk.[11] The creativity of language use—the fact that speakers do come up with novel ways of saying things—belies such a simplistic approach. I-language needs to be characterized in such a way that it is able to sanction new and innovative expressions, and for this to be possible some degree of abstraction, or generalization over encountered utterances, has to be incorporated. The units over which generalizations are made are not, however, words as such. Speakers do not, most of the time, encounter words in isolation. Words are encountered in contexts—the immediate linguistic context in the first instance, but also the context of previous utterances and previous exchanges, and the context of the interaction itself. It is these contexts of use over which generalizations are made. These generalizations take the form of CON-STRUCTIONS, which link up the form of an utterance with information about its meaning and use. Constructions are the interface between language as experienced and language as represented in the brains of its speakers.

Studying E-language—not such a simple matter!

I have suggested a dialectic relation between E-language and I-language. I-language is acquired through exposure to E-language, while E-language is the output of speakers' I-language. The contents of I-language, however, cannot be directly observed; they can only be inferred. The main source of evidence has got to be E-language.

The study of E-language might seem a straightforward matter. What could be easier, one might ask, than finding out what speakers of a language 'actually say'? The matter is far from straightforward, however.

One possibility is to go up to people and ask them. There are many ways in which the question might be phrased. Would you say such-and-such? Do you think that other people would say such-and-such? In situation X, would you say Y? Do you think that other people would say Y? How likely is it that you (or other people) would say XYZ?

---

[11] The same might also go for the language production of young children; see Lieven *et al.* (2003).

The problem with this approach is that no matter how we phrase the question we are appealing to informants' intuitive judgements about language use. In this respect, the approach scarcely differs from that of the Chomskyan linguists with their focus on the grammaticality judgements of native speakers. Most people, I daresay, would regard the questions 'Would you say such-and-such?' (a question about their usage) and 'Is such-and-such a grammatical expression?' (a question about grammaticality) as more or less equivalent. Both require the informant to introspect about the kinds of expressions that are likely to occur in the language.

Unfortunately, introspective judgements about usage do not always accord with observed usage. A striking example of such a mismatch is reported in Labov (1996). How do you close a conversation, whether face-to-face or on the telephone? What is the last thing you say before leaving the other person or before putting down the telephone receiver? What is the most frequently used closing formula? (The reader may wish to answer these questions before proceeding.) Labov reports that when people were asked this question, they claimed that they closed their conversations with expressions such as *So long, See you, Good-bye*. Observation of actual conversations, however, revealed that these leave-taking formulas were not used particularly frequently. The most frequent closing expression by far was *Bye-bye*. When presented with the evidence, Labov's subjects reacted with incredulity. *Bye-bye* is 'baby talk', and few people seem to want to admit that they close a conversation with such an infantile expression.

Labov explains the unreliability of reflective judgements in this case by reference to the potentially stressful and "problematic" (1996: 94) nature of leave-taking. You have to terminate an interaction but you do not wish to jeopardize the relationship. What a person might say spontaneously in such a situation can diverge from what they believe, on reflection, that they should say, or would say. The same goes for many other stressful and potentially face-threatening situations. What do you say when insulted, embarrassed, or threatened? Intuitions in this regard are likely to be coloured by considerations of propriety, etiquette, and self-image.

There are other circumstances in which intuitions may not be entirely reliable. Speakers may be reluctant to admit that they use forms which, on reflection, they might perceive as 'substandard', 'illogical', or even 'wrong'. Not many speakers are willing to admit that they use the 'double-*is*' construction, illustrated in (2):

(2)   a. The funny thing is is that they didn't say anything about it.
       b. The problem is is that she already paid for it.
       c. The issue is is that there is no budget anywhere for it.

The repeated *is* in these examples looks like a case of faulty planning and might therefore be dismissed as an error. Yet, as a number of researchers have documented, the construction is not at all uncommon in spoken English, and its properties are fairly consistent amongst the speaker groups investigated (Bolinger 1987; Brenier and Michaelis 2005; Massam 1999; Tuggy 1996).

Intuitive judgements are also likely to be suspect when we are dealing with variable usage. When different linguistic forms are in competition, speakers may be unsure about which form they actually use or which form they use more frequently. Many English speakers will be aware of alternative pronunciations of words like *schedule* and *either*, yet may be hard pressed to state which of the pronunciations they themselves habitually use or which they encounter more often. Many adjectives can form their comparatives by use of the *-er* suffix or by means of the analytic construction with *more*. Sometimes the choice is easy: *more profound* rather than *profounder, prettier* rather than *more pretty*. But can you say with certainty that you would never use the less preferred options? Sometimes, the options seem to be more evenly balanced: *sexier* or *more sexy*?[12]

Innovative forms may sometimes pass below the threshold of consciousness. The following (anecdotal) example provides an illustration.

What is the plural of the noun *process*? English speakers to whom I have put this question all give the same unequivocal answer: *process* forms its plural in the 'regular' way, by suffixation of [əz], or, in some accents, [ɪz]. What one sometimes hears, however, especially in academic discourse, is the plural form ['prəʊsəsiːz] (British accent), or ['prɒsɛsiːz] (American accent). The innovative plural terminates in [iːz], with a tense vowel, instead of the expected [əz], with a short schwa-like vowel. It is as if the word is being assimilated to the pattern of 'Greek' nouns such as *thesis, hypothesis*, and *analysis*, all of whose plurals end in [iːz]: *thesis* ['θiːsɪs] ~ *theses* ['θiːsiːz], and so on. But whereas the 'Greek' nouns form their plural by replacing a final [ɪs] by [iːz], the innovative plural of *process* is formed by adding the suffix [iːz].

At a conference I attended a few years ago, I asked some of the presenters whether they were aware that they had used the innovative plural of *process* in their lectures. They all denied that they had. In the course of the conference, I heard plenary speakers (native English speakers) use two further pseudo-Greek plurals. One was ['baɪəsiːz], the plural of *bias*, the other was ['prɛməsiːz], the plural of *premise*. The speakers reacted with surprise and disbelief when I pointed out to them that they had used these forms in their presentations.

In view of the above, we should take 'what speakers say they say' and 'what speakers think they say' with a large grain of salt. We need to turn to actual data, records of what people 'actually say'. Again, the matter might seem straightforward. Anyone with a pair of ears (and eyes) is confronted, almost minute by minute, with what people 'actually say' (or write). The difficulty is not so much finding the data, but knowing how to handle it.

Linguists studying a hitherto unfamiliar language have kept field notes, recording as faithfully as possible what their informants have said. An important resource for

---

[12] The choice of comparative forms will be addressed later, in Chapter 9.

the study of first language acquisition has been the data diaries in which linguists have recorded the things that young children (often their own) say, sometimes on a regular day-to-day basis (Ingram 1989). Many linguists also keep notes of unusual or innovative pronunciations or turns of phrase that they encounter. Fromkin's (1973) study of speech errors, or 'slips of the tongue', was based on a set of errors that she had jotted down and assembled into a reference corpus; likewise for Stemberger (1982). For myself—and I would imagine that most linguists do the same—I keep a record of unusual turns of phrase or unusual pronunciations that I hear on the radio or on television or from friends and colleagues. While such observations are random and sporadic, they may nevertheless be indicative of trends in the language at large and suggestive of matters which deserve further investigation (for a case study, see Taylor and Pang 2008). Not to be overlooked, too, are a number of other resources for the study of actual usage, such as the published concordances of important words in literary and religious texts, as well as dictionaries—the OED being a preeminent example—with their lists of attested citations.

The breakthrough in the study of actual usage came with the possibility of electronic data processing.[13] With the possibility of automatic parsing and part-of-speech tagging of texts, more sophisticated queries can be made, concerning the syntactic environment of words and word combinations and the incidence of syntactic constructions. Once texts are available in a computer-readable format, data on the usage of individual words and word combinations can be easily and quickly retrieved. Questions about word frequency, or the incidence of word combinations, can be answered in a matter of seconds. Before this technological revolution, anyone wishing to find out whether a particular word or expression was in use in the 'language at large' had to search manually through potentially vast quantities of material, a procedure which was not only time-consuming and intellectually numbing but also prone to errors of attention. Even such a basic question as how frequently a word is used could be answered only after days, weeks, or even years of drudgery. It is sobering to recall that Kaeding (1898), for his study of the frequency of letters, letter combinations, syllables, and words in written German, employed up to a thousand research assistants over a period of five years for the filing and cross-referencing of millions upon millions of index cards. (Kaeding's corpus comprised a total of 20 million syllables, or 11 million words.) All the more remarkable, therefore, are the findings on word frequency (as well as the frequency of other elements, such as phonemes, morphemes, verb inflections, and the like) reported by earlier

---

[13] The role of technology in linguistic study deserves more attention. The advent of the tape recorder made it possible, for the first time in human history, for linguistic utterances to be contemplated at leisure. More recently, the possibility of video recordings has initiated the study of the gestural accompaniments of speech. Conversely, technological innovations feed back into our conception of what language is and of how we use it.

researchers such as Zipf (1935) and Greenberg (1966). Nowadays, the kinds of questions that these researchers asked can be answered in a matter of minutes by anyone with an Internet connection. I was able to state, earlier in this chapter, that *total failure* was a more frequent expression by a ratio of about 4 to 1 than *total success* by looking up the two phrases in the British National Corpus (BNC).[14] Searches in other corpora, such as the Corpus of Contemporary American English (COCA), confirmed the finding.

Corpora and their representativeness

In this book, I will make frequent reference to data derived from the BNC. The BNC consists of about 100 million words of text and is meant to be a snapshot of (British) English in the late twentieth century. It includes texts (and text fragments) on different subject matters, such as biology, linguistics, and cooking; texts from different genres, such as newspaper articles, popular novels, and technical manuals; texts from different kinds of speakers (young and old, well-educated and not-so-well-educated); texts produced in formal situations and directed at an audience of strangers alongside informal conversation between close friends and intimates; and so on. The hope was that the assembled texts would be representative of the language at a given period in time.

Representativeness is the holy grail of corpus linguistics (Biber 1993; Leech 2007). However, the very notion of a representative corpus brings with it some serious conceptual problems. What, in brief, is a corpus supposed to be representative of?

Consider the matter from the point of view of an opinion pollster or market researcher. You ask a sample of eligible voters about their party political allegiance. To the extent that the sample is representative of the voting population, you will be able to project the opinions expressed by the sample onto the population as a whole. One way to obtain a representative sample of voters is to make a random selection; in principle, each eligible voter has an equal chance of featuring in the sample. You might check on the representativeness of the sample by checking out its make-up against what is known about the make-up of the population. If, for example, it is known that, say, 52 per cent of the eligible voters are female, you would expect that about 52 per cent of your randomly sampled voters should be female. If 20 per cent of the voters are known to live in one-person households, you should expect about the same percentage of the sample to have this characteristic. Alternatively, you can put

---

[14] The reader may be wondering whether the higher frequency of *total failure* vis-à-vis *total success* might not be attributable to the higher overall frequency of *failure* in the language. It turns out, on the contrary, that *success* is the more frequent word, by a factor of about two to one (13,243 occurrences vs. 7,687 in the BNC).

together the sample by ensuring that its members exhibit the known demographic properties of the voting population as a whole.

With respect to the opinion pollster, we can be confident of the representativeness of a sample only if the sampled population is well-defined. Moreover, the representativeness of the sample can, in principle, be subjected to empirical validation. The accuracy of an opinion poll can be tested against the results of a general election.

There are certainly situations in which linguistic sampling does meet the criterion of a well-defined population. The complete works of Jane Austen; all the articles in all the issues of the *Daily Telegraph* published in the 1990s; the complete text of all the books published in the UK in 2007—these all constitute well-defined populations.[15] We can create our sample in such a way that each sentence of the population has an equal chance of appearing in the sample; alternatively, we might construct a balanced sample by ensuring that it reflects the known make-up of the population. Moreover, we could, in principle, test the representativeness of the sample against the total population.

However, when it comes to studying E-language 'as a whole', we simply do not know what its properties are. We simply assume that, by assembling texts from various sources, and in varying proportions, we have made a more or less representative sample of everything that is in the E-language. Decisions regarding what to include, and in what proportions, are ultimately a matter of personal judgement. The BNC includes extracts from Mills and Boon novels. The novels are certainly widely read, but what proportion of the E-language do they constitute (and what proportion is constituted by any single novel)? We are reminded of Chomsky's strictures on the indeterminacy of E-language.

Instead of trying to capture the language 'as a whole', we might focus on the reception of texts by individual members of a speech community. Certain texts—the evening news on television, advertising slogans, lyrics of popular songs, joke lines of popular sitcoms—reach millions of individuals. Other texts—enigmatic poetry, abstruse academic papers, complex legal decisions—might reach only a couple of dozen readers. There might be grounds, when compiling a corpus, to give greater weight to texts with the widest reception. Paradoxically, however, the texts which probably make up the bulk of most people's linguistic experience are those with the smallest reception, namely, one-on-one conversation and everyday chit-chat.

Yet another approach might be to focus on the linguistic experience of the individual. For any individual speaker, it might be possible in principle (though scarcely in practice) to assemble all the language that they have been exposed to over a period of weeks, years, or even their entire life. More realistically, the linguistic experience of an individual, over a given time span, could be sampled. Individuals,

---

[15] For earlier stages of a language, or for dead languages, the text population may indeed be essentially closed.

though, differ with respect to their linguistic experience; think of the kind of language encountered by an academic researcher, a lawyer, a social worker, or a call-centre operative. Thus arises a second-order sampling problem. We need a representative sample of the linguistic input experienced by a representative sample of individuals.

Consider the matter from the perspective of individual speakers. To what extent does the linguistic experience of an individual in a speech community overlap with that of other individuals? Which kinds of individuals are most representative of the speech community with respect to their linguistic experience? What is the degree of variance between the representative speakers and the outliers—those speakers whose experience diverges from that of the norm? Here, a somewhat malicious question arises. Might professional linguists be amongst the group of outliers? In this case their intuitions as to what is 'in the language' might be very suspect, for reasons which go beyond those already discussed.

We could also consider the matter from the perspective of linguistic expressions themselves. It is likely that certain linguistic phenomena are common to just about all text types and occur in the experience of just about all speakers of the language. Presumably, these phenomena will be adequately represented in the larger corpora such as the BNC. Other phenomena, though, might occur in the experience of only certain groups of individuals, and then, only in certain kinds of texts to which they are exposed. Their occurrence in one of the available corpora will be subject to a high degree of sampling error. Hints as to this state of affairs may in fact be gleaned from corpus-based studies. Based on the British component of the International Corpus of English (ICE-GB),[16] Stefanowitsch and Gries (2003) identified verbs which were strongly attracted to the imperative construction. One of these verbs was *fold*. Subsequent inspection of the data showed that all examples of imperative *fold* occurred in a single text file, one dealing with origami. Gries (2008) addressed the issue in terms of the notion of DISPERSION. Some linguistic forms are dispersed over many text files; others are restricted to a small selection of files. Statements about raw frequency of occurrence need to be moderated by such considerations.

The BNC and linguistic experience

In spite of the conceptual problems raised by the available corpora, I shall, in this book, rely quite heavily on the evidence of the BNC, supplemented, when appropriate, by data from other readily available sources.

The BNC consists of about 100 million words. How does this stack up with respect to a person's linguistic experience?

---

[16] http://www.ucl.ac.uk/english-usage/ice-gb/

Let us assume an average speaking rate of 120 words per minute (Biber, Conrad, and Reppen 1998: 27). At ten hours per day, this comes out at 26.28 million words per year. Under these conditions, it would take just under four years for the total content of the BNC to be read out loud.

Individuals differ with respect to the amount of language they are exposed to each day, month, or year of their lives.[17] Very few people, I daresay, listen to continuous speech for ten hours per day. We also read, and speed readers, especially, are able to process text at a much faster pace than 120 words per minute. On the other hand, there are reclusive individuals who might be exposed to an hour or two of language a day, at most. With respect to second language and foreign language speakers, the amount of exposure might be assumed to be very much smaller than that of native speakers. According to a 'back-of-the-envelope' calculation by Ellis, Simpson-Vlach, and Maynard (2008), native speaker students at an American university are exposed to about 30,000 words of academic English per day (equivalent to about 10 million words per year). Overseas students—not least because of their lower reading speed—might be exposed to, generously, 10,000 words per day. Another factor to consider is the role of one's own linguistic productions. Does inner speech contribute to the E-language that a person is exposed to? Does this sentence that I am now composing count as input to my linguistic experience?

The questions raised here are particularly pressing with regard to expressions which are represented only very infrequently in a corpus, or perhaps not at all. Suppose that a word or expression is recorded only once or twice in the BNC. Assuming that the BNC is representative of what a representative English speaker is likely to have experienced, we should have to assume that the expression is encountered only a couple of times every four or five years, at most. Given its rarity, we should not be surprised that some speakers of the language simply do not know the expression. Suppose, on the other hand, that the form in question is widely known. We could explain this situation by pointing to the inadequate sampling in the corpus. Another possibility is that speakers learn the expression on only minimal exposure.

Foster (2001: 81) noted that expressions which "would be considered a normal part of any native speaker's repertoire" did not appear even in the 300 million word corpus of the Bank of English. Moon (1998: 60) failed to find many common idioms in the 18 million word Oxford Hector Pilot Corpus (OHPC). To be sure, the Hector corpus is relatively small and is heavily weighted towards journalistic English. Nevertheless, the absence of such well-known phrases as *bag and baggage, by hook or by crook, kick the bucket, out of practice*, and *speak for yourself* is remarkable.

---

[17] Hart and Risley (1995) estimated that children of academics hear an average of 2,150 words per hour in their first year of life; for children of working-class and welfare households, the estimates are 1,250 and 620 words per hour, respectively.

Take the case of *kick the bucket*. Everyone knows this expression. Indeed, it is often cited as a parade example of an idiom. Yet it seems to be not particularly frequent. (Ask yourself: When was the last time you heard the expression or used it yourself?) A BNC search of *kick(s)(ing)(ed) the bucket* returns only thirteen instances. Of these, only five constitute genuine uses of the idiom; the remaining eight examples occur in texts with a linguistics content, where *kick the bucket* is cited as an example of an idiom. It is very likely that at least some English speakers have learned this expression after having encountered it only a handful of times.

The World Wide Web: a "fabulous linguists' playground"[18]

There now exists a resource that is many times more powerful than any constructed corpus, namely, the World Wide Web, in association with various search engines (Hundt, Nesselhauf, and Biewer 2007). It has been estimated that in 2002 the Google search engine was able to access a database of over 3,000 million indexed Web pages, more than any of its rivals (Notess 2002). Nowadays, the amount of accessed text is presumably much larger, exceeding, by many orders of magnitude, the size of corpora such as the BNC. Whereas a search of the BNC returns fifty-six examples of *total failure*, a Google search of the same phrase (July 2010) returned almost five and a half million hits. The BNC contains eighteen instances of *total success*; a Google search returned about one and a half million hits. (Interestingly, in spite of the vastly different numbers involved, the ratio for the two phrases is about the same, with *total failure* being about four times more frequent than *total success*.) In the light of vast amount of material that can be accessed, the Web has turned out to be invaluable for the study of less frequent items, which are only very sparsely represented in the BNC and other corpora. Moreover, the Web offers a vista of the contemporary language, one as up-to-date as one can imagine. The possibility of regional searches further enhances its usefulness.

There are, to be sure, several objections which can be raised against accessing the Web for linguistic research. Unlike with established linguistic corpora, the composition of the Web is not controlled for factors such as genre, register, or the sociocultural background of the authors of the texts. The Web consists of anything and everything that people have wished to contribute to it. For this very reason, however, the question of representativeness may not even arise. Existing corpora aim to sample the total population of linguistic utterances. The Web is not a sample; it *is* the total population (of contributed material) (Kilgarriff and Grefenstette 2003).

A more serious objection has to do with data retrieval and the status of reported frequencies. It is impossible to determine the amount of text which is being accessed

---

[18] Kilgarriff and Grefenstette (2003: 345).

in a search. Search engine results, therefore, can give no indication of the absolute frequency of an item per so many million words. At most, we can gain a rough idea of the relative frequency of search items. Moreover, because of the ever-changing composition of the Web, search results are sensitive to the time at which a search is conducted. Additional factors are the workings of the search algorithm and the frequency reporting mechanism (Eu 2008). Webmasters are familiar with various tricks for increasing the hit rate for their documents; indeed, it is a common observation with many searches that some documents are reported more than once and some have a habit of always appearing on top. These distortions are most likely to be encountered on searches for topical content phrases, which are likely to be the subject of links to other Web pages. Even so, the number of hits for the rather anodyne and nondescript phrases which linguists are likely to be interested in will probably be unreliable to some unknown degree. In view of all this, it is of some comfort to learn that estimates of relative word frequency obtained from the Web have been found to correlate highly with data from established corpora (Blair, Urland, and Ma 2002). For multi-word searches, the results may even outperform those derived from a corpus. Keller, Lapata, and Ourioupina (2002; see also Keller and Lapata 2003; Lapata, McDonald, and Keller 1999) found that search engine frequencies for three kinds of bigrams (adjective–noun, verb–object, and noun–noun) correlated better with informants' acceptability judgements than data obtained from the BNC.

Another objection, frequently heard, is that Web-sourced data is corrupted by non-native contributions. Quite a lot of English language data on the Web is authored by non-native speakers. Perhaps this is not as great a problem as is sometimes imagined. Consider, again, the matter from the perspective of individual speakers and the kind of language that they are exposed to. In today's globalized world, quite a lot of a native English speaker's linguistic interactions are with non-native speakers. For my own part, a significant minority of the students that I teach, and of the colleagues that I interact with, are non-native speakers of English. Many of the people I interact with socially are non-native speakers. I also happen to be married to a non-native speaker. My situation is probably not all that untypical. The uncontrolled, heterogeneous nature of the Web could be its greatest advantage.

2

The dictionary and the grammar book: the generative model of linguistic knowledge

In his book *The Atoms of Language*, Mark Baker (2001) has an imaginary interlocutor ask the question 'What is English?' This might seem a rather odd question to ask. The discussion in Chapter 1 provides a context. The question, namely, has to do with how we conceptualize a language. Do we think of a language as an inventory of everything that its speakers have said? Baker does not endorse this option. He does not, for example, refer his interlocutor to one of the available corpora of English, nor does he gesture to a bookshelf full of English-language books and say 'That is English'. Instead, he regards a language as a mechanism for constructing sentences:

> Suppose someone were to ask you what English is.... You might say that English is the set of sentences that are constructed by combining the following ingredients (you hand her a massive dictionary that lists all the English words) according to the following rules of grammar (you hand her an equally massive English grammar).... [B]etween them they would tell the reader how to make any conceivable English sentence. (Baker 2001: 53–4)

This passage puts forward a conception of language which is, I think, deeply entrenched in contemporary thinking about language. I refer to it as the DICTIONARY PLUS GRAMMAR BOOK model, or, more succinctly, as the GENERATIVE MODEL. According to this model, a language comprises two components. One component is the dictionary, or lexicon, which lists all the words of the language. The other is the grammar, or syntax, which lists the rules for combining into sentences words taken from the dictionary. Cruse (2000*b*: 238) expresses this view somewhat less colourfully than Baker:[1]

---

[1] Pawley (1985: 86) parodies the dictionary plus grammar book model in terms of a linguist who has compiled both a grammar and a lexicon of a language and who then sits back with a satisfied sigh and says, "My job is done; I have described the language".

... the bare essentials for a language are, first, a set of basic units, and, second, a set of rules for combining them into larger, more complex units like phrases and sentences. A list of the basic units constitutes the lexicon of the language; a specification of the combinatorial rules constitutes the grammar.   (Cruse 2000b: 238)

The model also looms large in Jackendoff's *Foundations of Language*:

Since the number of possible utterances in a human language is unlimited, language users cannot store them all in their heads. Rather,...knowledge of language requires two components. One is a finite list of structural elements that are available to be combined. This list is traditionally called the "lexicon," and its elements are called "lexical items."...The other component is a finite set of combinatorial principles, or a *grammar*. To the extent that speakers of a language (or a dialect) are consistent with one another...we can speak of the "grammar of a language" as a useful approximation to what all its speakers have in their heads.

(Jackendoff 2002: 39)

For a first approximation, the lexicon is the store of words in long-term memory from which the grammar constructs phrases and sentences.   (Jackendoff 2002: 130)

It will be noted that Jackendoff adds a cognitive dimension to the model.[2] The word list is not some hefty tome that can be handed around; it is a mental dictionary, a "store of words in long-term memory". Speakers of a language also "have in their heads" a grammar, understood as a set of principles for combining items taken from the lexicon. A language, then, is regarded as a device for generating the sentences of a language which is located in the minds of individual speakers. In speaking of 'a language' we are generalizing over the mental states of its speakers, assuming for this purpose that their mental lexicons and mental grammars are largely congruent with one another.

Jackendoff, along with many others, motivates this conception of language by appealing to the ARGUMENT FROM CREATIVITY. As Jackendoff states, both the lexicon and the grammar are finite, that is to say, the words and the rules of a language can be exhaustively listed. The sentences that speakers produce, however, are not subject to any upper boundary. Speakers are constantly producing sentences which (most likely) have never been produced before in exactly the same form, and hearers, most of the time, have no problems in understanding them. Since the possible sentences cannot be enumerated, knowing a language cannot be equated with knowing a set of sentences. By the same token, learning a language cannot be a matter of learning sentences that one has encountered. Speakers possess the finite

---

[2] It is only fair to emphasize that Jackendoff's view of the lexicon as a "store of words" is but a "first approximation". In fact, Jackendoff's view of the lexicon is much more inclusive. It comprises not only words as such, but also idioms such as *kick the bucket* and *by and large*, as well as constructional idioms, of the kind that we will discuss in Chapter 6.

means for creating an infinite set of sentences. The dictionary plus grammar book model offers itself as an elegant and compelling explanation of this state of affairs.

An important component of the creativity argument is the claim that speakers do not regurgitate chunks of pre-learned language. "It is evident", Chomsky (1964: 7–8) stated, "that rote recall is a factor of minute importance in ordinary use of language." Citing Hermann Paul (1886), he claims (p. 8) that only "a minimum of the sentences which we utter is learnt by heart as such"; it would therefore be a "fundamental error" to regard linguistic utterances as "something merely reproduced from memory". The point was taken up by Langacker in one of his earlier publications, his introductory textbook *Language and Its Structure:*[3]

> One of the characteristics of language use is its creativity, its freedom of control on the basis of the past linguistic activity of the user. Almost every sentence that occurs is a novel one and has never occurred before. (Langacker 1967: 22)

Language use cannot therefore be based on the recycling of already heard expressions:

> [W]e do not go around collecting sentences to hold in memory for future use in speaking and understanding. Nor do we have to search through our personal linguistic archives . . . whenever we want to say something. (Langacker 1967: 22)

Even if a speaker does happen to produce the same sentence on two or more occasions the repetition is likely to be fortuitous:

> If a sentence duplicates one that has occurred previously, chances are that it was created anew the second time and that the repetition was purely coincidental. Talking does not consist of parroting sentences that have been heard and memorized. (Langacker 1967: 22)

The creativity argument can be found in just about any introductory textbook to linguistics. The authors of an especially popular and long-running textbook explain it as follows:

> If language is defined merely as a system of communication, then language is not unique to humans. There are, however, certain characteristics of human language not found in the communication systems of any other species. A basic property of human language is its creative aspect—a speaker's ability to combine the basic linguistic units to form an infinite set of 'well-formed' grammatical sentences, most of which are novel, never before produced or heard. (Fromkin *et al.* 2005: 23)

---

[3] Langacker's 1967 textbook predates his development of Cognitive Grammar (Chapter 6), which espouses a very different view of linguistic knowledge. Indeed, a central axiom of Cognitive Grammar is that linguistic knowledge is acquired on the basis of experience of the language. Every linguistic encounter has some impact, if only very minor, on the mental representation of the language. Repeated exposure to a structure or an expression can lead to its entrenchment in memory, while lengthy periods of non-use can lead to atrophy; see Langacker (1987: 59, 160, 376).

Fromkin *et al.* (2005: 26) ask their readers to ponder why it would be odd to say 'I learned a new sentence today', whereas it would be quite normal to say 'I learned a new word today'. The point which the textbook writers wish to bring home to budding linguistics students is that learning a language does not consist in the learning of sentences; it consists in learning the means for creating and understanding sentences.

Creativity, in the sense in which the word is being used here, is undeniably a feature of language use, though, as we will see in due course, its footprint may be somewhat smaller than often claimed. To be sure, it is easy to demonstrate that we do not go around regurgitating whole sentences that we have committed to memory; sentences, for the most part, simply do not repeat themselves. (Do an Internet search for this very sentence that you are now reading and you will almost certainly draw a blank.) It is less easy to dismiss out of hand a number of more modest claims; for example, that quite a lot of our linguistic activity consists in the stitching together of 'bits of sentences' that we have learned, or that novel sentences are created by filling in the slots made available by phrasal or sentence patterns that we have picked up. But even if we accept the premise of creativity at face value, we might still question the logical link to the generative model. Might there, for example, be other ways to guarantee creativity which are not based on the dictionary plus grammar book model? I address this topic in Chapter 12 of this book. In the meantime, however, I want to explore in more detail the generative model, its motivation, and, most importantly, its entailments. Its entailments frame a good deal of linguistic theorizing and practice. And it is when we examine its entailments that major cracks begin to appear in the generative model.

A rule-based approach to linguistic knowledge

The dominant approach in academic linguistics has been to view the mental grammar as a finite device which generates an infinite set of grammatical sentences. The prototype for this kind of device is provided by mathematics. Let us take a very simple example: the set of natural numbers $\{1, 2, 3, \ldots \infty\}$.

The set of natural numbers is infinite. It is impossible in principle to list them all and it would be absurd to ask whether a person has learned them or how many of them they have learned.[4] 'Knowing' the natural numbers consists in knowing the principle whereby the set is created. The principle is extremely simple, namely, addition: any natural number n (with the sole of exception of 1) can be created by

---

[4] For young children, who have not yet grasped the generative principle, the questions might not be so absurd. Initially, a child learns to name numerosities of like objects: three apples, five fingers, and so on. Subsequently, she learns to abstract from named numerosities and realizes that there is no end to the numbers that can be counted; see Lakoff and Núñez (2000).

adding 1 to an already existing number. The rule of addition can be stated using the RE-WRITE formalism widely adopted by linguists:

(1)   n → n + 1

According to (1), any natural number n can be 'rewritten', or analysed, as a natural number plus 1. Alternatively, adding 1 to a natural number creates another natural number.

To be sure, language is vastly more complex than the set of natural numbers. Nevertheless, the parallels between the numbers and a language will be evident. The set of possible sentences in a language, like the set of natural numbers, is infinite. We do not learn the sentences or the numbers; we learn the principles whereby sentences and numbers are generated. Two aspects of the number rule are especially relevant for a generative account of language:

- The number rule is RECURSIVE, that is to say, it can apply to its own output. Any number n, created by the number rule, can be the input to a new application of the rule. The process can be repeated an infinite number of times.
- The rule refers to a VARIABLE. The variable in this case is n. The variable does not designate any particular number, but can take on the value of any natural number.

It is the first characteristic which guarantees infinite membership in the set. Thus, in order to guarantee the creativity of language we need grammatical rules which are recursive. To give a very simple example: we need a rule which can generate, not only *an old man* and *a very old man*, but also *a very very old man*, *a very very very old man*, and so on. There is in principle no end to the number of times this rule can apply.

It is the second feature, the role of variables, that I wish to focus on here. Consider a fairly unremarkable English sentence, such as (2):

(2)   The farmer shot a rabbit.

This is probably not a sentence that you have encountered in your previous linguistic experience. (A Google search—March 2008—returned no hits.) We can nevertheless agree that the sentence is grammatical. We recognize the sentence as grammatical because the words are combined 'correctly', in accordance with the rules of English syntax. Since we know the meanings and the pronunciations of the individual words, we also know what the sentence as a whole means and how it is pronounced. It is these intuitions that the generative model is meant to explain.

As a matter of fact, the thumbnail sketch of the generative model offered by Baker and Jackendoff in the passages quoted previously oversimplifies the matter by leaving out the role of variables. For it is not the case that the rules of a language stipulate how words as such are combined; rather, the rules stipulate how words of a certain category are combined. The generative model does not provide us with a rule which states that the word *farmer* can combine with *the*, nor, for that matter, is there a rule which allows the word *shot* to occur before the word *a*. If such were the case we would need a truly gigantic battery of rules, one for each of the combinatory possibilities of every single word in the dictionary. Furthermore, adding just one new word to the dictionary would bring with it the need to add a vast set of rules pertaining to all the possible contexts in which the word could be used. What we have, instead, are rules which stipulate that words of a certain category can combine with words of another category in order to generate an item of a higher order category. Other rules stipulate the ways in which these higher order categories can themselves combine. With respect to (2), the rules refer to items of the categories noun (N), determiner (Det), and verb (V). Determiner plus noun gives us a unit of the category noun phrase (NP), a verb plus noun phrase gives us a verb phrase (VP), while a noun phrase plus verb phrase gives us a sentence (S):

(3)   a. NP → Det N
      b. VP → V NP
      c. S → NP VP

In order, then, for the syntactic rules to be able to apply, it is necessary that items listed in the lexicon are TYPED, that is, they are assigned to the various LEXICAL CATEGORIES (these are, of course, the traditional parts of speech, such as noun, verb, determiner, preposition, and so on). The resulting combinations also need to be typed, namely, as PHRASAL CATEGORIES such as noun phrase and verb phrase. This is because sentences are constructed, not by combining words of particular categories, but by combining phrasal units belonging to certain categories.

As the reader will no doubt have realized, rules like those in (3) are liable to massively overgenerate; if applied mechanistically, they will create all sorts of manifestly ungrammatical and nonsensical sentences. Assuming that *sneeze* is typed as a verb, the rules will give us the nonsensical *A farmer sneezed the rabbit*; assuming that *spinach* is typed as a noun, the rules generate *A spinach shot a farmer*, and similar absurdities.

To a large extent, the history of generative grammar over the past half century can be read as a prolonged attempt to fine-tune the model in order to get it to work. The aim is that the model will generate only grammatical sentences and none of the absurd specimens just cited. Let us briefly consider three such strategies, familiar to us at least since Chomsky's *Aspects of the Theory of Syntax* (1965).

Subcategorization

The rules in (3) assume that items of a certain category all behave identically with respect to the relevant rules. Rule (3b), for example, will apply across the board to any item typed as a verb. Verbs, however, can participate in a number of different verb phrase structures. Here are some of them:

(4) a. VP → V
   b. VP → V NP
   c. VP → V NP NP
   d. VP → V PP
   e. VP → V NP PP

Not every item listed in the lexicon as a verb is able to occur in each of these VP structures:

(4a) accommodates so-called intransitive verbs (*She slept* is an OK sentence).

(4b) is valid for so-called transitive verbs, like *shoot*, as in *shoot a rabbit.*

(4c) is the structure appropriate for so-called ditransitive verbs, such as *give, forgive,* and *deny*: *give the dog a bone, forgive us our sins, deny them access.*

(4d) is for those intransitive verbs which require a prepositional phrase. It would be odd to say, quite simply, *He lived*; you need to say where, or when, the person lived: *He lived in London; He lived in the nineteenth century,* and so on.

(4e) refers to verbs like *put.* You cannot say *I put the book.* You have to state where you put the book, using a prepositional phrase: *I put the book on the shelf.*

We need, then, to recognize a number of sub-categories within the broader verb category. The traditional terms intransitive, transitive, and ditransitive cover the cases in (4a), (4b), and (4c). (There are, however, no traditional terms for the verbs which pattern as in (4d) or (4e).) The upshot is that each verb in the lexicon must be marked for the kind of VP it is able to occur in. A given verb may, of course, be able to occur in more than one SUBCATEGORIZATION FRAME (as these frames are known). *Give*, for example, can occur in the frame [_ NP NP], as in *give the dog a bone*, but also in [_ NP PP], as in *give a bone to the dog.*

Analogous strategies may be applied to other lexical categories. For example, the noun category can be subdivided into proper nouns (like *Mary*) and common nouns; common nouns, in turn, split into count nouns (like *farmer*) and mass nouns (like *spinach*). These distinctions affect the kinds of determiners that can occur with the nouns. We can have *a farmer*, but not **a spinach.*

An interesting question—explored by, amongst others, Wierzbicka (1988*b*)—is the extent to which subcategorization frames are a function of a word's meaning.[5] The fact that *give* occurs in the ditransitive frame is not unconnected with the fact that giving, by its very nature, involves two entities (in addition to the giver): the thing given and the person to whom it is given. Subcategorization may not be fully predictable from semantics, however. *Donate* is semantically similar to *give.* Yet

---

[5] We can, of course, reverse the argument and enquire whether a word's meaning might be (in part) a function of its subcategorization frame. Gleitman (1990) and Pinker (1994*b*) have indeed argued that subcategorization might be a valuable cue to some aspects of a verb's meaning.

donate sounds odd in the ditransitive frame; you donate money to a charity, you do not donate a charity money. In the last analysis, subcategorization frames are a property of a word which has to be specified in the lexicon and which, perforce, has to be learned by speakers of the language.

Selectional restrictions

The rules in (3) create a sentence with the structure [s NP [vp V NP]], the verb being categorized as transitive. However, not any randomly generated NP can feature in a transitive sentence. We want to avoid generating nonsense such as *The spinach shot a farmer* or *Sincerity admired the boy*. This problem is handled by means of SELECTIONAL RESTRICTIONS. These impose restrictions, usually semantic in nature, on the kinds of items a word can combine with. Thus, *admire* requires as its subject an NP referring to an entity capable of admiring, typically a human being. *Drink* requires its direct object to be a drinkable substance, that is, a liquid; *in* requires its complement to be a container; *put* requires its PP complement to refer to a place; *give*, in the frame [_ NP PP], requires that the PP designates a recipient, and so on. Selectional restrictions may sometimes COERCE a novel interpretation of a constituent phrase. Strictly speaking, it would be nonsensical to say *The University just telephoned*. The verb requires a human subject and a university is not a human entity. We make sense of the expression by assuming that *the University* does in fact refer to a person. Most likely, we would assume that *the University* refers to a person working for the institution and speaking on its behalf.

Agreement features

Nouns, in English, can be inflected for number (singular or plural) and determiners associated with the noun may need to agree with the noun in this respect. Number agreement rules out *a farmers*, as well as *many farmer*. Present tense verb forms also show number agreement with a subject NP. Agreement plays a much larger role in languages with elaborate gender and case systems. In German, members of a noun phrase, such as determiners, adjectives, and nouns, must agree with respect to number, case, and gender.

The generative model in relation to data

I have presented subcategorization frames, selectional restrictions, and agreement features as devices which are invoked in order to get the dictionary plus grammar book model to 'work', that is, to generate a grammatical output. How, though, do we decide whether an output is grammatical or not? What are the data against which the model is evaluated as 'working' or 'not working'?

The answer would appear to be obvious: a grammar which is supposed to model the linguistic knowledge of native speakers is evaluated against what native speakers actually say. In Chapter 1 I already raised some of the problematic issues associated with this seemingly simple notion. We also need to bear in mind that one of the motivations for the generative model has been the folly of basing a linguistic description on a corpus of attested utterances. A corpus is but an incomplete and accidental sampling of what is possible in a language. A different corpus, or data collected from different speakers, would provide a different sample. The new corpus might contain words not present in a previous sample or it might show old words combining in new ways or occurring in a different range of constructions; verbs, for example, might turn up in previously unattested subcategorization frames.

These matters were already touched on in Chapter 1. A set of encountered utterances only provides positive evidence of what has occurred in the language. It tells us nothing about the things that have not occurred. There are two options open to us. One is to regard the non-occurrence of an expression as simply due to the limited size of the corpus; if we increase the size of the corpus we might well come across the expression in question. The other possibility is that the expression is ungrammatical, which is tantamount to saying that the expression will never occur in a corpus, no matter how large it is. Increasing the size of a corpus will not enable us to decide between these two possibilities. Any corpus, no matter how large, is finite, and the non-occurrence of an expression cannot be taken as proof that the expression will not occur in any further data we collect.

Even the evidence of what people have said might be suspect. Speakers do sometimes make errors (Fromkin 1973, 1980; Stemberger 1982). Some errors might be put down to faulty planning and execution, as with false starts and slips of the tongue. Others might be attributed to imperfect knowledge of the language, as with malapropisms and (in the written language) spelling mistakes. Occasionally, speakers may become aware of errors in their own speech, immediately correcting a mispronunciation or a grammatical solecism; mostly, though, errors go uncorrected.[6] The mere fact of something having occurred in a corpus is no guarantee that it is a legitimate part of the language.

Rather than rely on corpus evidence, linguists, especially generative linguists, have appealed to another kind of data, namely, the intuitions of native speakers. The grammaticality of a sentence is not a matter of whether it is present in a corpus or has been recorded in the field. It is a matter of whether a native speaker (in many cases, the analysing linguist), drawing on the intuitions generated by his or her mental grammar, judges the sentence to be grammatical. Paradoxical as it might seem, what people say is not the yardstick by which the generative model is evaluated. It was, after all, on the basis of intuitions that we took *The farmer shot a rabbit* to be a

---

[6] We should also recognize the possibility that 'errors' might propagate themselves throughout the language, by being taken up by other language users; see pp. 268–9, 270–1.

perfectly grammatical sentence in English; whether or not the sentence occurs in a corpus is irrelevant.

The methodology rests on the assumption that grammaticality intuitions reliably reflect the contents of the mental grammar. But is this assumption warranted? In many cases, certainly, we feel very confident about our intuitions, so confident, in fact, that we may see no need to back them up by reference to attested data. For some example sentences, though, our intuitions might not deliver a clear-cut answer.[7] Sometimes, even, intuitions and corpus data might be in conflict. The situation is not at all infrequent. I discuss one such case below.

Explain me

Consider the verb *explain* and the VP frames it is able to occur in. If you explain something, you elucidate it, by providing additional information about it. Not surprisingly, *explain* can occur in a transitive frame (*explain the situation*). The information may be for the benefit of another person (*explain the situation to the audience*), in which case *explain* aligns itself with a large number of verbs which designate the transfer of something (goods or information) to another entity, usually another person or persons. Let us refer to the thing transferred as the THEME and the person to whom it is transferred as the GOAL. The prototypes of transfer verbs are *give* (for the transfer of goods) and *tell* (for the transfer of information) (Goldberg 1995). *Give* and *tell*, like many of the transfer verbs, can occur both in a ditransitive frame (*give the dog a bone, tell the children a story*) and in a frame in which the Goal appears in a *to*-phrase (*give a bone to the dog, tell a story to the children*).

When used in the transfer of information sense, one might expect *explain* to pattern like *tell*. However, this seems not to be the case. We say *Explain it to me*, not **Explain me it*; *Explain to me what happened*, not **Explain me what happened*. Huddleston and Pullum (2002: 309) state categorically that the Goal of *explain* can occur only in a *to*-phrase. According to Levin (1993: 46), there are a couple of dozen transfer verbs which resist the ditransitive frame; in addition to *explain*, these include *display, recommend, allege, confess,* and *entrust*.

If we refer to our intuitions, these accounts seem reasonable enough. *Explain me it* does sound rather bad, so much so that we might not even consider checking out the usage in a corpus. As a matter of fact, there are no instances of the word string *explain me* in the BNC as against 293 occurrences of *explain it*. But can we be confident that *explain* absolutely requires the Goal to appear in a *to*-phrase?

A Google search (April 2008) for the string *explain me* returned no fewer than 6 million hits; another 100,000 were returned for *explains/explained/explaining me*.

---

[7] The instability and unreliability of grammaticality intuitions is a well-known and well-researched phenomenon (Bolinger 1968; Carroll, Bever, and Pollack 1981; Greenbaum 1976; Luka and Barsalou 2005; Schütze 1996, esp. Chapters 1–5; Snyder 2000). I address the matter again in Chapter 9 (see pp. 215–16).

To be sure, not all the hits exemplify the ditransitive frame. In the following, *me* designates the Theme; the examples are fully consistent with Levin's (1993) claim.

(5) a. I need to **explain me** to myself.
  b. Do I want this therapist to **explain me** to myself?
  c. "You have **explained me** to myself, Harry," he murmured, with something of a sigh of relief. (Oscar Wilde, *The Picture of Dorian Gray*, Chapter 8).

It must also be recognized that quite a few of the hits are clearly to be attributed to non-native speakers; indeed, the use of *explain* in the double object construction is a common learner 'error':

(6) a. Could you **explain me** the exactly meaning of "Many Happy Returns of the Day!"?
  b. Can anybody **explain me** the difference between A GREAT DEAL OF and PLENTY OF? Thanks.

But now consider the following.

(7) a. Can someone **explain me** how PHP interacts with Java?
  b. Can someone please **explain me** how are aggregates stored in the database?
  c. We drove there with his private car and he **explained me** that he would get the expenses for the fuel back.
  d. Thank you all for your replies. They've **explained me** what I wanted to know. Now, I must check if my cable modem supports the VoIP bandwidth.

These exemplify the supposedly ungrammatical occurrence of the Goal (*me*) in immediate postverbal position without the preposition *to*.[8] Are the examples ungrammatical? Were the authors of these excerpts making errors? If I appeal to my native speaker intuitions, I have to confess that the citations do not sound all that bad. They are certainly not as bad as *Explain me it*.[9]

The supposed inability of the Goal to appear without the preposition *to* has consequences for passive sentences. If *explain me the problem* is ungrammatical,

---

[8] Supposedly ungrammatical uses of *explain* receive some discussion in Stefanowitsch (2007).
[9] A Google search returned about 200 hits for 'explain me it'. A quick perusal of the hits suggested that they were overwhelmingly from non-native speakers of English. On the other hand, *Explain me this* appears to have a different status. The following is recorded in the COCA corpus:

(i) Then **explain me this**, young pup: why do you want to join the expedition?

The usage may well be modelled on *Answer me this*. (*Answer* would not normally subcategorize for a ditransitive frame.) There are six examples of ditransitive *answer* in the BNC and twenty-one in the COCA, including the following:

(ii) **Answer me this**, Mason. Why did you enroll in the mounted police?
(iii) Daniel, **answer me this**. What's the square root of nine hundred sixty-one?
(iv) **Answer me this**—when your planes bombed the oil fields of Iraq, did you cry for those dark skinned men whose names you do not know?

then so too is *I was explained the problem* (the only possible passive sentence would be *The problem was explained to me*). As a matter of fact, there are no examples in the BNC of *I was explained, we were explained*, and the like, where passive *explained* has the Goal as its subject. Since we have found not a few instances of *explain me* on the World Wide Web, it is not surprising that we should also come across examples of the supposedly ungrammatical *I was explained*. As with the examples in (7), these do not strike me as being horribly ungrammatical, nor do the examples display any obvious indications of non-native authorship.

(8) a. On the first day **I was explained** what to do—and if I didn't understand something then I just had to ask someone—who would happily help me out.

b. **I was explained** on the phone what was included and what was delivered was not the same.

c. **I was explained** that the item was out of stock.

Are we to conclude from this little exercise that intuitions concerning the Goal of *explain* are totally unreliable? This would be too radical a conclusion. For one thing, there is the matter of frequency. Recall that there were no occurrences of the offending expressions in the 100 million word BNC corpus. And while 6 million Google hits seems like an enormous number, we must bear in mind the truly gigantic size of the Google database, as well as the fact that a not inconsiderable proportion of the hits were probably authored by non-native speakers. One would certainly not recommend that foreign learners of English should be instructed that *explain* patterns like *tell*, with *explain me* having the same status as *tell me*. The exercise does, however, teach us that we need to approach intuitive judgements with caution.

When intuitions and data are in conflict, a common strategy is to claim that usage is 'contaminated', and thus reflects the mental grammar only indirectly. Another strategy is to appeal to the researcher's idiolect. Intuitions are valid only for the mental grammar of the intuiting individual; other individuals have their own mental grammars, which might differ in small details one from another. Taking this line, we would say that the authors of the offending examples cited above spoke idiolects in which the examples are fully grammatical. In this way, we can preserve intact the view that intuitions reliably reflect the mental grammar of the speaker.

It would be a gross error to suppose that a language is represented identically in the minds of each of its speakers. With respect to lexical knowledge it is rather obvious that different speakers do differ from each other; some speakers know words that others do not and some use idioms that others are unfamiliar with. That speakers of the 'same' language should differ in their grammatical knowledge is not at all outrageous. (I shall shortly mention a case where differences in grammatical knowledge are clearly at issue.) But before we appeal to idiolectal differences we need to consider another possible reason for a disparity between intuitions and data.

Mostly, intuitions are brought to bear on invented sentences. These, of necessity, are decontextualized; they are also very often semantically impoverished, as with the example *explain me it*.[10] When the ditransitive construction is fleshed out with more contentful material, as in (7), we may find that the examples do not sound all that bad after all. We might even note some commonalities amongst the supposedly ungrammatical examples. In many cases, the Theme of *explain*—what it is that is explained, or to be explained—does not appear as a simple noun phrase and certainly not as a pronoun. The Theme is much more contentful. It may be a fully fledged *that*-clause, as in (7c), or, more typically, a *wh*-clause, that is, a clause introduced by interrogative *why, how, where*, and the like. Based on the cited examples, we might even want to identify a specific construction associated with ditransitive *explain*:

(9)   Can {someone / anyone / you} (please) explain me *wh*-S?

Let us return to the supposedly ungrammatical passive sentences in (8). On standard accounts, the Goal of *explain* cannot appear as the subject of a passive clause. But if (8c)—*I was explained that the item was out of stock*—is ungrammatical, what else is the speaker supposed to say? Here are two options:

(10)   a. It was explained to me that the item was out of stock.
       b. They explained to me that the item was out of stock.

We note that the 'acceptable' sentences are longer than the supposedly ungrammatical (8c). Also worth noting is that the 'ungrammatical' sentence fails to mention the speaker in sentence-initial position. When a person is reporting her experiences (concerning the explanation she has received), her first inclination is to mention herself at the very beginning of the sentence, typically by *I* in subject position. This is precisely what the speaker of (8c) has done.

There is another solution to the problem of how to report on an explanation one has been given and still use *I* in subject position. Consider these (Internet-sourced) examples:

(11)   a. **I was explained to** by my doctor that I needed some treatment but not a lot, and they relieved me of pain the same day.
       b. **I was explained to** that penicillin shouldn't be taken for very long.
       c. Six months ago, **I was explained to,** what <head> and <body> tags were.
       d. When I first called about the program, **I was explained to** that it would be a three or four month course.

To me, these are totally ungrammatical. When I came across the first of these examples while perusing hits for the phrase 'I was explained', I dismissed it as a

---

[10] Bolinger (1968: 36) in this connection speaks of "stripped-down sentences".

garbled error. It was only when I came across a second and a third example that I began to suspect that there was a pattern. Subsequent Googling of 'I was explained to' returned about 100,000 hits.[11]

What seems to be happening in these examples is that *They explained to me* is being passivized in the same way as *They spoke to me*, namely, by stranding the preposition:

(12)   a. They spoke to me ~ I was spoken to
        b. They explained to me (that ...) ~ I was explained to (that ...)

For me, the analogy fails. *Speak* and *explain* belong to different semantic types; *speak* designates a manner of communication, *explain* has to do with the communication of information. The verbs occur in different subcategorization frames and are passivized in different ways. For some speakers, however, it seems that the analogy does go through. In this respect, the mental grammar of these speakers differs significantly from my own (and probably from that of many other English speakers).

The lexicon

A crucial component of the generative model is the dictionary, or lexicon. So far I have referred to the lexicon simply as a list of all the words in a language. We need to expand on this statement. First, we need a definition of 'word' and a set of criteria for deciding what belongs in the lexicon and what stays out. Second, we need to consider the kinds of information that is associated with each of the dictionary entries. Our earlier discussion has already touched on this second issue. We have seen that each word needs to be marked for its category membership, as (count) noun, (transitive) verb, or whatever. Entries for some words, such as verbs, also need to give information on subcategorization frames and selectional restrictions. There is general agreement that the lexicon also needs to provide, for each word that is listed, information about what it means (its semantic representation) and how it is pronounced (its phonological representation). To the extent that we are concerned with the written form of a language, the lexicon needs to provide information about how each word is represented in writing.

What, though, is a word, and how do we determine whether a particular item counts as a word? The question seems trivial. 'Word' is a familiar, everyday concept, and literate speakers would have no problems in identifying the words in the present paragraph. Words, after all, are marked off by spaces.

---

[11] There is also one example of the usage in the COCA:

(i) And **I was explained to** by my Irish brothers and sisters in the North that they followed and modeled their civil rights movement, before Bloody Sunday in Derry, on Martin Luther King.

Appeal to the writing convention, though no doubt useful as a rule of thumb, begs the question of how words might be defined. What, after all, motivates the use of word spaces in our writing system? What are the characteristics of those linguistic units which are separated by word spaces? Words, in this sense, do share some common properties. Here are some of them:

- *Meaning*. Words, for the most part, designate concepts, that is, fairly stable units of meaning which are stored in a person's memory.
- *Internal structure*. Words are relatively stable units, both in pronunciation and in spelling. If their internal structure is changed—if, for example, one part of a word is replaced by something else—we have, at best, a different word with a different meaning, or, more likely, a piece of nonsense. Moreover, words cannot be interrupted by a pause, and do not tolerate the insertion of intervening material.
- *Freedom of occurrence*. Words are not particularly choosey with regard to material that may precede them or follow them; in appropriate circumstances, they can be preceded and followed by pauses.

This set of features seems to lie behind the writing convention of marking off words by spaces. On the above criteria, *farmer*, in *The farmer shot a rabbit*, is a word; the agentive morpheme *-er*, on the other hand, is not a word. Although associated with a fixed phonological form and with a determinate meaning, the suffix 'chooses' the items to which it attaches; the agentive suffix, namely, only attaches to verb stems.[12] Moreover, nothing can intervene between the verb and the suffix. Not every item that we might want to regard as a word exhibits each of the above properties. *The* has word status, even though it is not associated with a fixed concept. Neither is its pronunciation fixed: it may appear as [ðə] or [ðiː]. The crucial fact is that there are no particular restrictions on the items which may follow it: it may be followed by a noun (*the farmer*), an adjective (*the old farmer*), an adverb (*the rather old farmer*), a preposition (*the in my view old farmer*), and even by a pause (*the—erm—farmer*). The possibility of inserting material between *the* and *farmer* is the main reason why *the farmer* would be regarded as a sequence of two words.

The hedges which I used in the above paragraph ('fairly', 'relatively', 'particularly') suggest that the notion of word might not be rigidly circumscribed, and this is indeed the case (Taylor 2003b [1989]: 202–8). We need only consider variations in the use of word spaces to confirm this. Alongside *nevertheless* (written as one word), we occasionally find *never the less* (written as three words).[13] The BNC contains sixteen tokens of *toenail* and four of *toe nail*, along with two tokens of *toe-nail*. (This last

---

[12] The suffix has other semantic values and in these cases it can attach to other kinds of stem, as in *villager, back-bencher*, and *old-timer*. For the semantics of *-er*, see Panther and Thornburg (2001).

[13] The BNC has over 7,000 tokens of the one-word spelling and sixteen tokens of the three-word spelling.

example also raises the question of how to deal with hyphenated words—do these constitute two words or only one?)

According to the criteria for wordhood listed above, *farmer* and *farmers* are two different words. As such, both would need to be listed in the lexicon. On the other hand, we could argue that *farmers* does not need to be listed. This is because the plural form can be created through the application of a rule. In a sense, *farmer* and *farmers* are two forms of the same word. (The term LEXEME refers to this more abstract unit.) Pursuing this line, we might even decide that *farmer* does not need to be listed. It could be argued that *farmer* can also be created by rule, namely, by addition of the agentive *-er* suffix to the verb *farm*. What gets listed in the lexicon is the verb *farm*, the agentive suffix *-er*, and the plural suffix {s}. *Farmer* and *farmers* are generated by rules operating over these units.

This observation, if followed through, leads to a rather different conception of what belongs in the lexicon. The lexicon, namely, is the repository of those items which are not the output of some rule application. This criterion may exclude internally complex words like *farmers* from the lexicon. The same criterion, however, requires that quite a number of multi-word units do feature in the lexicon. Take the expression *by and large*. There are good reasons for regarding *by*, *and*, and *large* as words, each of which needs to be listed (along with their pronunciations and semantics). *By* will be listed as a preposition, designating amongst other things spatial proximity; *large* as an adjective having to do with size; while *and* is a coordinator, one of whose functions is to join together two words of the same lexical category (*old and young*, *men and women*, *come and go*, etc.). There is, however, no syntactic rule which enables *and* to conjoin a preposition and an adjective; as far as I am aware, *by and large* is the only example of such a structure in English. *By and large* cannot be generated by a syntactic rule operating over the words *by*, *and*, and *large*, neither can the meaning of the phrase be worked out from the meanings of its parts. For these reasons, the expression must itself be listed in the lexicon, and specified as a kind of adverbial.

The view of the lexicon as consisting only of those forms which cannot be generated by rule dates back at least to Bloomfield: "The lexicon is really an appendix of the grammar, a list of basic irregularities" (1933: 274). Bloomfield's view has been endorsed by many scholars. Thus, Chomsky and Halle (1968: 12) assert that lexical information is arbitrary or "idiosyncratic". More recently, Chomsky (1995: 235) reiterated the "rather traditional" view of the lexicon as "a list of 'exceptions'", comprising "whatever does not follow from general principles". Somewhat more colourful is Di Sciullo and Williams's (1987: 3) statement that "The lexicon is like a prison—it contains only the lawless, and the only thing that its inmates have in common is lawlessness".

Bloomfield's approach, and that of subsequent scholars, is based on the view that everything that occurs in a language can be put into one of two baskets. On the one hand, there are things which can be generated by the rule component (or, as Bloomfield understood the matter, by 'analogy'). Things that cannot be generated by rules belong in the lexicon. This, of course, is the very substance of the dictionary plus grammar book model. Notice, however, that the contents of the lexicon are not decided on the basis of an independent characterization of words. What counts as a word, for the purposes of the dictionary plus grammar book model, is dictated by the model itself. The lexicon does not consist of 'orthographical words', i.e. items separated by spaces and exhibiting the properties listed at the beginning of this section. Derivational morphemes such as agentive -*er* and inflectional morphemes such as plural {s} are listed as 'words', whereas forms such as *farmer* and *farmers* are not.[14]

This view of the lexicon and its contents raises a number of problems. I consider three of them.

Compounds

A compound is a word which consists of two words. English is particularly rich in compounds. Two nouns can be juxtaposed to create another noun (*toenail, airport, fish knife, dog house*, and countless more); less commonly, two verbs can come together to create a compound verb (*to sleep-walk, to drink-drive*), while two adjectives can form a compound adjective (*greenish-blue, icy cold*). One might even regard forms such as *into, onto, out of, away from*, and *off of* as compound prepositions, formed by juxtaposing two prepositions.

It would be easy to propose a rule which generates these compounds. A rule for [NN] compounds of the type *airport* and *fish knife* might look like the following:

(13)   N → N N

Since the same symbol N occurs on both sides of the re-write arrow we might expect the rule to be recursive, and this is indeed the case. Repeated applications of (13) make it possible to generate compounds of ever-increasing length: *airport, airport bus, airport bus route, airport bus route operating company*, and so on, in principle, indefinitely. In view of the fact that we can have VV and AdjAdj compounds, and perhaps even compound prepositions (*into, off of*), we might be tempted to propose an even more general rule, one which operates over any lexical category X to give a compound of the form [XX]:

(14)   X → X X

---

[14] As this discussion shows, the term 'word' is open to different interpretations. In general, I will use the term to refer to the orthographical word, marked off by spaces. Context should make it clear if other understandings of the term are indicated.

If compounds can be generated by rule (a rule, moreover, which possesses the hallmark of recursivity), one might conclude that compounds do not need to be listed in the lexicon, any more than expressions like *the farmer* or *a rabbit* need to be listed. This conclusion would be problematic, for a number of reasons. First, there is the question of the productivity of the rule. Nominal compounding is undeniably a productive process; speakers are constantly coming up with new compounds, suggesting that a rule such as (13) does have some validity. Moreover, as pointed out, it is not uncommon for an NN compound to be included within a further compound. VV compounding, on the other hand, is relative infrequent. One cannot create new ones at will. While *(to) sleep-walk* is a standard expression, *(to) walk-dream* is not. Recursive application of the rule is even more problematic; *(to) sleep-walk-dream* is just bizarre.

In spite of the existence of a rule which can create compounds from words, compounds themselves exhibit some typical features of words, for example, internal integrity. You cannot break up a compound by inserting other material; you have to say *major airport*, not **air-major-port*; *ingrowing toenail*, not **toe-ingrowing-nail*. In addition to this, quite a few compounds are associated with meanings which cannot always be predicted. *Airport* is the name of a particular kind of facility; given only the words *air* and *port* (and their listed meanings), one would be hard pressed to predict the conventionalized meaning of the compound. Indeed, it is quite possible that some native English speakers know and use the word *airport* without making any associations with the word *port*.

The case of compounds opens up a large chink in the generative model. On the one hand there is a rule which generates an infinite number of compounds (the number is infinite, since, as already illustrated, the rule is recursive). On the other hand, some outputs of the rule appear to have the status of established lexical items, which must be learned by speakers of the language and which must perforce be listed in the lexicon. However, it may not be possible to clearly circumscribe the set of established, lexicalized compounds from those that are created by rule application.[15] The notion of the lexicon as a finite list, whose members can be exhaustively enumerated, comes into question.

Derived words

A similar conclusion awaits us when we turn to another process of word creation, namely, the derivation of new words through the addition of suffixes (more rarely, prefixes) to an already existing word. A couple of paragraphs ago I wrote of criteria for 'wordhood'. Probably, if you are not a linguist well versed in the literature,

---

[15] Neither is it always clear whether an expression is to be regarded as a compound or not. Is *apple pie* an [NN] compound or an [Adj N] phrase? There are arguments both ways; see Taylor (2003*b* [1989]: 211).

wordhood will be a new word to you. (It is not accepted by the spell-checker that I am using.) Yet readers will hopefully have been able to comprehend the word. They will be familiar with the suffix *-hood*, exhibited in such words as *likelihood, sainthood, fatherhood*, and several more. The suffix attaches to an item X, usually a noun, sometimes an adjective, to create a noun referring to the status or quality of being X. There are perhaps a dozen or so established words in *-hood*.

In spite of the possibility of making a generalization over these dozen or so words, and even though it might be possible to create new words on the pattern (witness: *wordhood*), it will be appreciated that the process is not productive in the way in which generative rules are supposed to be productive. We have *fatherhood* and *motherhood* but not *sonhood*; *wordhood* is acceptable (at least, in a linguistics text), but *rulehood* sounds bizarre. The matter is complicated by the fact that some established words in *-hood* exhibit a range of semantic properties. *Brotherhood* does not refer to the status of being a brother, but rather to a (smallish) collection of males united in a common cause, typically with a secretive religious or political agenda; likewise with *sisterhood*. *Neighbourhood* does not refer to the status of being a neighbour, nor even to a collection of neighbours, but rather to a locality of a city.

The case of words in *-hood* is not untypical of the derivational process in general. We are able to create words through the use of suffixes such as *-al, -ity, -ization*, and also by prefixes such as *over-, out-*, and *in-*. We typically find that the process does not apply across the board to all the potential inputs (compare *wordhood* and *rulehood*). We have *overeat* ('eat too much'), but *overdrink* sounds very odd. The established items sometimes have their own idiosyncratic meanings. *Oversleep* does not refer to sleeping too much, but to sleeping beyond an expected wake-up time.

The examples of compounding and derivation call into question the clean distinction between the predictable and the unpredictable, between expressions which can be generated by rule and which speakers do not need to learn and items which must be listed in the lexicon and which must be individually learned. In some cases, the rules are less than fully productive—they do not apply to all eligible inputs and their outputs may have idiosyncratic properties which cannot be attributed to the rule and its operation. A basic assumption of the dictionary plus grammar book model thus comes under scrutiny, namely, the idea of the lexicon as a finite list of items. Even though word formation rules may be idiosyncratic in various ways, speakers are still able to use these rules to creatively extend the lexicon.

Syntactic constructions

Word formation rules—in particular, rules for compounding and derivation—are notorious for their only limited productivity and for their sometimes idiosyncratic outputs. We might expect a different picture to emerge with respect to rules for the creation of phrases and sentences.

It is true that many syntactic rules are highly productive. They seem to apply across the board to any eligible input and are able to generate expressions whose properties are entirely predictable. A candidate for such a rule is the one that generates a transitive clause of the type [NP V NP].[16] Nevertheless, the kinds of issues we encountered in connection with word formation rules also arise in connection with phrases and sentences.

Consider the following expression:

(15)   Off with his head!

Although unusual in many ways, the expression in (15) does allow some lexical variation. Here are some examples:

(16)   a. Down with imperialism!
        b. Up with equal education!
        c. Out with the old, in with the new!
        d. On with the show!
        e. Away with him!
        f. Off with you!

We might even be tempted to propose a syntactic rule which will generate these examples:

(17)   S → P with NP

The rule is unusual in several respects. First, the rule generates an odd kind of sentence, namely, a sentence which lacks a tensed verb, indeed, which lacks a verb at all. Second, it refers to a specific lexical item, the word *with*. Third, the element P ranges over only a subset of the English prepositions. These include *on*, *off*, *in*, *out*, *up*, *down*, and *away*. These designate a Goal, that is, the Place to which, or towards which, a thing is moved. However, other Goal prepositions, such as *above*, *over*, *across*, *below*, *near*, *from*, and *behind* are excluded. On the other hand, some directional prepositional phrases do seem to be compatible with the construction:

(18)   a. Upstairs with you, there's a good boy!
        b. Into the car with you all!
        c. Overboard with it!

There are also restrictions on the NP constituent. Nominals with definite reference (including pronouns) are strongly preferred, though *up with* and *down with* may be used with generic mass nouns.

---

[16] For a more nuanced view, see p. 144.

A notable feature of these expressions is their semantics. Expressions of this form express an exhortation, a wish that some act should be performed. The act itself is not named. However, if accomplished, the act will result in the referent of the NP being in a place, or a state, indicated by the preposition or prepositional phrase. Exactly how an expression is interpreted varies from case to case. Compare:

(19) a. Off with his head!
      b. Off with you!

The first expresses the wish that the person's head be cut off, the second that the person in question should 'be off', that is, should go away. Or take the following examples:

(20) a. On with the show!
      b. On with your clothes!

The first expresses the wish, not that the show should be 'put on', that is, staged, but that it should 'go on', or continue. The second invokes a different sense of 'put on', with reference, in this case, to the putting on of clothes. A feature of all these various interpretations is that they seem to have little to do with the normal semantic value of the one stable element in the construction, the word *with*. Elsewhere in the language, *with* is used to indicate accompaniment (*come with me*) or means (*cut it with a knife*). Neither accompaniment nor means can be worked into the interpretations commonly associated with the construction.

Some instances of the [OFF WITH] construction (as we might call it) are associated with special semantic values and specific conditions of use. *Up with NP* and *Down with NP* are slogans at protest meetings. *Out with it* is used to urge a person to be forthcoming with information. *On with the show* can be used as an encouragement to pursue some enterprise (not necessarily a theatrical show) in spite of interruptions or setbacks. Many English speakers will associate *Off with his head!* with the Queen of Hearts in *Alice in Wonderland*, though the expression had also been used by Shakespeare.[17] Nowadays, the phrase is sometimes used as a jocular reproach to a person who has said or done something that is silly or embarrassing.

In summary, the [OFF WITH] construction bears the hallmarks of limited productivity and idiosyncratic outputs that we found with word formation rules. Knowledge of the construction cannot be equated with knowledge of the generative rule (17). Knowing the construction consists in knowing its established instances and their conventional semantic and pragmatic values. Some of the established uses are to all intents and purposes lexically fixed; this is the case with *Off with his head*, especially when intended as a jocular reproach. On the other hand, the sloganeering *Up with*

---

[17] *Henry VI Part III* (I, iv); *Richard III* (III, iv).

NP contains an open slot which may be filled with the name of any fashionable cause. To this extent, even fixed expressions are compatible with a degree of creativity. Speakers may also creatively extend their repertoire by creating phrases on the pattern of one of the established uses. The use of *overboard* and *upstairs*, as in (18), can be seen in this light. Such extensions are, however, severely constrained by existing uses. They are not the result of the mechanistic application of the phrase structure rule.

By any measure, the [OFF WITH] construction is fairly marginal in English. In the first place, instances of the construction are not very frequent. One can easily imagine living for months in an English-speaking environment without ever once encountering the construction. The construction is marginal also with respect to its internal structure. It exemplifies a use of the word *with* which has no parallels elsewhere in the language, while its syntactic make-up, in association with its specific semantics, bears little resemblance to any other sentence type in the language. Nevertheless, as we shall see in the following chapters, the case of *Off with* is by no means untypical of the large number of constructions and idiomatic phrases which we find in a language. If we focus on only a single one of these marginal phenomena, we might be tempted to dismiss it as an idiomatic exception to the rule-governed rest of the language. Once we take into account a wider range of examples, however, it becomes increasingly difficult to dismiss them as peripheral. On the contrary, a very great deal of what is in a language displays the kinds of idiosyncrasies exhibited by the [OFF WITH] construction.

Compositionality

An expression such as *Off with his head* is problematic for the generative model, not only because of its strange syntax and limited productivity, but also because of the meaning which idiosyncratically attaches to it, a meaning, moreover, which cannot be built up from the meanings of its component parts. Similar remarks apply to cases of compounding and derivation. *Neighbourhood* is interpreted differently from *brotherhood*, and an airport is not really a kind of port at all.

On the generative model, the meanings of complex expressions are COMPOSITIONAL, that is, they can be worked out on the basis of the meanings of the component words and the manner of their combination. Assuming compositionality, speakers do not need to learn the meanings of complex expressions. They need only learn the semantic properties of the component words along with rules for their combination. Although compositionality is often taken to refer to the semantic properties of an expression, it can also be applied to its phonological properties. We do not need to learn how a complex expression is to be pronounced; we need only know the pronunciation of its component words and the rules for their combination.

The generative model is intimately tied up with the notion of compositionality. On the one hand, the generative model entails that complex expressions will exhibit compositionality. At the same time, the fact of compositionality is taken as a compelling argument in favour of the generative model.

Indeed, compositionality would appear to be a brute fact about language use—speakers do utilize known resources in order to create new sentences. Speakers do come up with novel combinations of words, and hearers, for the most part, are able to work out what they mean. The generative model offers an explanation for this state of affairs. On the basis of a finite lexicon and a finite set of combinatorial rules, speakers are able to produce, and hearers are able to understand, an infinite set of sentences.

In view of the failings of the generative model which we have hinted at in this chapter and which we shall discuss in greater detail in due course, we shall need to seek alternative means for dealing with linguistic creativity. In the meantime, I want to consider some of the entailments of compositionality.

The compositionality principle requires that each component of a complex expression contributes a fixed and stable chunk of semantic (and phonological) material to the expressions in which it occurs. In the ideal case, each item in the lexicon would contribute exactly the same chunk to whatever expression it occurs in. This ideal is rarely met. Words (and morphemes) are often pronounced differently, and have different meanings, according to the contexts in which they occur.

One way to handle this state of affairs would be to propose a set of rules for generating the full range of phonological and semantic variants of a word, while still associating the word with fixed and unique phonological and semantic representations. There are some cases in which this approach might be viable. Thus, the plural morpheme—at least with respect to its use in 'regular' plural forms—might be represented in the lexicon as an alveolar sibilant, unspecified for voicing. Whether the morpheme surfaces as [s] or [z] would be handled by rules of voicing assimilation: nouns terminating in a voiced segment form their plurals in [z], those terminating in a voiceless segment form their plurals in [s]. Plurals in [əz] would need a special rule of [ə]-insertion, applicable just in case the noun ends in one of [s, z, ʃ, ʒ, tʃ, dʒ]. For some other items, however, the approach is much less compelling. Consider the definite article. The definite article can appear as [ðə] or [ðiː]. We could, no doubt, come up with a rule for deriving the one pronunciation from the other (or for deriving both from a more abstract representation). The rule, though, would be entirely ad hoc and specific to this one item. The simplest solution is to associate the definite article with two different phonological representations and to specify the conditions of their use.

A lexical item can vary not only in its pronunciation but also in the meaning which it contributes to an expression. In some cases, the variation might also be handled by rule. For example, words such as *institute, museum, university,* and several more, can refer both to an institution (*work for the museum*) and to a building (*the museum burned down*). The variation is systematic for this set of nouns and the availability of the two different readings is largely predictable.[18] There might be grounds, in this case, for associating these words with a single semantic representation (Bierwisch 1983; for a counter view, see Taylor 1994, 2006*b*). Mostly, though, semantic variants will need to be separately listed. This is because the range of variants is very often specific to each lexical item. It would be pointless to propose a rule which derives the 'means' sense of *with* from the 'accompaniment' sense, or vice versa. Most words, quite simply, are POLYSEMOUS, often extensively so. This means that most words will need to be associated with two or more different semantic representations.

The existence of polysemy (and of pronunciation variants) does not in itself threaten compositionality. It does, however, considerably complicate the compositional process. *Cut the meat with the knife* draws on the 'means' sense of *with*; *stew the meat with the vegetables* implicates the 'accompaniment' sense. If the interpretations are crossed, we are left with nonsense. Compositionality, in other words, is not simply a matter of combining semantic units; the units that are to be combined have to be properly selected. This makes demands, both on the contents of the lexicon and on the compositional process itself. For compositionality to go through, it is necessary that each item in the lexicon is associated with a fixed number (one or more) of discrete meaning chunks, only one of which is selected in the compositional process. For each word, we shall need to specify (a) exactly how many different meanings it has, and (b) exactly what these meanings are. To the extent that these requirements are not able to be met (and these are issues we shall examine in Chapter 10), the very principle of compositionality (and the view of polysemy which it entails) come under threat.

In conclusion

According to the dictionary plus grammar book model, knowledge of a language consists of two components: a list of words (which comprise the dictionary) and a list of rules for combining words into grammatical sentences. It is impossible to overestimate the influence of this model on linguistic theory and practice. It has set the research agenda for at least half a century of academic linguistics and even when the model is not explicitly invoked its entailments have provided the context against which many issues of concern to linguists are discussed. The issues range from semantic compositionality and the nature of polysemy to syntactic theory and the status of lexical categories.

---

[18] Prepositions also exemplify a degree of systematicity in their range of semantic values, as we shall see in Chapter 10 (p. 234). Even so, individual items may have idiosyncratic properties with respect to these more general processes.

A critical examination of the model and its entailments, and their assessment in the light of actual linguistic data, reveal its tensions and inherent contradictions. Yet the power of the model is such that linguists have often felt obliged to accommodate recalcitrant data by some means or other. For example, expressions which manifestly do not conform with the workings of the dictionary plus grammar book model might be regarded as 'idiomatic' and thereby shunted off to the periphery of the language system, of little relevance to the language 'core'. There comes a point, though, when the periphery looms so large that it may no longer be an option to regard it as peripheral. We will need to abandon the model, its assumptions, and all that it entails.

3

Words and their behaviour

According to a common conception, knowledge of a language can be partitioned into two components: one is the lexicon, which lists the basic units of the language (the words), the other is the syntax, or rule component, which specifies how items selected from the lexicon can combine into larger expressions (phrases and sentences). The model, as discussed in Chapter 2, was motivated by the observation that speakers are able to produce, and hearers to understand, a potentially infinite number of novel sentences. This being the case, knowing a language cannot be equated with knowing a set of sentences. Rather, knowing a language consists in knowing the means whereby sentences are created (and understood). The dictionary plus grammar model offers itself as an explanation for this state of affairs.

Lexical categories (the traditional parts of speech) play a central role in this model. This is because the syntactic rules do not specify how lexical items *per se* can be combined. There is no rule which stipulates that *cat* can combine with *black* to produce the phrase *black cat*. If such were the case, we would need a battery of rules specific to every single item in the lexicon, stating each of its combinatory possibilities. With every new word added to the lexicon, the rule component would increase exponentially. This situation would defeat the very *raison d'être* of the generative model. Instead, the rules refer to categories and generalize over those lexical items which are members of those categories. It is necessary, therefore, in terms of the working of the model, that each item in the lexicon is marked for its membership in one of the available categories. *Black* is specified in the lexicon as an adjective, *cat* as a noun. *Black cat* is sanctioned by a rule which permits an adjective to combine with a noun.

What are the available lexical categories and how many of them are there? Their number, clearly, must be finite, since the rules of the grammar are themselves finite. Ideally, the number of categories will be quite small so as to maximize the generative capacity of the grammar. If the number of categories were anything like the number of items listed in the lexicon, we would be approaching a situation in which each word, or small set of words, would need a battery of syntactic rules in order to account for its use in the language. The idea of syntactic rules making reference to categories with a very small membership would defeat the very objective of the generative model. As a matter of fact, the consensus appears to be that the number of categories is highly restricted: noun, verb, adjective, preposition, adverb, determiner, conjunction, and a few more (the precise inventory depends to some extent on the linguistic theory). In any case, the number of categories is to be counted in the single digits or low teens, certainly not in the high tens or the thousands. Subdivisions within these categories may need to be recognized, of course. *Cat* would be classed, not just as 'noun', but also as 'common noun', more specifically, as 'common count noun'; *sleep* would be listed, not just as 'verb', but as 'intransitive verb'.

The account brings with it an important entailment, namely, that all members of a category are equally available to fill the relevant slots of the combinatorial rules. If a rule refers to the noun category, then any and every item marked as 'noun', or more specifically (as the case may be) as 'count noun', can stand as the value for the category symbol. For the purpose of the combinatorial rules, all members of a lexical category are equal and have the same distributional possibilities.

I do not, at this stage, want to question the notion of lexical category as such (I return to the matter in Chapter 6). It may certainly be useful, and insightful, to group different words together as members of a single category on the basis of their shared properties. I do, however, want to question the assumptions of the generative model with respect to lexical categories, specifically:

- that there exists a small, finite number of categories, to which all items in the lexicon can be assigned;
- that all members of a category behave identically with respect to the rules which refer to the categories.

If these assumption should turn out to be false, it would have major implications for the validity of the generative model. In order to know how to use a word, the speaker of a language would need to know specific facts pertaining to that word, facts which could only be acquired through exposure to how the word is used. It would not be enough simply to have a word labelled as noun, adjective, or whatever, or even as count noun or transitive verb. Such information would be inadequate for predicting how the word might be used in larger structures.

Lexical categories

The notion of lexical category, or part of speech, is as old as the study of language itself. It is based on the realization that it is possible to group words together on the basis of what they have in common. For example, a set of words may behave in similar ways with respect to how the words combine with other words, or they may share some semantic and even phonological commonalities.[1]

---

[1] The semantic commonalities are rather evident; nouns tend to refer to physical objects, verbs refer to actions or events, and so on. Phonological commonalities of the word classes are less expected. Research by

Chomsky, and, following him, many generative linguists, took the line that there exists a small, universal set of major categories; these are noun, verb, adjective, and preposition (Chomsky 1981). More recent versions of Chomskyan grammar, e.g. Chomsky (1995), recognize in addition a rather larger set of minor, or functional categories. The distinction between major and minor categories is based on the widely accepted contrast between content and function words, that is, between words which have conceptual content and those which have more grammatical functions. Functional categories include tense and aspect inflections, number inflections, markers of negation, and complementizers. It should be mentioned, however, that the categorization of these latter items is heavily theory-dependent. In older versions of Chomskyan grammar, a word such as *the* was assigned to a distinct lexical category, that of determiner; in more recent versions, determiners are analyzed as heads of noun phrases, and thus as nouns. Number (singular or plural) and case (nominative, accusative, etc.) used to be features of a noun phrase; in more recent accounts number and case are treated as minor categories.

The most robust of the lexical categories are undoubtedly noun and verb (Croft 1991; Givón 1984; Langacker 1987). The categories are based in the fundamental conceptual distinction between things and processes, between, on the one hand, entities of which existence can be predicated and, on the other, the events or situations in which these entities participate and which can be assigned a value of either true or false. The distinction is supported by distributional and morphological facts. Nouns (in English) can occur with determiners and quantifiers (*the*, *some*, etc.); many of them can pluralize; noun phrases can function as the subject of a verb. Verbs, on the other hand, may inflect for tense; they may be negated; and they may be used to predicate a state of affairs of a subject nominal. Probably, all languages exhibit the noun–verb distinction, or, perhaps fairer to say, all languages have words which can function as nouns and words which can function as verbs (Croft 2001: 65–70).

All other categories are parasitic on the noun–verb distinction and on syntactic categories based on nouns and verbs, that is, noun phrases, verb phrases, and clauses. Adjectives are items that specify, or serve to restrict the referential range of a noun, as in *old man, black cat*. Adverbs serve to restrict the referential potential of a verb: *sing loudly, leave early*. Prepositions may be regarded as items which serve to establish a relation to a thing; often it is a spatial relation but it could also be a temporal or other kind of relation: *a book on the table, the cat in the bag, sleep in the bed, walk in your sleep*. Conjunctions are items which establish a relation between

a number of scholars (e.g. Berg 2000; Kelly 1992; Monaghan, Chater, and Christiansen 2005; Sereno and Jongman 1990), however, has shown that correlations do exist. There is a slight bias for the stressed syllable in English verbs to have a front vowel, while stressed syllables in nouns prefer a back vowel; a final obstruent consonant is more likely to be voiced if the word is a verb than if it is a noun; and nouns, on the whole, are longer, in terms of number of syllables and number of phonemes, than verbs.

clauses, that is, between events or situations: *leave <u>while</u> the party is in progress, cry because you have lost your toys, go to work <u>although</u> you feel sick*. Complementizers serve to embed one clause as the complement of another: *believe <u>that</u> the earth is flat, wonder <u>whether</u> the sun will rise*.

Once we leave the relatively safe territory of nouns and verbs, classification of words into parts of speech becomes increasingly problematic. Adjectives, for example, can typically be used both attributively (*an old man*) and predicatively (*the man is old*). Attributive uses conform better with our earlier characterization of adjectives as items which restrict the referential range of a noun; the category 'old man' has fewer potential members than the category 'man'. The predicative use, on the other hand, is somewhat verb-like, in that a property is predicated of an individual. Not surprisingly, attributive and predicative uses are not always semantically equivalent. An 'old friend' is not necessarily a friend who 'is old' (Taylor 1992*b*) and while we might consume 'fast food' it would be odd to say that the food we are eating 'is fast'. A particularly heterogeneous category is that of the adverbs. In fact, the adverb category serves as something of a dumping ground for any word which somehow serves to modify the meaning of a verb phrase, clause, or sentence. Such diverse items as *very, frankly, honestly, however, indeed, never, nevertheless*, and even *not*, may be accommodated in this category.

It also turns out that many of the most frequently used words do not easily fit into any of the standard categories. What is the part of speech of *up* in *shut up*? It is not a preposition on our earlier characterization, nor is it an adverb (it does serve to specify in more detail the process of 'shutting'). It is sometimes regarded as a particle—another waste-basket category. And how would we categorize *yes, no, please, there* (as in *There's a man been shot*), or even *ago* (as in *three weeks ago*)? What about French *voici* and *voilà* and Italian *ecco*?

In spite of these strictures and problematic cases, there is no denying that large chunks of the vocabulary of English and other languages can be designated as nouns, verbs, adjectives, and so on. It does not follow, however, that each and every word of a language can be cleanly assigned to one of the commonly recognized categories. Some words turn out to be *sui generis*; in terms of their behaviour in the language they belong to a category with a membership of one. It would also be an error to assume that all members, even of the more robust categories like noun and verb, are essentially equal with respect to their distribution in the language. Lexical categories, in fact, are not unlike semantic categories such as 'fruit' and 'vegetable'. The validity and general usefulness of the fruit and vegetable categories by no means entails that all members of the categories share a set of common properties (Taylor 2003*b*). Neither is the classification of foodstuffs without its problems. Are tomatoes a fruit or a vegetable? What about cucumbers?

In order to investigate this matter thoroughly, it would be necessary to examine the usage range of a large number of individual lexical items—it would be necessary, in fact, to write a full grammar for each word. I will instead select a small number of words, as representative of the kinds of issues that arise.

Unique distribution of words

It is certainly true that a set of words can often be lumped together in a lexical category and that generalizations can be made about their distribution. It would seem fair to say that any common noun (whether count or mass) can combine with *the*, that any noun phrase (given semantic plausibility) can function as the subject of a verb (whether transitive or intransitive). However, once we start looking at individual cases in any detail, we find all manner of marginal, exceptional, and in other ways problematic examples. Many quite ordinary words have distributions which cannot easily be accounted for in terms of their membership in one of the standard lexical categories.

The point is not new. Gross (1979) reports a study in which he listed the syntactic properties of 12,000 French verbs. The properties included the type of complement the verb took, whether a preposition is involved, whether a clausal complement is in the indicative or subjunctive mood, whether the verb takes *être* or *avoir* as auxiliary, and so on. Gross states that no two verbs shared exactly the same set of properties. (See also Gross 1984.) He also points out that supposed generalizations concerning, for example, the English passive, may not hold across the board. It is commonly asserted that the *by*-phrase is optional in passives: *Max ate my soup ~ My soup was eaten (by Max)*. Yet there are cases where the *by*-phrase seems to be obligatory (Gross's examples):

(1)   a. The symbol ψ represents this function.
      b. This function is represented *(by the symbol ψ).

(2)   a. Sharp intuitions underlie his discourse.
      b. His discourse is underlain *(by sharp intuitions).

The availability of the passive may also be influenced by the choice of participating nominals. Gross's examples once again:

(3)   a. Max inhabits Manhattan.
      b. *Manhattan is inhabited by Max.

However, with a plural or 'collective' subject, the passive is claimed to work:

(4)   a. Rich politicians inhabit Manhattan.
      b. Manhattan is inhabited by rich politicians.

Gross goes on to draw implications of this state of affairs for acquisition. Alongside the need for children to learn "the basic mechanisms of sentence structure"—the province, presumably, of general syntactic rules—there must also be "an important amount of rote learning" (p. 876), concerning the specifics of individual lexical items and their behaviour in syntactic constructions. It is, for Gross, an open question how much of a language is subject to rote learning. The general tone of his paper, however, suggests that the amount is rather large. This is a point that I would also want to endorse.

These matters were taken up, a couple of decades later, by Culicover in his monograph *Syntactic Nuts* (1999). Unlike Gross, who was openly critical of the Chomskyan enterprise, Culicover firmly aligns himself with the generative approach. The import of his monograph is therefore all the more worthy of note (Taylor 1999*b*).

Culicover argues that a surprisingly wide range of phenomena in English (he also pays attention to Italian and French data) cannot be accounted for by appeal to general syntactic principles. His examples range from clause types, such as the imperative, to the behaviour of individual lexical items and classes of items. Thus, with respect to determiners and quantifiers—items such as *the, this, each, these, many, all*, as well as the numerals—Culicover points out that there is no general principle governing their use. In fact, their distribution in the language suggests that there are "almost as many categories as there are elements" (1999: 64). Culicover likewise brings his analysis to bear on the class of prepositions. There are 'odd' prepositions, like *ago* and *for*, and 'marginal' prepositions like *notwithstanding*. Even seemingly central members of the category, such as *in* and *out*, turn out to be rather different in their distributional possibilities. Another of his examples is the question phrase *how come?* As Kay and Fillmore (1999: 4) point out in a different context, *how come?* is not exactly equivalent to *why?* Whereas the latter merely asks for a reason, *how come* conveys that the queried situation is somehow unexpected or incongruous. In some contexts, *how come* and *why* distribute in a similar way. In the following, the two expressions are claimed to be equally available:

(5) a. He said he would leave early but he didn't say {why / how come}.
    b. {Why / How come} and when did you leave the area?
    c. I wanted to invite some weird people to the party. But {why / how come} Robin, of all people?

A peculiarity of *how come*, however, is that it does not trigger subject–auxiliary inversion. Moreover, unlike other *wh*-words, it cannot co-occur with *the hell, on earth*, and the like.

(6) a. Why did you leave?
    b. How come you left?
    c. *How come did you leave?

(7)   a. Why on earth did you leave?
       b. *How come on earth you left?
       c. *How come on earth did you leave?

The thrust of Culicover's account is that any syntactic rule or principle that one might wish to invoke in order to account for these facts simply re-states, or paraphrases, the facts and fails to offer any deeper insight into the phenomena in question. The language learner simply has to learn the facts as they are. And once the learner has done this, that's it, the relevant part of the language has been successfully acquired:

> Once the learner has identified the special properties and made the generalizations, the learner knows the relevant facts about the language in this domain, and we may say that the learner has 'acquired' this part of the language in some concrete sense. There is nothing more about the language that the learner acquires in virtue of assigning the various elements to the linguist's categories.   (Culicover 1999: 67–8)

The point is repeated:

> …it appears that the learner must acquire a precise knowledge of the facts about some phenomenon, and having done so, can be said to have learned the language, regardless of whether or how this knowledge is encoded into an abstract structural representation.
>
> (Culicover 1999: 68)

In order to acquire a "precise knowledge" of the facts, the learner must, "in many if not all cases…have access to all of the data" (p. 68). Moreover, the learner "does not go significantly beyond its experience", in other words, the learner is "conservative and attentive" (p. 68).

Culicover, in his monograph, raises the possibility that the number of lexical categories in a language might be very large and that a not insignificant number of these might have a very small membership, even a membership of one. This is tantamount to saying that a considerable number of lexical items are *sui generis* with respect to their occurrence in larger configurations. The properties of these words simply have to be learned; they cannot be derived from general syntactic principles.[2]

In the following, I look at some examples where the use of a word involves the knowledge of specific facts pertaining to the word. I start with a couple of words whose category status (as count nouns) is not in dispute. The words, however, fail to show the full distribution that one would expect of members of this category.

---

[2] Culicover (2004) reiterates this position in his review of Huddleston and Pullum's (2002) *Cambridge Grammar of the English Language*. "The devil", he writes, "is in the details" (p. 135) and the *Grammar* abounds in myriad descriptions of the "finest details" (p. 130) of usage. The issue, for the theorist, is then to explain "how in the world someone could have all of this stuff in his or her head" (p. 135). Culicover contends that it is in the head because it has been learned on the basis of "primary linguistic experience" and whatever generalizations the experience gives rise to; things that are not encountered, and which "fall[s] outside of a well-supported generalization", are not "in the head" (p. 131).

Laps and bosoms

Nouns, by common consent, are able to occur in noun phrases; selectional restrictions and subcategorization permitting, these noun phrases may stand as the subject or direct object of a verb. Given that a word is listed in the lexicon as a noun, the syntactic rules of the language will generate phrases and sentences with the noun appearing in these configurations.

Sinclair (2004: 18) drew attention to some words for which this broad generalization does not hold, an example being the word *lap*. As a noun, *lap* is homonymous between the meanings 'circuit in a race' and 'area between the upper legs, formed when a person is in a sitting position'. A lap, in this second sense, is a place which can support a sitting child, a small animal, or a tray with food while you are watching television. The racing and the body-region senses are of about equal frequency in the BNC. It is the body-region sense that Sinclair was referring to and it is the one that I want to focus on here.

Data from the BNC suggest, first of all, that body-region *lap* occurs almost exclusively in a possessive environment, mostly with possessive adjectives: *my lap, her lap*, etc., but also occasionally with a postnominal *of*-phrase: *the lap of a kindly angel, the lap of my trenchcoat, the lap of his dressing gown*. The possessive pattern is also exhibited by metaphorical uses—*the lap of luxury, the lap of plenty, power falls into his lap*. Adjectival modification of *lap* is rare: examples include *her ample lap, her rigid lap, his gasoline-soaked lap. Lap* also has uses as a premodifier, in such fixed expressions as *lap dog* and *laptop (computer)*.

The association of *lap* with possessive constructions is perhaps what one should expect, given that *lap* designates a part of a larger whole. (Part terms, especially body-part terms, are typically used with reference to the larger whole.) It may also not come as a surprise that the frequency of *her lap* is about double that of *his lap*; this is no doubt because a 'lap' is better defined if the person is wearing a skirt or a dress.

A second notable aspect of the way *lap* is used is that the possessive noun phrases are virtually restricted to occurring as the complement of a preposition. Here are some examples (from the BNC):

(8) a. the baby asleep in her lap
    b. dropped it into her lap
    c. dropped an envelope in my lap
    d. sit on her lap
    e. she dropped her hands to her lap
    f. holding a large cardboard box on her lap
    g. she let the dog slide from her lap to the floor
    h. the cat jumped off his lap

Also of note is the fact that not all the prepositions are equally favoured. A BNC search shows that the configuration [possessive adjective + lap] occurs predominantly after the prepositions *on* (239 uses) and *in* (244 uses). *On* is a preposition which, in its spatial sense, takes as its complement an entity which is construed as a supporting surface (*the book on the table, the fly on the wall*). *In*, in its spatial sense, construes its complement as a containing volume: *the car in the garage, the money in the box*. The data suggest, therefore, that a lap is regarded both as a surface and as a container, to approximately equal degrees.

The spatial prepositions of English make a three-way distinction between relations of Place (where something is), Goal (where something goes to, or is moved to), and Source (where something moves from, or is removed from). The complex preposition *into* and *onto* explicitly designate a Goal relation. We often find, however, that *in* and *on*, without the addition *to*, can also express Goal. Thus, (8c) clearly has the Goal sense; the case of (8d) is ambiguous between a Place and Goal reading. The Source relation requires a different set of prepositions. Corresponding to *on/onto*, we have the source preposition *off*. Corresponding to *in/into* we have *out (of)*. Just as you can put something on, or onto your lap, you can also take it from your lap. But whereas you can put something in, or into your lap, the Source relation *out of your lap* is not attested in the BNC.

How does the preposition *at* fit into the picture? *At* construes its complement as a zero-dimensional point (*the lines intersect at A*); alternatively, the dimensionality of the complement entity is not an issue: *I met her at the supermarket, the plane landed at Heathrow*. Often, *at* implies the functionality of the complement entity: if I sit *at* my desk, I am using my desk for the purpose for which it is intended, namely, as a work place. Similarly with *at work, at the office, at school*, and many more. The corresponding Goal preposition is *to* (*go to the office*), the Source preposition is *from* (*drive from Oxford to Birmingham*). *Lap* rarely occurs with *at*, though *to* and *from* are occasionally encountered.

The occurrence of these prepositions with [possessive adjective + lap] is shown in Table 3.1. The rows refer to the dimensionality of the complement entity, the columns distinguish the kind of spatial relation. Note that the entries for the Goal relation with respect to surfaces and containers underestimate the incidence of these

TABLE 3.1. **Prepositions associated with *lap* (data from the BNC)**

	Place	Goal	Source
Zero-dimensional point	at 9	to 20	from 13
2-dimensional surface	on 239	onto 10	off (off of) 13
3-dimensional volume	in 244	into 50	out of 0

categories. This is because *on* and *in* regularly can encode both the Place and the Goal relations.

Prepositions other than the ones listed in Table 3.1 are rare. In the BNC, *over* is attested twice: there are no cases of *across*, *under*, *beneath*, or *above*.

(9) a. She sat down and examined it minutely—spread it **over her lap** and investigated.
     b. She said: 'He wanted me **over his lap**, so my feet were off the ground.'

The data presented above might strike the reader as unremarkable and just what one might expect, given our understanding of what a lap is. If you know what the word means, then you can be fairly confident about how it will be used. Such judgements are easy to make after the fact. (We could, for example, reverse the argument and claim that we know what the word means, precisely because we know how the word is used.) The corpus data, however, are not without their surprises. The almost equal distribution of container and surface construals is not, I would maintain, something that could have been predicted from introspecting about what a lap is. Moreover, given the slight preponderance of the container conceptualization (the uses of *in* and *into* total 294, as against 249 for the combined *on* and *onto* uses), one might have expected at least a small number of cases in which something is removed *out of* a person's lap. Yet such uses are not attested, at least, not in the BNC.

We can bring the distinctiveness of the data into focus by comparing *lap* with another body-region term, *bosom*. This denotes the front top half of the torso, typically of a woman and involving her breasts. Like *lap*, *bosom* is associated with possessive contexts, whether prenominal (*her bosom*) or post-modifying (*the bosom of…*). Not surprisingly, *her bosom* outnumbers *his bosom* by a ratio of 5:1. Metaphorical uses go with post-modification (*the bosom of the family*, *the bosom of the Lord*). There are also some well-entrenched uses as a nominal premodifier, in particular *bosom friend* and *bosom pal*.

In contrast to the *lap* data, adjectival modification is not uncommon, *ample bosom* being a particularly frequent collocation. Another difference is that the word features quite often in subject and object noun phrases. A point of similarity with *lap*, on the other hand, is the fact that *bosom* frequently occurs in prepositional phrases. Interestingly, though, the prepositions are different, the most frequent preposition being *to*.

(10) a. she clutched it to her bosom
      b. Clara, clasped to the young man's bosom, reflected…
      c. take her to your bosom
      d. clutching to her bosom the file of notes and sketches
      e. thrust it under her raincoat and pressed it to her bosom
      f. holding the brown teapot to her bosom
      g. she pressed a hand to her bosom

Especially noteworthy in these examples is the distinctive value of the preposition. In Table 3.1 *to* is classified as a Goal preposition. The above examples, however, do not involve a dynamic relation whereby one entity moves to the place of another entity (as in *go to the shops, put it to one side*). Rather, something is held or maintained in a location, typically a position of contact with respect to some other entity. You can (metaphorically) *put your nose to the grindstone* (the Goal sense of *to*), and, having done this, you *keep your nose to the grindstone*. The 'maintaining in position' sense is exemplified by some common expressions such as *Keep to the left* ('continue driving on the left-hand side of the road'), *Keep it to yourself* ('don't talk about this to other people'), and *Hold to your principles* ('do not depart from your principles').

The choice of verbs in (10) bears out this analysis. *Clutch, clasp, hold*, and *press* all have to do with exerting energy in order to maintain something in position and are commonly found with the preposition *to*:

(11)   a. She clutched her handkerchief to her mouth.
       b. He lightly pressed his finger to her lips.
       c. He pressed his ear to the door.
       d. She held her hand to her head.
       e. She held her head to his.

Verbs such as *grip* and *grasp*, which have to do with establishing contact, are not attested with the 'positioning' sense of *to*.

Fun

Next, let us consider a rather more frequent word than *lap* or *bosom*.

At first blush, *fun* would appear to be easily categorized, namely, as a (singular) mass noun. We should expect it to behave in much the same way as other mass nouns, such as *patience, music,* and *happiness*, and in many respects this is indeed the case. In addition to the fact that they lack a plural form, a distinctive feature of mass nouns is that they can occur without a determiner (*have fun, listen to music, lack patience*). Determiner-less *fun* features in a number of idiomatic expressions, such as *make fun of* and *poke fun at*. Mass nouns can, however, occur with *the, more, (not) much, lots of*, and *no*, and in this respect also *fun* is in no way remarkable:

(12)   a. Don't spoil the fun.
       b. We had lots of fun.
       c. We didn't have much fun.
       d. You'll have more fun with me.

A closer inspection of the contexts in which *fun* occurs, however, reveals some rather distinctive distributions. Consider the following:

(13)   a. It's no fun (being suspected of murder).
       b. It wasn't much fun (being accused of something you didn't do).
       c. It won't be much fun (for you).
       d. (Standing there) wasn't much fun.
       e. There's no fun (in reading it).
       f. There isn't all that much fun (in going around with a married bloke).

In these contexts, *fun* is not readily replaceable by other items commonly regarded as mass nouns. You cannot use *patience* or *money*, or even words semantically close to *fun*, such as *enthusiasm* or *enjoyment*, in the context [It's no___ V-ing]. You can't say *It's no enjoyment meeting them*, or *It's no enthusiasm reading that book*. The words that *are* appropriate in this context constitute a rather odd group; they include *use*, *good* (construed, unusually, in this context as a mass noun), and a few others such as *joke* (*It's no joke*) and *big deal* (*It's no big deal*). When we consider the other environments in (13), however, we discover that the sets of items which can take the place of *fun* only partially overlap.

(14)   a. It's no {fun, good, use, joke, big deal} trying to do it.
       b. It won't be much {fun, good, use} trying to persuade them.
       c. It won't be much {fun, use} for you.
       d. Doing that wasn't much {fun, good, use, help, consolation}.
       e. There's no {fun, point, use, harm, sense} in reading it.
       f. There isn't all that much {fun, point, use, sense} in trying.

There are two ways of looking at these data. On the one hand, we can regard the different environments in (14) as so many constructions, each of which contains a slot which can be filled by an item selected from a specified list. The construction [It's no___ V-ing] can be filled by an item selected from {fun, good, use, joke, big deal}. The construction [There's no___ in V-ing] selects from {fun, point, use, harm, sense}. The other way of looking at the data is to list, for each lexical item (*fun*, *point*, *use*, etc.), the contexts in which it may occur. *Fun* can occur in all the contexts in (14), *sense* only in the last two. The two approaches are complementary. Knowing how to use the word *fun* involves knowing the constructions in which it can occur; at the same time, knowing the constructions involves, *inter alia*, knowing which items can fill its various slots. Although there is certainly some overlap in the words available for the constructions, we are not able to identify a unique set of items which are available to fill the slots in all of the constructions.

Nevertheless, the constructions in (14) do share a common semantic feature. The constructions, namely, are used to express the speaker's evaluation of a situation or a course of action. *Fun* is able to occur in the constructions because the word is compatible with this semantic value. Consider the following examples, where the evaluative sense of the word is particularly prominent.

(15)   a. That'll be fun.
        b. That wasn't much fun.
        c. It won't be much fun for me.

In these examples, a property (that of 'being fun') is predicated of the subject referent. In this respect, *fun* is aligning itself with predicative adjectives. *That'll be fun* is parallel to *That'll be great, That'll be fine, That'll be nice,* and so on.

In the examples in (15), the subject referent most likely is a situation or activity: *Seeing that movie a second time wasn't much fun.* We also find *fun* being predicated of an individual. Note that in (16b) *fun* is coordinated with *rich.* Since *rich* is uncontroversially an adjective, the same status needs to be accorded to *fun.*

(16)   a. She wasn't even fun.
        b. He was fun and rich and she clearly enjoyed his company.

From here, it is but a short step to using *fun* as an attributive adjective in prenominal position and, indeed, as a full-blown adjective modified by *quite*:

(17)   a. It was a fun little piece.
        b. We were involved in some fun collaborations.
        c. It might be quite fun to do a kind of singing and dancing cabaret act.

If *fun* is indeed able to function as an adjective we should expect to find comparative and superlative forms. *More fun* and *most fun* are attested in the BNC, in contexts which clearly testify to their adjectival character. Note in particular that in (d) and (e) below *most fun* is explicitly set alongside forms which are undeniably adjectival: *best, quickest,* and *cheapest.*

(18)   a. It's so much **more fun** being a winner than a loser.
        b. She was **much more fun** after a few drinks.
        c. Think of ways to make life **more fun** together.
        d. They advised me of the best route to take home—and by the best they meant **the most fun,** not the quickest.
        e. The cheapest way to eat—and **the most fun**—is at the open-air food markets.

What we do not find in the BNC are the inflected forms *funner* and *funnest.* These are, however, attested in the COCA corpus, where we find nineteen examples of *funner* and twenty-five of *funnest.*[3]

---

[3] This development was anticipated by Algeo (1962). He wrote, half a century ago:

The future development of adjectival *fun* needs watching. We can surely expect to find pure intensifiers used with it: *a very fun party* is only a matter of time. We may even anticipate being told that one car is funner than another, and that will be the funnest thing of all. (Algeo 1962: 159)

On the semantic–syntactic properties of *fun*, see also Bolinger (1963) and Denison (2001).

(19) a. Learning geography this way is much **funner**.
      b. some of the **funner** things that you can get online
      c. It's not the **funnest** way to get herpes.
      d. Use the kookiest, prettiest, **funnest**, most interesting or elegant cocktail glasses you can find.

Internet searches turn up numerous further examples:

(20) a. Making computing easier, **funner** and safer
      b. It's **funner** and more challenging
      c. How to have your **funnest** summer ever
      d. the **funnest** game in the world

Huddleston and Pullum (2002: 1643) discuss *fun* in the context of conversion; the word, which is basically a noun, comes also to be used as an adjective. The data, however, suggest that the situation is much more complex than this. It is not just that *fun* can be used both as a noun and as an adjective; the word has a range of uses in a number of distinct constructional environments. These uses have to be learned; they cannot be predicted from the categorization of the word as a noun and/or adjective. Speakers of English clearly have learned these distinctive uses, presumably on the basis of their exposure to them.

Pluralia tantum

An interesting sub-category of nouns are the so-called pluralia tantum, or plural only nouns. Here are some examples:

(21) a. I bought some **groceries**.
      b. The caretaker lives on the **premises**.
      c. His **whereabouts** are unknown.
      d. go to the **movies**
      e. wash the **dishes**
      f. I need some new **glasses**.
      g. How are your **folks** keeping?
      h. How are **things** with you?
      i. the great **outdoors**
      j. You can see the **Alps** from here.

Many of these nouns do not have singular forms; one cannot speak of 'an Alp' or of 'an outdoor'. In cases where a singular form does exist, the singular and the plurale tantum have distinct meanings. *Movies*, in (d), does not refer to a plural number of films; it refers to a place in which films are shown. Likewise, if you 'wash the dishes' you are not washing a number of dishes; you are cleaning all manner of articles after they have been used for cooking and eating.

The pluralia tantum category is far from homogeneous, both semantically and syntactically (Wierzbicka 1988a). Many of the items display highly idiosyncratic distributions. *Whereabouts* is virtually restricted to occurring in a possessive environment (*his whereabouts, the whereabouts of the suspect*); *Alps, outdoors,* and *movies* occur only with the definite determiner; *things* and *folks* are best with a possessive determiner. *Premises* is somewhat more versatile. It can occur in a prepositional phrase, mostly with *in* and *on* (*on the premises, in these premises*), and also as the subject of a clause; in this case, it may even take singular verb agreement (*the premises is/are located...*). Many pluralia tantum nouns do not tolerate any kind of quantification; one cannot ask 'how many Alps' are visible. And while one might say that a person owns 'six premises', it would not be possible to say that he bought 'six groceries'. You would have to say 'not many groceries', using a vague expression of quantity. Some pluralia tantum nouns are even more limited in their distribution, in that they are restricted to occurring in fixed idiomatic phrases: *odds and ends, bits and bobs, (to) all intents and purposes, the ins and outs (of a situation), the ups and downs (of life), comings and goings.*

As we inspect the pluralia tantum in finer detail, it becomes apparent that their occurrence in the language cannot be predicted from some general purpose rule governing the use of plural nouns. On the contrary, many of these nouns have a distribution which is virtually unique to themselves. The set of environments in which *whereabouts* can occur hardly overlaps at all with the set of environments in which *premises* can occur. At the finest level of description, we need to state the properties of each noun individually. It is almost as if there are as many subcategories as there are items (Taylor 2002: 376).

Much

It is often the most frequent, 'little' words that defy classification into traditional parts of speech. Take, as a case in point, the word *much*.

In some of its uses, *much* appears to function as a noun, more precisely, as a pronoun, standing in for 'many things', or some such. (In spite of this paraphrase, *much* is always construed as singular.)

(22)   a. Much has happened since we last met.
      b. There is much in this essay which I disagree with.
      c. Much of what you say is common knowledge.

Especially characteristic is its use in a partitive *of*-construction. This is exemplified in (c) above, where *much* has the sense 'a large part (of)' or 'many aspects (of)'. Curiously, when pronominal *much* appears in direct object position or as the complement of a preposition, it prefers a negative or interrogative context. In the absence of such a context, an alternative form, such as *a lot*, is required.

(23) a. I didn't buy much; We didn't talk about much; Did you learn much about it?
    b. I bought {??much, a lot}; we talked about {??much, lots of things}.

If *much* is a (pro)noun, it is not a run-of-the-mill example. It can take a demonstrative determiner: *That much I know, This much is clear*, though other determiners are ruled out: **The much has happened*. Nor can it be preceded by an adjective: **Interesting much has happened*. It can, however, be preceded by *not*, *too*, and *(not) very*—words which typically modify an adjective or adverb: *Not (very) much has happened, Too much has been said, Not very much is known*.

The adjectival status of *much* is evident from such uses as *(not) much money* and *too much work*, while *I liked it very much* and *How much did you like it?* testify to its adverbial status. Consistent with its status as an adjective/adverb is the existence of comparative and superlative forms (*more money, most money; I liked it more, Who likes it most?*). Yet the word does not distribute like 'normal' adjectives. While we have *this much money* and *that much beer*, the word cannot occur with articles or possessives: **the much beer, *his much money*. Predicative uses are also excluded: **His money is much*.

(It might be noted in passing that *many*—a form which might be regarded as the plural form of *much*—is compatible with some of these adjectival contexts. *His many friends* is fine, as is *the many friends that he has*. We even encounter predicative *many* in the slightly archaic *Our sins are many*. In terms of their distribution, *much* and *many* cannot be lumped together in a single category.)

In addition to the uses already illustrated, *much* can function as a kind of hedge to a following noun phrase. We can distinguish at least three distinct patterns:

(i) the [MUCH THE SAME] construction. In the following, *much* hedges the strict entailments of *the same* and *the best*:

(24) a. We came to **much the same** conclusions.
    b. They provided **much the best** explanation.

In uttering (24a), the speaker is not committing herself to the claim that the conclusions were exactly the same as other people's but that they were to all intents and purposes, or roughly speaking, the same. Likewise, in (24b), the speaker hedges her claim that the explanation was the best of all possible ones. I have dubbed this the [MUCH THE SAME] construction since this use of premodifying *much* is particularly frequent in the context *much the same*.

(ii) the [VERY MUCH NP] construction, illustrated by the following:

(25) a. He was **very much the product** of the patriarchal system of the day.
     b. This is **very much the case** between mothers-in-law and sons-in-law.
     c. He was **very much the professional consultant**.

(26) a. This is **very much a matter of negotiation**.
     b. It was **very much a family event**.

In this construction, the occurrence of *very* is obligatory: **He was much the product of his times*. The function of *very much* is to comment on the categorization implied by the following nominal. Two cases can be distinguished according to the definiteness of the nominal. With a definite nominal (very much the N), the construction points to the exemplary status of the category member. Thus, the man referred to in (25c) is claimed to be, not merely a professional consultant, but an exemplary member of this category, a 'paragon' exemplar, to use Lakoff's (1987) term. With indefinites, the categorization is claimed to be particularly appropriate. In (26b), the event referred to is not merely 'a family event', but a stereotypical, or prototypical example of such an event.

(iii) the [(NOT) MUCH OF A N] construction, illustrated by the following:

(27) a. It didn't come as **much of a surprise**.
     b. I'm not **much of a cook**.
     c. It's not **much of a life** for you.
     d. Not **much of a country girl**, are you?
     e. There's **not much of a difference** between them.
     f. I'm not **much of a one** for talking.
     g. Is it **much of a place**, Caernarvon?

This construction prefers a negative or, more rarely, an interrogative context: **I am much of a cook*. The feature is shared with some uses of pronominal and adjectival *much*, mentioned above. Another characteristic is the obligatory occurrence of *of*. In this respect, the construction harks back to the 'partitive' use of *much*, mentioned above on the example *Much of what you say*. There is, however, an important difference with respect to the partitive use. Compare:

(28) a. We didn't eat much of the meal (that she cooked).
     b. It wasn't much of a meal.

What is meant in (28a) is that a large part of the meal was not eaten. The (28b) sentence, however, does not refer to a part of the meal; rather, the meal in question is claimed to be a not particularly good example of the category. Whereas in (28a), *much* picks out a portion of the meal, in (28b) it invokes a degree of category membership. Thus, in (27b) above, the speaker is not saying that she is not a cook, only that she cannot be considered a particularly good example of the category, or that she can be considered a cook only to a limited degree. Interestingly, this construction is only found with singular indefinites: *We aren't much of cooks, *He isn't much of the professional consultant.*

Like some other uses of *much*, this construction is compatible with *too, so, how,* and even *however*:

(29) a. I don't think that is **too much of a problem**.
      b. I don't want to make **too much of a fuss**.
      c. It was **too much of a coincidence**.

(30) a. You can only have **so much of a good thing**.
      b. Sometimes people are in **so much of a hurry** that they run.

(31) a. **How much of a problem** had the noise been?
      b. **How much of a check** do they actually go into if somebody makes a claim?

(32) a. By the end of that first evening I'd discovered that, **however much of a rebel** your younger sister might be, you were made of tougher, truer steel.
      b. **However much of a bastard** he may be, you can't help liking the guy.

The construction even permits the comparative *more of (a)* and its converse *less of (a)*:

(33) a. This is **more of a problem** for children than it is for adults.
      b. She was **more of a man** than any of them.
      c. I thought you were **more of a man** than that.

(34) a. Storage is **less of a problem** than it used to be.
      b. That doesn't make him **less of a man**.

Considering the above data, it would, I believe, be grossly inadequate to say, following Hudson (2007: 167), that *much* is a 'mixed category', inheriting properties of both the noun (more specifically, pronoun) category and the (attributive) adjective category. What we find, instead, is a cluster of uses, some of which, admittedly, are (pro)nominal in character, while others have distinctly adjectival (or adverbial) properties; certain uses, such as *Not very much has happened* (p. 168), might even be said to exhibit both adjectival and pronominal properties. This, however, is a far cry from claiming that the nominal and adjectival uses of the word can be predicted from general rules pertaining to the distribution of these two word classes. The hedging uses, in particular, would seem to be idiosyncratic to this lexical item.

In stressing the uniqueness of *much*'s distribution, I am not denying that the various uses are related by criss-crossing similarities. For example, the [MUCH OF A N] construction bears some formal and semantic affinities to the partitive [(NOT) MUCH

OF NP] construction. Nevertheless, the conclusion has to be, I think, that *much* is *sui generis*—a word which requires its own grammar and whose range of uses cannot be predicted from more general syntactic principles. In the last analysis, the word belongs to a category with a membership of one. There are, to be sure, several other words with a quantifying semantics, such as *many, more, most, few, less, some, all, none, nothing*, as well as *a lot (of)*, which may be compatible with some of the contexts reviewed above. None of them, however, shares exactly the same distributional properties as *much*. In fact, a fine-grained analysis of these other words, while recognizing some family resemblances, would probably show that each of them is also *sui generis*.

Verbs and their subcategorization

In Chapter 2 I raised the possibility that the subcategorization properties of a verb reflect the verb's meaning. Verbs which designate the transfer of an entity to a recipient are likely to be used in a ditransitive frame [V NP NP]. Conversely, the use of the ditransitive construction is likely to be restricted to verbs which are compatible with the semantics of transfer. Ideally, we should like to be able to predict the subcategorization properties of a verb from its semantics. In this way, subcategorization information would become redundant. If you know what a verb means, then you should be able to work out what kind of complement, if any, it takes. Much effort has gone into identifying the semantic principles underlying subcategorization patterns: see e.g. Huddleston and Pullum (2002: Chapter 14) and Wierzbicka (1988*b*), and, for more recent accounts, Duffley (2006), Egan (2006, 2008), and Smith (2009). A particularly fruitful approach has been to attribute rather abstract meanings to the various subcategorization patterns, claiming that a verb can occur with that pattern just in case its semantics are compatible with the semantics of the pattern. For example, it might be claimed that a *to*-infinitive complement designates a potential or future event, while a V-*ing* complement designates a generalized notion of the activity in question. In this way, we can account for the contrast between *I would like to go for a walk* (which refers to a potential event in the future) and *I like going for a walk in the evening* (which refers to the activity as such).

Although a good number of broad generalizations do seem to be possible in this area, a detailed examination of individual verbs often reveals idiosyncrasies of usage which cannot be derived from more general principles. Consider, as an example, the case of prepositional verbs, such as *insist (on)*, *agree (to)*, or *rely (on)*. These are verbs which cannot be followed directly by a nominal complement; rather, the complement is introduced via a preposition. The preposition can be followed either by a regular nominal (a noun phrase, a proper noun, or a pronoun) or by the nominalized form of a verb phrase, that is, by a gerundial V-*ing* form. The following illustrate these possibilities:

(35) a. I must insist on an early departure.
      b. I must insist on leaving early.
      c. I must insist on everyone leaving early.

(36) a. I rely on you.
      b. I rely on people's honesty.
      c. I rely on people being honest.

(37) a. I can't agree to this proposal.
      b. I can't agree to signing this contract.
      c. I can't agree to you signing this contract.

(38) a. The sales people talked me into the most expensive one.
      b. The sales people talked me into buying the most expensive one.

(39) a. They talked me out of the investment.
      b. They talked me out of making that investment.

Not surprisingly, the pattern generalizes over sets of verbs with similar semantics. You can be talked, pushed, forced, cajoled, enticed, tempted, charmed, or shamed into or out of something, into doing something, or out of doing something.

The snag is, these alternatives do not generalize to all prepositional verbs. There are one or two verbs where the preposition can take a nominal complement but not a gerundial complement:

(40) a. We prayed/longed for a speedy recovery.
      b. *We prayed/longed for his recovering quickly.

There are, on the other hand, a few verbs which take a gerundial complement but which reject the preposition plus nominal complement option. *Prevent, stop,* and *prohibit* are examples.[4]

(41) a. You're not going to prevent me from trying.
      b. *You're not going to prevent me {from it, from the attempt}.

(42) a. He tried to stop me from leaving.
      b. *He tried to stop me {from it, from my departure).

(43) a. You are prohibited from engaging in commercial activities.
      b. *You are prohibited from these activities.

These examples might suggest the presence of a minor generalization, involving verbs which have to do with causing someone not to do something. Such a possibility raises the question of why such a restriction should apply. Why should verbs of

---

[4] The case of *prevent* is mentioned by Hudson (2007: 187).

stopping and preventing behave differently from verbs of insisting or agreeing? We should not put too much effort into searching for an explanation, however, since the generalization does not hold. *Talk out of* readily takes a regular nominal complement—see (39a)—while *dissuade* and *discourage* do not show a categorical rejection of NP complements:

(44)   a. I tried to dissuade him from buying those options.
      b. I tried to dissuade him from that purchase.
      c. I was dissuaded from that strategy.

(45)   a. Don't discourage me from trying.
      b. Don't discourage me from that.

The conclusion, unpalatable as it may seem, is that *prevent, stop,* and *prohibit* are exceptions to the general principles governing prepositional verbs. Their idiosyncratic properties simply have to be learned. Considering the almost categorical rejection of the starred examples in (41) to (43), speakers seem to have learned this peculiar property of these words exceedingly well.

Zero-complements

Consider, next, the situation in which the direct object of a normally transitive verb can be omitted. A number of scholars have commented on this phenomenon: see e.g. Fillmore (1986), Goldberg and Ackerman (2001), Lemmens (2006), and Levin (1993). An often-cited example is the contrast between *eat* and *devour*. Both verbs designate a similar kind of process involving the same kind of entities (a person who does the action and the food which is ingested). *Devour* absolutely requires that the ingested food is mentioned in a direct object nominal: *He devoured the meal, He devoured everything,* **He devoured quickly. Eat,* on the other hand, can easily be used intransitively, the ingested food being inferred from context (*Here, eat*) or understood generically (*Have you eaten yet?*).

Eat is a general purpose (and relatively high frequency) verb, used for the ingestion of any kind of solid food. *Devour,* on the other hand, is not a high frequency verb and it refers to a particular manner of eating, namely, eating large quantities of food with speed. One might be inclined to infer a general principle from these two verbs, namely that general purpose ingestion verbs do not need an overt complement, whereas manner of ingestion verbs do. The generalization holds only in part.

General purpose ingestion verbs, such as *drink* and *smoke,* resemble *eat* in many respects. Both can be used intransitively. One can ask *Do you smoke?* and *Do you drink?* But whereas the former refers to any kind of smoked substance (cigarettes, drugs, etc.), the latter specifically refers to the ingestion of alcoholic liquids. One could not, for example, ask someone *Did you drink yet?*, with the meaning 'Did you drink anything—water, orange juice, milk—since getting up?' On the other hand, if the direct object of the verb is inferable from context, intransitive *drink* may indeed refer to the ingestion of any liquid substance. You can hold out a glass of water to someone and say, *Here, drink*, where the direct object of the verb is understood from the context. Any generalization that we might make with regard to *eat, drink*, and *smoke* is, however, upset by other general purpose ingestion verbs—*ingest* itself, as well as *consume*. These absolutely require an overt direct object.

What about the verbs which denote a specific manner of ingesting? Some, such as *gobble (up), guzzle (down), nibble*, and *gnaw*, are like *devour*, in that they require an overt direct object. You would have to say that a person gobbled up their food, not that they, simply, 'gobbled up'. On the other hand, many of the manner verbs are very compatible with an intransitive use: *swallow, chew, much, chomp, slurp, suck, sniff*, and *inhale*. Possibly, semantic factors other than the one we have mentioned—concerning, for example, whether the verbs refer to the sound emitted whilst food or drink is being consumed—might be relevant. Even so, the sound-emitting *slurp* behaves differently from *guzzle*. We seem to be confronted, once again, with a great deal of idiosyncratic usage. Speakers simply have to learn the usage facts of the individual words. Since many of the words are not high frequency, the learning takes place on the basis of rather sparse input.

For another example of the idiosyncratic nature of zero-complementation, compare the verbs *try* and *attempt*. These near synonyms share similar complementation patterns. Both can be followed by a *to*-infinitive (*try/attempt to do it*), by a V-*ing* complement (*try/attempt doing it*), and also by a nominal complement (*try/attempt it*). Where they differ is in the possibility of a zero-complement. Compare:

(46)   This is quite difficult, but you should still $\left\{ \begin{array}{l} \text{try it / try to do it / try}. \\ \text{attempt it / attempt to do it / *attempt.}^5 \end{array} \right\}$

As we see, *try* is compatible with a zero-complement, *attempt* is not. Other phrases with a similar meaning pattern like *try*.

(47)   You should $\left\{ \begin{array}{l} \text{make an attempt.} \\ \text{make an effort.} \\ \text{have a shot.} \\ \text{have a go.} \\ \text{have a try.} \end{array} \right.$

The odd-man-out, in this paradigm, is the verb *attempt*. Idiosyncratically, it absolutely requires some kind of complement, even though the phrasal expression *make*

---

[5] Note also the contrast between *Give it a try* (a rather common phrase) and *Give it an attempt*. The latter is not recorded in either the BNC or the COCA, though numerous examples are to be found by Googling the phrase.

an/the attempt does not display this feature. Once again, the conclusion has to be that speakers of English have learned this peculiar feature of this not particularly frequent verb.

Defective verbs

One of the most robust of all lexical categories is that of verb. Verbs have the unique function of predicating a property of a subject nominal. As such, in English, they inflect for tense and (in the present tense) show number agreement with the subject nominal. They also appear in a several non-finite forms (infinitive, past participle, and present participle). No other category of word shares this set of properties.

In terms of the above properties, the so-called modal verbs (*can, must, will*, etc.) are something of an anomaly. They do not, for example, take the -*s* inflection with a third person singular subject, they do not have non-finite forms, they are negated by the addition of *not*, while interrogatives are formed by inversion of the modal and its subject. The category of modal verbs is not homogenous, however. Mostly, *ought (to)* behaves like the other models; occasionally, however, we come across expressions where the word appears to function like a regular verb: *We didn't ought to do it* instead of the expected *We oughtn't to have done it*. Another marginal modal is *used to*; *Did you use to smoke?* would probably be preferred over *Used you to smoke?*

Leaving aside the modals, one might reasonably expect that any verb will exhibit the full set of verb properties. This expectation, however, is not fully borne out. There are, namely, some verbs which are defective with respect to the forms in which they appear.

A striking example is *beware*. This verb is virtually restricted to occurring in its non-inflected base form, typically as an imperative (48) or infinitive (49).

(48) a. Buyer beware!
      b. Beware of the dog!
      c. Beware of appearing over aggressive or unnecessarily rude.

(49) a. We should beware of falling victim to a fairly common fallacy.
      b. Let us always beware of jumping to conclusions.
      c. We must beware that we do not exaggerate.

The use of *beware* with a subject nominal (such as *I always beware of dogs*) is completely ruled out. Even the use of *beware* in association with negation (*Don't beware of the dog*) is not attested.

A somewhat less clear-cut case is that of compound verbs, such as *babysit, sleep-walk, drink-drive, sight-see,* and *grandstand*. These are most commonly used as infinitives or with the -*ing* inflection: *We were sight-seeing in Paris; The foreign minister loves to grandstand; Can you babysit our little boy?* Present and past tense forms are less common. Past tense forms, in particular, tend not to be acceptable at all if the compound has, as its final element, a so-called strong verb, that is, a verb which forms its past tense other than by means of suffixation of -*ed*. For me, the following become increasingly bad:

(50) a. I don't think I ever sleep-walked before.
      b. They babysat our little boy.
      c. We sight-saw in Paris.
      d. Who ghost-wrote her memoirs?
      e. The foreign minister once again grandstood in parliament.[6]

A particularly interesting case are the French words *voici* and *voilà*. Historically, these were imperatives: *vois ci* 'see here', *vois là* 'see there'. Contemporary usage is consistent with these verbal origins (Bergen and Plauché 2001, 2005). Thus, *voilà* can take what looks like a direct object, the direct object can appear as a clitic pronoun, and the word can take other verbal clitics such as *y* and *en*; these are all typical verbal properties. The word can also take what looks like a clausal complement and can itself appear in a subordinate (relative) clause. In the informal spoken language, *voilà* can even appear in what looks like a subject–verb inversion construction, complete with a linking 't' (cf. *il aime* 'he loves', *aime-t-il?* 'does he love?)

(51) a. Voilà mon oncle. Le voilà.
         'There's my uncle' 'There he is'
      b. Nous y voilà.
         'Here we are'
      c. En voilà des étudiants.
         'There are some students'
      d. Voilà que la fin s'approche.
         'The end is now approaching'
      e. Mon frère a vu l'homme que voilà.
         'My brother saw the man (who is) there'
      f. Ne voilà-t-il pas ton frère?
         'Isn't that your brother over there?'

What distinguishes *voilà* from a 'true' verb is the fact that it cannot bear the usual person and tense inflections of a verb. Notwithstanding the usage in (51f), neither can it appear with a 'true' subject nominal.

---

[6] To the extent that the reader finds these examples unacceptable, the question arises, what else is one supposed to say? If you don't like *We sight-saw in Paris*, how else can you express the thought? One possibility is the periphrastic *We went sight-seeing in Paris*, thereby avoiding the problem of using a past tense of *sight-see*. *Grandstand* is rather different. The preferred solution would appear to be the past tense form *grandstanded* (attested eight times in the COCA).

Semantically, *voilà* differs from other members of the verb class in that it does not predicate a property of an entity; rather it draws attention to the presence of an entity in the current discourse space. In this respect, it resembles the presentational *there (is)* of English (Bergen and Plauché 2005). The range of contexts in which it can appear, however, differs very considerably from that of its English counterpart. To this extent, *voilà* is indeed *sui generis*.

In conclusion

My aim in this chapter was to show that the ways in which a word is used are often specific to the word itself; its usage cannot be predicted from the categorization of the word as a noun, verb, or whatever, in association with syntactic rules operating over these categories. Indeed, some words seem to resist part-of-speech categorization at all and some have a distribution which is unique to themselves. A competent speaker of the language needs to have learned all these distinctive usage patterns.

My account has, of necessity, been very selective. I believe, however, that the data reported in this chapter are not untypical for the language at large. Many more examples of idiosyncratic usage, which lie outside the scope of the dictionary plus grammar book model, will be cited in the following chapters. This kind of data has important implications for what it means to know a language. It strongly suggests that knowledge of a language can only be attained through exposure to actual usage events, whose particularities are noted and laid down in memory.

4

Idioms

It is a testament to the authority of the dictionary plus grammar book model of language that idioms are commonly understood against the assumptions and predictions of the model (Fillmore, Kay, and O'Connor 1988; Jackendoff 2002, 2010; Nunberg, Sag, and Wasow 1994). An idiom, namely, may be defined as any expression whose properties, whether semantic, syntactic, or lexical, cannot be accounted for in terms of syntactic rules operating over the lexicon. This is not, to be sure, the only approach to idioms, as we shall see in the next chapter. In the meantime, however, I want to go along with the above definition and consider the kinds of expressions which fall under its scope. Three broad categories can be recognized:

(a) SEMANTIC IDIOMS. These are expressions whose meaning cannot be worked out from the meanings of the component words, as these are listed in the lexicon. Parade examples include *kick the bucket* 'die', *spill the beans* 'reveal confidential information', and *pull someone's leg* 'tease a person'. From a syntactic point of view these are unremarkable, each being a verb phrase with the structure [V NP]. Given their regular syntax, idioms of this kind are usually ambiguous between a literal, compositional reading and an idiomatic meaning.

(b) SYNTACTIC IDIOMS. These are expressions whose syntactic structure cannot be generated by the general syntactic rules of a language. We have already examined a number of examples, ranging from fixed expressions such as *by and large* (p. 34) through to syntactic configurations exemplified by *Off with his head!* (p. 38). Unlike semantic idioms, syntactic idioms are not usually ambiguous between a literal and an idiomatic meaning, since, being syntactically anomalous, they do not have a literal meaning.

(c) LEXICAL IDIOMS. These have to do with usage patterns associated with specific lexical items. Much of the data cited in Chapter 3 and elsewhere in this book falls into this category. The usage range of *fun* cannot be predicted from the specification of the word as a mass noun, nor even by recognizing that the word has dual status as both mass noun and adjective.

To these, we can add a fourth category, that of phrasal idioms:

(d) PHRASAL IDIOMS. These are word combinations, often quite short and with the internal syntax resembling that of a phrase, but with an established and not fully predictable meaning. Particularly à numerous in English are expressions with the syntax of a prepositional phrase, often with an adverbial function. Examples include *of course, at most, in fact, under way* 'in progress', *(learn) by heart* 'memorize', *on-line, on purpose* 'intentionally', *on foot, out of practice, at any rate*, to name just a few.

The above categories are by no means mutually exclusive. Many expressions exhibit more than one kind of idiomaticity. A phrasal idiom such as *under way* exemplifies idiomatic uses of the lexical items *way* and *under*; moreover, its internal syntax is not fully regular, in that the count noun *way* is being used, exceptionally, without a determiner. Also cross-cutting the above categories are the so-called phrasal verbs of English, such as *come to* 'regain consciousness', *put up with* 'tolerate', *go off* 'explode', and *work out* 'calculate'. These combine a verb with words which elsewhere in the language function as prepositions. The category of phrasal verbs is by no means homogeneous, from both a semantic and a syntactic point of view. The above-cited example of *come to* functions as an intransitive verb, while *put up with* functions as a transitive, roughly equivalent to *tolerate*. For some phrasal verbs, the prepositional element—sometimes referred to as a 'particle', in order to emphasize its distinctive status vis-à-vis regular prepositions—can be separated from the verb: *work out the answer* ~ *work the answer out*.[1] In some cases, the prepositional element has a spatial, directional sense: *put the cat out, bring in the washing*. Often, however, it is not possible to predict the semantic properties of phrasal verbs (and quite a number of them have more than one conventionalized meaning). To be sure, some minor generalizations can be made: *eat up, drink up, finish up, clean up*, and several more, all seem to share the notion of doing something to completion, while *hand out, spread out*, and *share out* involve the notion of dispersal. We might even be able to perceive some relation between the meaning of the prepositional element and the 'basic' spatial sense of the preposition; see in this connection the pioneering study of Lindner (1981) on the use of *up* and *out* in phrasal verbs. Nevertheless, in the final analysis, as every foreign learner of English knows, phrasal verbs simply have to be learned.[2]

Neither are the above categories themselves entirely unproblematic. I defined semantic idioms in terms of their non-compositional semantics; the meaning of an

---

[1] On the distinctiveness of the verbal particles vis-à-vis the prepositions, see Cappelle (2005). The categories are by no means coextensive. Consider examples such as *bring together, put back, take apart*, and even *push open*. Arguably, these function like many other phrasal verbs; for one thing, they can be interrupted by an intervening nominal: *bring the parts together, push the door open*, etc. However, *together, back*, and *apart* are not prepositions (neither, of course, is *open*). On the basis of examples such as *take (something) to pieces*, we might even need to recognize the word combination *to pieces* as a particle.

[2] A study of phrasal verbs aimed at foreign learners of English, and which highlights the semantic motivation of the expressions, is Rudzka-Ostyn (2003).

expression cannot be computed from the meanings of its parts, as these are listed in the lexicon. Suppose, however, that we were to list 'divulge' as one of the meanings of *spill* and 'confidential information' as one of the meanings of *bean(s)*. In this way, we could claim that the meaning of *spill the beans* is fully compositional. The snag, of course, is that *spill* means 'divulge' only in the idiom; likewise for *beans* in the meaning 'confidential information'. The matter is not so clear, however, in the case of what we might refer to as CRANBERRY WORDS.[3] These are words which are virtually restricted to occurring in a single set phrase. An example, from many, is the word *once-over*. If you give someone or something 'the once-over' you make a quick inspection, with a view to deciding on the merits of the person or whatever it may be. The word *once-over* clearly makes a semantic contribution to the expressions in which it occurs; its meaning, presumably, is 'quick inspection'. To this extent, *give someone/something the once-over* is interpreted in accordance with the dictionary meaning of *once-over*. On the other hand, *once-over* is not freely available to occupy the N-slot of a noun phrase; the word is virtually restricted to occurring in the cited phrase. (Note, in this connection, the virtually obligatory use of the definite determiner.) The phrase, along with its conventional meaning, has to be learned as such.

Not surprisingly, generative linguists have paid little attention to idioms, preferring to focus their efforts on the system of rules governing the non-idiomatic 'core' of a language. Idioms, almost by definition, are peripheral to the language system, the idiosyncrasies of individual expressions and particular lexical items having little bearing on the generative potential of the language. Being exceptions to general rules, idioms can be shunted off into the limbo of the lexicon, the province of the irregular, the unpredictable, and the 'badly behaved'.[4]

Such an approach might be all well and good if it were possible to make an exhaustive list of the idiomatic expressions of a language and if these could be clearly demarcated from the non-idiomatic 'rest' of the language. It would also help the generativist case if the number of idioms were quite small, in the hundreds, say, rather than the tens of thousands.

These conditions cannot be met. On the contrary, it turns out that the idiomatic reaches into every nook and cranny of a language, so much so that it might not be

---

[3] The term is based on the notion of the 'cranberry morpheme' (Taylor 2002: 550). A cranberry morpheme is a morpheme, like *cran-* of *cranberry*, which occurs in only one word. Correspondingly, a cranberry word is a word which occurs only in a specific phrase. The word *intents* is an example; this word is restricted to occurring in the phrase *to all intents and purposes*.

[4] Idioms do, however, play a minor role in generative theory, in that they are sometimes cited as evidence for syntactic transformations and for the need to posit an underlying structure distinct from surface structure (Radford 1988). *Spill the beans* and *the beans were spilled* exhibit the very same co-occurrence restriction between the verb and the noun phrase. There are grounds, therefore, for listing the idiom and the selectional restriction only once and for deriving the passive sentence by means of a passive transformation. For a critical review of this argument, see Ruwet (1991).

outrageous to claim that just about everything in a language is idiomatic to a greater or lesser degree and in some way or other. If anything, it is the fully regular, the fully compositional, that is exceptional.

In this chapter I first examine some properties of semantic idioms; this is followed by a discussion of syntactic and phrasal idioms. The discussion aims to demonstrate, first, the very wide range of phenomena in a language which might be labelled as idiomatic. It should also become apparent that the idiomatic cannot always be cleanly separated from the rule-governed rest of the language. The idea of the idiomatic as an "appendix to the grammar"—to use Fillmore *et al.*'s (1988: 504) phrase—cannot be maintained.

Semantic idioms

When people think of idioms they tend to think of semantic idioms, especially those whose literal meaning invokes a highly imageable and sometimes bizarre scene. Examples of such prototypical idioms include the following:

(1) a. kick the bucket ('die')
     b. spill the beans ('divulge confidential information')
     c. pull someone's leg ('tease someone')
     d. rain cats and dogs ('rain heavily')
     e. fly by the seat of one's pants ('have to make decisions moment by moment')

As already noted, these expressions are in principle ambiguous between a literal and an idiomatic interpretation. Syntactically, however, they are run-of-the-mill verb phrases. Indeed, it is their syntactic regularity which makes a literal, compositional interpretation possible.

Although their idiomatic meanings cannot be worked out, in many cases it might still be possible to make sense of an idiom, once it has been learned (Keysar and Bly 1999). With some idioms, we can perceive metaphorical correspondences between elements of the literal and idiomatic interpretations. In *spill the beans*, the beans evidently correspond to pieces of information. Prior to their being spilled the beans are securely located inside a jar or other container, just as the information is tightly lodged inside a person's brain. If the jar is accidentally tipped over the beans spill out on the floor, for anyone to pick up; likewise, if the person holding the information inadvertently lets it slip out it becomes public knowledge, available to all and sundry (Gibbs 1992; Gibbs and O'Brian 1990).

As is now widely recognized, metaphors are ubiquitous in everyday language (see Lakoff and Johnson 1980, and much subsequent research). Yet metaphorical expressions, such *waste time* or *demolish an argument*, would probably not normally be classed as idioms, or at least, not as idioms on a par with those in (1). The reason is that the expressions are based on what Lakoff and Johnson have called CONCEPTUAL METAPHORS; these are highly productive and sanction a wide range of metaphorical expressions.[5] You can not only waste time, you can also save it, invest it, or fritter it away. These expressions exemplify the conceptual metaphor TIME IS MONEY; expressions we use to talk about money can be transferred to talk about time. Likewise, you can not only demolish a person's argument, you can shoot it down, knock it over, undermine it, or topple it. You can also strengthen it, buttress it, support it, and ensure that it has good foundations. These are all elaborations of the conceptual metaphor ARGUMENTS ARE BUILDINGS; the way we talk about buildings can be transferred to talk about arguments. In the case of *spill the beans*, however, the metaphor is not productive (Clausner and Croft 1997). One cannot, outside of the idiom, speak of information as beans. It would be bizarre to ask where a person got the beans from, in the sense of where they got the information. Neither does the idiom tolerate any lexical variation. You cannot 'tip over the beans' or 'spill the rice' to refer, metaphorically, to divulging information. *Spill the beans* exemplifies a one-off metaphor. It is, if one will, an idiomatic metaphor.[6]

Not all semantic idioms are metaphor-based. Metaphor is not an issue in *rain cats and dogs*. The expression is perhaps best characterized as an exuberant (and colourful) hyperbole. Neither, I would suggest, is metaphor relevant to proverbial expressions such as *take the bull by the horns* and *shut the stable door after the horse has bolted*. These expressions invoke a narrative which is taken as emblematic for the state of affairs under current consideration, the former having to do with how to tackle a difficult situation, the latter with taking precautions after a mishap has occurred. It is not the case that some aspect of a current situation is being metaphorically construed as a bull, or as a bolting horse.

This said, there remain some idioms which are largely opaque. The often-cited *kick the bucket* is one such example. Another is *pull someone's leg*. It is by no means obvious why this expression should refer to teasing someone, by making statements which, though plausible, are not in fact true.

Although the picturesque idioms are in principle open to both a literal and an idiomatic interpretation, they are rarely used in their literal sense and cases of genuine ambiguity between the two readings—jokes and word play excepted— are hardly likely to arise. It is as if the expressions are so strongly associated with the idiomatic meaning that the literal interpretation is inhibited. *Pull someone's leg* is a case in point. There may, indeed, be occasions in which a person's or an

---

[5] Although conceptual metaphors are productive, in the sense that they sanction a large and open-ended set of metaphorical expressions, they may still be subject to idiomatic constraints, particularly concerning the lexical choices that are available. You can attack, storm, or assault an enemy's position; in accordance with the ARGUMENT IS WAR metaphor you can also attack the position which your debating partner adopts. However, you cannot storm or assault an argument (Vervaeke and Kennedy 1996).

[6] Recall from Chapter 3 that metaphorical uses of *lap* and *bosom* are largely restricted to a few set phrases, such as *lap dog, bosom pal, live in the lap of luxury, in the bosom of the Lord*. These might also be referred to as idiomatic metaphors (or metaphorical idioms).

animal's leg is (literally) pulled. In describing such situations, speakers seem careful not to use the wording associated with the idiom. There are thirty instances of [pull * leg(s)] in the BNC. The twenty-seven idiomatic uses have a possessive determiner in the [*] slot. The three literal uses deviate from this pattern. In (2a)—which refers to an injured animal—the definite determiner is used, also in association with the prepositional element *up*, thus signalling that the idiomatic meaning is not in play. In (2b), the occurrence of plural *legs* blocks the idiomatic interpretation.

(2)   a.   We tried to **pull the leg up** so that he wouldn't put so much weight on it, but then he only found it even harder to walk straight.
      b.   I'm stuck... amidships. My damned hips... "**I'll pull your legs**." "No, don't. Push'em. If I can lever myself by hanging on to this... No, God, that's worse, much worse. You'll have to **pull my legs**. I'm absolutely stuck fast."

Symptomatic of the priority of the idiomatic meaning is the fact, noted by numerous researchers (see Gibbs 1994 for an overview), that the idiomatic meaning of potentially ambiguous expressions like those in (1) can be accessed more rapidly than the literal meaning.

Another feature of picturesque idioms which is worth mentioning is that they are on the whole not particularly frequent (Grant 2005). A BNC search of *kick(s)(ing)(ed) the bucket* returns only thirteen instances, and of these more than half (8) pertain to metalinguistic usage, where the expression is cited as an example of an idiom. *Rain cats and dogs* scores just as badly. The combination *cats and dogs* occurs forty-three times in the BNC, but *rain(s)(ing)(ed) cats and dogs* only a paltry three. *Fly by the seat of one's pants* is recorded only once, though *spill the beans* fares somewhat better, with thirty-nine instances. To the extent that the BNC is representative of the kind of language that native English speakers are exposed to in the course of their daily lives, a reasonable inference would be that *kick the bucket* is not encountered very often. Indeed, based on the estimates presented in Chapter 1, it is an expression that one might expect to hear once or twice a year, at most.

Given the relative infrequency of idioms of the kind discussed here, it is remarkable that speakers have such an accurate knowledge of them, indeed, that they should be so widely known at all.[7] English speakers not only know the expression *kick the bucket*, they also know that it is not just a synonym of *die*. You would not say that people 'kicked the bucket' in a car accident, nor would you apply it to pet animals. (But see below, p. 80, on how the idiom can be extended to apply to machines.) It seems that people are able to learn these expressions after only minimal exposure; they notice and remember

---

[7] Possibly because of their relatively low frequency, knowledge of idioms is liable to vary from speaker to speaker. I have even encountered linguistics students (native English speakers) who claim not to know the expression *spill the beans*. It is perhaps not all that implausible that a 20-year-old may actually have never heard this expression. Moreover, some idioms are restricted geographically. *Shoot the breeze* ('chat aimlessly') is virtually unknown to non-American speakers.

the circumstances in which the expressions are used and assimilate them to their linguistic knowledge. Interestingly, people's familiarity with idioms is such that they tend to overestimate their frequency of occurrence. Popiel and McRae (1988) asked subjects (graduate and undergraduate students) to give a subjective estimation of the frequency of idioms on a seven-point scale, ranging from 1 (= never used) to 7 (= seen, heard, or used every day). Remarkably, subjects rated *kick the bucket* at 5.9. (For comparison, *pull someone's leg* was rated at 6.54 and *spill the beans* at 5.75.)

While knowledge of (relatively infrequent) idioms might be cited in support of the mental corpus hypothesis, in that speakers appear to have learned these expressions after only minimal exposure, it could also be argued that the existence of idioms need not threaten the dictionary plus grammar book model. If we restrict our attention to expressions of the kind discussed above, it seems fair to say that picturesque idioms are rather marginal to the language as such. It is not just that they occur infrequently; they constitute tightly bound associations of words which are nearly always used in the idiomatic meaning. A person who did not know—or who never used—expressions like those in (1) could still be judged to be a competent speaker of English.

To the extent that picturesque idioms could be exhaustively listed—and assuming that their number is fairly limited—they need not pose an insurmountable problem to the dictionary plus grammar book model of language. The idioms would simply be listed in the lexicon as multi-word expressions, with, however, the peculiarity that they would be labelled, not for their part of speech, but for their syntactic category. Thus, *kick the bucket* would be listed as a fully formed verb phrase, with *kick* as a verb and *the bucket* as its direct object nominal.

In brief, if the idiomatic in a language comprised only the kinds of expressions discussed above, it would be of no particular interest to linguistic theory, and would not pose a serious threat to the generative model.

Idiom variability

Although the terms 'idiom' and 'fixed expression' are often used in close proximity (a Google search for 'idioms and fixed expressions', in October 2009, returned 60,000 hits), the two are by no means synonymous. There are, to be sure, a number of multi-word expressions, such as *of course, by the way*, and *on purpose*, which are to all intents and purposes fixed and which in some linguistic theories would count as single items in the lexicon. However, when it comes to clausal and sentence-length idioms, the number of truly fixed idioms, which permit no lexical or syntactic variation whatsoever, is extremely small.

One of the very few examples that comes to mind is the greeting formula *How do you do?* (Another candidate is *Break a leg!*, supposedly said to actors about to go on stage.) *How do you do?* cannot be changed in any way. You cannot say *How do you all do?*, *How do you both do?*, or *How did you do?* Neither is it possible to embed the formula under a main clause: *He asked me how I did*, *Go and ask him how he does*. Just about the only way of combining the formula with other material is to cite it under a quotative introducing direct speech: *He shook my hand and said: "How do you do?"*. Even the response to the greeting is fixed. The standard response is not *Very well* or the like, but a repeat of the greeting, or, indeed, nothing at all.[8]

Very few idioms—even those that might be referred to as fixed expressions—display this kind of rigidity. For many idioms, what is fixed is the lexical material; their syntactic form, however, is subject to variation. The idiomatic character of *spill the beans* lies, precisely, in the association of the verb *spill* with the direct object *(the) beans*. If either of these two components is replaced even by a near-synonym the expression loses its idiomatic meaning. As we have seen, *pull someone's leg* ceases to be idiomatic if *leg* appears in the plural form or even if *leg* takes a non-possessive determiner. These idioms are, however, compatible with a greater or lesser degree of syntactic and morphosyntactic variation. The verb can appear with the full range of tense and aspect markers; the expressions can be negated; they can appear in interrogatives and imperatives and can take the full range of modal auxiliaries: *spill the beans*, *spilled the beans*, *may have spilled the beans*, etc. Moreover, many verb-phrase idioms are compatible with a range of syntactic configurations, such as the passive or relative constructions. Sometimes, even, the nominal component can take a modifying adjective.[9]

(3)   a. Armored assault boats did exist back in England, but they remained a well-guarded secret; heaven forfend invaders would use them and thus **spill the British beans**. (COCA)

   b. For three years, the government wrestled with **the beans Boesky had spilled**, trying to come up with airtight felony counts. (COCA)

   c. There . . . **the beans are spilled**! And here's another little surprise. (BNC)

   d. We **spilt a few beans** and touched the odd (female) nerve and laughed off a few fiascos. (BNC)

Many idioms do, however, permit a degree of lexical variation. Sometimes, the amount of variation concerns a choice from a smallish set of items. You can hit the

---

[8] The circumstances in which the expression can be used are also rigidly circumscribed. The expression, namely, is restricted to a situation in which one person is formally introduced to another. It cannot be used as a generalized greeting formula, in the manner of *How are you?*

[9] Some idioms seem to resist this kind of syntactic variation. Passivization or relativization of *kick the bucket* is scarcely possible: *The bucket was kicked (by the old man)*, *the bucket that the old man kicked*. As Nunberg *et al.* (1994: 507) observe, speakers of a language are not explicitly taught which idioms passivize and which do not. Their suggestion is that the degree of syntactic flexibility correlates with an idiom's semantic transparency. As already mentioned, the 'beans' of *spill the beans* can be identified with confidential information; for this reason, according to Nunberg *et al.*, the idiom can be easily passivized. There is, however, no semantic unit which corresponds to 'the bucket' of *kick the bucket*; accordingly, it would make no sense to state what happens to 'the bucket'.

bottle, the booze, or the whisky (Gibbs 2007). Sometimes, more than one item in an idiom is subject to variation. You can pour oil on the flames or add fuel to the fire (in the sense 'exacerbate a dangerous situation, typically by means of a provocative remark'). In this example, the speaker has three choices available to her: (a) oil vs. fuel, (b) flames vs. fire, and (c) pour on vs. add to. In principle, permutations of these three choices generate eight possible expressions, though not all the permutations might be equally likely.

For a more complex example, consider expressions which idiomatically refer to being frightened. The following data are from the BNC, with the number of attested examples being given in parentheses:

(4) scare the shit   (11)
     scare the life   (9)
     scare the living daylights   (6)
     scare the wits   out of someone   (4)
     scare the hell   (4)
     scare the daylights   (3)
     scare the stuffing   (1)
     scare the pants   off someone   (7)

     total with *scare*: 45

(5) frighten the life   (23)
     frighten the living daylights   (2)
     frighten the daylights   (1)
     frighten the hell   out of someone   (1)
     frighten the wits   (1)
     frighten the shit   (1)

     total with *frighten*: 29

(6) terrify the life   (1)
     terrify the wits   out of someone   (1)
     terrify the living daylights   (1)

     Total with *terrify*: 3

This degree of lexical variation prompts the question of how the idiom should be stated and how it might be represented in the mental grammar. One strategy would be to identify the idiom with its most frequent variant, which in this case is *frighten the life out of someone*. We would also need to state the range of possible variation, noting, for example, that the verb *frighten* can be replaced by *scare* or *terrify*. Another possibility is to list all the attested variants as so many distinct idioms, perhaps with a cut-off point to exclude the most infrequent. Although this approach might be descriptively adequate, in the sense that it would accurately describe the data at hand, it would miss the generalization that all the above examples are constructed on the same pattern and invoke much the same image. It would ignore the possibility that speakers might use the idiom creatively, coming up with new permutations of the various elements, or perhaps slotting in a different verb or noun.

A third possibility is to state the idiom in the form of a schema or frame (Moon 1998: 161), that is, as a syntactic configuration containing of a number of slots, with, for each slot, a list of the items which are able to fill it. The idiom in question might be stated as [V THE N OUT OF SOMEONE], with the stipulation that V designates a verb of frightening (*frighten, scare, terrify*) while the N-slot selects from a heterogeneous set of items including *life, hell, shit, (living) daylights*, and *stuffing*. The full set of idiomatic expressions would then be generated by permutations of the verbs and the nouns.

A more sophisticated account would rank the listed options for their relative frequency. With regard to the verb slot, *scare* would be marked as the most frequent exponent, *terrify* as the least probable. Even so, it is not the case that each of the three verbs shows equal preferences for the noun exponent. The most frequent variant with *scare* is *scare the shit out of*, while the most frequent variant with *frighten* is *frighten the life out of*. While *scare the life out of* is also quite frequent, *frighten the shit out of* is not recorded. The data therefore not only reflects the relative frequency of the constituent items, it also shows certain co-occurrence preferences between the verb and the noun.

The question of co-occurrence preferences also arises in connection with an expression which the suggested schema does not generate, namely, *scare the pants off someone*. Here, *pants* specifically selects the preposition *off*.

It will be noted that not every verb which signifies frightening can occur in the idiom's verb slot. *Startle*, for example, is not attested, perhaps because this verb does not designate a strong enough emotion. In spite of this, *startle* does occur in an idiom frame which exploits a similar image to that exemplified above, an idiom, moreover, which confirms the association of *scare* with *shit*:

(7)   scared shitless   (13)
       scared witless   (6)
       terrified witless (1)
       startled witless   (1)

While the verbs that occur in these idiom clusters obviously share some semantic commonality, the same can hardly be said for the nouns. What do *life, shit, wits, (living) daylights*,[10] and *hell* have in common, apart from the fact that they are used in the idiom? Interestingly, a substantially similar set of nouns occurs in a further set of

---

[10] *Daylights* is a further example of a cranberry word (see footnote 3). The word is hardly used outside of the idiom clusters discussed here. The OED gives the definition 'the eyes', and by extension 'any vital organ'. I doubt, though, whether many English speakers associate the word with these definitions. There is also the question of why eyes, or vital organs more generally, should be characterized as 'living'. The 'meaning' of *daylights* is, quite simply, the possibility of its use in the idiom clusters.

expressions, this time involving, not frightening, but hitting and beating. Overall, the hitting and beating cluster occurs less frequently than the frightening cluster.

(8) beat the hell   (4)
     bash the hell   (4)
     beat the living daylights   (2)
     smash the living daylights   (2)
     hit the life   } out of someone   (1)
     kick the shit   (1)
     blow the hell   (1)
     blast the hell   (1)
     spank the daylights   (1)

A partially overlapping set of nouns is encountered with the verb *knock*. This evokes an unpleasant surprise, perhaps tinged with the notion of (metaphorical) beating and causing an element of fear.

(9) knock the stuffing   (16)
     knock the wind   (2)
     knock the shite   } out of someone   (1)
     knock the guts   (1)
     knock the daylights   (1)
     knock the socks   off somebody   (2)
     knock [POSS] socks off   (2)

Note that it is in association with the verb *knock* that *stuffing* (attested only infrequently in the fear-expressions) comes into its own.

Let us summarize:

- There are grounds for recognizing an idiom schema [V THE N OUT OF SOMEONE]. There is a minor variant [V THE N OFF SOMEONE].
- The dominant use of the idiom is to refer to an event which causes fear. It can also be used, albeit less frequently, to refer to a beating, and, less frequently still, to a sudden and unpleasant surprise.
- Each of the semantic values of the idiom selects from a different set of verbs. The verbs differ with respect to their frequency of occurrence in the idiom.
- The idiom is associated with a rather heterogeneous set of nouns. It is generally the case that a specific verb combines preferentially with certain nouns; conversely, that a certain noun tends to occur with certain verbs.
- Some instantiations of the idiom schema occur more frequently than others.
- The idiom schema is able to generate a large set of specific expressions, perhaps even an open-ended set. The lists in (4)–(9) are almost certainly not exhaustive. Searching in a larger corpus would very likely throw up many more expressions, perhaps involving new items for the V and N slots.

Let us return to the question posed earlier of how to represent the idiom in the mental grammar. Do we represent the idiom as a schema, supplemented by a list of the items which are able to fill its various slots? Do we state the relative frequency of the noun and verb options, along with co-occurrence preferences between a given verb (noun) and the noun (verb) options? Do we list specific instances of the idiom, with perhaps a cut-off point for the less frequent? The answer, I suggest, is 'all of the above'. Knowledge of the idiom consists, in the first instance, of familiarity with its specific wordings, together with their distinctive semantic values, internal structure, and frequency of occurrence. Speakers are also likely to perceive co-occurrence and statistical patterns in the data, and on this basis are able to productively extend their repertoire, coming up with the less frequent examples which we have cited. Indeed, if we fail to attribute this kind of knowledge to speakers of a language, it is difficult to explain how they are able to produce utterances with the properties that we have documented.

Allusions to idioms

We have seen that most idioms are subject to greater or lesser degrees of variability, both in their lexical material and their syntactic structure. In this section I consider another phenomenon which conflicts with the idea of idioms as rigidly fixed expressions. This is the possibility of alluding to idioms.[11] Of special interest is the fact that the allusions can themselves give rise to new idioms, undermining further the notion that the set of idioms in a language is rigidly fixed.

We can illustrate on the old chestnut, *kick the bucket*. From the point of view of its semantics, the expression is notable for its lack of transparency. The 'bucket' of the idiom does not correspond, even metaphorically, to any conceptual unit, nor can the deceased be understood to have done something to this entity. After all, *kick the bucket* is a transitive phrase, designating an action performed by an agent on a patient, whereas its idiomatic meaning 'die' is intransitive, denoting a process which the subject entity undergoes. In view of its opaque semantics, it is not surprising that the idiom admits very little formal variation; it cannot, for example, be passivized (**The bucket was kicked*). The form of the idiom, however, is not totally fixed, as illustrated by the following Internet-sourced examples:

---

[11] Creative play with idioms, especially in journalistic writings, has been extensively documented by Moon (1998); German examples are discussed in Gehweiler, Höser, and Kramer (2007). One of their examples pertains to the German idiom *die erste/zweite Geige spielen* 'to play first/second fiddle' and its recent extension *keine Geige spielen* 'to play no fiddle', that is, 'to have no role to play', 'to be irrelevant'. The expression appears to be used, not so much of persons, but of abstract entities, including the content of previous discourse, as in the following (Internet-sourced) example:

    (i) Ob das nun Ausbildungskosten sind oder nicht—*es spielt keine Geige* meiner Meinung nach.
    'Whether they are educational costs or not—it is irrelevant in my opinion.'

(10) a. what would he do if I **kicked the old bucket?**
      b. It made me think what people would say and do when I finally **kick the old bucket.**
      c. not long after Francis **kicked the earthly bucket.**

Neither is the idiom restricted to human subjects, being used of vehicles, technological devices, and even commercial enterprises:

(11) a. I'm also going to go on a quick little road trip down to Jacksonville to pick up a pickup truck seeing as how the old blazer finally **kicked the old bucket.**
      b. To recap: My Kindle **kicked the metaphorical bucket** on the 25th.
      c. wouldn't bat an eyelid if Versace (the company) **kicked the hypothetical bucket** and folded.

Particularly interesting, however, are the following examples.

(12) a. The old fool **finally kicked it.**
      b. My old computer **finally kicked it.**

It, in these examples, does not refer to some identifiable entity in the situational context. If the word refers to anything at all it is to 'the bucket' of the idiom. The examples play on the presumption that the hearer knows the full idiom. Other aspects of the examples are worth mentioning, such as the collocation with *finally* and the reference to 'old' entities, as well as the fact that the idiom is able to be applied, not only to decrepit humans, but also to worn-out pieces of machinery—aspects which are already in evidence in examples (10) and (11). In brief, the supposedly 'frozen' idiom *kick the bucket* has given rise to a new idiom, *kick it*, whose usage range only partially corresponds with that of its source.[12]

In some cases, allusions to an idiom are more frequent that the idiom itself. This is especially the case with proverbial sayings. Consider the expression *Make hay while the sun shines*. Most English speakers are probably familiar with this saying. It evokes an agricultural scene and advises farmers to make good use of the fine autumnal weather before winter sets in. This scene is taken as emblematic of a more general situation, the moral being that one should take advantage of favourable conditions while they last. As mentioned, most people seem to know the proverb and are able to recite it. Interestingly, though, the proverb is rarely encountered in its entirety (there

---

[12] Another extension of the idiom is illustrated by *kick one's last*. Some Internet examples:

(i) proud of his marksmanship, he watched as the rat **kicked its last.**
(ii) the big bullfrog **kicked his last.**
(iii) Dr. Orbell has hopes that the little (turkey-sized) Anomalopteryx moa has not yet **kicked its last.**

A further play on the idiom is the expression *bucket list*, after a 2008 movie title. The term refers to a list of things one would like to do before one dies.

are only four instances in the BNC[13]). Mostly, speakers merely allude to it (Barlow 2000). Political commentators might urge opposition parties to make hay while the government suffers embarrassments or companies can make hay while their competitors are embroiled in strife. In brief, the proverbial expression has given rise to a new locution, *(to) make hay*, which refers to the optimizing of one's situation while circumstances allow. Although many speakers will be aware of the source of the expression, others—foreign learners, for example—may not.

Another example is provided by the proverbial saying *The early bird catches the worm*. The scene is taken as emblematic of the more general situation where people who are first on the scene get the best deal. Of the twenty-seven instances of *early bird* in the BNC only two occur in a full citation. Some instances play on the proverb, slightly changing its terms:

(13)   It's the early bird watcher that catches the best bird song.

Otherwise, *early bird* seems to have developed two distinct uses. One concerns a person who rises early in the morning; here, the 'early bird' contrasts with the 'night owl'. When used attributively, the expression characterizes the favourable deals which are available to those who are first in line. Conference organizers may offer discounted early bird rates for those who register before a certain date, while retailers may entice shoppers with early bird bargains. Once again, some speakers may be aware of the proverb which motivates these uses. For those who are not, *early bird* is just another (and rather curious) idiomatic phrase.

Take, as a further example, the saying that 'every cloud has a silver lining'. The expression evokes the scene of a dark storm cloud obscuring the sun. The outer edges of the cloud may be noticeably brighter than its dark interior. The expression is odd in a number of respects. First, it is manifestly not true that every cloud does have a silver lining. Another odd thing about the expression is the word *lining*. Normally, the word would refer to the piece of cloth attached to the interior of a garment, not to the bright edge of a dark object. And even assuming that a dark cloud may have a bright edge, why should this be characterized as silver in colour? Be all that as it may, the proverb encapsulates the folk wisdom that even a bad situation may have some positive aspects.[14]

There are fifty-two instances of *silver lining* in the BNC, only seven of which occur in full citations of the proverb. Some examples play on the association of *silver lining*

---

[13] Recall my earlier observation (pp. 16–17) concerning the status of corpus data with respect to an individual's linguistic experience. If we assume—conservatively—that the 100 million words of the BNC correspond to four years' linguistic experience, the average English speaker will encounter the full proverb about once a year, at most.

[14] Another proverb offering the same piece of wisdom concerns the ill wind that blows no one any good. Once again, allusions to the proverb by far outnumber its citations.

and *cloud*, as in (14a) and (14b). Note that (14c) cleverly reverses the proverb, claiming that there are bad aspects even to good situations. Otherwise, *silver lining* is used in the general sense of 'positive aspects to a bad situation', as exemplified in (14d).

(14) a. even the home secretary, Kenneth Clarke, usually a man to find **a silver lining in**[15] **the blackest cloud**, admitted that the government was in "a dreadful hole."
      b. **The tiny bit of silver lining on the cloud** is a new application by National Wind Power.
      c. maybe it's true what they say about **every silver lining having a cloud**.
      d. The current difficulties may have **a silver lining**.

Allusions to well-known sayings—not only proverbs—can be an important source of phraseological innovation. Consider the expression *sea change*. The source is not a proverb, but *Full Fathom Five*, a song in Shakespeare's *Tempest*:

> Full fathom five thy father lies;
> Of his bones are coral made;
> Those are pearls that were his eyes;
> Nothing of him that doth fade,
> But doth suffer a sea-change
> Into something rich and strange.

The term is now almost totally dissociated from its original context, being used to refer to any change which is complete, total, or profound. Some representative examples from the BNC:

(15) a. My own belief is that we have had a **sea change** in the nature of employment in Britain and in other western societies
      b. How shall we explain such a **sea change** in the dominant theory of legislation?
      c. will Cadbury effect the **sea change** in attitudes and practices necessary to restore standards of corporate governance in the UK
      d. All this makes for a **sea change** in our lives.
      e. Recent years have witnessed a **sea change** in the fortunes of car safety as a marketable quantity.

Syntactic idioms

I have suggested the need for a schematic representation for the cluster of idioms illustrated in (4)–(6). In terms of its internal structure, however, the schema

---

[15] In terms of the proverb, the silver lining should be *on* the cloud. The use of *in* suggests that the image of the cloud and its lining is no longer active.

conforms to a much more general verb phrase pattern in English, namely [V NP PP], where V indicates some action which causes the referent of NP to be in a place designated by the PP. Examples of this pattern include *put the book on the shelf, drive the car out of the garage,* and (with metaphorical displacement) *move the lecture onto the Tuesday.* From a syntactic point of view, therefore, the idiomatic expressions are not particularly remarkable. Their idiomaticity resides in their selection of specific lexical items and in their conventionalized meaning.

For many expressions, however, their idiomaticity does reside in their syntax. We have already discussed the fixed expression *by and large* (formed by coordinating a preposition and an adjective). Other syntactically odd expressions include *how come?* 'Why?', *far be it from me to V* 'I do not wish to V', *all of a sudden, come to think if it, more fool you, believe you me, methinks* 'I think', *no matter* 'It doesn't matter', *Long time no see*[16] 'It's a long time since we last saw each other'.[17]

The above examples are lexically fixed. We cannot have, on the pattern of *methinks*, expressions such as **usthinks* 'we think', **himbelieves* 'he believes', **meseems* 'it seems to me', and the like.[18] A large number of syntactic idioms are, however, compatible with lexical variation. Such idioms are best characterized in terms of a syntactic pattern associated, mostly, with a specified semantics with one or more slots which can be filled by lexical material which is consistent with the idiom's meaning. These syntactic idioms, or CONSTRUCTIONAL IDIOMS, are productive to a greater or lesser extent, in that the pattern can be instantiated by a number (in some cases, a very large, or even open-ended number) of specific expressions.

An example, already discussed, is the [OFF WITH] construction, exemplified by *Off with his head!, On with the show!, Down with globalization!* The pattern is (mildly) productive, in that it is able to sanction new expressions, albeit within the tight constraints imposed by the construction's formal and semantic specifications.

Although the [OFF WITH] construction itself might be somewhat marginal to the language as a whole, it is by no means untypical of the very large number of syntactic idioms that one finds in a language. Below I discuss a few examples of syntactic idioms whose properties—indeed, whose very existence—cannot be predicted from the generative model.

the more the merrier

This construction—schematically [the X-er the Y-er]—is commonly referred to as the CORRELATIVE CONSTRUCTION (Culicover 1999: 83–5; Culicover and Jackendoff 1999; Fillmore, Kay, and O'Connor 1988). It conveys that any increase (or decrease) in the

---

[16] This jocular attempt at pidgin English appears to be a translation of Chinese *hǎo jiǔ bú jiàn* 'very long-time not see'.

[17] For further examples, see Moon (1998: 81–2).

[18] For the historical development of *methinks*, see Wischer (2000).

value of X is associated with, and may even be construed as the cause of, an increase (or decrease) in the value of Y. A notable feature of the construction is the fact that the word *the* which features in it is not a determiner and is therefore not to be identified with the definite article *the*. Some instantiations of the construction:

(16)   a. The more I know the more I worry.
      b. The less they have to say the more they talk.
      c. The bigger they are the harder they fall.
      d. The earlier you start the more chance you have of being successful.
      e. The bigger the risk the bigger the payout.
      f. The less said the better.

It is also worth noting that although the correlative construction is highly unusual, given the general principles of English syntax, it is not totally isolated from the rest of the language.[19] There are, in fact, quite a few bipartite expressions in which the first element is presented as the cause, precondition, or explanation for the second. Like the correlative construction, these expressions lack a finite verb. Here are some examples:

(17)   a. Garbage in, garbage out.
      b. Out of the frying pan (and) into the fire.
      c. Easy come, easy go.
      d. Cold hands, warm heart.
      e. Once bitten, twice shy.
      f. Out of sight, out of mind.
      g. Once a whinger, always a whinger.[20]
      h. One for me (and) one for you.
      i. First come, first served.
      j. Nothing ventured, nothing gained.

Another bipartite pattern, in which the conjuncts are linked by *and*, is exemplified by the following (Culicover and Jackendoff 1997):

---

[19] Another way of putting this is to say that the correlative construction, in spite of its strangeness, is nevertheless MOTIVATED, in that at least some aspects of the construction can be linked up with other things in the language. In Taylor (2004a) I discuss the phenomenon on the example of the [BANG GOES] construction, exemplified by *Bang goes my weekend*, showing how the semantic, syntactic, and even phonological characteristics (the latter pertaining to the onomatopoeic character of the ideophone *bang*) of the construction are related to other phenomena in the language.

[20] This expression instantiates the construction [ONCE A N, ALWAYS A N]. Examples from the BNC include *once a Catholic, always a Catholic*; *once a Russian, always a Russian*; *once a misfit, always a misfit*; *once a dealer, always a dealer*. The construction conveys that a person is not able to change their personality or their entrenched behaviour.

(18) a. One more beer and I'm off.
      b. Another botch-up like that and you're fired.
      c. Three hours and we'll be home.

These have the schematic structure [NP and s], where the initial noun phrase names an entity which is involved in some unnamed and usually future or hypothetical event; this event, once it has materialized, is the precondition for the occurrence of another event, named in the second conjunct. Thus, (18a) conveys that after I will have had one more beer I will leave, while (18c) states that we will be home after three hours of travelling. The initial NP constituent can invoke a wide range of different situation types; the inferred relation between the invoked situation and the clausal conjunct is equally broad. Here are some further examples (from Culicover 1970):

(19) a. A little water in the face and he goes indoors.
      b. The first sign of cold weather and John says he's going to put his snow tires on.
      c. My only pen and you went and lost it.
      d. Twenty-five centuries of language teaching and what have we learned.

him write a novel!?

This construction is commonly referred to as the INCREDULITY RESPONSE CONSTRUCTION (Fillmore *et al.* 1988; Lambrecht 1990; Taylor 1998, 2002: 568–70). Although apparently possessing elements of a clause, with its subject–predicate structure, the construction is remarkable for the fact that the 'subject' nominal fails to appear in nominative form and that the verb lacks tense and person inflections. (If the verbal element is the copula *be* it is typically omitted, as in (20d) below.) Semantically, the construction serves to pick up on a proposition which has already been introduced into the discourse and dismisses it as absurd, unrealistic, preposterous, or whatever. Indeed, the construction may well be followed up by a remark such as 'nonsense', 'impossible', 'you must be joking', 'I don't believe it'. In principle, the construction is able to sanction a very large number of possible instantiations. Some examples:

(20) a. Him write a novel!?
      b. Me let you down!?
      c. What do you mean? Me go back?
      d. Your parents going to get divorced!? I don't believe it.

A further notable feature of the construction is its pronunciation: the 'subject' and 'predicate' need to be spoken on separate tone units, usually with a rising, querying intonation. Moreover, the construction allows some word order variation. For example, the 'predicate' may appear in initial position, followed by the 'subject'.

(21) a. Write a novel? Him?
      b. What!? Go back!? Me!?

What about me?

Also very productive is the [WHAT ABOUT X] construction, where the speaker draws the interlocutor's attention to some matter that may have been overlooked:

(22)   a. What about the workers?
        b. What about on Tuesday?
        c. What about saying so?
        d. What about you going without me?
        e. What about if she says no?
        f. What about where you're going to live?

Observe, in particular, the wide range of items which can occupy the X-slot. These include noun phrases, prepositional phrases, V-*ing* phrases, and certain kinds of subordinated clauses (those introduced by *if, when, where, before,* and *after,* for example, but not those with *because, since, although,* or *unless*). These various kinds of items cannot be brought under a more general syntactic category.

that idiot of a man

This is one of several constructions which feature an EPITHET, in this case, the word *idiot*. Some examples of the construction (from the BNC):

(23)   a. that blustering fool of a priest
        b. it had been a bastard of a night
        c. that clown of a teacher
        d. this noisy oaf of a bus driver
        e. a crotchety old prick of a man
        f. that wretched old witch of a woman
        g. that genius of a brother of yours (meant ironically)
        h. a saucy chit of a girl
        i. some quack of a psychology professor

Huddleston and Pullum (2002: 380–1) define an epithet as "an emotive expression which serves to indicate annoyance with the individual concerned rather than to give an objective description".[21] The definition is probably too narrow in that epithets can, if somewhat less frequently, express a positive attitude of approval or admiration, as in the following:

---

[21] A distinctive feature of epithets is their nominal character. As Huddleston and Pullum observe, epithets are used with reference to persons and (more rarely) things. Other emotive expressions, such as *damn, bugger off, stuff you,* belong to the category of EXPLETIVES.

(24) a. that angel of a girl
       b. it's one blockbuster of a film
       c. behind a plain exterior is a gem of a hotel
       d. he scored a real beauty of a goal

The epithet construction is unusual in a number of respects. Consider, first of all, its structure. The cited examples appear to consist of two noun phrases linked by the preposition *of*. The following analysis suggests itself:

(25) [that idiot] of [a man]

The *of* in the construction is clearly different from possessive *of* in *the father of the bride* and from partitive *of* in *a piece of the cake*. Since the referent of (25) is a man, who is also characterized as an idiot, the expression might be regarded as an example of appositional *of* (Taylor 1996: 329), where the preposition links two nominals with the same reference, as in the following:

(26) a. the state of California
       b. the city of Dublin
       c. the problem of what to do with it

California is characterized as 'a state', Dublin as 'a city', while 'what to do with it' constitutes 'the problem'. Similarly, the referent of (25) is characterized both as 'a man' and as 'an idiot'. There is a snag, however. Semantically, *that* appears to go with *man*, whereas *a* seems to go with *idiot*. A paraphrase would be 'that man, who is an idiot', rather than 'that idiot, who is a man' or 'a man, who is that idiot'. A structure more in line with the semantics might therefore be following, where *idiot of a* serves as a kind of modifier to *man*. Needless to say, there are no general rules of syntax which generate such a phrase.[22]

(27) that [idiot of a] man

This structure is perhaps even more compelling for examples such as *my idiot of a husband*, where *my* is clearly to be construed with *husband* (Aarts 1998).

According to (27), the word *a* which occurs in the construction does not form a noun phrase with the following noun. Nevertheless, there appears to be a strong

---

[22] Nevertheless, there are other cases where this kind of analysis may be indicated. Consider expressions such as *those kind of people*, where plural *those* is in agreement with *people*, not with *kind*, suggesting the analysis [those [kind of] people] (Davidse, Brems, and de Smet 2008). The usage is not uncommon. In fact, *those kind of* (63 tokens) is more frequent in the BNC than *those kinds of* (38 tokens). Take, as another example, the phrase *a strong cup of coffee*, where *strong* modifies *coffee*, not *cup*, suggesting the analysis [a strong [cup of] coffee]. Although, then, the structure proposed in (27) looks decidedly odd, it is not totally isolated from other facts about the language.

requirement that the noun is compatible with the singular indefinite determiner, namely, that it is a singular count noun.[23] Mass nouns therefore do not fit into the construction. Examples such as *that horrible din of a music* and *this bastard of a weather we are having* do not work. It also turns out to be very difficult to pluralize expressions of the kind *that idiot of a man*. *Those idiots of a men* is ruled out, because of the clash between singular *a* and plural *men*. The only option would be to omit the word *a*: *those idiots of men*. The option is rarely taken; the only example of this pattern that I have been able to find in the BNC is *the fools of aristocrats he had been brought up with*.[24]

Also problematic in the construction is the use of a proper name in the final slot. When used with unique reference, this kind of noun would be incompatible with the use of an article. I have not been able to find any such examples in the BNC or the COCA. Nevertheless, *that tyrant of a Josef Stalin* does seem preferable to *that tyrant of Josef Stalin*. Austin (1980) cites *that clever little wretch of a Rebecca*, which he attributes to Thackeray, *that goose of a Mr Cox* (Mrs Gaskell), and *that interfering prig of a Westcott* (Hugh Walpole). In spite of their occurrence with indefinite determiner *a*, these examples appear to refer to unique individuals. (Austin also cites, from Thackeray, *that confounded old ass of Benson*, where the proper name suppresses the occurrence of the indefinite determiner.)

Another curious fact about the construction is that it tends to prefer either an initial demonstrative (*this* or *that*) or an indefinite determiner (*a* or *some*); see the examples in (23) and (24). Expressions with initial *the* can, however, be found. The BNC has *the idiot of a captain* as well as the above-cited *the fools of aristocrats*.[25]

Two further observations are in order. The first concerns the set of items which can function as epithets. Some words have an entrenched status as epithets, such as *idiot, fool, bastard,* and *oaf.*[26] The category, however, is not closed. The use of an emotive adjective can often render a nominal compatible with the construction:

---

[23] Another way of putting this is to say that *a*, in *that idiot of a man*, has dual allegiance, as part of the modifier phrase *idiot of a* and as part of the noun phrase *a man*.

[24] Note that the rarity of the plural variant of the construction is not a matter of the semantics. There is nothing in the least anomalous in referring to a group of men and declaring that they are idiots.

[25] Epithet constructions, similar to the one under discussion, though with some differences of detail, are found in Dutch (Paardekooper 1956) and in Romance languages (Ruwet 1982). Thus, in French, we have *cet idiot de Paul* 'that idiot Paul', *cet idiot de mon mari* 'that idiot of my husband', alongside *mon idiot de mari* (Hirschbühler 1975). Italian has *quel idiota di tuo fratello* 'that idiot of a brother of yours', *quel idiota di Mario* 'that idiot Mario', and so on.

[26] There are also some words which have specialized uses in the construction, as exemplified by the following:

   (i) We had a whale of a time.
   (ii) She'd had a dickens of a lot to drink.
   (iii) They had a hell of a row.

It is interesting to note that *hell of a* is sometimes written as *helluva*, supporting the syntactic analysis proposed in (27).

(28)   a. ?a hut of a house
       b. a ramshackle wooden hut of a house

(29)   a. ?a skyscraper of a building
       b. a monstrous skyscraper of a building

(30)   a. *that architect of a man
       b. that incompetent architect of a man

A second observation concerns the other constructions in which epithets are able to occur. It turns out that epithets have a number of distributional possibilities not shared with 'normal' nouns. Here are just a few:

(31)   a. You fool!
       b. Bastard!
       c. Bernard just confessed, the idiot.
       d. I'll kill him, the bastard.
       e. You are such an idiot.
       f. Don't be more of an idiot than you can help.

If we replace the epithets in these examples with a non-emotive word, such as *architect*, the special value of the epithet constructions becomes apparent. The following are bizarre:

(32)   a. You architect!
       b. Architect!
       c. Bernard just confessed, the architect.
       d. I'll kill him, the architect.
       e. You are such an architect.
       f. Don't be more of an architect than you can help.

Another distinctive feature of epithets is that they can be used anaphorically, to refer back to a previously mentioned referent (with, of course, the added emotive nuance):

(33)   A: What do you think of Harry?
       B: Can't stand **the bastard**.

(34)   I thought for a second she was smoking so I avoided her and I don't think she noticed me. When I came out, there was Shelima's science book in a wash-basin smoldering away. **The idiot** had set fire to it.

that'll teach you!

The expression is addressed to a person who has done something stupid and who has had a bad experience as a consequence. The disapproved behaviour can be stated in an infinitive clause:

(35) That'll teach you to booze at lunchtime!

Note that the import of (35) is that the person should not booze at lunchtime. The negative import of the expression can be made explicit: *That'll teach you not to booze at lunchtime*[27] (Croft 2000: 135). Substandard usage also has *learn* instead of *teach*: *That'll learn you.*[28]

what's it doing raining?

A well-known example of a syntactic idiom is the [WHAT'S X DOING Y] construction (Kay and Fillmore 1999). The following exemplify:

(36) a. What are all these people doing here?
b. What's a nice girl like you doing in a place like this?
c. What are you doing with all that money?
d. What are you doing, going through my mail?
e. What's this scratch doing on the table?
f. What's it doing raining on my birthday?

Some of these examples are open to a 'literal' interpretation. For example, (a) could be a straightforward enquiry into what the people are doing. (The literal reading is more compelling if the final *here* is omitted.) In other cases, however, a literal interpretation is not available. It makes no sense to enquire what an inanimate entity, such as scratch, is 'doing', since a scratch is not able to 'do' anything. On the other hand, it might be possible to enquire what 'it' (in the meteorological sense) is doing: for example, someone looks out the window and you ask, 'What's it doing out there?'. However, this account is hardly available for (f), since the query itself already states what 'it' is doing, namely, 'raining'.

---

[27] A BNC example: *That will teach you not to walk over the moors in bad weather.*

[28] Readers may recall the dispute in Chapter 11 of Kenneth Graham's *The Wind in the Willows* on the proper use of *teach* and *learn*. (Incidentally, the excerpt exemplifies yet another variant of the [THAT'LL TEACH YOU] construction, namely *I'll teach/learn them.*)

The Toad, having finished his breakfast, picked up a stout stick and swung it vigorously, belabouring imaginary animals. 'I'll learn 'em to steal my house!' he cried. 'I'll learn 'em, I'll learn 'em!'

'Don't say "learn 'em," Toad,' said the Rat, greatly shocked. 'It's not good English.'

'What are you always nagging at Toad for?' inquired the Badger, rather peevishly. 'What's the matter with his English? It's the same what I use myself, and if it's good enough for me, it ought to be good enough for you.'

'I'm very sorry,' said the Rat humbly. 'Only I *think* it ought to be "teach 'em," not "learn 'em."'

'But we don't *want* to teach 'em,' replied the Badger. 'We want to *learn* 'em—learn 'em, learn 'em! And what's more, we're going to *do* it, too!'

'Oh, very well, have it your own way,' said the Rat. He was getting rather muddled about it himself, and presently he retired into a corner, where he could be heard muttering, 'Learn 'em, teach 'em, teach 'em, learn 'em!' till the Badger told him rather sharply to leave off.

On their idiomatic interpretation, these examples do not enquire at all into what some entity is 'doing'. Rather, the speaker observes a certain state of affairs—the presence of a large number of people, your possession of a large amount of money, the presence of a scratch on the table, the fact that it is raining—and finds the situation unusual, unexpected, or in some way incongruous. The speaker conveys her surprise at the state of affairs and requests an explanation. Strictly speaking, therefore, the speaker is not asking a *what*-question at all, but a *why*-question, or, as Kay and Fillmore suggest, a *how come*-question. (Recall, p. 49, that *how come*, in contrast to *why*, usually conveys that the speaker finds the queried situation anomalous or incongruous.[29])

Kay and Fillmore dub the construction the WXDY construction, where W is the *wh*-word *what*, X is a nominal, D is the verb *do* (typically in present progressive form), and Y is a non-finite descriptive phrase, such as a prepositional phrase, an adverbial, a participial V-*ing* phrase, or a participial V-*ed* phrase. Together, the X and Y constituents refer to the queried state of affairs, while the speaker's query is conveyed by the W and D components.

Some variation in the form of the idiom is possible. For example, the introductory *what* may be elaborated by various expletives. These serve to emphasize the speaker's sense of surprise or even outrage.

(37)   What the hell are you doing, going through my mail?

Another elaboration involves the parenthetic *do you think*, perhaps with an introductory *just*:

(38)   (Just) what do you think you are doing, going through my mail?

Note that (38) illustrates an 'idiomatic' use of *do you think*. The phrase is not being used to enquire into the addressee's thoughts: it adds a sarcastic nuance to the speaker's demand for an explanation.[30]

---

[29] The potential ambiguity between the literal and idiomatic meaning of the construction is exploited in the following joke (Kay and Fillmore 1999: 4):

DINER: Waiter! What's this fly doing in my soup?
WAITER: I think it's doing the backstroke, sir.

[30] On the possible values of *do you think*, consider the following:

   (i) Who do you think I should ask to make my wedding dress?
   (ii) Who do you think I could trust with that hanging over my head?
   (iii) Who do you think came into the store yesterday? Your friend Edward!

Example (i) can be interpreted as a genuine request for the addressee's opinion. In both (ii) and (iii), however, the speaker has no expectations that the addressee can answer the question. Example (ii) is a so-called rhetorical question, with the implication that no one can be trusted. Example (iii) illustrates the topic-introducing function of an interrogative, discussed below.

Kay and Fillmore illustrated the WXDY construction on examples commencing with interrogative *what*. However, the idiomatic meaning associated with the construction is by no means restricted to expressions involving *what*, nor even to expressions with the main verb *do*. Consider the following:

(39)   Where are you going, dressed up like that?

While this could be taken as a straightforward query about the person's destination, it more likely demands an explanation: it expresses the speaker's surprise or even outrage that the person is going on an outing dressed up as they are. (Imagine the question asked by a parent of their teenage daughter.) Again, the same kinds of elaboration are possible:

(40)   a. Where in heaven's name are you going, dressed up like that?
        b. (Just) where do you think you are going, dressed up like that?

The sense of outrage associated with the construction may be present even if the appended Y component is missing. In order for the idiomatic meaning to be guaranteed, one or more of the interpolations is usually indicated. *Who are you?* and *What are you doing?* would (probably) be taken as genuine enquiries into the addressee's identity or activity. Not so the examples in (41):

(41)   a. (Just) who (the hell) do you think you are?
        b. Just what do you think you are doing?

Both express the speaker's outrage at some aspect of the addressee's behaviour. In (41a) the suggestion is that the addressee's behaviour is not in keeping with their status, while (41b) demands an explanation for their activities.

The fact that the 'idiomatic' meaning associated with the WXDY construction turns up with a wide range of interrogatives, with verbs other than *do*, and even in expressions which lack the final Y constituent, suggests that it might not be a straightforward matter to differentiate idiomatic interrogatives from their regular, non-idiomatic counterparts. The standard account of interrogatives is that they request information. A yes–no, or polar question, formed by subject–auxiliary inversion (*Are you leaving early?*) requests the addressee to specify the polarity (affirmative or negative) of a proposition. *Wh*-questions, on the other hand, request information which fixes the value associated with the *wh*-variable. *Where* requests a specification of place, *who* a specification of a person, *how* a specification of manner, and so on.

There are, no doubt, situations in which interrogatives do indeed have their regular, compositional value, and little else. Mostly, however, people ask questions with an ulterior motive. If I ask 'Is there an Internet café around here?', my main concern is not to establish whether there is, or is not, an Internet café in the vicinity; I want to be directed to such an establishment, if one exists. If I ask 'Who was that man you were talking to just now?', I want to know more than just his identity; I am curious about your relationship to him. 'What do you think about X's latest film?' is likely to serve as a preliminary to me offering my opinion of the film, or at least as a means of introducing the topic of the film into the current discourse. These effects might be dismissed as merely pragmatic overlays to the compositional value of the interrogatives. It is remarkable, however, that many interrogatives have acquired a conventionalized idiomatic value. *Well, what do you know?, How about that?, Who would have thought it?* are little more than expressions of speaker surprise; they are not really questions at all, and certainly not questions into 'what', 'how', or 'who'. *Who knows?*, possibly accompanied by a shrug of the shoulders, conveys a general ignorance: nobody knows, or could possibly know. A speaker can gloat over the accuracy of some prediction she previously made with *What did I tell you?*

Conflicting with the compositional value of interrogatives are those questions which the speaker herself is perfectly capable of answering. Pedagogical and quiz-show questions are asked, not because the speaker wishes to establish the value of the *wh*-variable, or because she is ignorant of the truth value of a proposition, but because she wants to find out whether the addressee knows the relevant facts.[31] In the case of so-called rhetorical questions, the answer is evident to the speaker and presumably also to the hearer. Their function is to structure an ongoing discourse, highlighting facets which the speaker deems to be important. We should also not overlook the fact that requests for information need not take the form of interrogatives. A statement such as *So, you're leaving early tomorrow* (even if spoken with a falling, declarative intonation) would likely be meant, and taken, as a request for confirmation ('Is it true that you are leaving early tomorrow?').

The WXDY construction thus fits into a larger picture of interrogatives and their semantic–pragmatic values. Interrogatives can be used to introduce a topic into the discourse; they can serve as proxies for an unstated request; they can be used sarcastically to humiliate the addressee; they can express the speaker's attitude, such as surprise, astonishment, or outrage; and they can prompt the addressee to offer an explanation for some manifest state of affairs. Situations in which an interrogative merely has its 'literal', compositional value are probably the exception rather than the rule.

Phrasal idioms

At the beginning of this chapter I proposed the category of phrasal idioms, citing examples of prepositional phrases whose meaning cannot be derived from the

---

[31] Questions in the foreign language classroom may be even further removed form the canonical value of interrogatives. The language teacher asks a question, not because she wishes to know the answer, nor even because she wants to find out whether the learner knows the answer, but to find out whether the learner is able to formulate the answer in the foreign language.

meanings of the constituent elements and which, moreover, tend to be used as adverbial modifiers.

There are many such phrasal idioms in English, each of which, on close examination, would have its own story to tell. Here, by way of illustration, I examine the phrase *on end*.

A first comment is that this phrase, like many phrasal idioms, is mildly irregular from a syntactic point of view. Elsewhere in the language, *end* is a count noun; as such, its use without a determiner is prohibited. To be sure, count nouns can sometimes be used with the syntax (and semantics) of mass nouns. Consider a prototypical count noun such as *cat*. In *After the accident there was cat all over the road*, the noun refers, not to a cat-individual, but to cat-substance; the cat-concept has been construed as mass, rather than count. This type of semantic coercion (Michaelis 2003), however, is not apparent in the phrase *on end*. The determiner-less use of the noun is a feature of the phrasal idiom. It is almost as if the absence of the determiner signals the fact that the noun is being used in an idiomatic environment.

On end has two principal uses. The first has to do with an elongated entity standing upright, 'on its end' (or, more accurately, on one of its ends). A typical usage is with reference to hair.

(42)   His hair stood on end.

It may be the case that when certain animals—a dog or a cat, for example—are aroused by fear or anger, their fur, especially around the nape of the neck, may tend to stand erect. This phenomenon, though, is hardly to be observed with humans. We refer to a person's fear or anger by invoking a characteristic animal response. To talk of a person's hair standing on end is to invoke the conceptual metaphor A PERSON (IN A STATE OF EMOTIONAL AROUSAL) IS AN ANIMAL.

The second major use of *on end* is illustrated by the expression *for hours on end*. It is as if the hours are laid out in succession, one after the other, or end to end (another phrasal idiom!). The expression, however, does not simply refer to a period of time comprising an unspecified number of hours. It suggests the subjective experience of the passage of time. A participant is so involved in, or so bored by, a situation that she is no longer aware of how many time units have elapsed. The following illustrate this semantic nuance.

(43)   a. He would listen spellbound to their stories **for hours on end**.
         b. ... the little Polish stations where we sometimes waited **for hours on end**.
         c. They have short attention spans so don't expect them to sit **for hours on end** without fidgeting, yawning or falling asleep.

Needless to say, other time units can be slotted into the idiom. The idiom might thus be represented by the schema [FOR NP ON END], where NP is the plural form of a noun designating a unit of time. It is worth noting, however, that not all time units are equally attracted to the idiom. BNC searches indicate that the most frequent exponent of the NP slot is *hours*. Other options, listed in order of declining frequency, are given in (44).

(44)   for {hours, days, weeks, months, years, minutes, nights, centuries} on end

This ranking is broadly what we might expect, given the subjective nuance of the idiom. The subjective experience of unchanging monotony is more likely to concern the passing of hours, days, and weeks, rather than minutes or centuries. Interestingly, the one time unit which is not attested in the BNC is *second*. Again, this should not be too surprising, since a second is too short a unit to be compatible with the idiom's meaning.[32]

The idiom permits some variation from its canonical form. One variant involves a repetition of the time noun; another permits the coordination of two time nouns. Note that the items in question are selected from the more frequent end of the rank in (44).

(45)   a. for hours and hours on end
       b. for weeks and months on end
       c. for days and nights on end

Another variant refers to a specific number of time units.

(46)   a. some will stand there reading Rapeman **for eight hours on end**.
       b. Beaten in the field, their farms harried **for eleven years on end**, the Milesians held out, getting food by sea.
       c. He was denied sleep for **five days on end**.

These examples appear to conflict with our initial characterization of the idiom, as referring to the laying out, end to end, of an unspecified number of time units. They testify, once again, to the subjective value of the idiom. *Five days on end* conveys that the time period is perceived as interminably long (for the activity in question).

Especially curious is the use of the idiom with respect to a single time unit.

(47)   but what is really incredible is to see him improvise **for an hour on end** and in doing so give rein to the inspiration of his genius

Here, there is no question of time units being placed end to end. The hour is simply presented as an excessively long period, for the activity in question.

The above discussion has brought into focus the internal structure of the *on end* idiom cluster. On the one hand, a schematic characterization of the idiom is certainly

---

[32] The idiom is used mostly with reference to units of time. Other repeated activities are also compatible with the construction. One such example from the BNC is the following:

(i) The quotations go on in this vein **for pages on end**.

One might, in this case, argue that the pages are construed metonymically to refer to a time period needed to read or scan the pages.

possible, namely [FOR NP ON END], with the stipulation that the NP slot is occupied by the plural form of a noun designating a period of time. This schematic characterization is inadequate, however, for two reasons. First, some time-denoting nouns are more frequent in the idiom than others. Second, some deviations from the canonical structure are permitted. Nouns other than those which denote a period of time may be used (see footnote 32); the NP constituent can consist of coordinated nominals; the NP can refer to a specific number of time units, even, in the limiting case, to a single time unit. These deviations are not frequent and appear to be restrained by the properties of the more frequent instances of the idiom. Thus, we have *for an hour on end*, whereas *for a century on end* is not attested. These facts, taken together, strongly reinforce the status of *for hours on end* as the idiom's prototype.[33]

Minor (ir)regularities

On the margins of the idiomatic are the very large number of minor (ir)regularities that we find in a language. I use the hedging parentheses to emphasize that the phenomena in question may be considered regular with respect to general syntactic principles even though their lexical form is idiosyncratic. At the same time, the expressions in question can often be brought under low-level generalizations and with respect to these generalizations the expressions can be considered to be not at all irregular.

Why do we say *on Tuesday* but *in the morning* and *at Easter*? Why don't we say *at Tuesday*, *on the morning*, and *in Easter*? These are facts of usage which bedevil foreign learners of English, and indeed foreign learners of any language. For example, in German, we use different prepositions for 'on Tuesday' (*am Dienstag*) and 'on holiday' (*auf Urlaub*, or for some speakers, *im Urlaub*).

From one point of view, the above-cited expressions are perfectly regular. They are examples of a prepositional phrase, headed by a preposition with a noun phrase complement. The issue for the learner is the selection of a specific preposition (*on, at, in*) in association with a certain kinds of noun phrase (*Tuesday, Easter, the morning*).

Appeal to the semantics of the prepositions scarcely explains the usage. When used of the spatial domain, *in, on,* and *at* are associated with different kinds of complements (see p. 52). *In* takes a three-dimensional container as its complement (*in the box, in the house*), while for *on* the complement is a supporting surface, typically two-dimensional (*on the floor, on the ceiling*). *At* may invoke a zero-dimensional point (*at the intersection of the two lines*); alternatively, it construes the relation in functional terms. If you are *at* your desk, you are using the desk in the way it is intended, for work or for study. The dimensionality of the desk is not really an issue.

---

[33] For further examples of idioms and their prototype structure, see Taylor (2002: 228).

Some temporal uses of the prepositions seem to derive from their spatial uses. *At* is typically required for a point in time: *at midnight, at 4 o'clock*. One could also argue that periods of time may be metaphorically construed as containing the events which occur within their boundaries; hence *in the morning*. The problem, of course, is that we should have to say that some periods of time, such as the days of the week, are metaphorically construed as supporting surfaces (*on Tuesday*) while others, such as Easter, are construed either as points or as invoking a functional relation. The only evidence for such construals is the prepositional usage itself. This kind of explanation turns out to be hopelessly circular (Taylor 2006a).

When we consider the range of nouns which are compatible with each of the prepositions, however, a good deal of regularity can be observed. Thus, specific days generally require the preposition *on*. This applies not only to named days of the week (*on Friday*, etc.) but to other unique days: *on my birthday, on Christmas Eve, on my wedding anniversary, on the centennial of her birth, on the 21st of next month*. We even use *on* when only a part of specific day is referred to: *on the morning of the 19th of February*. There is clearly a generalization to be made here. The generalization, however, is rather low-level, involving the word *on* and a narrowly defined set of expressions which can function as its complement, that is, those which refer to specific days. In like manner, temporal *in* would be associated with parts of a day (*in the morning, in the afternoon*), as well as other definite time periods (*in March, in 1970, in the twentieth century*), while *at* is reserved for named calendar events (*Easter, Christmas*).

Even so, some variation in usage is to be observed. What, for example, is the prepositional usage associated with *weekend*? According to Leech and Svartvik (1975: 77), British usage has *at*, whereas American usage has *on*. The situation is probably much more complex. Table 4.1 shows the incidence of the two variants in three regional varieties of English. The data were obtained using the Google search engine (June 2006), restricting the results to sites from the three geographical areas. The data suggests that *at the weekend* is indeed the preferred option in British English, whereas Australian English is biased towards *on the weekend*. New Zealand English—to judge from the Googled data—straddles the two variants, with a more balanced distribution of the two alternatives.

TABLE 4.1. Incidence of *at the weekend* and *on the weekend* in three regional varieties of English. Googled data. From Taylor (2006a).

	at	on	on:at ratio
UK	1,630,000	343,000	1:4.8
AU	286,000	616,000	1:0.4
NZ	55,400	50,900	1:1.1

Competition between the two variants is probably due to the fact that a weekend is not a particularly good example of a calendar event (the proposed value of the *at*-construction). Conversely, since for most people a weekend consists of two days, *weekend* is not an optimal candidate for the *on*-construction. At the same time, we need to recognize *at the weekend* and *on the weekend* as themselves having the status of idioms, whose degree of entrenchment differs in different English-speaking communities and even, one might suppose, for individual speakers.

The example with the temporal prepositions is not untypical of the kinds of issues which arise whenever we describe facts of usage in fine-grained detail. Some expressions, to be sure, can be brought under high-level, broad-ranging generalizations. They can be assembled in accordance with very general principles and their properties (including their semantics) are fully predictable. There is nothing remarkable about *the money in the box*, about how it is assembled, and what it means. A great deal of what occurs in a language, however, cannot be handled in this way. Some expressions—recall our earlier example *by and large* (p. 34)—are outright exceptions to general principles. Others, such as the temporal expressions discussed above, have properties that are not fully predictable from general principles. Even though low-level, narrow-ranging generalizations may be possible, and these may indeed exhibit a limited degree of productivity, in the limiting case it is the individual expressions themselves which need to be learned.

5

Speaking idiomatically

In Chapter 4 I considered as an idiom any expression whose properties cannot be predicted on the basis of general syntactic rules operating over items selected from the lexicon. Idioms, on this approach, range from expressions with a non-compositional semantics (*kick the bucket*), through constructions with an unusual syntax (*by and large*), to uses of words which cannot be predicted from specifications contained in the lexicon (*weeks on end*). An interim conclusion would be that a very great deal of what people say is idiomatic in some respect or other. A major failing of the generative model, then, is that it massively UNDERGENERATES. The model fails to predict a very large number of the things which are known to proficient speakers of a language.

The generative model fails on the other side of the ledger, too. It not only undergenerates, it also OVERGENERATES. A person armed only with the dictionary and the grammar book could well come up with expressions which are fully grammatical and with meanings which can easily be worked out but which happen not to correspond to what speakers of a language would normally say.

Suppose you want to find out a person's age. There are many ways to formulate your request. Here are some of the questions you could ask:

(1) a. What is your age?
     b. How long ago were you born?
     c. How many years ago were you born?
     d. How many years ago is it since you were born?
     e. How much time has elapsed since the moment of your birth?

All of these are perfectly grammatical and their meanings are fully predictable. They are not, however, the way to ask the question. The 'idiomatic' thing to ask, in English,[1] is *How old are you?*[2]

---

[1] German follows English in this respect: *Wie alt bist du?* Not so Italian and Spanish: *Quanti anni hai? ¿Quántos años tienes?* (literally: 'How many years do you have?').

[2] This is not to say that there might not be situations in which it would be appropriate to ask a person to state 'their age' rather than 'how old they are'. Suppose you are entering a person's data on an official form.

A similar structure, with *how* and a degree adjective, is used for enquiries into other properties of a person or a thing. To enquire into a person's height we ask *How tall are you?*, not *What is your height?* To enquire into the length of a thing we ask *How long is it?*, not *What is its length?* If we want to know the distance from here to there, we ask *How far is it?*, rather than *What is the distance?*

How in association with a degree adjective is not used in all cases, however. (There are, if one will, idiomatic exceptions to the idiomatic way of asking this kind of question.) We would not enquire into a person's weight with the question *How heavy are you?* One might suppose that we avoid this wording because we do not wish to imply that the person might be 'heavy'—a rather sensitive issue, for many people. Even so, the wording would probably be avoided even with reference to a new-born infant, where 'being heavy' might be considered a positive attribute. Whether with reference to an adult or a baby, or even a sack of potatoes, the appropriate question to ask is with *How much?*: *How much do you weigh? How much did the baby weigh?* We also use a *How much?* question when we enquire into the price of an article. We do not ask *How expensive is it?* or *What is the price?* The idiomatic way to make the enquiry is with the question *How must does it cost?*, or, quite simply, *How much is it?*

These few examples suggest a very different approach to the idiomatic than the one pursued in Chapter 4. The idiomatic way of saying something need not be syntactically or semantically unusual in any way at all. The idiomaticity of an expression resides in its conformity with native speaker norms.

This alternative view of the idiomatic is cued by the language itself. Consider some of the ways in which the term *idiomatic* is used.[3] On the one hand, we can characterize

---

The form has boxes for 'nationality', 'age', 'profession', 'marital status', and so on. In this situation it would be quite natural to ask 'What is your nationality?', 'Your age?', and similarly for each of the boxes. Awareness of the contextual appropriateness of the different wordings is yet another aspect of what is involved in being proficient in a language.

[3] Collins English Dictionary (1979), in its first entry under *idiom*, gives the following definition:

idiom 1. a group of words whose meaning cannot be predicted from the meanings of the constituent words, as for example (It was raining) cats and dogs.

This definition, with its reference to non-compositional semantics, accords with the approach pursued in the last chapter. The dictionary gives a second definition, which appeals to usage that accords with native speaker norms:

idiom 2. linguistic usage that is grammatical and natural to native speakers of a language.

While perhaps more appropriate to the adjective *idiomatic* than to the noun *idiom*, this second definition is more in keeping with the approach taken in this chapter. As a matter of fact, the Collins Dictionary lists two further senses of *idiom*:

idiom 3: the characteristic vocabulary or usage of a specific human group of subjects

idiom 4: the characteristic artistic style of an individual, school, period, etc.

Sense 3 would appear to be a specialization of sense 2. Whereas sense 2 appeals to the linguistic usage of native speakers as a whole, sense 3 refers to the linguistic usage of a subset of speakers, street youth, for example. Sense 4, on the other hand, may be seen as an extension of sense 2, referring, not specifically to *kick the bucket* as an idiomatic expression, whose idiomatic character resides in its idiomatic (that is, non-compositional) meaning. On the other hand, we might praise a foreign learner for their idiomatic command of a language, or we might criticize a translation, not because it is inaccurate or ungrammatical, but because it is not idiomatic. Idiomatic, in these cases, does not refer to the use of idioms, as we discussed them in the previous chapter. Peppering your speech with picturesque expressions of the kind *kick the bucket* or *rain cats and dogs* is no guarantee that you will be speaking idiomatically. Conversely, you can display an idiomatic command of a language without needing to use picturesque idioms. As we have seen, picturesque idioms may be not all that frequent, anyway.

If, on this alterative approach, we understand the idiomatic in terms of conformity with usage norms, the question arises as to how these usage norms are to be characterized. The matter is far from straightforward and there are many aspects to it. In the following I outline two broad approaches. The first has to do with the appropriateness of linguistic expressions with respect to a reality which strictly speaking is external to the language itself. The second concerns language-internal relations, largely independent of the contexts in which language is used.

Language and context of use

One approach to usage norms concerns the relation between linguistic expressions and a non-linguistic reality. A useful way to approach this matter is in terms of Halliday's (1985) three-way distinction between the ideational, interpersonal, and textual functions of language. An expression that a speaker chooses must be appropriate to the conceptual content which she wishes to verbalize (the IDEATIONAL perspective); the expression must take account of the relation between speaker and addressee(s), and, more generally, the context of utterance (the INTERPERSONAL perspective); finally, the expression must contribute to the structuring of the ongoing discourse (the TEXTUAL perspective). Let us briefly consider each of these in turn.

---

linguistic usage, but to those features which characterize a musical, artistic, literary, or other type of creative activity.

If we consult the BNC returns for the term *idiom*—ignoring for this purpose the metalinguistic uses—we find, somewhat surprisingly, that senses 3 and 4 predominate. Here are some examples:

(i)　　a. Much of their propaganda was produced in a popular **idiom**, such as poems and broadsides.
　　　　b. for one culture some years ago when Romeo and Juliet were transposed into the **idiom** of youth group clash in modern New York in West Side Story.
　　　　c. Some musicians find the constant changes and surprises inherent in Berlioz's dramatic **idiom** disrupting.
　　　　d. the judgement of Fats Navarro was the first recorded tenor solo in the bebop **idiom**.
　　　　e. We talked of the influences of both Brahms, and also of traditional Irish folk **idioms** on Stanford's output.

As we saw in the above example of how to enquire into a person's age, there are many ways (in principle, an open-ended number of ways) in which the speaker's intent could be verbalized. Not all of these are sanctioned by the usage norms of the language. Moreover, as pointed out in footnote 1, the norms may differ from language to language. Translators are acutely aware that the transfer of conceptual content from one language to another is not just a matter of replacing the words in the source language with words in the target language. (This is hardly likely to be viable option, anyway, since a word in one language rarely has an exact translation equivalent in another in terms of the concept which it designates and the range of entities it may refer to.) Rather, it is a matter of selecting a form of words in the target language which matches the source with respect to the conceptualization which it symbolizes.

Consider, for example, the ways in which motion events are described in different languages (Slobin 2006; Talmy 1985). Arguably, the 'reality' is the same for all speakers. However, in describing motion events, English speakers like to make use of verbs describing specific manners of motion (*run, dash, hurry, crawl, jump, limp, scuttle,* and many more), with the path or direction of motion expressed in a prepositional phrase (*into the house, out of the room, up the stairs, across the field*). Speakers of the Romance languages, on the other hand, express the path and direction by means of a verb ('enter', 'exit', 'ascend', 'cross'), with the manner of motion expressed in an optional adverbial adjunct ('running', 'in a hurry', 'on all fours', and the like). Thus, in English, one 'runs out of the house', while in French 'on sort de la maison en courant', that is, one 'exits the house running'. While 'exit the house running' would no doubt make sense to an English speaker, it is not the idiomatic way to describe the event. Consider, in this connection, the stereotypical ending of a Western, where the cowboy 'rides into the sunset'. In many languages, it would be necessary to construe the event very differently, by saying something like 'the cowboy departed on his horse going in the direction of the sunset'.

A second kind of reality relevant to usage norms is that of the communicative situation itself, concerning, in particular, the relation between the speaker and the addressee(s) and their mutual expectations. An important topic here concerns the prevailing conventions for the performance of different kinds of communicative acts, especially those which are potentially face-threatening and which, if handled inappropriately, are liable to lead to embarrassment and conflict. How to ask a favour of someone? How to decline a favour? How to express disagreement, without causing offence or insult? How to break off an interaction? Contrastive studies (e.g. Wierzbicka 1991) have revealed major differences between the communicative norms in different language communities. The British, especially, are known for their indirectness. Thus, a boss might instruct his secretary with some roundabout instruction like 'I don't suppose you could finish this off by this afternoon, could you?' Translated literally into another language, this might well border on the risible.

Equally important are conversational strategies. How do you avoid answering an embarrassing question? How do you handle a question which you really do not know how to answer, without displaying your ignorance? How to fudge? How to make small talk with someone you really have no interest in, without making your disinterest too obvious? How to 'spin' bad information, so that it doesn't look too bad after all? These are matters which, regrettably, career politicians and their appointed communications personnel are only too proficient in!

Another aspect of speaker–hearer relations concerns the matching of language to the degree of formality of a situation and to the medium of communication (spoken or written). Are you speaking to one or two people with whom you are personally involved or to a large audience of unknowns, as when giving a public lecture? Are you writing to a long-standing colleague or composing an academic paper? The different situations will be associated with a distinctive range of linguistic features, even though the informational content of what you say may remain more or less constant (Biber, Conrad, and Reppen 1998: Chapter 6).

Certain recurring situations of everyday life trigger conventionalized linguistic responses. There are prescribed ways of greeting and leave-taking, of answering the telephone, of apologizing when you inadvertently step on someone's foot. If someone does you a small favour, you are expected to acknowledge the act with 'Thank you'; in the case of a large favour, the other person might respond to your 'Thank you' with 'Don't mention it', 'It's nothing', or some such. Failure to act in the appropriate way might mark you out as uncouth, socially gauche (or indeed as a non-native user of the language). In some situations it might be appropriate to say nothing.[4] For example, do you say 'Thank you', or some such, when the supermarket cashier hands you your change? In many cultures, such a response would to be out of order. After all, the cashier is not actually doing you a favour; she is only giving you what belongs to you. And if you were to say 'Thank you' in such a situation, what would be the appropriate behaviour of the cashier? Would she feel obliged to acknowledge your thanks in some way?

Continuing with Halliday's taxonomy, we might consider, next, the textual dimension of language, that is, the way in which linguistic expressions are used to structure a discourse and to manage an interaction. A current utterance needs to link up with preceding discourse and might anticipate what is to follow. Speakers need to know how to sum up, how to introduce a new topic, how to return to a topic after a digression, how to introduce a digression, and how to underline the importance of a claim. Speakers also need to negotiate turn-taking: how to signal that your turn is coming to an end, how to take the floor in a group discussion, how to keep the floor, how to fill in potentially embarrassing pauses, and such like.

---

[4] A well-known example concerns what people say at the start of a meal. Foreign learners of English are puzzled by the fact that there is no English equivalent to French *Bon appétit* or German *Guten Appetit.*

A focus on the norms of language use might suggest that speakers are at the mercy of the conventions and that they are unable to innovate. To a degree, this is indeed the case: to be proficient in a language means, precisely, knowing the conventional way to behave linguistically. This is not to say that speakers may not flout the conventions, for special effect. There are occasions on which one might wish to be rude and offensive, or to appear arrogant or morose. These effects, however, are to be achieved against the conventions. There is a difference between being rude intentionally, and coming across as rude inadvertently.

As suggested here, usage norms pertain to recurring facets of context, whether ideational (what the speaker wants to say), interpersonal, or textual. On the other hand, it could be argued that every context of use is bound to be unique: it is different, if only minimally, from all others. The thought that I wish to verbalize on one occasion will not be identical with the thoughts that I, or indeed anyone else, have entertained on other occasions; the audience I am addressing today will be different from audiences I have addressed in the past. We can counter this argument by pointing out that linguistic (and communicative) proficiency consists in the ability to categorize a present reality with respect to norms, as these have been established through previous experience with the language and interactions with its speakers. This is not to deny that sometimes new situations can arise for which no established conventions are at hand. Consider, for example, the etiquette of electronic communication. In the old days, when people communicated with formal letters, there were strict conventions for the salutation (*Dear Sir, Dear Mr X, Dear John*, etc.) and the sign-off (*Yours sincerely, Yours faithfully*, etc.), an important parameter being whether the recipient was known to the sender, and, if so, what the nature was of the relationship. These conventions were largely abandoned with the advent of electronic email communication. How, for example, do you start an email? Older people, I suspect, experience some uncertainty here, and may feel slightly uncomfortable when a total stranger addresses them with *Hi*.

Words and collocations

The above section considered usage norms from the point of view of the relation between linguistic expressions and a reality which is, strictly speaking, outside of the language itself—the intended conceptualization, the speaker's communicative goals, the relation between the interlocutors, and the non-linguistic situation. There is, however, a language-internal dimension to speaking idiomatically. At its most basic, this is a matter of grammatical correctness, as this would be understood by generative linguists, indeed, by linguists of just about any theoretical persuasion. *I believe to be correct*, with the meaning 'I believe that I am correct', is unidiomatic for the reason that it is ungrammatical, that is, it fails to conform with any of the established subcategorization frames of the verb *believe*. In this section, however, I would like to focus on another aspect of language-internal norms and one largely ignored by generative linguists. This has to do with adherence to the statistical norms of the language.

Some words occur more frequently than others; some word combinations occur more often than other, equally plausible combinations; some constructions are in more common uses than others. Generative linguists have had little to say about these matters. The fact that passive clauses might be less frequent, overall, than active clauses, or that passive clauses with a *by*-phrase might be less frequent than agent-less passives, is deemed to be outside of their area of competence. Frequency data, such linguists might argue, are a matter of E-language, not of I-language. The I-language makes available these various options; how a speaker makes use of the options is not their concern.

In some cases, it is true, relative frequency might seem to be an essentially non-linguistic matter. Frequently occurring events are likely to be named more often than rare events, while entities which we encounter every day of our lives are likely to be the topic of our conversation more often than things which are outside of our experience. Thankfully, catastrophes occur less frequently than accidents. Not surprisingly, the word *catastrophe* is less frequent than the word *accident*. On the other hand, the word *mishap* is even less frequent than *catastrophe*, even though mishaps are an everyday occurrence. In the vast majority of cases—a point I shall argue in Chapter 7—the frequency of a word, expression, or construction has to be regarded as a fact about the language itself, largely independent of the vicissitudes of the world and the communicative needs of language users.

Adherence to statistical norms is not just a matter of the relative frequencies of particular words, phrases, and constructions. We also need to consider the frequency of words relative to other words and the frequency of words relative to constructions. This is a matter of knowing which words go with which other words and of knowing which words are associated with which syntactic configurations.

The central notion here is that of COLLOCATION. The term, and the way we understand it, is from Firth (1957a: 194). Collocation is a matter of "mutual expectancy" (Firth 1968 [1957]: 181), of "the company [that a word] keeps" (p. 179). Very often, the use of a word or expression generates expectations as to the surrounding words in the discourse. The phenomenon is easy to demonstrate. Read the following, and try to predict the next word in the expressions.

(2)   a. In the foreseeable...
      b. It was an unmitigated...
      c. It was an unqualified...
      d. It was a foregone...

Probably, you will have completed these fragments to create the expressions *the foreseeable future, an unmitigated disaster, an unqualified success,* and *a foregone conclusion*. The very fact that speakers of English are able to complete the fragments in this manner indicates that they 'know' the collocational preferences in question. This knowledge constitutes just one small aspect of what it means to have an idiomatic command of the language.

Although *the foreseeable future* has the status of a set phrase, it probably would not qualify as an idiom, certainly not on the criteria discussed in the previous chapter. First, the meaning of *foreseeable future* is just what we should expect, given the meanings of the component words. Second, in spite of the strong expectancy set up by *foreseeable*, other candidates are also available. A large number of things might be qualified as 'foreseeable'. One could speak about a foreseeable outcome, foreseeable results, or foreseeable consequences. Equally, there are many adjectives that can qualify *future*: we speak of the near future, the immediate future, the distant future, and so on.

The mere fact that two words tend to occur together is not in itself evidence of a collocation. The first example in (2) has *in* occurring adjacent to *the*. Although this combination might well be very frequent (there are in fact over half a million examples in the BNC), it may not be of any special interest. The status of *in* as a (transitive) preposition requires that it is followed by a noun phrase, and noun phrases are often introduced by the determiner *the*. Moreover, *in* and *the* are themselves words of high frequency; the probability of their occurring together is therefore inherently greater that the probability of less common words occurring together. The matter might, though, be of interest if it should turn out to be the case that the frequency of the combination *in the* were to be significantly higher (or lower) than what one would expect on the basis of the frequency of each of the two items, within expressions of the form [PNP].

Let us consider *foreseeable future* in the light of these remarks. *Foreseeable* is not a particularly common word; it occurs only 427 times in the BNC. It turns out, however, that just over two-thirds of these uses (294) are in the phrase *foreseeable future*. The matter is even clearer when we differentiate between attributive uses of the adjective (that is, when something is characterized as a 'foreseeable N') and predicative uses (when something is said to 'be foreseeable'). As it happens, *foreseeable* is used predominantly in the attributive position (352 instances). Four-fifths of these examples consist of the expression *foreseeable future*; other uses, with only a handful of examples each, include *foreseeable consequences, results, losses*, and *circumstances*. On the other hand, predicative uses of the adjective show no particular attraction to the word *future*. Things that are characterized as being '(not) foreseeable' include damage, consequence, circumstances, injury, and side effects.

The attributive use of *foreseeable* creates a strong expectation that the following word is going to be *future*. Does the preference work in the other direction? Does an occurrence of the word *future* evoke the word *foreseeable*? *Future* is a rather common word (22,378 instances in the BNC). As we have seen, a miniscule 287, barely more than 1 per cent, occur with *foreseeable*. One might conclude, therefore, that the collocational preference goes one way only. However, if we focus on the frame [Adj future], a slightly different picture emerges. The frame is attested 2,669 times. The most frequent combination is *near future* (585 examples), with *foreseeable future* in second place (294 examples). Further preferences, in declining order of frequency, are *immediate future* (131), *distant future* (77), and *uncertain future* (71).

In recent years, sophisticated statistical procedures have been brought to bear on these issues. The null hypothesis is that the probability of two words occurring adjacent to each other is the product of the probability of each occurring on its own. Attested frequency of word combinations may be indicative of a significant attraction, or significant repulsion, between the words. Such mutual information statistics—which are available online from the Bank of English website[5]—need, however, to be interpreted with caution. Unlike with tossing a coin—where the probability of the coin landing tails is independent of how it landed on the last throw—the probability of word occurring at a specific point in the discourse may be conditional on the syntactic category of the word itself, the syntactic category of a previous word, and of the construction in which the word features. Word occurrences thus need to be seen in the context of their syntactic category and the syntactic configuration in which they occur. The probability of *a* and *the* occurring together is virtually zero, in spite of the fact that each is a very common word, the reason being that there is no syntactic configuration which would sanction this combination. Our discussion of *foreseeable* also illustrated the importance of the containing construction. The association of *foreseeable* and *future* is only attested in the attributive construction [Adj N], not at all in the predicative construction [NP be ADJ].

In spite of these strictures, the notion of collocation has provided valuable insights into the use of words. An interesting application of the notion has to do with the differentiation of near synonyms. Very often, near synonyms are differentiated by their collocational preferences, or, as the case may be, their collocational dispreferences. Consider near synonyms such as *high/tall*, *big/large*, and *small/little*. You prepare a big (*large) surprise for someone and pay a large (*big) amount of money for something. Often, the collocational preferences may be indicative of subtle semantic differences between the words. For example, *big* and *little* tend to carry affective and evaluative connotations, whereas *large* and *small* tend to refer only to the size of a thing. Significantly, *nice* and *horrible* collocate with *big* and *little*, but not with their near synonyms: *a nice big house*, *a horrible little man*. Sometimes, though, collocational preferences seem to be a matter of brute usage. Given the meaning of *merry*, there is no obvious reason why birthday celebrations should not be as merry as Christmas celebrations. Yet we do not wish someone a 'merry birthday', we

---

[5] www.titania.bham.ac.uk.

wish them a 'happy birthday'. (*Happy*, on the other hand, goes equally well with both nouns.)[6]

A well-studied case concerns adjectival modifiers which emphasize the absolute degree of something (Partington 1998, 2004). There are quite a few such words in English:

(3)   utter, complete, absolute, perfect, total, sheer, downright, outright, out-and-out, unqualified, unadulterated, pure

Consider, for example, which of these words could be used to modify the following nouns: *nonsense, delight, pleasure, disaster, lack, embarrassment, disgrace,* and *stranger.* As will be readily apparent, each of these nouns tends to go with only a subset of the modifiers. We might characterize something as 'an absolute disgrace' in preference to 'a downright disgrace', as an 'outright lie' but not as a 'sheer lie', we win an 'outright victory' but suffer a 'total defeat', and, as mentioned in Chapter 1, 'total failure' is a more common collocation than 'total success'.

Another domain has to do with adjectives which signify that something is 'really' what it is claimed to be, or, conversely, that it is not really such:

(4)   a. real, true, genuine, authentic, bona fide, valid, legitimate
      b. false, fake, artificial, synthetic, counterfeit, bogus, sham, mock, phoney, faux, spurious, fraudulent

Each of these has its own collocational profile. We have 'artificial cream' but 'counterfeit money', a 'fake gun' but 'false teeth', we make a 'bogus claim' but a 'false statement'.

Closely related to collocation is Firth's concept of COLLIGATION. Whereas collocation has to do with the lexical context in which a word occurs, colligation has to do with its syntactic environment. Recall our discussion of the word *lap* in Chapter 3 (pp. 51–3). There it was noted that *lap* occurs almost exclusively with possessive determiners—*her lap, my lap,* and so on. Whereas some possessives might be more frequent than others, the basic insight was that *lap* co-occurs with a certain class of words. Moreover, the possessive phrases themselves occur preferentially within a prepositional phrase: *on her lap, into my lap,* etc. Again, the preference is not for any particular preposition (though, as we saw, some prepositions are more frequent than others) but with prepositions (more accurately, a subset of prepositions) as a group. The notion of colligation is also relevant to my earlier remarks on the word *foreseeable.* In addition to its preferred collocation with the word *future* (*the foreseeable future*), we also noted that the word is preferentially used in attributive position rather than predicatively.

---

[6] Collocational dispreferences—as exemplified by *merry birthday, large surprise,* and *big amount*—are sometimes referred to as ANTI-COLLOCATIONS (Inkpen and Hirst 2005). See also Renouf and Banerjee (2007).

Firth's notion of the company that a word keeps extends beyond the immediate context of use. A word may extend its influence over a span of discourse. We can illustrate with the example of the word *cause* (as both noun and verb). One could argue that any and every happening in the world is part of a causal chain. The happening itself has a cause and will itself be the cause of future events. We need not go into the philosophical ramifications of causal chains. Of interest to us is how the word *cause* is used in the language. Remarkably, we find that the word is used predominantly of 'bad' events. (Stubbs 1995). We are more likely to talk about the causes of the Great Depression than about what caused the subsequent recovery. We ask what caused a company to go bankrupt rather than what caused a company to flourish. We talk about the cause of death and the cause of an accident rather than the cause of a person's good health or the cause of her success. This facet of the meaning of *cause* has been referred to as a SEMANTIC PROSODY (Louw 1993).[7]

There is one further aspect of Firth's approach that I would like to emphasize. In stating that one knows a word by the company it keeps (Firth 1968 [1957]: 179) he is implying that the meaning of a word can to some extent be stated in terms of how it is used. He cites the example of the word *ass*, as used in the following expressions:

(5)   Don't be such an ass, You silly ass!, What an ass he is!

He commented: "One of the meanings of ass is its habitual collocation with such other words as those quoted above" (p. 179).

To a modern reader—recall that Firth was writing in the 1950s—the expressions in (5) may seem rather quaint and a little dated. For my part, I cannot imagine myself exclaiming 'what an ass' of someone. This, however, by no means detracts from the point that Firth was making. On the contrary. The very fact that modern readers might perceive Firth's examples to be somewhat dated merely shows that the usage norms have changed over time, and this, for Firth, would be indicative of a change in the meaning of the word.[8]

The Firthian notion of collocation played a central role in the theoretical and descriptive work of John Sinclair. Sinclair opposes two "organizing principles" of language (p. 109)—what he calls the open choice principle and the idiom principle. The OPEN CHOICE PRINCIPLE is based on the dictionary plus grammar model of language (though Sinclair does not refer to it as such) and views linguistic structure from a

---

[7] The negative prosody associated with *cause* does not, however, manifest itself in academic scientific discourse—at least, in those contexts where the causal relations are between events which have little direct impact on human concerns (Hunston 2007).

[8] The BNC suggests that the collocation *silly ass* was still current in the 1990s, there being five instances of the expression, followed by *pompous ass* (four examples). The BNC also testifies to a usage not mentioned by Firth, namely, *The law is an ass*, with some fifteen examples. A further dimension to the use of the word concerns its phonological closeness to *arse*. Speakers may use *ass* euphemistically as a phonetic distortion of the tabooed word.

processing perspective, that is, from the point of view of a speaker producing discourse or of a listener comprehending incoming language. He describes the principle as follows:

At each point where a unit is completed (a word or a phrase or a clause), a large range of choice opens up and the only constraint is grammaticalness.... This is probably the normal way of seeing and describing language. It is often called a 'slot-and-filler' model, envisaging texts as a series of slots which have to be filled from a lexicon which satisfies local restraints. At each slot, virtually any word can occur.   (Sinclair 1991: 109)

Let us illustrate on a concrete example. After the occurrence of a determiner (*the*, let us say), several choices open up: the next word could be a noun (*the farmer*), an adjective modifying a subsequent noun (*the rich farmer*), or an adverb modifying a subsequent adjective which in turn modifies a subsequent noun (*the incredibly rich farmer*). These choices complete the phrasal category of noun phrase. (Precisely these kinds of forward predictions are central to the processing model of Hawkins 1994, 2004.) Any item specified in the lexicon as 'noun', 'adjective', or 'adverb' is available to complete the phrase. *The vicariously empty farmer* and *the voraciously green lap* would count as equally valid continuations of a phrase initiated by *the*. One might, to be sure, eliminate these bizarre outcomes by appeal to the semantic incompatibility of the various elements, in accordance with selectional restrictions specified in the lexicon. Thus, the determiner + adjective sequence *the foreseeable* needs to be completed with a noun designating a 'foreseeable' entity. There are many such candidates. Of these, however, just one is the preferred choice—*future*. The selection of this noun goes beyond matters of grammaticality and semantic compatibility. Contrary to the open choice principle, words are not "independent items of meaning", each constituting "a separate choice" (Sinclair 1991: 175).

Opposing the open choice principle is the IDIOM PRINCIPLE, according to which "the choice of one word affects the choice of others in its vicinity" (Sinclair 1991: 173). The language user has available to her "a large number of semi-preconstructed phrases that constitute single choices, even though it might appear to be analyzable into segments" (p. 110). The phrase *the foreseeable future* does not represent three separate and independent choices; it represents a single choice, even though, as we have noted, the expression is both syntactically and semantically unexceptional.

In this particular example, the speaker has available to her a fully preconstructed phrase. In the above quotation, Sinclair also spoke about 'semi-preconstructed phrases'. These constitute syntactic patterns which may permit some degree of lexical variation: they have 'open slots' which may be filled by items which satisfy the specific demands of the occasion. Recall our earlier example of how to enquire into an attribute of a person, thing, or place. One semi-preconstructed phrase commences with *how* followed by a dimensional adjective: How old/tall are you? How far is it? Another commences with *how much*: How much does it cost? How much does he weigh? In some cases, the available pattern makes no reference to specific lexical items. As a description of a motion event, *he ran out of the house* is constructed on the general pattern of [manner-of-motion verb + directional prepositional phrase], in contrast, say, to [change-of-location verb + manner-of-motion adverbial]. The idiomaticity of the English expression does not reside in the choice of specific words but in its adherence to a more general constructional schema. Sinclair's definition of 'idiom' as "a group of two or more words which are chosen together in order to produce a specific meaning or effect in speech or writing" (1991: 172) is therefore too narrow; the 'idiom' may consist in the appropriateness of a syntactic configuration. The definition may be too restrictive in other ways. For example, a single word may have its idiomatic uses. *Cheers*—said whilst raising a glass—is the conventional thing to say in that kind of situation.

Learning to speak idiomatically

The goal of any foreign language student (and their teacher) is an idiomatic command of the target language.

We have considered a number of aspects of the idiomatic. In the last chapter we looked at expressions which fall outside the scope of the dictionary plus grammar book model, such as picturesque idioms with their unpredictable semantics, and groups of words with their unusual syntax, as well as lexical and phrasal idioms of various kinds. In this chapter I have considered the idiomatic from the perspective of the usage norms of a language. Two aspects of usage norms were highlighted. The first concerns the need to match language to the 'external' circumstances of its use (the conceptual content to be verbalized, the interaction in progress, the text that is being created). The second concerns language-internal relations, in particular, respect for the statistical norms of usage. Some words tend to co-occur with other words, while some words and word groups are more frequent than others. Constructions may also create expectancies with regard to the items that occur in them, while the items themselves might feature predominantly in some constructions rather than others.[9]

It is easy to see how some facets of the idiomatic might be incorporated into a teaching syllabus. Picturesque idioms (*spill the beans, pull someone's leg, rain cats and dogs*) might feature on the learning agenda, as might the phrasal verbs and various syntactically irregular phrases (*by and large, weeks on end*). Learners might have their attention drawn to specific verb–noun combinations—*conduct a study, reach a decision, achieve a goal*—perhaps on the basis of the perceived utility of these phrases for a given learner group (Nesselhauf 2003). Frequent collocations (*Merry Christmas, happy birthday, utter nonsense*) might be taught as such. The same goes for formulaic

---

[9] I discuss the interaction of words and constructions in more detail in Chapters 7 and 8.

expressions which are tied to a specific context of use (*Good Morning, Cheers, How do you do?*). Students might be coached in Anglophone (Francophone, Russophone, or whatever) strategies for making requests, for asking favours, for apologizing, and for politely disagreeing. Tertiary students might be instructed in the characteristic ways of structuring a piece of academic writing—how to describe the conduct of an experiment, how to report the findings, how to discuss the findings against previously reported research.

In the final analysis, however, many aspects of 'speaking idiomatically' might not be amenable to pedagogical instruction at all. This is especially the case with statistical norms of usage. It would be futile, I suspect, to instruct learners in the relative frequency of lexical items and highly counterproductive to teach a construction, only to inform learners that the construction is not particularly frequent and should not be overused. In any case, the statistical properties of language are so all-pervasive, and of such subtlety, that it would be a major task to draw up a profile even for a single word, let alone incorporate these findings into a pedagogical programme. Indeed, it is only in recent times, with the availability of electronic corpora, that language-internal usage norms have been able to be studied at all. In some cases, to be sure, the relative frequency of words and word combinations are available to introspection, a matter we address in Chapter 7. A good deal of what constitutes speaking idiomatically, however, lies below the conscious awareness even of linguistically sophisticated speakers (and language teachers).

Rather, what seems to happen is that learners 'pick up' language-internal usage norms through exposure and ongoing experience with the language. As all language learners (and their teachers) know, extensive exposure is crucial to successful language acquisition. What is not obvious is what, precisely, learners are acquiring through exposure, over and above what they learn through classroom instruction. My suggestion is that they are building up a store of statistical knowledge. It is as if they are keeping a tally of the number of times a word has been used relative to other words, noting and cross-referencing these uses with the linguistic and extra-linguistic context (Ellis, Simpson-Vlach, and Maynard 2008). The study of a limited set of selected texts, such as might be available in a language-teaching classroom, is insufficient for this purpose. Learners need extensive exposure to language as used in a range of contexts. The knowledge that they pick up is mostly implicit and rarely available to introspection. Language users come to 'feel', without being able to say why, that *total failure* 'sounds better' than *total success*, and that *unqualified success* 'works better' than *unqualified disaster*.

Given the crucial importance of exposure, and the subtlety and complexity of the statistical norms of language use, it is remarkable that second-, and especially foreign-language learners are able to achieve a native-like proficiency at all, in spite of their only limited exposure to the language.[10] This is not to say that non-native productions, even those with a seemingly impeccable grammatical and lexical structure, may not diverge in subtle ways from native-speaker norms. Granger (1998) found that collocations such as *acutely aware, readily available*, and *vitally important* were rare in the productions of advanced French learners of English. The learners tended to opt for 'safe' alternatives, with *totally, highly*, and *completely*. When asked to judge the acceptability of collocations with *highly* and *fully*, they were inclined to endorse combinations which strike English speakers as unusual, such as *fully different* and *highly difficult*.

In the final section of this chapter, I present a case study which demonstrates the subtlety and pervasiveness of language-internal statistics.

A case study: *X-minded*

The following article appeared over fifty years ago in *Time* magazine. To be sure, the subject matter of the article wears its date on its sleeve. But can we say the same about the language? How dated is the text, linguistically speaking?

Security in Space
The world is about to watch a strange and exciting show: U.S. industry, led by scientists and engineers and backed by the U.S. Government, is headed for outer space. The cost of the campaign will be as astronomical as its objective, but the men who lead it consider its success a national necessity. They point out that the earth's atmosphere is an insignificant film, thinner in proportion than the skin of an apple, and that military technology is about to outgrow it, as it outgrew the earth's surface two world wars ago. Navigation of the air-film is no longer enough. No nation will be safe unless it can also navigate the vacuum that hangs overhead.

The new status of space flight, formerly made suspect by visionaries and fiction writers, was not defined in public until the Convair Division of General Dynamics Corp. held its Astronautics Symposium at San Diego (TIME, March 4). Planned as a small confab of space-minded missile men, the conference ballooned into a crammed mass meeting of engineers and scientists representing airplane, electronic and instrument companies as well as universities and all three armed services. A few years ago most of these hardheaded characters would not have attended a space-flight meeting except incognito. Now they are eager.

Dollars for Space. The change in their attitude was caused by Government money tossed into guided missiles in billion-dollar chunks. Everyone at the San Diego meeting realized that missiles will soon replace aircraft as prime consumers of taxpayers' funds. For forward-looking space-flight workers that is already history. Next step beyond missiles is true space navigation, and no manufacturer who wants to stay on the Government's contract list can afford to neglect it. So practically every outfit even remotely connected with aircraft or missiles was represented at San Diego, and trying hard to look as space-minded as possible.   (*Time*, 11 March 1955)

---

[10] For evidence that foreign learners do indeed pick up subtle features of the target language, see Gries and Wulff (2005).

Many features of the text are surprisingly modern—with one notable exception, the word *space-minded*. The word occurs twice, once as an attributive adjective (*space-minded missile men*), once as a predicative adjective (*trying hard to look as space-minded as possible*). The word is not in my productive repertoire; in fact, I am not aware of having heard it at all. It is not recorded in the BNC, though a Google search (February 2008) returned about 500 hits (including the text cited above).

I stumbled across the *Time* article while following up some remarks which Firth had made in his 1935 essay 'The technique of semantics'. Firth commented on the popularity of what he called "'old school-tie' comedians" and their use of "public school cant", an allusion which will probably be lost on modern readers (myself included). Then, after touching on the sociological dimension of language change, he writes:

> While 'old school tie' makes the success of a comic turn, the word *plan* with its derivatives provides some of the magic words of the age. Compounds like *air-minded*, *traffic-minded*, are fairly common. The other day I saw *beacon-minded* and *flat-minded* in a newspaper. Such compounds have favoured the rather un-English formation *likemindedness* as some sort of equivalent of the German magic word *Gleichschaltung*. Cases like this are interesting because they are often sociologically symptomatic.   (Firth 1957*b* [1935]: 13)

According to Firth, then, fashionable words in the 1930s included *plan* and its derivatives as well as compounds in *-minded*. While *plan* is still very much with us, the expressions *air-minded* and *traffic-minded* are definitely not. For a modern reader, *beacon-minded* is virtually uninterpretable.[11]

Being curious about Firth's observations concerning compounds in *-minded*, I turned to the TIME Magazine Corpus (Davies 2007–). Ideally, I would have preferred an archive of a British newspaper, such as the London *Times* (a newspaper which Firth would probably have read). Unfortunately, the online *Times* archive does not date back to the 1930s. The following data on *-minded* therefore pertain to American journalistic usage. This does not, however, invalidate the issues that arise from the data.

There are ninety-one instances of *air-minded* in the 100 million word TIME Corpus. Table 5.1 lists the number of occurrences per decade (there are no occurrences after the 1960s). The data suggest that *air-minded* was fairly popular in the 1930s and 1940s, as Firth indeed suggested, with its use peaking in the '30s.[12] Thereafter it gradually fell into disuse.

Intrigued by this pattern, I checked out other compounds formed by the addition of *-minded* to a noun. Remarkably, they all tell a similar story. With one exception (*business-minded*, which saw a sudden jump in frequency in the 2000s) they all

---

[11] Also puzzling are Firth's remarks on German *Gleichschaltung* and its supposed equivalence to English *likemindedness*. The German word refers to the bringing into line, or the synchronization, of different policies or agendas.

[12] *Traffic-minded*, another term mentioned by Firth, is attested only once, in the 1950s. *Flat-minded* and *beacon-minded* are not recorded.

enjoyed a peak of popularity in the mid-decades of the last century. Thereafter, their use has declined (see Table 5.2).

TABLE 5.1. Incidence of the term *air-minded* per decade in the TIME Corpus (Davies 2007–).

	Occurrences	Frequency per million
20s	8	1.0
30s	33	2.6
40s	37	2.4
50s	7	0.4
60s	6	0.4
70s and beyond	0	0

TABLE 5.2. Frequency of compounds in *–minded* per decade in the TIME Corpus (Davies 2007–).

	Overall frequency	Peak decade	Frequency (per million) in peak decade
reform-minded	173	1960s	3.4
economy-minded	98	1950s	2.0
air-minded	91	1930s	2.6
business-minded*	42	2000s	0.9
fascist-minded	32	1940s	1.6
tradition-minded	30	1960s	0.6
budget-minded	26	1970s	0.5
expansion-minded	19	1960s	0.5
world-minded	19	1940s	1.0
security-minded	18	1950s	0.3
publicity-minded	18	1940s	0.5
science-minded	16	1960s	0.4
war-minded	13	1930s	0.4
farm-minded	10	1940s	0.5
space-minded**	7	1950s	0.2

Notes: * Leaving aside a spurt in the 2000s, the peak decade for *business-minded* was the 1950s.
    ** Only attested in the 1950s and 1960s.

In these examples, the initial part of the compound is a noun, and many of the compounds do indeed sound dated. On the other hand, compounds in *-minded* where the initial element is an adjective, such as *high-minded, open-minded, strong-minded, single-minded, fair-minded*, and *tough-minded*, are very much part of the modern language. Interestingly, though, these words also peaked prior to the 1960s. One exception is *like-minded*, whose use gradually increased into the 2000s. On the other hand, *like-mindedness*, which Firth considered to be "rather un-English", seems not to have taken off. There are only three instances, one in the 1940s and two in the 1980s.

What is perhaps even more surprising is that the trend identified above is not restricted to compounds in *-minded*. In fact, it seems to apply more generally to compounds of the structure [X-Yed], where X is an adjective and Y names a body part. Data on some of these compounds, again from the TIME Corpus, are given in Table 5.3. Also shown in the table is the most frequent of the body-part compounds in the peak decade. The majority of these compounds peaked in the 1930s or 1940s;

TABLE 5.3. Frequency of compounds of the type [X-Yed], where Y names a body part, in the TIMES Corpus (Davies 2007–).

	Total frequency	Peak decade	Per million in peak decade	Most frequent type in peak decade
-eyed	6688	1940s	106.0	blue-eyed
-headed	1556	1930s	42.0	red-headed
-handed	1247	1930s	16.3	left-handed
-legged	971	1930s	13.0	long-legged
-blooded	728	1930s	10.7	full-blooded
-cheeked	701	1940s	15.3	pink-cheeked
-skinned	641	1940s	9.0	brown-skinned
-hearted	633	1930s	14.6	light-hearted
-footed	530	1950s	7.4	fleet-footed
-necked	468	1930s	7.7	bull-necked
-chested	347	1940s	5.2	barrel-chested
-eared	314	1940s	6.1	jug-eared
-fingered	266	1950s	4.2	light-fingered
-boned	155	1930s	3.6	big-boned
-brained	146	1930s	2.5	crack-brained
-kneed	120	1920s	2.0	weak-kneed

this is true of the more common types, with -*eyed* and -*handed*, as well as of the less frequent types, with -*brained* and -*boned*.

What about the other fashionable word that Firth cites, namely *plan*? The word can hardly be regarded as dated nor, on the face of it, subject to fashion. Remarkably, however, the TIME Corpus suggests that the historical profile of this word may not be too dissimilar from those discussed above. Its use peaked in the 1940s (244 per million), declining to a low of 167 per million in the 1960s. Thereafter, it appears to have regained its popularity, hitting another peak in the 2000s (256 per million).

These data—even bearing in mind possible differences between British and American usage—would suggest, if nothing else, that Firth had a rather good ear for detecting upcoming linguistic fashions of his day.

The data are instructive in other respects, too. First, it is evident that the fashion for words in -*minded* which Firth commented on was not a property of these words alone. Rather, it appears to have been part of a wider trend favouring compounds with the structure [X-Yed]. Corpus data are able to show that this trend continued for a couple of decades after Firth was writing; thereafter, it declined. The effects are both subtle and wide-ranging, and, I venture to say, go well beyond what might be intuited by a native speaker. To be sure, words such as *air-minded*, *barrel-chested*, and *crack-brained* sound a little dated; I cannot envisage myself using any of them. Even *tradition-minded* sounds, to my ears, rather unidiomatic; I should prefer *traditionally minded*.[13] On the other hand, *left-handed*, *light-hearted*, and *blue-eyed* do not seem remarkable in any way; they are part and parcel of modern English usage. How else is one to describe a person who writes with the left hand, or who has blue eyes?

The discovery of patterns such as the one identified above raises the question of how such patterns can come to exist at all. People use a word such as *left-handed*, one would have thought, whenever they wish to characterize a person as, precisely, left-handed. One would not, a priori, expect to find any particular pattern in the frequency of this expression in journalistic prose over the past eight decades. After all, the percentage of left-handers in the population remains more or less constant. At most, one might expect some random variation from decade to decade. All the more remarkable, therefore, is the fact that the use of *left-handed* should have peaked in the 1930s (according to the corpus evidence), and in conformity with a more general pattern that the corpus data reveal.

The conclusion has to be, I think, that the incidence of expressions such as *left-handed*, *air-minded*, and even *blue-eyed*, is guided by the usage norms for the

---

[13] The BNC confirms my intuitions. There are no instances of *tradition-minded* as against five occurrences of *traditionally minded*: examples include *a traditionally minded bishop* and *the traditionally minded paterfamilias*. On the other hand, we should not discount the possibility of a subtle difference between British and American usage. The COCA records twelve examples of *tradition-minded*, including *tradition-minded Bishops* and *tradition-minded Jews*, against five examples of *traditionally minded*.

morphological pattern which they instantiate. The usage norms in question are not categorical—they are not of an either/or nature prescribing that a usage, at one time or place, is acceptable, at another time and place, unacceptable. The norms are statistical in nature, having to do with the probability of occurrence of a certain pattern and of the expressions which instantiate it.

As stated in the preceding section, these usage norms cannot reasonably be taught. It would be absurd to attempt to coach foreign learners of English (or indeed native speakers of English) in the frequency with which they should use compounds of the kind [X-Yed]. But while the usage norms cannot be taught, they clearly have been learned. The patterns that we have discerned emerge from the usage of innumerable individuals—writers, journalists, interviewees, the authors of press releases, copy-editors, and so on. The individuals have modelled their own usage on the patterns that they have observed around them. They have also contributed, through their own linguistic productions and their dissemination in the wider linguistic community, to the entrenchment of these very patterns.

6

Constructions

In previous chapters I have referred on several occasions to constructions. The term is common in linguistic discourse. We can refer to the passive constructions, the relative clause constructions, and the conditional constructions of a language. Students of Latin will recall having learned about the ablative absolute construction. Although familiar, the term is far from uncontroversial. Generative linguists have tended to dismiss constructions as epiphenomena, the product of more fundamental principles, of no particular interest in themselves. Others, however, take a different view, putting constructions in centre stage and regarding them as one of the most basic of all linguistic constructs. In fact, in many construction-based grammars, constructions perform the work which in generative theories is performed by rules.

There are, as we shall see, a number of different ways in which constructions can be characterized. Thus, something which might be regarded as a construction on one approach might turn out not to be a construction on other approaches. In order to provide some background to a discussion of these different approaches, I first present the basic assumptions of Langacker's theory of Cognitive Grammar. Later in the chapter I address some of the issues arising from an approach to language which gives preeminence to constructions over rules, even to the extent that rules (or at least, rules as traditionally understood) are no longer needed.

Cognitive Grammar: some basic concepts

Langacker began working on the theory of Cognitive Grammar in the mid-1970s, in part as a reaction to the generative theories of the time.[1] The standard presentation is the two-volume *Foundations of Cognitive Grammar* (Langacker 1987, 1991); a more recent account is Langacker (2008). In this section I introduce some basic principles of the theory, especially as these pertain to constructions.

Let us begin by considering language in the broader context of communication. Humans (and other animals) communicate by means of signs. A SIGN is a perceptible

---

[1] For the historical background to Cognitive Grammar, see Taylor (2007).

object or event which stands for something else. Observing only the sign we can infer the something else for which it stands. Language is, of course, a sign system *par excellence.*

There are several ways in which a sign can mean (Taylor 2002: Chapter 3). In the case of INDEXICAL signs, the perceptible event can be traced back to its presumed cause. Smoke is a sign of fire: if we observe smoke rising into the air, we presume there is a fire which causes the smoke. Medical diagnosis proceeds on the basis of observed (and reported) symptoms. Some aspects of language are indexical. Slurred speech might be taken to signify the inebriated state of the speaker; a deep baritone voice communicates that the speaker is a male of the species; hearing a Scottish accent we reasonably infer that the speaker is Scottish.

Another way in which signs can mean is though an ICONIC relation between the form of the sign and its meaning. The sign in some way resembles the meaning which it stands for. Many road traffic signs belong to this category, as do the onomatopoeic words in a language. Aspects of text structure may also display iconicity. To mention event A before mentioning event B can convey, iconically, that event A happened before event B.

Although language may display elements of indexicality and iconicity, language is primarily neither indexical nor iconic. Linguistic signs are meaningful in another respect, namely, in virtue of a SYMBOLIC relation between form and meaning. Symbolic signs do not resemble what they mean, neither is there a causal relation between a sign and what it signifies. The relation, instead, is purely a matter of convention, which all users of the sign have to learn and comply with. An important feature of symbolic signs is that they are under the control of the agent who uses them. A person chooses to use the sign, and does so with the intention of representing the associated meaning.

Cognitive Grammar is based on the view that language is inherently and quintessentially symbolic. Given this assumption, the study of language involves the study of three kinds of object:

(a) the linguistic signs themselves, that is, language in its perceptible form, prototypically as sound, but also encompassing written forms and (in the case of sign languages) hand movements. Following Langacker, I will use the term PHONOLOGICAL REPRESENTATION to refer to this aspect of language.[2]

(b) the symbolized meaning. Meaning is being used here in a rather broad sense, to refer not only to propositional content and referential intent, but also to the expression of the speaker's attitudes and beliefs. I refer to this aspect of language as the SEMANTIC REPRESENTATION.

(c) SYMBOLIC RELATIONS between elements of (a) and elements of (b).

---

[2] Evans (2009) introduced the term VEHICLE to refer to the physical manifestation of a linguistic sign, in whatever medium.

Symbolic relations are most clearly illustrated with reference to words. A word such as *tree* associates a phonological representation [triː] with the concept 'tree'. The notion of symbolic relation applies to many other linguistic phenomena, however. Indeed, a distinctive claim of Cognitive Grammar is that *all* of language can be described in terms of the three kinds of entities listed above. Cognitive Grammar is therefore a MINIMALIST theory of language, indeed, a RADICALLY MINIMALIST theory.[3]

In its insistence on the symbolic nature of language, Cognitive Grammar is at variance with most mainstream theories. Other theories of language certainly acknowledge that language is a means for relating sound and meaning. They insist, however, that the relation is not a direct one but is, rather, mediated by intervening levels of organization. These intervening levels have their own distinctive structural principles, involving elements and relations which are unique to these levels. The most important of these intervening levels is syntax, which is structured from uniquely syntactic elements such as the lexical categories (noun, verb, etc.), the phrasal categories (noun phrase, verb phrase), and the various relations which can hold amongst these elements (such as the relation of subject-of a clause). The Cognitive Grammar claim, on the other hand, is that syntax can be fully described in terms of symbolic relations between phonological structures and semantic structures.

On the Cognitive Grammar view, then, a language does not comprise a set of rules for generating well-formed syntactic objects. Rather, it consists of an INVENTORY OF LINGUISTIC UNITS. A UNIT is any element of a language (whether phonological, semantic, or symbolic) which has become established, or ENTRENCHED, in the speaker's mind as a result of the frequency of its previous use (whether in production or reception). Since units are established as a consequence of usage, the inventory of units which constitute a language is open-ended. Using a language is a matter of drawing on the available inventory in order to realize one's present needs. Learning a language is a matter of expanding one's repertoire of linguistic units and becoming expert in their use. Language learning, on this view, is a life-long process. Even for competent adult speakers, the inventory of linguistic units is subject to change. New units are added as a consequence of entrenchment, while previously established units may atrophy through lack of use.

---

[3] Cf. Culicover (2004: 132): "the most radical form of minimalism in linguistic theory is one that starts from the premise that ... if you can't 'see' it, that is, if it isn't concrete, it isn't there. What is concrete in the case of language is meaning and sound." One might, to be sure, take issue with the claim that meanings are 'concrete' and can be 'seen'. Be that as it may, Culicover's notion of 'radical minimalism' would seem to exclude all structural elements which are not directly relatable to the surface form of an expression. In this connection, Langacker (1987: 53–4) proposed the CONTENT REQUIREMENT, according to which the only structures permitted in the grammar are those that actually occur in linguistic expressions, or else emerge by abstraction or categorization of the primary data. Structures which diverge from surface forms in terms of their constituency or their linear sequence are inadmissible.

Importantly, the inventory of units which make up a language does not constitute a random, unorganized list. Units may be related to each other in various ways. Three kinds of relation are important:

(a) the PART–WHOLE RELATION. One unit may be part of a larger unit. Conversely, a complex unit can be analysed into its constituent parts. The specification of a unit may include information regarding the larger units of which it may be a part.

(b) the SCHEMA–INSTANCE RELATION. This has to do with the abstractness of a unit. One unit can be SCHEMATIC for units which are specified in more detail. Conversely, a unit may INSTANTIATE a more schematically characterized unit.

(c) the BASED-ON RELATION. One unit may be structured on the basis of its similarity with another unit.

These relations pertain to phonological, semantic, and symbolic units alike. Moreover, the relations may be recursive. For example, [A] may be part of [B], which in turn is part of [C], or [X] may be an instance of [Y], which in turn is an instance of [Z].

To get a flavour of how this model might work, consider an example from phonology. The word-form [sɪŋ] is an established phonological unit, associated with the concept 'sing'. We can analyse the unit into its parts, namely, the segments [s], [ɪ], and [ŋ]. Each of these constituent units instantiates more schematic units: [s] and [ŋ] are instances of [CONSONANT], [ɪ] is an instance of [VOWEL], while the complex form [sɪŋ] is an instance of the syllable schema [CVC]. The syllable schema [CVC] may be divided into its parts, namely, an onset unit, consisting of the initial [C] component, and a rhyme unit, consisting of the [VC] component. Accordingly, [sɪŋ] may be analysed in terms of its onset [s] and its rhyme [ɪŋ]. Units of intermediate schematicity might also be recognized. Thus, [ɪ] is not only a vowel but also a short (or lax) vowel as well as a mid-high front vowel; [ŋ] is not only a consonant but also instantiates [NASAL CONSONANT] and [VELAR CONSONANT]. A peculiar feature of [ŋ] in English is its restricted distribution. The sound can only occur in syllable-coda position and only after a short (or lax) vowel;[4] [ŋɪs] and [siːŋ] are not possible syllables in English. These facts can be accommodated by proposing, as part of the specification of [ŋ], that the sound can only occur in a syllable rhyme containing a lax vowel. The impossibility (or, if one will, the ungrammaticality) of [ŋɪs] and [siːŋ] follows from the fact that these forms are not sanctioned by any existing phonological schema of English.

With this background information in mind, let us now turn to the notion of construction.

---

[4] But not, however, after all of the short vowels. There are in English no syllables terminating in [ʊŋ].

Constructions

The term 'construction' has been used in the linguistics literature in a number of ways (Langacker 2005; Taylor 2004*b*). There is, as we shall see, some overlap amongst the different uses, in the sense that there are phenomena which would count as constructions on any of the approaches. Equally, some things which might count as a construction on one of the approaches would be excluded on other understandings of the term.

(a) Constructions as internally complex entities

In keeping with the internal make-up of the word (*construction* is a noun derived from the verb *(to) construct*), a construction is any linguistic form which can be analysed into its parts. The phonological form [sɪŋ] is a phonological construction, in that it can be analysed as a sequence of three sound segments as well as into an onset constituent and a rhyme constituent. The word *singer* is a symbolic construction, in that it can be analysed into its parts, [sing] and [-er], each with its own meaning and pronunciation. The sentence you are now reading is a construction, in that it can be broken down into its component words and phrases. On a more restrictive view, and one more in keeping with the traditional use of the term, construction refers, not so much to actual words and expressions, but to the patterns by which these are put together. Constructions, in other words, are schemas for the combination of smaller units. The phonological form [sɪŋ] instantiates the syllable construction [CVC]. The word *singer* instantiates the agentive noun construction [V-er]. We may likewise speak of noun phrase constructions, transitive verb constructions, relative clause constructions, and so on. This understanding of constructions was quite widespread during the middle decades of the twentieth century, especially in the writings of linguists influenced by Bloomfield. Here is Rulon Wells explaining the different readings of *old men and women* in terms of the different constructions which the word string can instantiate:

> In the meaning 'women and old men' the sequence belongs to that construction (noun or noun-phrase + and + noun or noun-phrase) which has the meaning of conjunction; the first noun-phrase belongs to the construction modifier + noun or noun-phrase. But in the meaning 'old men and old women' the sequence belongs to the construction modifier + noun or noun phrase; the noun phrase in turn belongs to the construction noun or noun-phrase + and + noun or noun-phrase.   (Wells 1957 [1947]: 195)

Let us use Nom as a cover term for Wells's 'noun or noun phrase'. Wells identifies two distinct Nom constructions. The one has the structure [Modifier + Nom], the other may be stated as [Nom and Nom]. These specifications state how a Nom expression can be assembled from its parts (alternatively, analysed into its parts). A feature of Wells's account is that the one construction can be embedded into the other. For example, the Nom constituent of the [Modifier + Nom] construction may be instantiated by an expression with the structure [Nom and Nom]. Equally, a Nom constituent of the [Nom and Nom] construction may be instantiated by an expression with the [Modifier + Nom] structure.

(b) Constructions as pairings of form and meaning

On an alternative approach, constructions are defined, not in terms of the part-whole relation, but in terms of the symbolic relation between form and meaning. On the most liberal interpretation of this view, any association of a form and a meaning constitutes a construction. The word *tree* is a construction, since it associates a concept with a phonological form. The sentence you are now reading is, once again, a construction, in that it associates a phonological (or graphological) form with a meaning. A narrower approach restricts the term to form–meaning pairings which have unit status. 'Construction' thereby becomes synonymous with the symbolic unit of Cognitive Grammar. On this more restricted understanding, the sentence you are now reading is not a construction, since this specific combination of words and phrases has not become established through usage. Note that this approach excludes the possibility of phonological constructions, such as [sɪŋ] or the syllable schema [CVC]. A syllable may, of course, feature as the phonological pole of a symbolic unit. However, considered simply as an element of the sound structure of a language, a syllable is not in itself a symbolic unit.

A more restrictive view still is to regard as constructions only those form–meaning pairings whose properties (whether formal or semantic) cannot be derived from the properties of any other constructions (Goldberg 1995).[5] Prime examples of constructions, on this more restricted view, are the constructional idioms—more precisely, the schematic representations of these idioms—that were discussed in Chapter 4. *The more the merrier* would not be regarded as a construction; constructional status would, however, attach to the schema which the expression instantiates, namely [THE X-ER THE Y-ER]. Note that on Goldberg's approach, the word *sing* would be a construction since we cannot predict, from anything else we might know about the language, that this concept will be symbolized by this particular combination of sounds. On the other hand, the word *singer* might not be regarded as a construction. The word certainly has unit status. On the other hand, it could be argued that it inherits its phonological and semantic properties from the schematic [V-er] construction and from the unit which instantiates the [V] constituent.

---

[5] According to Goldberg's (1995: 4) definition, "C is a CONSTRUCTION iff$_{def}$ C is a form–meaning pair $<F_i, S_i>$ such that some aspect of F_i or some aspect of S_i is not strictly predictable from C's component parts or from other previously established constructions".

(c) Constructions as units

The two approaches outlined above differ in their coverage. As we have seen, phonological constructions are impossible on approach (b). On the other hand, morphologically simplex words, such as *sing*, are excluded on approach (a). Otherwise, the data covered by the two approaches overlap considerably. It may be no accident that many authors tend to slip between one and the other understanding of the term.

Taking elements from each of the above approaches, we can propose a third definition of 'construction', referring to whatever a speaker of a language has specifically learned. On this definition, *singer* might well have the status of a construction. Although the phonological and semantic properties of the word can be derived from its component parts and from the schema whereby they are combined, it is unlikely that speakers who use the word do in fact put it together from its parts. The word is stored, and accessed, as a whole. Similarly, *How old are you?* is likely to have the status of a construction since this phrase is available as a ready-made whole; it does not have to be assembled in accordance with a more schematic interrogative construction. 'Construction' thus becomes synonymous with the Cognitive Grammar 'unit'. In brief, a construction is any element of a language that has been learned and that forms part of a speaker's linguistic knowledge.

As noted earlier in this chapter, it is axiomatic in Cognitive Grammar that a language can be exhaustively described in terms of established units (or, if one will, constructions), whether semantic, phonological, or symbolic. There is, in this scheme of things, no place for rules—or at least, no place for rules as they are commonly understood, namely, as instructions for the composition of larger configurations.

There are undoubtedly many phenomena in a language which are best analysed in terms of constructions. These include idiomatic expressions of various kinds, in particular the constructional idioms discussed in Chapter 4 and elsewhere. Constructional idioms, it will be recalled, are idiomatic in the sense that they cannot be generated by general syntactic rules. Moreover, the items which are able to fill their various slots can often not be brought under any of the generally recognized syntactic categories, and a construction's meaning, more often than not, cannot be derived compositionally. At the same time, the constructions are productive to a greater or lesser extent, in that new instances can be created in accordance with the constructional schema. It is worth noting that a major impetus for the development of construction-based grammars came from the study of constructional idioms in the 1980s and 1990s (Fillmore, Kay, and O'Connor 1988; Kay and Fillmore 1999).

For other phenomena, however, the need for a construction-based account is less evident. In spite of the ubiquity of the idiomatic and the idiosyncratic—a feature of language that I have emphasized in the preceding chapters—there is still, one might suppose, a place for generative rules. *The farmer shot a rabbit* is not obviously idiomatic, nor is the process whereby the overwhelming majority of count nouns form their plural, namely, by suffixation of {s}. These phenomena, one might suppose, are best handled by rules of the traditional kind. One option, then, might be to propose a division of labour between generative rules and a battery of idiomatic constructions, as argued, for example, by Pinker (1999) on the example of verb morphology. Thus, in Pinker's account, the rules generate the regular past tense forms, by suffixation of {t}, whereas irregulars are learned as such.

In the next part of this chapter I compare a rule-based and a construction-based account of the regularities in a language. Although seemingly equivalent, there are some substantive differences between the two approaches and the predictions which they make. The discussion will also allow us to reconsider the nature of rules and how they are applied. I then turn to one of the entailments of a construction-based grammar. As noted earlier in this chapter, Langacker's radically minimalist theory of language brings with it the rejection of syntax as a distinct level of organization mediating between phonological and semantic representations. (Recall the claim that the only objects of study in Cognitive Grammar are phonological representations, semantic representations, and symbolic relations between phonological and semantic representations.) The very fact of syntactic structure could therefore be a crucial argument against one of the underlying assumptions of Langacker's theory. I shall argue, on the contrary, that far from threatening the theory, syntax in fact provides a very strong argument for the primacy of constructions.

Constructions or rules?

With respect to the regular expressions in a language, the sceptical reader may be wondering whether a construction-based account is little more than a notational variant of a rule-based approach. On the constructionist account, we might represent one type of noun phrase by means of the schematic unit [Det N]. Exactly this same structure could be generated by means of a re-write rule of the kind NP → Det N. On the constructionist account, the expression *a rabbit* is sanctioned by the fact that *a* instantiates [Det] while *rabbit* is an instance of [N]. On the rule-based account, *a* and *rabbit* can slot into the rule output in virtue of the fact that *a* is marked in the lexicon as a determiner, *rabbit* as a count noun. The reader may also have noticed how the rather tortuous formulations that Wells employed in the above citation (see p. 124) can be easily, and perhaps more perspicaciously, expressed in phrase-structure terms. Essentially, Wells was proposing that *old men and women* can be parsed in two alternative ways. Again using Nom to cover Wells's 'noun or noun phrase', we can represent the two structures as follows:

(1)   a. [$_{Nom}$[$_{Nom}$old men] and [$_{Nom}$women]]
       b. [$_{Nom}$[$_{Adj}$old [$_{Nom}$men and women]]]

Each of these structures could be generated by a set of rules for the formation of Nom phrases. The rules would include the following:

(2) a. Nom → Adj Nom
     b. Nom → Nom and Nom

The ambiguity of *old men and women* follows from the ordering of the rules and the way in which the one 'feeds' into the other. If (b) is applied after (a), we have the structure [Adj [Nom and Nom]]; applying (a) after (b) we can generate the structure [[Adj Nom] and [Nom]]. (Many other outcomes can of course be envisaged, due to the fact that the rules can be applied recursively.)

Again in the spirit of re-write rules, we could represent the content of the syllable construction [CVC] as follows:

(3) a. Syllable → Onset Rhyme
     b. Onset → C
     c. Rhyme → VC

Additional rules might specify that [C] could be re-written as [p], [s], and so on, while [V] could be rewritten as [iː], [ɪ], etc.

Given the seeming equivalence of rules and constructions, it is legitimate to ask whether there is any substantive difference between the two approaches. Is a constructionist account simply a notational variant of the generative account? If constructions are nothing other than the output of generative rules, there may be no compelling reason to prefer a constructionist account, at least with respect to fully regular, non-idiomatic expressions. Constructions, as Chomsky (1995: 170) has stated, would be little more than epiphenomena, the secondary consequence of rules operating over a lexicon.

Although the two approaches might be descriptively equivalent, in the sense that they are able to accommodate the same range of data, they differ with respect to what a speaker of a language is claimed to have learned. A construction-based approach tolerates a good deal of REDUNDANCY. The same fact about a language may be stated in more than one place. A pattern may be stated in a schematic construction; the same pattern is manifest in each of the established instances of the schema. The generative model, on the other hand, strives to eliminate redundancy from the grammar. If a form can be generated by rule it does not need to be listed. The only things that need to be listed are the irregular and non-predictable forms of a language (see pp. 34–5). However, to the extent that knowledge of a language does contain redundancies, the construction-based account might be psychologically more plausible.[6]

---

[6] Langacker (1987: 29) in this context speaks of the RULE/LIST FALLACY. This refers to the (as he claims, unwarranted) assumption that if a specific statement can be derived from a more general statement, the specific statement does not need to be listed.

Take the case of nouns and their plurals. In principle, every count noun can be pluralized. The pluralization rule, in English, is very simple: add {s} to the singular form. The matter is complicated somewhat by the fact that there are a couple of dozen exceptions to this rule. Exceptional plurals such as *men*, *children*, and *mice* must obviously be listed and must be learned as such by all speakers of a language. The question arises, though, whether we also need to count, as part of a person's linguistic knowledge, those plurals which can be formed according to the rule. Do we want to say that a person who knows how to form the plural of the noun *eye* also stores in memory the plural form *eyes*? If our aim is to minimize redundancy in the grammar, the answer would have to be 'no'. There are, however, good reasons for believing that in the case of high-frequency plurals at least, these are indeed stored as such.

Consider the matter from the point of view of acquisition. Although the pluralization rule is very simple, it still has to be learned and this can only happen on the basis of an array of examples. It is only after having noticed that plural nouns (in the main) end in {s} that the learner is able to hit upon the rule. For the learning process to be possible at all, the learner has to have an array of plural forms available in memory. On the no-redundancy approach, we should have to assume that the moment the rule is abstracted the instances on which it is based are immediately erased from memory. This is somewhat implausible. More likely, the already learned plural forms, especially if they are in frequent use, are retained.

Support for this view comes from LEXICAL DECISION TASKS. On a lexical decision task, a subject is presented with a sequence of letters and must decide, as quickly as possibly, whether the sequence constitutes a word or not. Several factors influence the speed of the decision, one being the frequency of the word in the language. Consider, now, recognition speeds for singulars and plurals. If plurals are always generated from the singular, the recognition speed for plurals should correlate exactly with the recognition speed for singulars. Sereno and Jongman (1997) report that this is not the case (see also Alegre and Gordon 1999). Some nouns, such as *kitchen* and *village*, tend to be used predominantly in the singular. Other nouns, such as *window* and *expense*, are biased towards the plural. Sereno and Jongman found that the recognition speed of plurals reflected the frequency of the plural forms, rather than the frequency of the singulars. The finding entails that high-frequency plurals are stored and accessed as such; they do not need to be generated by the pluralization rule, nor analysed into their component parts, on each occasion of their use.[7]

---

[7] It is also worth noting that the singular and plural forms of a noun might have their own characteristic distributions in the language. As Sinclair (2004: 31) observed, plural *eyes* typically has a literal, referential sense (as when we say that a person 'has brown eyes'), whereas singular *eye* commonly has a metonymic or metaphorical sense, often in association with fixed expressions (*keep an eye on, have an eye for, in the*

The decision paradigm has also shown that speakers are sensitive to the overall frequency, not only of words, but also of word combinations. In a recent study, Arnon and Snider (2010) displayed four-word strings on a screen and asked subjects to decide as quickly as possible whether the strings were grammatical. More frequent combinations (as determined by corpus data), such as *don't have to worry*, elicited faster responses than less frequent strings, such as *don't have to wait*.[8] The effect cannot be accounted for in terms of the higher frequency of *worry* vis-à-vis *wait* (in fact, according to the BNC, *wait* occurs more frequently in the language than *worry*), nor indeed in terms of the higher frequency of *to worry* vis-à-vis *to wait* (again, BNC data indicate that *to wait* is the more frequent combination). Nor is it a matter of the plausibility of the semantic content of the two expressions. According to ratings elicited by the researchers, both strings were judged to be equally plausible. Rather, it would seem, subjects are responding according to the frequency of the four-word phrases as a whole, as laid down in memory on the basis of their previous experience with the language.

These findings suggest that frequently used items, whether internally complex words or multi-word units, tend to be accessed as wholes, even though, in principle, they can be analysed into their component parts. The other side of the coin is that the component parts of a complex unit may not be immediately apparent to language users. The matter has been investigated using the MONITORING paradigm, where subjects are asked to listen out for a particular item and to press a key the moment they hear it (Connine and Titone 1996). Several studies have shown that sound segments take more time to identify in the flow of speech than the syllables of which they are parts, and that syllables take more time to identify than the words of which they are parts (Foss and Swinney 1973; Savin and Bever 1970; Segui, Frauenfelder, and Mehler 1981). In some respects, this finding is paradoxical. One might suppose that in order to identify the word *cactus*, a listener must identify the first syllable as [kæk], which in turn requires that the first sound of the syllable is identified as [k]. One might expect that monitoring times would reflect this compositional sequence. The fact that it does not suggests that it is the larger, entrenched units that are more immediately available for processing than the parts of which they are composed.

---

mind's eye, in the public eye, more than meets the eye, etc.). Also from a language-internal perspective, therefore, there are good reasons for supposing that the singular and the plural forms of the noun are associated with distinct representations.

[8] Comparable findings are reported by Bod (2000; cited in Bod 2006: 316) and by Bannard and Matthews (2008). Bod showed that frequently occurring sentences, such as *I like it*, are recognized as grammatical more quickly than less frequent sentences, such as *I keep it*, even after plausibility and word frequency are taken into account. Bannard and Matthews found that two- and three-year-olds were able to repeat multi-word sequences that had frequently occurred in child-directed speech, such as *When we go out*, more quickly and more accurately than low-frequency combinations, such as *When we go in*.

Sosa and MacFarlane (2002) showed that the degree of entrenchment of a larger expression, as measured by its frequency of occurrence, delayed the recognition of a component word. Subjects were asked to listen out for the word *of*. When the word occurred in high-frequency combinations, such as *kind of*, *some of*, and *out of*, responses on a monitoring task were longer than with less common sequences, such as *sense of*, *example of*, and *care of*. It seems that the high-frequency phrases had been stored as such, rendering their internal analysis less salient.

Other experimental results point to a similar conclusion. Wheeler and Schumsky (1980) asked subjects to divide written words up into their constituent parts. They report that about half their subjects failed to mark any internal divisions in the word *baker*, suggesting that for these subjects, at least, the word had become so entrenched as a lexical unit that it was no longer felt to be related to the base verb *(to) bake*, neither was the final *-er* suffix recognized as such. Consider, also, work reported in Nordquist (2004). She presented subjects with isolated words and asked them to construct, for each word, three sentences containing the word. One of the words tested was the pronoun *I*. Corpus data indicate that the personal pronoun is typically used in expressions such as *I think*, *I guess*, and *I suppose*. These high-frequency phrases tended not to be elicited in the experiment, precisely because, according to Nordquist, they are stored and accessed as wholes, rather than being compiled compositionally. One of the sentences proffered by her subjects was the rather bizarre combination *I cough*, a phrase which had evidently been put together on the basis of the schematic [NP V] schema.

Evidence that regularly formed expressions may be stored in memory also comes from within the language itself. Internally complex expressions, once they have acquired unit status, are liable to undergo what Bybee (1985) has referred to as DRIFT (see also Taylor 2002: 310–11). Although such expressions can in principle be generated by rule, they tend to be stored and accessed as wholes. As a consequence, they are liable to take on a life of their own, independent of their compositional value. I mentioned above that *singer* is assembled in accordance with the agentive noun schema [V-er]. This account may not be strictly accurate. *Singer* does not simply refer to 'one who sings' (the compositional value). It comes to be used only of persons who sing well, competently, or professionally. The word has acquired a meaning which is not fully predictable from its compositional structure. Likewise, *baker* does not simply denote 'one who bakes (things)' (its compositional meaning). The word can be used of a retailer who sells baked products, such as bread and cakes (not, though, potatoes), irrespective of whether he has himself baked these products. Indeed, as noted above, some speakers apparently do not even perceive the word to be an agentive noun at all. *Murderer*, on the other hand, refers to any person who has committed the crime: you do not have to be a competent or professional killer to be named by this word. Often-used phrases can also acquire specialized meanings, over and above, or even at variance with their compositional value. *Would you believe it?* is not really a yes–no question, enquiring whether the addressee would, or would not, believe something. It is more an expression of speaker surprise and does not require a 'yes' or 'no' response. *I don't know* can be used not only to express the speaker's ignorance of some matter, but as a kind of hedge, conveying lack of commitment.

Drift also characterizes phonological structure, in that frequently used combinations tend to exhibit a greater degree of phonological reduction, involving assimilations, elisions, and the like, than less frequent combinations or combinations which are assembled ad hoc. *I don't know*, especially when used in its hedging function, typically shows reduction of *don't* to [ɾə], or even to [ə] (Bybee and Scheibman 1999). Palatalization of [dj] to [dʒ] is more likely to occur in the frequently occurring phrase *did you* [dɪd juː] → [dɪdʒuː] than in the incidental combination *had yesterday* (Bush 2001). Krug (2003) observed a similar phenomenon in the written language. High-frequency strings such as *I have* and *you have* are often written as *I've* and *you've*; elision is less common with less frequent strings such as *they have*, *there have*, and *where have*. In fact, Krug discovered that the frequency of a string correlated quite well with the frequency of the elided spelling.

The converse of drift—what we might call PERSISTENCE—can also be observed in many places in the grammar.[9] Frequently used forms may fail to undergo changes which are operative elsewhere in the language: their very frequency (and their corresponding entrenchment) protects them from change. In earlier stages of English, verbs could be negated by means of *not* (*they sang* ∼ *they sang not*) and interrogative forms required subject–verb inversion (*they sang* ∼ *sang they?*). Nowadays, so-called *do*-support is virtually obligatory for negated and interrogative forms: *They sang* ∼ *they did not sing* ∼ *did they sing?* (Modal verbs are, of course, the exception: *He can sing* ∼ *he cannot sing* ∼ *can he sing?*—a fact which is probably not unrelated to their high frequency: Bybee and Thompson 1997.[10]) Even now, however, one occasionally encounters expressions which have held out against *do*-support. The greeting formula *How goes it?* is recorded twice in the BNC. *I think not* is often used instead of the expected *I don't think (so)*. *Go* and *think* are amongst the most frequent of the English verbs.[11] An especially curious relic is the expression *methinks*,

---

[9] 'Persistence' is being used in a slightly different sense from Hopper (1991).

[10] The usage of some of the less frequent modals, such as *dare* and *need*, oscillates between forms with and without *do*. Alongside *you needn't go* we have *You don't need to go*. Past tense forms of *dare* tend to require *do*-support: *I didn't dare (to) go*, while present tense forms do not: *I daren't do it*. Note also the fossilized form *How dare you!*, uttered as a challenge to the addressee. *How do you dare? would be totally ruled out.

[11] Frequency, however, cannot account for the jocular *I kid you not*, with eleven attestations in the BNC. Possibly, the archaic syntax is being used in order to enhance the jocular character of the expression. Significant, though, is the fact that the expression is virtually frozen: no other subject or direct object NP is allowed, neither can the expression be used in the past tense. There are no attestations of *They kid(ded) him not*, and the like.

in the sense 'I think'. This harks back to a now archaic impersonal construction, in which the experiencer (the thinker) is expressed by dative *me* while the verb takes the third person singular inflection.

The requirement for speakers to generate each and every complex expression that they utter, applying the rules of grammar to items from the lexicon, is implausible from another perspective: it would severely compromise the fluency of speech. Speakers have at their disposal a vast repertoire of ready-made and semi-preconstructed expressions, which they can reel off without the need to assemble them, even though the expressions may be perfectly regular in terms of their internal make-up. You wish to gently discourage someone from some course of action. There is a ready-made expression for this: *I wouldn't do that if I were you.* You find fault with the way your interlocutor has expressed himself, but you don't want to be too direct. Again, a fixed expression is available: *I wouldn't put it like that.* You want to express your indifference; out comes another ready-made formula: *I couldn't care less.* In summary, there is evidence from various sources that speakers do learn frequently encountered forms and have recourse to these in their day-to-day use of the language.

Applying a rule: What kind of process is it?

As many researchers have emphasized (Pawley 1985; Pawley and Syder 1983; Sinclair 1991, amongst others), quite a lot of what people say is formulaic in nature. It is equally clear that not everything that people say consists in the parroting of ready-made formulae. Speakers are creative and do come up with forms which have not been learned as such. Here, one might suppose, the rule-based approach will come into its own. Should you have occasion to talk about more than one portcullis, you will need to come up with the plural form of the noun. Given that the noun is rather infrequent, and its plural more infrequent still, it is highly improbable that you are able to retrieve the ready-made plural from memory. You have to create it.

Applying a rule is often thought of as an operation performed on an input. With respect to pluralization, the input is the singular form and the operation consists in adding {s}. There is, however, another way to conceptualize the process. The task is to come up with an output which conforms with the plural construction, namely [N {s}].

On the face of it, the two mechanisms appear to be exactly equivalent. Whether you add {s} to an input form, or aim to produce an output which consists of the base noun plus {s}, amounts to much the same thing. In order to be able to differentiate the two approaches we need to turn to cases where a speaker innovates with respect to the prevailing norms of the language, or, if one will, where a speaker 'makes a mistake'.

One type of innovation consists in the regularization of an irregular form. Several English nouns have a mildly irregular plural form, in which the final voiceless fricative of the singular is replaced by its voiced counterpart. Thus, the plural of *thief* is *thieves* instead of the expected *thiefs*. *House* is another such noun (though in this case the irregularity is not represented in the spelling). Children often fail to produce the standard plural [hauzəz], instead forming the plural in the 'regular' way: [hausəz]. Their mistake can be explained equally well on either of the two approaches. On the rule-based account, we might suppose that the speaker's lexicon has failed to tag the noun *house* as an exception to the plural rule; alternatively, that the speaker has inadvertently overlooked the tag. On a constructionist approach, we should say that the irregular plural has not yet become entrenched; the speaker therefore must fall back on the plural schema.

More interesting, from our perspective, is the reverse phenomenon, whereby a regular form is replaced by an irregular. One such case of irregularization was mentioned in Chapter 1.[12] Alongside ['prəʊsɛsəz]—the 'regular' plural of *process*— one sometimes hears, especially in academic discourse, the form ['prəʊsɛsiːz], with a tense [iː] vowel in the final syllable rather than the expected [ə]. What could occasion this seemingly bizarre innovation?

The innovative plural resembles the plurals of 'Greek' nouns, such as *theses* (plural of *thesis*), *hypotheses*, *analyses*, *parentheses*, and several more. These plural forms share several properties. Apart from the fact that they all end in [siːz], they consist of at least two syllables, often more, in which case word stress mostly falls three syllables from the end. The regular plural of *process* almost conforms with the plural schema for these nouns. The innovation consists in the plural being made to fully conform with the schema. That *process* comes under the influence of the schema may well be due to the fact that words such as *hypothesis, thesis,* and others are associated with scholarly academic discourse; the innovative plural of *process* seems to be largely restricted to this context. As also noted in Chapter 1, the pattern seems to be being extended to other plurals, such as *biases* and *premises*. These are forms which, once again, tend to be restricted to academic contexts.

The example of *processes* ['prəʊsɛsiːz] suggests that the innovative plural has been formed, not by the application of a rule to an input form (prior to the creation of the innovative form there was no such rule), but by the desire to make the plural conform with a plural schema, a schema, moreover, which is probably quite well entrenched for speakers familiar with academic discourse.[13]

---

[12] Another example is provided by the word *roof*. Mostly, the word forms its plural in the regular way: *roofs*. Occasionally, however, the form *rooves* is encountered; there are five examples in the BNC against 658 examples of *roofs*, while the COCA has 2,015 instances of *roofs*, with only one solitary example of *rooves*. The irregular plural would appear to have been formed on the pattern provided by the dozen or so nouns which exhibit fricative voicing in the plural. See Pierrehumbert (2003) for a discussion of this example in terms of her notion of probabilistic phonology.

[13] For languages with more complex morphology, such as German, the role of output schemas over input rules is even more compelling; see Köpcke (1998).

For a further illustration of the role of output schemas, consider the irregular past tense forms of certain verbs (Bybee and Slobin 1982; Bybee and Moder 1983). There is a small set of verbs in English which are unchanged in the past tense (*put, cut, set, let,* and, for some speakers, in some of its uses, *fit*). These are verbs which already terminate in a typical exponent of the past tense, namely [t]. It is as if the verbs already 'look' to be past tense forms; hence, no further inflection is necessary. For a more complex example, consider the following mildly irregular past tense forms.

(4) a. dwell ~ dwelt   spell ~ spelt
     b. bend ~ bent   spend ~ spent
     c. keep ~ kept   creep ~ crept
     d. feel ~ felt   dream ~ dreamt
     e. leave ~ left   cleave ~ cleft

We may discern a number of distinct patterns here.

- In (a) the past tense is formed by suffixation of [t]. This is unusual, in that a past tense form in [d] would be expected. Compare *quell* ~ *quelled, compel* ~ *compelled.* For some verbs, such as *spell,* the 'irregular' *spelt* co-exists with the regular *spelled.*
- In (b) nothing is added; rather, the final [d] is replaced by [t].
- In (c) there is the suffixation of [t], as in (a). In addition, the stem vowel shortens from [iː] to [ɛ].
- In (d) there is once again suffixation of [t] along with the shortening of the vowel to [ɛ]. Since the base verb ends in a voiced consonant, suffixation of [d] would be expected.
- In (e) there is again vowel shortening in association with the suffixation of [t]. In addition, the final stem consonant devoices: [v] → [f].

It would be possible to capture these five different processes by means of five different rules, each performing a different operation on a different kind of input. Such an approach would conceal the fact that the rules all conspire[14] to create a past tense form with a certain structure. The past tense forms are all monosyllabic; the vowel is in all cases a short [ɛ]; and the past tenses all end in a voiceless consonant cluster, the second member of which is [t].[15] There is a sense, therefore, in which all the verbs in (4) undergo the very same process: they are made to conform to the past tense schema [... ɛCt].

[14] On the notion of conspiracy, see Kisseberth (1970). The term refers to the fact that diverse rules, operating over different kinds of input, may all serve to create a common output.
[15] It is the voiceless final [t] which occasions the change of [v] to [f] in *left* and *cleft.* According to a very well-entrenched phonological construction in English, obstruent clusters must agree in voicing.

A striking example of the power of an output schema in contrast to source-oriented rules is provided by the much-discussed *way*-construction (see e.g. Goldberg 1995; Jackendoff 1997). Here are some instances:

(5) a. I pushed my way to the exit.
     b. I lied my way through the interview.
     c. The government hopes to spend its way out of recession.
     d. We ate our way through France. (from a travel report)

The construction is associated with a rather specific semantics. The subject entity moves (either literally or metaphorically) to a place designated by the PP, by V-*ing*. (There is also the nuance that some difficulty and effort are involved.) The construction is remarkably productive, in the sense that a very wide range of verbs can feature in it. (Curiously, however, motion verbs such as *go*, *walk*, *run*, and *drive* tend not to be attracted to the construction.) Observe that the verbs appear in what looks like a transitive frame, more specifically, in a [_ NP PP] frame. Yet the construction easily tolerates verbs which are not subcategorized for such a frame. Elsewhere in the language, *lie* ('speak untruthfully') is intransitive, while *spend*, though transitive, cannot take *way* as its direct object (except in the *way*-construction). It is the construction itself which sanctions this particular use of the verbs. The demands of the construction override the properties of the participating verbs.

In summary, evidence from within language itself, as well as from various experimental paradigms, strongly supports a construction-based account of linguistic knowledge. Complex expressions are formed, not by rules operating over an input string, but with reference to constructions, specified at various levels of abstraction. Even regular processes, such as regular plural formation, can be understood in these terms. Before we rush to endorse a constructionist approach, however, there is an important issue that we need to tackle. This concerns the supposed autonomy of syntax. If valid, the autonomy of syntax argument would undermine a central claim of Cognitive Grammar and, with it, the basis for a constructionist account of syntax. I address these issues in the next section.

Constructions and the autonomy of syntax

As was mentioned at the beginning of this chapter, the Cognitive Grammar view of language departs significantly from mainstream and especially generative views in its approach to syntax. On mainstream views, syntax constitutes an independent level of organization, based on categories such as noun, verb, preposition, noun phrase, and the like, as well as on relations between these elements, such as subject-of (a verb), direct object, and so on. Linguistics students learn very early in their career that these categories and relations cannot be defined in semantic terms, even less, in phonological terms. You cannot identify the subject of a clause by searching for the actor which instigates an event (consider: *The rabbit was shot by the farmer* or *The next day saw our departure*); nor is it possible to classify a word as a noun or a verb simply by referring to its semantics. It won't do to define 'noun' as the name of a person, place, or thing, or to define 'verb' as the name of a state or action. *Explosion*, undeniably, is a noun. We do not arrive at this judgement by contemplating the word's semantics. Instead, we look at the syntactic behaviour of the word. The word distributes as a noun: it can take definite and indefinite determiners, it can pluralize, and it can be preceded by an adjective. If it behaves like a noun, then it is a noun, even though, arguably, it has verb-like semantics.

Considerations such as these easily lead to the view that syntax constitutes an autonomous level of linguistic organization, mediating between, but independent of, both phonological and semantic structures. Such a view is inconsistent with the Cognitive Grammar claim that language is basically and quintessentially symbolic, consisting only of phonological and semantic representations and symbolic relations between them.

One way to counter the autonomy of syntax argument would be to address head-on the claim that syntactic categories lack an identifying semantic content. This has been Langacker's strategy. Langacker (1987) strongly argued that noun and verb can be associated with a schematic semantic content, the former having to do with the status of the referent as a 'thing', the latter designating a 'temporal relation'.[16] He has also proposed schematic values for other elements of syntactic description, such as the subject and object relations, the subject of a clause being the more 'prominent' entity in the relation designated by the verb. A problem with this account is that it runs the danger of circularity. 'Thing' is defined so broadly (namely, as a 'region in a domain') that practically anything can be brought under its scope, the only criterion for the correctness of the analysis being, precisely, the fact that concept in question is referred to by a nominal expression (Hudson 1990). In the last analysis, we determine that a word is a noun because of its distribution, not because of its meaning, and we identify the subject of a clause on the basis of syntactic criteria, not by reference to its prominence. This is not to dismiss out of hand Langacker's semantic characterizations. It could well be, however, that the semantic properties of nouns and subjects that Langacker identified derive from their syntactic status, rather than their syntactic status being the consequence of their semantics.

Another approach was pursued by Croft (1991). Croft sought a functional account of the major categories of syntax, appealing to such notions as reference (a function

---

[16] Taking a slightly different tack, Givón (1984) appealed to the semantic properties of prototypical nouns and verbs. Thus, the prototypical noun refers to a time-stable entity while a prototypical verb refers to a transient or changing phenomenon. The trouble with this account is that while *explosion* may well be a non-prototypical noun in terms of its semantics, it displays all of the distributional properties of prototypical nouns. In terms of its syntactic behaviour, *explosion* is not at all a non-prototypical noun.

of nominals), predication (a verbal function), and modification (characteristic of adjectival and adverbial elements). Deviations from this state of affairs—as when an adjectival or verbal form is nominalized, thus making it possible to predicate some property of the derived concept—are typically marked in some way, by special morphology, for example. Thus, *explosion* (a nominal) is marked vis-à-vis verbal *explode* by means of the nominalizing *-ion* suffix.

In more recent work, Croft (2001, 2007) has suggested a more radical approach, one which effectively turns the autonomy of syntax argument on its head. We do not hesitate to classify *explosion* as a noun, neither are there any doubts about the verb status of *explode*. This is not because of what the words mean but because of the way they distribute in the language, that is, on the basis of their syntactic and morphological properties. Now, to assign a word to a lexical category on distributional grounds is to appeal to the constructions in which the word can occur. If we say that a word is a verb because it can take a past tense inflection we have effectively defined the verb category with respect to the past tense construction. If the ability to form a noun phrase in association with the definite determiner is a feature of (common) nouns, we have defined (common) noun with respect to a noun phrase construction. By the same token, 'noun phrase' would be defined with respect to those constructions which have noun phrases as a constituent, while clausal subjects are defined with respect to clausal constructions, and so on.

A phonological analogy illustrates the issues (Taylor 2004b). The distinction between vowels and consonants is fundamental to any phonological theory. We might propose to define the two categories in terms of their inherent phonetic, that is, their articulatory–acoustic properties, claiming that vowels are relatively sonorous elements, produced with relatively free flow of air through the oral cavity, whereas consonants are produced with some kind of constriction of the air flow. We do not, however, identify the sounds of a language as vowels or consonants simply by inspecting their phonetic properties; we refer to their role within a larger construction, namely, the syllable. (In fact, were it not for the role of the syllable in phonological structure, there would be no point in making a distinction between consonants and vowels in the first place.) Acoustically, the initial sound of *yes* is very similar to the final sound of *say*. Yet we would regard the initial [j] of *yes* as a consonant and the [j] off-glide of *say* as a vowel. This is not because of their inherent acoustic–articulatory properties but because of their role within the syllable construction. The [j] of *yes* occupies the consonant slot of the syllable construction; the [j] of *say* occupies a vowel slot. While no doubt grounded on facts of articulation, membership in the categories is defined, in the last analysis, in terms of the (phonological) constructions in which they occur.

Seen in this light, constructions are primary and syntactic and lexical categories are derivative on the constructions in which they are eligible to occur. This approach suggests that it may be an error to speak of nouns or noun phrases as such, and likewise for all the other commonly recognized lexical and syntactic categories. Rather, we should be speaking of noun phrase and so on as a shorthand way of referring to the set of items which are able to occupy a certain slot in a specific construction. In principle, then, there are as many noun phrase categories as there are constructions which have, as one of their parts, a noun phrase constituent. We should have to recognize [Noun Phrase]$_X$—this being the noun phrase category defined with respect to construction X—alongside [Noun Phrase]$_Y$, the noun phrase category defined with respect to construction Y, and so on. To the extent that these noun phrase categories are coextensive there may be no harm in speaking of noun phrases *tout court*, and similarly for all the other commonly recognized lexical and syntactic categories. However, the possibility of construction-specific differences should not be overlooked.[17]

As an illustration, let us consider a couple of constructions which refer to noun phrases. One is the clausal construction [NP VP], where the subject slot is occupied by a noun phrase. Another is the prenominal possessive construction [NP POSS N], where NP constitutes the possessor, POSS is the possessive morpheme (typically *'s* or one of its variants), and N is a noun designating the possessed entity. By and large, NPs which can occur in the transitive construction are also able to function as possessors, and vice versa. *The farmer* is an NP in the clausal construction (*The farmer shot a rabbit*) as well as in the possessive construction (*the farmer's wife*). There are, however, some discrepancies. *Mine* can function as an NP in the clausal construction, but not in the possessive construction:

(6) a. Mine was expensive.
     b. *Mine's price

Arguably, presentational *there* and meteorological *it* constitute the NP subject in clausal constructions. Thus, in interrogative contexts, these items invert with respect to an inflection-bearing auxiliary verb, this being a typical property of a clausal subject. However, presentational *there* and meteorological *it* are excluded from featuring as possessors:

(7) a. There is a man at the door ∼ Is there a man at the door?
     b. *There's man

(8) a. It was raining ∼ Was it raining?
     b. *Its weather

---

[17] Croft's approach entails that syntactic categories are not only construction-specific but also language-specific. There may be no basis, other than terminological convenience, to refer to nouns, noun phrases, and so on, as universal categories, applicable to all languages.

The upshot is that the noun phrase category defined with respect to the possessive construction is not the same as the noun phrase category defined with respect to the clause construction.[18]

Collostructional analysis

A basic assumption of the dictionary plus grammar book model is that all members of a category behave identically with respect to the rules which refer to the category. All items marked in the lexicon as a common noun are equally available to feature in the noun phrase structure [DET N]; all noun phrases can function as the subject or direct object of a transitive verb or as the complement of a preposition; all transitive verbs are equally eligible to appear in a passive configuration, and so on. Indeed, it is these very equivalences which justify the recognition of the lexical and syntactic categories in the first place. *Explosion* is regarded as a noun precisely because it distributes in the language like other members of the category.

The discussion in the preceding section suggests a radically different view of the relation between the lexicon and the syntax, between words and the configurations in which they occur. On the one hand, a construction specifies the kinds of words which are eligible to occur in it. At the same time, words are specified for the range of constructions in which they are eligible to occur. Thus, to take up one of our earlier examples (see pp. 51–3), *lap* occurs preferentially in a possessive environment, while the possessive expression itself—*my lap, the lap of luxury*, and so on—occurs preferentially as the complement of a preposition, typically *in* or *on*. Again with reference to an earlier example (see p. 55), the noun slot in the [THERE'S NO N IN V-ING] construction is occupied, preferentially, by *fun, point, use, harm*, and *sense*, while the noun slot in the [IT'S NO N V-ING] construction is occupied, preferentially, by *fun, good, use, joke*, and *big deal*. The two sets of nouns only partially overlap. An important aspect of knowing a word such as *fun* is to know just which constructions it is able to occur in.

The interaction of linguistic expressions and the contexts in which they occur has been insightfully studied by Gries and Stefanowitsch in terms of COLLOSTRUCTIONS (Stefanowitsch and Gries 2003; see also Gries, Hampe, and Schönefeld 2005; Gries and Stefanowitsch 2004). (The term itself is a blend of *collocation* and *construction*.) The starting point for a collostructional analysis is a construction, understood as an internally complex syntactic configuration containing one or more open slots. The

---

[18] See Chapter 4, footnote 1, for a further example of a word category defined with respect to a construction. At issue is the set of items which are able to occur as 'particles' in so-called phrasal verbs, such as *take up, bring in, set out, put aside, take apart*, etc. In the main, the particles are members of the category of preposition. Yet the categories of preposition and verb particle are not coextensive. *Aside* and *apart*, for example, are not prepositions. What counts as a particle with respect to phrasal verbs is determined by the set of phrasal verbs.

analysis aims to identify those items which collocate with the construction, that is, which are able to occur in the open slot positions. By taking account of the number of potential candidates available to fill a slot, and the overall frequency of these candidates in the construction and in the language at large, it is possible to estimate the degree of attraction (or, conversely, repulsion) between an item and the construction.[19]

To illustrate, let us consider a couple of Stefanowitsch and Gries's examples. The first concerns the past tense construction, schematically [V + past tense]. All verbs— with the exception of some of the modals and a few other defective verbs (see p. 60)—can occur in the construction.[20] Yet not all verbs are equally likely to occur in the past tense. Some verbs, such as *say*, *become*, and *tell*, are biased towards occurring in the past tense vis-à-vis the norm for verbs as a whole; others, such as *hope*, *remember*, and *work*, are biased towards occurring in the present tense. Another of their examples concerns the *waiting to happen* construction:

(9)   (It was) [a N] waiting to happen.

In principle, any event-denoting noun can occur in the construction. Examples (from the COCA) include *crisis*, *tragedy*, *scandal*, *injury*, *nightmare*, *revolution*, *riot*, *overdose*, *crime*, *bad ending*, and *another Enron*. It will be noted that all these nominals refer to 'bad' events; the construction thus exhibits a negative prosody (p. 110). One can, of course, imagine 'good' things appearing in the construction: *It was a marriage waiting to happen*. Such expressions, however, tend not to be attested. Not only is the construction associated with 'bad' events, the two most common words to occur in the construction are *accident* and *disaster*. The BNC contains twenty-six tokens of the construction, exemplifying nine different nouns. Of these, *accident* and *disaster* each occurs nine times, together making up about two-thirds of all tokens.

By shifting the perspective of the analysis we can focus on a word or some other linguistic unit and consider the kinds of construction in which it preferentially occurs. While the [WAITING TO HAPPEN] construction is very strongly associated with the words *accident* and *disaster*, these two words show no particular association with the construction. There are 6,300 tokens of *accident* and 2,770 tokens of *disaster* in the BNC; only a minuscule proportion of these occur in the *waiting to happen* environment.[21]

---

[19] Strictly speaking, collostructional analysis is based, not on the notion of collocation, but on the concept of colligation. Collocation, it will be recalled (see p. 106), concerns the degree of attraction between words, while colligation (see p. 109) has to do with the preferred syntactic environment of an item.

[20] Whether a verb forms its past tense through regular suffixation of {t} or by other means is not relevant to the discussion.

[21] In spite of this, it could be argued that *disaster* is somewhat more closely associated with the construction than *accident*. Overall, *disaster* is a less frequent word than *accident*. This being so, a slightly greater percentage of all instances of *disaster* occur in the [WAITING TO HAPPEN] construction than is the case with *accident*.

Some words are very choosy with regard to the constructions in which they occur.[22] Examples already discussed include *lap* and *whereabouts*. Multi-word phrases, too, can be highly selective. The double negative *not for nothing* occurs mainly in two environments. The favoured environment is as the initial element of the negative inversion construction; this environment accounts for about 80 per cent of all instances in the BNC.

(10)   a. **Not for nothing** was he known as "the Destroyer".
       b. **Not for nothing** are black holes called black.
       c. **Not for nothing** have the invitations dwindled a bit over the years.

The remaining instances occur in a focusing construction introduced by *it is/was*:[23]

(11)   a. It is **not for nothing** that scabies is commonly known as the itch.
       b. It was **not for nothing** that he was chosen as Mr Squeaky Clean after the sexual and financial aberrations of his two predecessors.

Neither of these constructions shows a particularly strong association with *not for nothing*; practically any negative expression can introduce the negative inversion construction, while a wide range of items are able to occur in the focusing construction.

In the examples discussed, there are notable asymmetries in the relation between a construction and the items that can occur in it. In some cases, a construction is very strongly associated with a particular word, or small set of words; in other cases, a word or larger expression is strongly attracted to a certain construction, or small set of constructions. Sometimes, however, the relation between word and construction is more evenly balanced. A very large number of different verbs are able to occur in the ditransitive [V NP NP] construction. However, the verb which is most strongly attracted to the construction, and the one which the construction most strongly attracts, is the verb *give* (Goldberg 2006; Gries and Stefanowitsch 2004). Goldberg has argued that this strong mutual attraction between a verb and a construction contributes significantly to the learnability of a construction, in both its formal and semantic aspects. This is a topic which I will take up again in Chapter 8.

Acquisition

Given the assumptions of the generative model, one might suppose that once the learner has acquired a syntactic rule, the rule will apply across the board to every item

---

[22] Cranberry words (see p. 71), by definition, occur only in a specific environment. *Intents* is restricted to the context *to all intents (and purposes)*, *once-over* occurs in the context *give (someone or something) the once-over*, and so on.

[23] It is also worth noting that the majority of examples of *not for nothing* emphasize the appropriateness of the way in which something has been named.

which fits the specification of the rule. Thus, once a child starts producing passive clauses—evidence that she has acquired the passive rule—one might suppose that every transitive verb in the learner's lexicon will be available for use in passive clauses. This, however, is not how acquisition proceeds (Tomasello 2003, 2006). Constructions are acquired on a piecemeal fashion, verb by verb. Passive clauses, for example, are associated, in the first instance, only with specific verbs (Brooks and Tomasello 1999). Initially, therefore, a passive clause has the status of a verb-specific idiom. It is only at a later stage, when a critical number of such idioms have been learned, that generalization to new verbs occurs. The same goes for the structure of noun phrases, and indeed for many other constructions. One might suppose that once the learner starts using nouns in a range of NP constructions, with a range of determiners such as *the, a, this, my,* and so on, every eligible noun will appear with the full range of determiners. It turns out, however, that initially certain nouns are closely associated with particular determiners (Pine and Lieven 1997). It is only at a later stage, when a critical mass of lexically specified constructions has been acquired, that the learner proceeds to the appropriate generalization, namely, that any (common) noun can be used with the full range of determiners. Even so, as our case study of *lap* and *bosom* showed, distributional preferences may persist, even into the adult language.

Constructions all the way up?

In discussing constructional idioms of the kind *Off with his head,* I stated that these expressions were idiomatic to the extent that their properties could not be derived from the general syntactic rules of the language (see p. 40).

This formulation suggests that alongside idiomatic constructions there exist other constructions which are not at all idiomatic and which can be generated from the general combinatory rules of the syntax. The implication is that the expressions in a language can be partitioned into two sets. One set comprises expressions which are in some way idiomatic, idiosyncratic, or exceptional; the other set comprises perfectly regular expressions which conform to general syntactic rules. Whereas *Off with his head* needs to be described in terms of a low-level construction, involving, amongst other things, the construction-specific use of the word *with,* other expressions, such as *The farmer shot a rabbit,* can be generated by the syntax operating over the lexicon.

The discussion in this chapter suggests that this distinction may not be valid. The [OFF WITH] construction and the transitive clause construction differ only with respect to their generality, not in terms of their status as constructions. The former, as we have seen, imposes tight restrictions on the kinds of items that can occur in it; it is also associated with a specific semantics. The transitive clause construction, on the other hand, is relatively unconstrained, both with respect to the items which can feature in it and with respect to its semantics.

The crucial word here is 'relatively'. As a matter of fact, the transitive clause construction is not entirely free of idiosyncratic aspects. The idiosyncrasies are language-specific and therefore have to be learned (Taylor 2003*b*: Chapter 12). Consider the range of verbs which are eligible to occur in the construction. These are commonly referred to as transitive verbs. While a semantic characterization of (some) transitive verbs is certainly possible—we would probably want to say that the verbs designate some action performed by an actor which impinges on, and affects, another entity, a patient—what counts as a transitive verb is ultimately decided by the possibility of the verb occurring in the construction. In English, *remember* counts as transitive: *I remember that day*. The French and German translation equivalents of *remember* are not transitive: *Je me souviens de ce jour, Ich erinnere mich an den Tag*. In both languages, the verbs are reflexive, with the English direct object appearing in a prepositional phrase.

The notion becomes even more compelling when we consider some other major sentence types, such as the ditransitive [V NP NP], as in *give the dog a bone*. Such a construction simply does not exist in the Romance languages. In French, Italian, and so on, the goal, or recipient, must appear in a prepositional phrase: 'give a bone to the dog'. For those languages which do have a ditransitive construction, such as Korean or the Bantu languages, the range of application of the construction may differ very considerably from that of English (Jackendoff 1996). Consider the following Zulu examples (Taylor 1997):

(12)   a. Umama   unika   amantombazana   imali.
          Mother   gives   (the) girls   money

       b. Umama   utschela   amantombazana   indaba.
          Mother   tells   (the) girls   (the) news

(13)   a. Bayikhuthuza   indoda   isikhwama sayo.
          They robbed   (the) man   his wallet
          'They robbed the man of his wallet'

       b. Udokotela   ukhipe   umfana   izinyo.
          The doctor   extracted   (the) boy   (the) tooth
          'The doctor extracted the boy's tooth'

       c. Angimazi   lomuntu   igama.
          I do not know   this person   (the) name
          'I do not know this person's name'

The examples in (12) correspond to their English equivalents. In (13), however, we see that the ditransitive construction is used where English would have a different wording. In (13a) the postverbal nominal refers to a person who is deprived of something, in (13b) the nominal refers to a person who is affected by virtue of a process directed at a body part, while in (13c) the nominal indicates a possessive relation.

In brief, even the most general syntactic patterns of a language, concerning the major sentence types, need to be regarded as constructions. Their perceived generality is due to the fact that a very wide range of items can occupy their various slots; semantically, too, the constructions are compatible with a range of possibilities. Nevertheless, the constructions are not without their idiosyncratic properties, which will need to be specifically learned. Not only this, but the very fact that a construction exists in a language at all is something which needs to be learned. The idea that constructions are no more than the output of rules operating over the lexicon cannot be maintained. It's constructions all the way up.

7

Frequency

Things in a language occur with different frequencies. This is true wherever we look, whether at the phonology, the morphology, the lexicon, or the syntax. Some vowels and consonants are used more often than others; some consonant–vowel combinations occur more frequently than we might expect given the frequencies of the individual items, while some combinations might not occur at all. If the verbs of a language fall into several conjugations, as in French or Latin, some conjugations will have more members than the others and some will occur more often in running text than the others; the same goes for noun genders and noun declensions (in languages which have them). Inflected forms of nouns and verbs also differ in their frequency. Although every count noun can, in principle, appear in both the singular and the plural, they typically do so at different rates. The same goes for the various forms of a verb (present tense vs. past tense, for example). Constructions, too, differ in their frequency of occurrence while the items which are eligible to fill the slots of a construction will do so at different rates. Perhaps the best known and most intensively studied example of frequency, however, pertains to words. Everyone is aware that some words in a language are relatively rare while others are bound to crop up in just about any piece of text. It is not only words as such which occur with different frequencies; words also differ with respect to the company that they keep, with certain word combinations occurring more frequently than other, equally grammatical and semantically plausible combinations.

One's first inclination, when approaching frequency data in a language, is to consider these as reflecting the interests and concerns of speakers and of the environment in which they live. A word is in frequent use, one might suppose, because the kind of thing that the word refers to is a feature of our day-to-day existence. We encounter cats and dogs more often than giraffes and aardvarks; accordingly, the words *cat* and *dog* are more frequent overall than the words *giraffe* and *aardvark*. In the world outside of language, certain events may tend to be associated with another kind of event. Since a clap of thunder generally occurs with a flash of lightning, it comes as no surprise that the words *thunder* and *lightning* should also tend to occur in close proximity.

A functional account, appealing to the kinds of things that speakers are likely to refer to, may be valid in a small number of cases. It cannot, however, be the whole story. In the first place, frequency effects pertain not only to the meaning-bearing elements of a language, such as words and word combinations, but also to those elements which of themselves do not convey meaning, such as the vowels and the consonants, the declensions and the conjugations. There can be no reference-based explanation for the fact that the short DRESS vowel in English occurs about twice as often in running speech as the short TRAP vowel,[1] or for the fact that of the four tones of Mandarin, Tone 4 (the falling tone) should be more frequent than any of the others (Liu and Ma 1986). Neither can it explain why the majority of French verbs are in the -er conjugation (Bybee 1995) or why almost 50 per cent of the most frequent nouns in German text form their plurals by suffixation of -(e)n rather than by any of the other half dozen or so pluralizing patterns which are used in the language (Janda 1990; Taatgen 2001). In fact, a reference-based explanation fails even for word frequency. Why does the word *accident* occur more often than the word *mishap*? (The ratio is about 60:1.) Is it because accidents are so much more numerous than mishaps? Hardly. Neither can we gain much traction by arguing that people are more likely to categorize an event as an accident than as a mishap. The only evidence for such a claim is the frequency data itself. To take this line is simply to re-state the fact that we use the word *accident* more often than *mishap*. We need to regard the relative frequency of the two words as a fact about the language, not as a fact about the world or about the interests and concerns of speakers. Consider the above-mentioned example of thunder being associated with lightning. The standard phraseology in English is *thunder and lightning*. Yet, in the world outside of language, the lightning precedes the thunder. If language mirrored the world, we should expect the expression *lightning and thunder*.

A further remarkable fact about frequencies is that they tend to be stable across different text samples, even (in cases where comparisons are appropriate) across different languages. Greenberg (1966) found that in languages with a singular–plural contrast in nouns, the singular is more frequent than the plural by a factor of at least three to one, while in languages which classify nouns in terms of masculine and feminine genders, the masculines always outnumber the feminines. If a language contains a series of voiced and voiceless stops, the voiceless sounds will be more frequent than the voiced ones. Hudson (1994) discovered (to his considerable surprise) that "about 37% of word-tokens are nouns", not only in written and spoken English, but also in Swedish, Welsh, and New Testament Greek.

---

[1] Here I follow the practice, due to Wells (1982: 120), of referring to English vowels by the name of a lexical set. The DRESS vowel is the vowel which occurs in *dress*, as well as *pet, send, friend*, and so on, while the TRAP vowel is the vowel in *trap, cat, band, ant*, etc.

It has also been established that different registers typically exhibit a distinctive frequency profile (Biber 2000). Of the relative pronouns *that* and *which*, the former is more frequent in the 'imaginative' texts of the LOB corpus, while the latter dominates in 'informative' texts (Johansson and Hofland 1989: 23). To be sure, some of the linguistic features of different kinds of discourse are open to a functional explanation. It is not really surprising that past tense forms are likely to predominate in historical narratives, that passive clauses are more common in scientific reports than in telephone conversations, or that the words *I* and *you*, common in face-to-face interaction, are virtually absent in legal contracts (Biber, Conrad, and Reppen 1998). One could, however, take a reverse perspective and argue that the different registers are constituted by the relatively stable frequencies of their linguistic features (Halliday 1991: 33). A piece of text counts as a scientific report or as a historical narrative or as informal chit-chat precisely because it exhibits the features characteristic of these registers.[2] Moreover, language users appear to be sensitive to these facts of usage (Hayward 1994). Given only a small fragment of a text, even one as short as five words, we can usually hazard a good guess as to the kind of document it was taken from, whether a novel, a government report, an academic paper, a transcript of a face-to-face interview, and so on.

These and similar considerations lead to the conclusion that frequencies are very much 'in the language'. They are not an epiphenomenon, contingent on speakers' interests and the environment in which they find themselves. Neither is it an option to regard frequencies merely as a feature of language-as-used, that is, of E-language. There is abundant evidence that speakers know, at least implicitly, the relative frequencies of the words, constructions, collocations, and all the other elements of their language (Diessel 2007; Ellis 2002; Robinson and Ellis 2008a). Frequency influences performance on all manner of experimental tasks, such as lexical decision, reading speed, and the processing of ambiguous sentences; it might even be argued that judgements of grammaticality reflect knowledge of language statistics. Furthermore, frequency has been implicated in the productivity of constructional schemas, as well as in language change, whether in syntax, morphology, phonology, or semantics (Bybee 1985, 2001, 2007). Frequency thus belongs firmly in the system of knowledge which constitutes I-language. To know a language involves, *inter alia*, knowing the relative frequency of the various elements which comprise the language.

While an explanation of frequencies in terms of speakers' referential intentions cannot be defended (except perhaps in a small number of cases), a functional explanation may still be indicated, albeit at a higher level. The very ubiquity and pervasiveness of frequency effects suggests that these may not be an accidental or

---

[2] It is also worth bearing in mind that speakers of a language often need to be trained in the characteristics of a register, as when students must learn the linguistic conventions of term papers and oral presentations.

fortuitous property of human languages. Imagine a language without skewed frequencies, a language in which no one vowel occurred more frequently than any of the others, or in which each of the verb conjugations contained the same number of members, and likewise for all the other areas where frequency effects have been observed. Would this hypothetical language be viable? I shall argue in the next chapter that it would not. Skewed frequencies, I shall argue, could well be a design feature of language, one which facilitates its efficient use and enables its transmission from one generation of speakers to another.

In this chapter, in addition to documenting a number of examples of skewed frequencies, I address the question of where, in a description of a language, frequency information belongs. Chomsky's position—which I review below—is that statistical properties of language merely reflect the ways in which a speaker deploys her linguistic competence; frequencies do not inhere in the language system as such. Frequencies, in other words, are located firmly in the E-language, not in the I-language. This position is inconsistent with the dialectic relation between language-as-used and language-as-represented in the mind, proposed in Chapter 1. Even though some frequency effects may well derive from a speaker's communicative needs, knowledge of these effects may still constitute an aspect of a speaker's internal grammar. As I shall document in this chapter, there is abundant evidence, from various sources, that such is indeed the case.

Chomsky on frequency: the Dayton Ohio argument

Chomsky's first major publication, *Syntactic Structures* (1957), opens with a discussion of grammaticality. Grammaticality, it is argued, is independent of meaningfulness. *The child seems sleeping*, though ungrammatical, is easily interpreted, while *I saw a fragile whale*, though nonsensical, is nevertheless grammatical. Neither, Chomsky insists, can grammaticality be thought of in statistical terms. He takes issue with Hockett's (1955: 10) contention that 'impossible in a language' is to be equated with zero, or close to zero probability of occurrence. For Chomsky, a sentence is grammatical if it can be generated by the rules of the language, whether or not that sentence has been attested in a corpus of utterances and irrespective of whether it approximates, in some statistical sense, to attested usage. "We are forced to conclude", he writes, "that grammar is ... independent of meaning, and that probabilistic models give no particular insight into some of the basic problems of syntactic structure" (p. 17).[3] Chomsky did not, however, completely reject the value of statistical studies:

---

[3] The idea that grammaticality (understood in terms of what is possible in a language) can indeed be equated with probability has recently been promoted by Sampson (2007). Responses to Sampson's leading article ranged from the incredulous (Pullum 2007) to the sympathetic (Stefanowitsch 2007).

Given the grammar of a language, one can study the use of the language statistically in various ways; and the development of probabilistic models for the use of language (as distinct from the syntactic structure of language) can be quite rewarding.   (Chomsky 1957: 17)

The passage makes clear that for Chomsky statistical aspects are relevant only to the use which speakers make of their language, not to the grammatical system which underlies the use. In terminology which Chomsky was to introduce later, frequencies and probabilities are facets of E-language, extraneous to I-language.[4]

Chomsky's scepticism towards probabilistic data was made clear in a remark he is reported to have made in a lecture at the Summer Institute of the Linguistic Society of America in July 1964.[5] He quipped that in a corpus of American English sentence (1a) is likely to occur more often than (1b):

(1)   a. I live in New York.
      b. I live in Dayton Ohio.

Since New York City has more inhabitants than Dayton Ohio, one might expect there to be more occasions on which (1a) is likely to be uttered. The relative frequency would be totally unremarkable and would have no bearing whatsoever on the grammar of English. Both sentences, namely, are legitimized by the fact that the verb *live* subcategorizes for a locative phrase. The subcategorization of *live* is a fact about the grammar of English; the relative frequency of one locative phrase over another is a fact of usage, not of the grammar.

It is unlikely that Chomsky's statement about the relative frequencies of (1a) and (1b) was based on corpus data. In fact, the kind of corpora from which such information could be extracted hardly existed in the 1960s. Presumably, Chomsky was appealing to his intuitions—not his intuitions about grammaticality, but his intuitions about probabilities in the E-language. The matter has, however, been taken up by Stefanowitsch (2005). Drawing on results from Internet searches, Stefanowitsch not only validated Chomsky's intuitions that (1a) is indeed more frequent than (1b); he also discovered that the relative frequencies correspond almost exactly to the relative populations of the two cities. New York City (according to census data) has about fifty times more inhabitants than Dayton Ohio, while sentence (1a) returned about forty-seven times more hits than (1b). The relative frequencies of (1) are almost exactly what one would expect on the basis of extra-linguistic data. The correspondence is indeed, as Stefanowitsch (p. 229) observes, "eerie". A point not made by Stefanowitsch is that the correspondence also offers an indirect and equally 'eerie' endorsement of the validity of Internet search data.

---

[4] Newmeyer (2003), while conceding that some aspects of grammar may be subject to explanations in terms of language use, has vigorously defended Chomsky's position. In particular, he dismisses any relation between frequency and grammaticality.

[5] The episode is reported in Halliday (1991: 42).

On the face of it, Stefanowitsch's findings would seem to give some credence to the view that, in some cases at least, relative frequencies mirror the contingencies of the world. Let us pursue this matter by examining a couple of similar sentences.

(2)   a. He lives in New York.
       b. She lives in New York.

On the reasonable assumption that the male and female inhabitants of New York are roughly equal in number, we should predict that the incidence of the two sentences in (2) should also be roughly equal. This, however, is not what we find. Google searches (October 2007) show that (2a), with 624,000 hits, is about twice as frequent as (2b), with 339,000 hits. Interestingly, the ratio of 2:1 happens to be about the same as that for the words *he* and *she* in the BNC (6,407 per million vs. 3,528 per million) as well as in the smaller (and older) LOB corpus (9,068 tokens vs. 4,090) (Johansson and Hofland 1989).

We might try to explain the skewed frequencies by supposing that speakers have more occasions to refer to males and where they live than to females and where they live. It is by no means obvious why this should be the case. In fact, the only evidence that it is indeed the case is the linguistic data itself.

Taking a different tack, we might note that *he* often functions (or used to function) as a default pronoun, used when the gender of the referent is not known or is not relevant. What is remarkable, though, is that the frequency ratio for the two sentences in (2) is roughly the same as that for the two pronouns in two independent corpora. The similar ratios raise the suspicion that the relative frequencies of *he* and *she* may actually be a fact about the language, not about the circumstances of its use.

A similar issue arises when we consider another pair of sentences.

(3)   a. He lives in New York.
       b. He lived in New York.

We might suppose that the people who formerly lived in New York by far outnumber the present inhabitants. On this basis, we should predict that (3b) will be more frequent by far than (3a). But this is not what we find. Google searching of (3a) returned more hits, by a ratio of about 3:2, than (3b). To this, one might respond that speakers have more interest in a person's present place of residence than to their past places of residence. There is no way of verifying this claim other than by pointing to the linguistic data. Once again, the only evidence for the *explicandum* is the *explicans*.[6] The argument in terms of speakers' referential intentions turns out to be irredeemably circular.

---

[6] The *explicandum* is the situation which is to be explained, the *explicans* is the situation which explains the *explicandum*. The terms were popularized by Karl Popper. For Popper, the *explicans* "must be independently testable, so that it is not *ad hoc*. This means that the *explicandum* must not be the only evidence relevant to the *explicans*" (Hickey 1995/2005: 36).

Verb complements

I now turn to another example where a functional account may seem to be indicated, at least on a first approach. A glance at a wider range of data, however, shows that appeal to speakers' communicative needs is bound to fail as an explanation of relative frequencies.

There are several different kinds of complement which a verb may take. The possibilities include a nominal complement: *I see the problem*; a clausal complement with or without the complementizer *that*: *I see (that) there is a problem*; a non-finite *wh*-complement: *I know what to do*; a *to*-infinitive: *I want to leave*; a V-*ing* complement: *I remember meeting them*, as well as prepositional complements: *I believe in him, I rely on you*. It is not uncommon for a verb to be able to take more than one complement type. *Know* may take either a nominal or a clausal complement: *I know the story, I know that it's true*; *insist* can take either a clausal or a prepositional complement: *I insist that you all leave, I insist on it*; and so on. Which complement types a verb is able to take, and the possible semantic factors which might motivate the various possibilities, have been studied quite intensively (see p. 62). Here I want to look at the relative frequency of some of the available options.

I begin with an example where the relative frequencies would seem to be semantically motivated. The verb *decide* can occur in a number of syntactic frames, including the following:

zero complement	We have to decide.
to-infinitive	We decided to leave.
non-finite *wh*-complement	We must decide where to go.
that-clause	We decided that we should leave.
prepositional complement	We decided on a new car.

Hunston (2003) examined the incidence of *that*- and *wh*-complements in the 450 million word Bank of English corpus. She found that overall these two complementation patterns accounted for about 25 per cent of all uses of the verb, with *wh*-complements being about 50 per cent more frequent that *that*-complements. She also found that the two complement types were distributed unequally over different forms of the verb. Specifically, *that*-clauses were mainly associated with the inflected form *decided*, whereas *wh*-complements occurred mainly with the uninflected form *decide*.

As Hunston observes (2003: 37), these patterns are not entirely unexpected. A *that*-clause is typically used to state the content of a decision already taken, while a *wh*-complement introduces a variable whose value is still to be fixed. It is not surprising, therefore, that reports of decisions already taken (and which typically involve the inflected form *decided*) should take a clausal complement. The uninflected form, on the other hand, is likely to be used for decisions yet to be taken, often in association with modal elements (*have to decide, must decide, will decide*, etc.). Interestingly, examples where uninflected *decide* takes a *that*-complement often involve a hypothetical, future, or otherwise irrealis situation (*Suppose you decide that...*, *You may well decide that...*, *Before you decide that...*). In brief, the distribution of the two complementation patterns for *decide* would appear to follow from the semantics of the two complement types, in association with the typical contexts of use of the inflected and uninflected forms of the verb.

This kind of explanation cannot, however, be extended to a wider range of examples. Quite a number of English verbs can be followed either by a nominal complement (4a) or by a clausal complement (4b):

(4) a. argue the issue, confirm the rumour, believe the interviewer
     b. argue (that) the issue was irrelevant, confirm (that) the rumour should have been stopped, believe (that) the interviewer had been dishonest

Which of these two patterns is likely to be more frequent? Speculative reasoning is not going to deliver a reliable answer. As a matter of fact, some verbs (*believe, argue, suggest*) are biased towards a clausal complement, some (*confirm, emphasize, establish*) are biased towards a nominal complement, while others (*concede, declare, know*) show no preferences either way (Gahl and Garnsey 2004; Garnsey, Pearlmutter, Myers, and Lotocky 1997). It does not seem possible to explain these biases by reference to the circumstances of how speakers use their language and what they might be interested in talking about. There is no basis—other than the linguistic evidence—for supposing that speakers believe propositions (as in *believe that the interviewer had been dishonest*) more often than they believe people (as in *believe the interviewer*). (I discuss this and similar examples in more detail later in this chapter.)

Words

Everyone is aware that some words in a language are rare while others are rather common. Amongst the most frequent words in English are the articles *a* and *the*. This is hardly surprising. After all, practically every clause contains at least one noun phrase and noun phrases are typically introduced by an article. For content words we might suppose that their frequency reflects the role which the referents play in our day-to-day life: recall the above example of *cat* and *dog* vs. *aardvark* and *giraffe*. This kind of explanation, however, cannot be generalized to the lexicon at large.

A good way to appreciate the independence of word frequencies vis-à-vis real-world contingencies is to compare words from a single semantic field which denote similar kinds of entities. Table 7.1 lists some words which refer to 'bad things' that can happen.

The frequency of the words correlates only imperfectly with the frequency of occurrence of the designated events, if indeed it is possible at all to determine the frequency of catastrophes, cataclysms, and debacles in contrast to accidents, disasters, and tragedies, independently of the frequency with which the words are used. Intuitively, though, one would like to think that catastrophes and cataclysms are

TABLE 7.1. **Number of occurrences of some words in the BNC.**

Singular		Plural		Singular+Plural
accident	6300	accidents	1964	8264
disaster	2770	disasters	515	3285
tragedy	1745	tragedies	185	1930
catastrophe	397	catastrophes	61	458
misfortune	374	misfortunes	88	462
fiasco	244	fiascos*	15	259
debacle	131	debacles	6	137
calamity	105	calamities	30	135
mishap	103	mishaps	40	143
cataclysm	25	cataclysms	4	29
Total	12194		2908	15102

* The BNC records one example of the spelling 'fiascoes'.

rather less common than accidents, and the frequency data do bear this out. But what about calamities and mishaps? Mishaps happen all the time; calamities, fortunately, do not. Yet the words differ hardly at all in their usage frequency.

Each of the nouns listed in Table 7.1 occurs in both the singular and the plural. Considering the data as a whole, we see that the plurals occur with about one-quarter of the frequency of the singulars. However, the ratio of singular to plural is not constant from noun to noun. *Accident* occurs rather more often in the plural than we might expect, while *disaster* is biased towards occurring in the singular. Once again, the relative frequencies of the singular and plural forms have little to do with the vicissitudes of the world. If anything, catastrophes and calamities come one at a time, so we should expect the words to be used overwhelmingly in the singular. While *catastrophe* clearly is biased towards occurring in the singular, the same does not go for *calamity*. We are lead once again to the conclusion that the relative frequency of the inflected and uninflected forms is a fact about the language, not a fact about the concerns of speakers.

Data on the singular and plural forms of a given noun need to be assessed against the frequency ratio for singulars vs. plurals in the language as a whole. In the BNC, there are 15,277,527 singular nouns and 5,323,109 plural nouns. The ratio is approximately 3:1 (more precisely, 2.87:1).[7] As rule of thumb, therefore, we can say that a noun is biased towards the singular or plural form if the singular–plural ratio

---

[7] The reader may note that the singular and plural nouns constitute just over 20% of the total word count of the BNC corpus, seemingly at variance with Hudson's (1994) observation that about 37% of word types are nouns. The discrepancy is due to what is to be counted as a noun. Hudson's count included proper nouns as well as pronominal forms. The latter category, on Hudson's theory of grammar, comprises

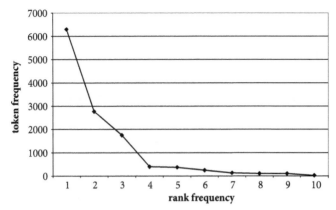

FIGURE 7.1. Frequency distribution of the words of Table 7.1.

diverges markedly from the 3:1 ratio. The 'bad event' nouns would appear to be skewed towards occurring in the singular. Other kinds of nouns—some body part terms, for example—are heavily skewed towards the plural form. *Eye, finger, toe,* and *foot* are actually more frequent in the plural than in the singular.

Inspection of Table 7.1 shows that of the word tokens which refer to bad events, somewhat more than half are taken up by the word *accident.* Moreover, the two most frequent words, *accident* and *disaster,* account for more than two-thirds of the data. The less common words, such as *cataclysm, mishap,* and *debacle,* make up a tiny proportion of the total of word tokens.

This aspect of the data is shown in Figure 7.1, which plots the number of tokens of the singular form of each word against the word's rank frequency. The figure shows a reverse-J curve, beginning with a steep decline, followed by a fairly level tail.

The distribution suggests a logarithmic relation between rank order and token frequency. If we plot rank position against the logarithm of token frequency, we obtain a more nearly linear relation (Figure 7.2).

The frequency distribution illustrated here is not unique to this set of data. It is in line with one of the most important discoveries of a pioneer of frequency studies, George Kingsley Zipf (1935). Suppose we list all the word types in a text or a collection of texts, from the most to the least frequent. If we then plot the rank frequency of the words against the number of occurrences of each word we obtain a graph with a shape similar to that of Figure 7.1. If, on the other hand, we plot the data on logarithmic scales, we get a linear, or almost linear relation.[8] Zipf found that this

---

not only items such as *I, he,* and *it,* but also pronominal uses of demonstratives (*this, those,* etc.) and interrogatives (*who, what,* etc.).

[8] Deviations from the linear relation are likely to be due to words of very high and very low frequencies (Ha *et al.* 2009).

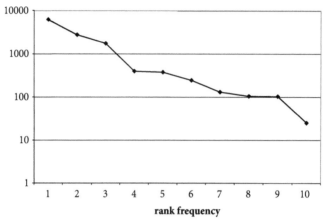

FIGURE 7.2. Frequency distribution of the words of Table 7.1 (logarithmic scale).

relation held for samples of English, Latin, and Mandarin. The relation is often referred to as ZIPF'S LAW. Roughly speaking, if the most frequent word in a corpus accounts for *x* per cent of all word tokens, the second most frequent word accounts for *x*/2 per cent of the corpus, the third most frequent word for *x*/3 per cent, and so on. What this means, concretely, is that a small number of very common words make up the bulk of a text, a fair number of moderately frequent words constitute a somewhat smaller proportion, while a very large number of infrequent words account for only a tiny amount of a text.

Zipf's law has some interesting implications for the question of how many words exist in a language, or indeed in a person's mental lexicon. In any text (or corpus), of whatever size, we will find quite a number of words which occur only once. These are the so-called HAPAX LEGOMENA.[9] As the size of a corpus increases, we would expect to find more tokens of each of the word types already encountered. The hapaxes of the smaller corpus will be used a second or even a third time. Equally, as the corpus increases in size, new hapaxes will make their appearance (Baayen and Lieber 1991; Baayen and Renouf 1996). One might suppose that as we keep on increasing the size of the corpus, adding ever more text samples, there will come a point at which all the words of the language have occurred at least once. We will, essentially, have recorded every single word of the language. (Alternatively, if we are collecting text samples from a single individual, we might expect to reach a point at which we have elicited tokens of every word in the speaker's mental lexicon.) Further increasing the size of the corpus will not increase the number of different word types, merely the number of tokens of each of the already encountered word types.

---

[9] The term is Greek: *hapax* 'once', *legomenon* (plural: *legomena*) 'thing(s) said'.

Statistical modelling indicates that this conclusion may be false (Kornai 2002; Sichel 1975). There may be no point at which the lexical resources of a language (or of an individual speaker) have been exhaustively recorded. As the size of a corpus approaches infinity, so too does the number of word types. This result goes counter to the view of the lexicon as a finite list of items, a cornerstone assumption of the dictionary plus grammar book model of language. Yet the result should not really surprise us. In Chapter 2 we already had reason to query the assumption of a finite lexicon. Speakers are able to creatively extend the word stock of their language, by compounding and derivation. Another process of word creation is blending, a topic we will examine in Chapter 12. The idea that the number of words in a language can be exhaustively enumerated cannot be upheld.

The Zipfian relation holds not only for words and their frequencies, but for many other elements of a language; a case in point will be mentioned in Chapter 8 (p. 193).[10] An interesting example is reported in Sampson (2007: 9). Sampson's data concerned the internal structure of noun phrases and the frequency of occurrence of different noun phrase types. The 131,302 word corpus which Sampson analysed contained 34,914 noun phrases. Sampson gives no information on how many different types these 34,914 noun phrases belonged to. He does, however, tell us that the most frequent type was a singular personal pronoun (such as *I* or *he*), the second most

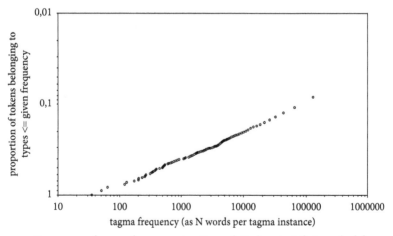

FIGURE 7.3. Frequency of noun phrase constructions plotted against their ranked frequencies (Source: Sampson 2007: 9; reproduced with permission).

---

[10] As Zipf himself discovered, the relation is found in other aspects of human behaviour. Zipfian distributions, for example, are exhibited by such diverse phenomena as the population sizes of cities in a country and the number of times different books are borrowed from a library (Pustet 2004).

frequent type being an article + a singular common noun (such as *the man*). These are represented by, respectively, 3,749 and 2,605 instances in the corpus. At the other extreme are the 2,904 noun phrase types which are represented only once. Figure 7.3 plots, on logarithmic scales, the frequency of the types (in terms of how many times the type occurs per N words of the corpus) against the number of tokens of each of the types. The relation, it will be observed, is virtually linear. Sampson ventures the prediction that the almost linear relation will continue to hold, no matter how far the database is expanded (p. 12). In other words, as the database becomes progressively larger, we can expect to find ever more noun phrase types making their appearance, with, at the same time, the most frequent types being used again and again.

Collocations (again)

According to the data in Table 7.1, we should expect to find, on average, sixty-three occurrences of the word *accident* in every one million words of text, or one occurrence every 15,873 words. Zipf, in this connection, spoke about a word's "wave length" (1935: 45). The word *accident* has a wave length of 15,873, that is to say, any two successive occurrences of the word will be separated, on average, by 15,873 words of text; the word *disaster* has a wave length of 36,101; while the wave length of *catastrophe* is 251,889.

These calculations assume that words occur randomly in a text. The assumption is, of course, unwarranted. For one thing, the probability that a word will be used appears to be enhanced by the recent use of that same word. As a consequence, tokens of a word tend to cluster in certain regions of a text (Ellis 2002; Szmrecsanyi 2006). Moreover, some words may be highly dependent on the occurrence of other words. An occurrence of *unmitigated* massively increases the probability that the following word will be *disaster*. The probability of *disaster* in this context is no longer 27.7/1,000,000, i.e. 0.0000277; as we shall see below, it is more in the vicinity of 0.25. Here it is a question, not of the overall probability of *disaster* occurring at a certain point in a text, but of the TRANSITIONAL PROBABILITY of the word's occurring, given the preceding context. Transitional probabilities lie at the heart of the notions of collocation and colligation, discussed in Chapter 6.

Interestingly, a Zipfian distribution can often be observed with respect to the collocational preferences of a word. Take the above-mentioned example of the word *unmitigated*. This is not a very common word, occurring only sixty times in the 100 million word BNC corpus. If something is judged to be 'an unmitigated X', it means that there is nothing that might detract from its description as X. Given this definition, one might expect that *unmitigated* could modify a large number of nouns, such as *success, happiness, failure*, and so on. If something were an unmitigated success, the success would be total, with no contrary or negative aspects. Likewise, an

TABLE 7.2. **Number of hits returned by the Google search engine for expressions of the form [unmitigated N] (January 2008).**

unmitigated	disaster	158,000
	success	19,400
	failure	15,100
	joy	8,450
	catastrophe	4,310
	tragedy	3,900
	calamity	1,400
	misfortune	895
	fiasco	809
	happiness	627
	accident	341
	debacle	201
	cataclysm	7
	mishap	1

unmitigated failure would be a total failure, with no redeeming features. As a matter of fact, the BNC does show that *unmitigated* can indeed combine with a wide range of nouns, including *joy, rubbish,* and *anger*. These combinations, however, are recorded only once. By far the dominant use of the word is in the phrase *unmitigated disaster*. This accounts for more than a quarter of all uses of the word (seventeen examples). Native speakers—at least, those who are familiar with the word *unmitigated*[11]—appear to know this fact. Given the phrase *It was an unmitigated...,* speakers invariably complete the sentence with *disaster*. Internet searches confirm this collocational preference. Table 7.2 lists the number of hits obtained from the Google search engine for various phrases of the form [unmitigated N]. The table is selective and does not pretend to list every noun which can be modified by *unmitigated*. It is apparent, however, that the bulk, by far, of [unmitigated N] expressions concern the word *disaster*; a couple of other words (*success* and *failure*) occur a fair number of times; while the tail of the distribution is occupied by options which occur exceedingly rarely.

Considering both the BNC and the Googled data, it would appear that *unmitigated* collocates predominantly with nouns designating 'bad events'. In the light of this, I have included in Table 7.2 all the 'bad event' nouns listed in Table 7.1. It is

---

[11] I once tried out the collocation test with a class of 2nd year undergraduate students of English. About a third (!) claimed not to know the word.

interesting to compare the rank frequency of these nouns in the BNC with their ranking in collocation with *unmitigated*. Nouns such as *cataclysm, debacle*, and *fiasco* are low on both lists. Nevertheless, some big discrepancies can be observed. Overall in the language, *accident* is more frequent than *disaster*; yet in collocation with *unmitigated*, the relation is dramatically reversed.

From a semantic point of view, there is no particular reason why *unmitigated* should collocate so strongly with *disaster* but show such a weak association with *success, failure*, and the other words listed in Table 7.2.[12] Unless, that is, one were to take the view that one aspect of the meaning of *unmitigated* is, precisely, the fact that this word preferentially occurs with *disaster*. This, no doubt, would have been Firth's position (see p. 110). To know the word involves knowing the contexts in which the word is used, where 'context' refers, not to the situations in the world which speakers wish to talk about, but to the linguistic context in which the word is used.

The collocational preferences illustrated above pertain only to attributive uses of the word *unmitigated*, not to its predicative uses. As a matter of fact, there are no examples in the BNC of *unmitigated* being used predicatively, although a couple of examples are found in the COCA.[13] Other forms derived from the verb *(to) mitigate* also show distinctive distributional patterns. Take, for example, the use of *mitigating* as an attributive adjective. There are fifty-six instances in the BNC, of which almost half (24) involve the phrase *mitigating circumstances*, followed by *mitigating factors* (8 instances) and *mitigating factor* (6 instances), while the singular *mitigating circumstance* is attested only once. Interestingly, however, the verb itself and its inflected forms—*mitigate, mitigates, mitigated*—show no association at all with *disaster* and *circumstances*, the preferred collocates of *unmitigated* and *mitigating* respectively. These observations suggest that each of the derived and inflected forms of a word may have its own, unique set of collocational preferences, distinct from those of the base word.

We have already seen an example of this phenomenon in our discussion of the complementation patterns associated with the verb forms *decide* and *decided* (p. 152): the uninflected form is biased towards a *to*-infinitive, whereas the inflected form

---

[12] The etymology of the word might go some way towards explaining why *unmitigated* tends to collocate with 'bad event' nouns: the word is from Latin *mitigatus*, past participle of *mitigare*, which derives from the adjective *mitis* 'soft, gentle'. Strictly speaking, therefore, to mitigate is to make less bad or less severe. Current usage, however, is not governed entirely by the etymology. First, some bad event nouns are more strongly attracted to *unmitigated* than others; compare *unmitigated disaster* and *unmitigated failure*. Second, appeal to etymology would entail that *unmitigated success* was not only less usual, but outright incorrect. Appeal to etymology as an explanation of usage is dubious in many other cases. Etymologically speaking, circumstances are conditions which surround an event or situation. The etymology dictates the usage *in these circumstances*; the frequently used alternative *under these circumstances* would have to be regarded as conceptually incoherent.

[13] An example of predicative use is the following:

(i) The emotional loss, many would even say the spiritual loss, **was unmitigated**.

favours a *wh*-complement. Tao (2003) noted that the choice between transitive and intransitive uses of *remember* and *forget* correlates with the tense (present or past), mood (imperative or indicative), and the person of the verbs. Newman and Rice (2006) come to a similar conclusion with respect to transitive and intransitive uses of the verbs *eat* and *drink*. They discovered subtle and unexpected patterns concerning the tense of the verbs and the features of their subject. For example, intransitive uses of *eat* tend to be associated with plural subjects (first and third person). In this connection, Newman and Rice propose the notion of an INFLECTIONAL ISLAND. Each inflected form of a word has its own distinctive distributional properties, which speakers need to learn. In the limiting case, the properties of one form of a word are independent of other forms.[14]

[I]nflected verb forms have their own semantic and constructional properties...and these merit serious descriptive and theoretical consideration. To that end we propose the notion of an *inflectional island*.... Syntactic/semantic properties tend to inhere in individual inflections of a verb in a register-specific manner. Furthermore, these properties may not extend across all the inflections to characterize the lemma as a whole. For us, the notion of a dictionary entry based on a lemma is still inadequate.   (Newman and Rice 2006: 255)

The matter is perhaps of even greater import in languages with more elaborate patterns of verbal and nominal inflection (Dąbrowska 2004). Children learning Polish do not learn the full paradigm of each noun in one fell swoop; they learn the more frequent forms and their appropriate contexts of use. It is, after all, the contextualized uses of a word that speakers encounter, not the lexeme as such.

Phonology

I now turn to frequency effects in the sound system of a language. These are of particular interest to our topic since speech sounds are not in themselves meaningful. One might suppose that a language will tend to make the most efficient use of the available phonological resources, with each of its vowels and consonants being exploited to an equal degree in the make-up of its words and morphemes. This, however, is not what we find. Skewed frequencies are manifest in each of the ninety-five languages surveyed by Tambovtsev and Martindale (2007), the skewing being particularly evident in languages with large phoneme inventories.

Table 7.3 shows data on the sounds of British English, based on Fry's (1947) analysis of the 17,000 sounds of transcribed text. Token frequencies refer to the occurrences of the sounds in the text comprising the corpus; type frequencies are the number of occurrences in the word types in the text.

---

[14] A similar point was made by Sinclair (2004). See also Stubbs (2009).

TABLE 7.3. **Frequency of English consonants.**

Consonant	Token frequency	Type frequency
n	7.58%	6.48%
t	6.42%	6.95%
d	5.14%	4.32%
s	4.81%	6.88%
l	3.66%	5.56%
ð	3.56%	0.12%
r	3.51%	4.68%
m	3.22%	3.01%
k	3.09%	4.56%
w	2.81%	0.93%
z	2.46%	4.05%
v	2.00%	1.22%
b	1.97%	2.21%
f	1.79%	1.79%
p	1.78%	3.16%
h	1.46%	0.75%
ŋ	1.15%	1.86%
g	1.05%	1.27%
ʃ	0.96%	1.24%
j	0.88%	0.72%
ʤ	0.60%	0.79%
ʧ	0.41%	0.54%
θ	0.37%	0.33%
ʒ	0.10%	0.07%

Vowel	Token frequency	Type frequency
ə	10.74%	6.29%
ɪ	8.33%	10.52%
ɛ	2.97%	2.30%
aɪ	1.83%	1.51%
ʌ	1.75%	1.45%
eɪ	1.71%	2.08%

iː	1.65%	1.36%
əʊ	1.51%	1.36%
æ	1.45%	2.35%
ɒ	1.37%	1.62%
ɔː	1.24%	0.96%
uː	1.13%	0.97%
ʊ	0.86%	0.40%
ɑː	0.79%	0.86%
au	0.61%	0.44%
3ː	0.52%	0.63%
eə	0.34%	0.20%
iə	0.21%	0.85%
ɔɪ	0.14%	0.16%
uə	0.06%	0.21%

Skewings are also apparent when we consider the sounds which make up the subsystems of English. Table 7.4 shows the token frequency of the nine stop consonants of English, classified according to their manner of articulation (voiceless, voiced, and nasal) and place of articulation (bilabial, alveolar, and velar). We see that voiceless stops as a whole are more frequent than the other manners of articulation, while alveolars are more frequent than the other places of articulation. The most frequent sound turns out to be the voiceless alveolar /t/, which occurs about six times more often than the least common sound, the voiced velar /g/.

TABLE 7.4. **Frequency of nine stop consonants in running English text (Source: Fry 1947).**

	Voiceless	Voiced	Nasal	Row total
Bilabial	p 1.78	b 1.97	m 3.22	6.97
Alveolar	t 6.42	d 5.14	n 7.58	19.14
Velar	k 3.09	g 1.05	ŋ 1.15	5.29
Column total	11.29	8.16	11.95	31.40

Combinations of vowels and consonants can have frequencies of occurrence which are at variance with what one might predict, given the probability of occurrence of their component elements. Kessler and Treiman (1997) examined 2,000 uninflected English monosyllables and found that some consonants, such as /b/, are more likely to occur in syllable onset position, whereas others, such as /ð/ and /z/, are more common in syllable codas. With respect to codas, some twenty-one VC combinations occur more often than what one might expect on the basis of the frequency of the V and C segments alone; these include /ʌf/, /ʌg/, and /ɒp/. Conversely, /æl/, /ʌl/, and /ɒf/ occur with less than chance frequency. Some possible combinations, such as /ɛŋ/, /iːb/, and /aɾʃ/, are not attested at all.

I would like to illustrate these frequency effects on another set of data: Chinese tones. As is well-known, each syllable in Mandarin is a meaningful morpheme, represented in the writing system by a single character. The majority of the syllable-morphemes are associated with one of four tones. Following the usual practice, I will refer to the tones as Tone 1 (high level), Tone 2 (high rising), Tone 3 (low falling), and Tone 4 (falling). A small number of morphemes do not have an inherent tone; rather, they acquire their tone as a function of a preceding morpheme. Following normal practice, I refer to these morphemes as bearing the 'neutral' Tone 5. With the exception of Tone 5—which tends to be associated with particles and other 'grammatical' elements—the tones would appear to be distributed randomly over the morphemes, independent of meaning and syntactic category. Nevertheless, the tones do not occur with equal frequency. Table 7.5 is from a study by Liu and Ma (1986). The table shows the frequency of the tones in the 7,776 different morpheme types which occurred in a corpus of 104,123 characters; also shown is the token frequency of the tones in the corpus.[15]

TABLE 7.5. **Relative frequency of tones of Mandarin Chinese (Source: Liu and Ma 1986).**

Tone	Characters (types)		Occurrences (tokens)	
	Characters	Per cent	Tokens	Per cent
Tone 1 (high level)	1,959	25.19%	24,690	23.71%
Tone 2 (high rising)	1,972	25.35%	25,130	24.13%
Tone 3 (low falling)	1,300	16.71%	17,853	17.15%
Tone 4 (falling)	2,488	32.00%	33,560	32.25%
Tone 5 (neutral)	58	0.75%	2,890	2.78%
Total	7,777		104,123	

[15] I am indebted to Dawei Han for assistance with the Mandarin data.

TABLE 7.6. Token frequency of Chinese tones in two-character morphemes (Data from Liu and Ma 1986).

	Tone 1	Tone 2	Tone 3	Tone 4	Tone 5 (neutral tone)
First character	9,910	8,623	6,283	10,404	
Second character	6,516	8,425	5,749	12,583	1,947
Total	16,426	17,048	12,032	22,987	1,947

We see that Tone 4 occurs in about one-third of all tokens; also, about one-third of all morpheme types bear this tone. Tone 5—the neutral tone—is comparatively rare amongst the morpheme types, but slightly more frequent in the token count, a fact which probably reflects the association of the tone with frequently occurring grammatical particles.

The uneven distribution of the tones becomes apparent from other aspects of Liu and Ma's study. Consider, for example, the incidence of tones in two-character (that is, bimorphemic) words. Data in Table 7.6—shown graphically in Figure 7.4— summarize over the 35,220 bimorphemic sequences in the data. We see that Tone 1 tends to be preferred in initial position, while Tone 4 is favoured in final position. The so-called neutral tone—whose actual value is determined by the preceding tone—is, not surprisingly, unattested in initial position. The skewing is even more in evidence if we consider specific tonal sequences (Figure 7.4). While all possible sequences are attested, some are considerably more frequent than others. By far the

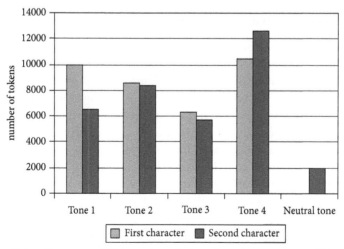

FIGURE 7.4. Token frequency of Chinese tones in two-character morphemes (Data from Liu and Ma 1986).

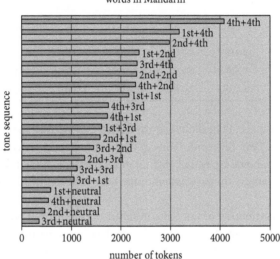

Frequency of tone sequences in bimorphemic words in Mandarin

FIGURE 7.5. Frequency of tone sequences in bimorphemic words in Mandarin.

most common pattern is Tone 4+Tone 4, which is about ten times more frequent than the least common, Tone 3+the neutral tone.

Ambiguity resolution and garden path sentences

The existence of skewed frequencies, in all areas of language structure, is beyond dispute. There is also abundant evidence that speakers of a language know these frequencies, at least implicitly and even, in some cases (as we shall see), explicitly. Evidence comes from performance on various psycholinguistic tasks. In fact, frequency turns out to be relevant to just about every experimental paradigm that has been devised. Frequency may even be implicated in judgements of acceptability and grammaticality (Lapata, Keller, and Schulte im Walde 1999).

Frequency is relevant to both the production and reception of speech. It has been found, for example, that the speed with which pictures are named depends on the frequency of the picture names (Oldfield and Wingfield 1965; Alario, Costa, and Caramazza 2002), suggesting that the more frequent names are more readily available than the less common ones. More frequent words tend to be articulated more rapidly than less frequent words; the effect shows up in the case of supposed homophones, such as *time* and *thyme* (Gahl 2008). The frequency effect also shows up on word identification tasks, both visual (Howes and Solomon 1951) and auditory. Consider, for example, the question of how easily spoken words can be identified against various levels of background noise or when the speech signal has been subjected to different amounts of filtering. (Much of the early research was sponsored by telephone companies, interested in determining the minimal needs of telephonic transmission consistent with intelligibility.) An early finding was that the recognition of degraded signals was dependent on word frequency, with the more common words of a language being easier to identify in noise than less common words (Black 1952; Savin 1963). Interestingly, the frequency effect disappears when listeners are presented with a small set of options from which they have to choose (Pollack, Rubenstein, and Decker, 1959). The multiple-choice format of listeners' responses effectively overrides the frequency biases.

In this section, I want to focus on just one kind of experimental task, concerning the interpretation of ambiguous sentences. Readers will no doubt be familiar with the following joke, attributed to Groucho Marx:

(5)   Time flies like an arrow; and fruit flies like a banana.

When the two phrases are coordinated we become aware of the ambiguity of each of them. The way we parse *Time flies like an arrow* primes us to parse the second phrase in a similar way; conversely, the normal interpretation of *Fruit flies like a banana* invites us to revisit the first phrase and impose a similar syntactic analysis. Thus, on the one hand, we have an image of flying fruit; on the other, we are invited to imagine a hitherto unknown kind of creature, the time fly. As a matter of fact, there is third reading of *Time flies like an arrow*. On this reading, *time* is an imperative. The sentence exhorts us to take out our stopwatches and to time the flies in the same way as we would time an arrow.

Probably, a very great deal of what we read and hear is multiply ambiguous, if examined analytically. Consider the following, seemingly innocuous sentences:

(6)   a. I cut the cheese with the knife.
      b. I stewed the meat with the vegetables.

The first exemplifies the instrumental sense of *with*: I use the knife as an instrument for cutting the cheese. The second exemplifies the accompaniment sense of *with*: I stew the meat together with the vegetables. Crossed readings would be absurd: using the vegetables as an instrument for stewing the meat or cutting the cheese along with the knife. There are, of course, cases where both interpretations are plausible:

(7)   I saw the man with a telescope.

On one reading, I use a telescope in order to see the man; on the other, I see a man who has a telescope.

One might expect that ambiguity would seriously impede the flow of linguistic interactions. Most of the time, however, this seems not to be the case. Usually, only one of the possible readings of a sentence is semantically coherent or relevant to the context at hand and this is the one that we unfailingly select. It seems that we do not even entertain the alternative and possibly nonsensical interpretations. Indeed, it may take quite a lot of reflection for us even to be aware of them. The point of the Groucho Marx joke is that it forces us to parse the well-known aphorism in a way which we might never before have considered.

It is unlikely that sentence interpretation is driven solely by a search for semantic plausibility. How, for example, can we come to know that one particular reading is more plausible than all the others, unless we have first worked out all the possible readings and then compared them? Comprehension of even the simplest of sentences would require a phenomenal amount of cognitive processing. In this connection the examples in (6) are by no means exceptional. Most words, especially the more common words in the language, are many-ways polysemous. Even the shortest and seemingly most straightforward of sentences may turn out to have a large number of possible readings.

Listeners, clearly, need some strategy which leads them directly towards the most plausible reading, without the distraction of having to consider the sometimes bizarre alternatives. The strategy, I suggest, relies on frequency-based expectations (Lapata, Keller, and Schulte im Walde 2001; MacDonald 1993; MacDonald, Pearlmutter, and Seidenberg 1994; McDonald and Shillcock 2001). In brief, a word, or word string, will be interpreted in line with its status in the listener's previous linguistic experience. We can expect the strategy to work, in most cases, since speakers also produce language in accordance with frequency norms prevailing in the language. How else do the frequency norms become established, if not through the accumulated produc- tions of a speech community? Should the strategy fail, the listener may need to backtrack and consider other, less likely possibilities. This, however, will involve additional cognitive work on the part of the listener and will result in a slowing-down of the comprehension process.

There is evidence that listeners begin to process an incoming message as soon as the first word has been identified (Trueswell, Tanenhaus, and Kello 1993); listeners do not need to wait until the full sentence is laid out before them. Even the processing of a word may commence as soon as the initial phonetic segments have been identified (Morton 1969). Let us suppose, as an example, that the first word of an utterance is identified as the word *time*. The word could be a noun or a verb; if a noun it could constitute a noun phrase or it could be the first item in an NN compound. Let us further suppose that these various options are kept open until a disambiguating context is encountered. If the second word is *the*, we decide that *time* is a verb; if the second word is *has*, *time* would be identified as a noun, indeed, as a noun phrase; if the second word is *machines*, *time* would be analysed as the first item in an NN compound. Ambiguities might still persist. If the second word is *limits*, we could be dealing with a noun–verb configuration or a nominal compound. The same would be true if the second word happens to be *flies*.

These various options are not equally probable. Corpus data suggest that there are overwhelming odds in favour of *time* being a noun, not a verb,[16] and this is an interpretation which a listener would reasonably choose, in the first instance at least. On the other hand, the probability of *time* constituting the first item of an NN compound is rather low, with *time limit(s)*, *time period(s)*, and *time scale* being the preferred options. In the light of these probabilities, and independently of any semantic considerations, a listener would reasonably opt for analysing *time flies* as a noun–verb sequence. In comparison, *fruit flies* would more likely be taken to be compound noun, not only because *fruit fly* is an established term, but because *fruit* has a pattern of occurring as the first element of a compound. (About one-quarter of all instances of the word in the BNC occur in such a context.)

Probability-based analyses may occasionally be incorrect. We might expect such cases to be comparatively rare. Speakers, no less than listeners, behave in accordance with the probabilities of their language. It could hardly be otherwise.[17] Any occurrence of the word *time* is likely to be a noun, precisely because speakers overwhelmingly use the word as a noun.

The possibility of listeners being misled by initial parsings has been fruitfully mined by psycholinguists investigating the processing of language. There is, namely, a large body of literature devoted to the understanding of so-called GARDEN PATH SENTENCES. These are sentences where initial expectations are frustrated by subsequent context. Garden path sentences are difficult to process, as manifested in the increased time taken for comprehension. The garden path paradigm sheds light on which of the various possibilities a listener or reader initially selects. To the extent that initial parsings are in conformity with frequency data, they provide evidence that listeners not only 'know' the relative frequencies of things in their language, they also draw on this information in language comprehension.

---

[16] Searches of the BNC using part-of-speech tags indicated that nominal uses of *time* (almost 150,000) far outnumber verbal uses (685); a similar ratio was found in the COCA. These numbers, however, turned out to be unreliable. Manual inspection showed that many of the supposedly verbal uses, in both corpora, were in fact nouns. (For example, *time allocations were not specified* was incorrectly reported as a verbal use.) The percentage of verbal uses of *time* is therefore likely to be extremely low. This suspicion was confirmed by manual inspection of 100 randomly selected instances of the word. No examples of *time* used as a verb were found.

[17] Pinker (1994a: 213) aptly notes that garden path sentences are "one of the hallmarks of bad writing". Good writers are those who edit their work from the perspective of a potential reader. It is perhaps worth noting in this connection that examples of ambiguity that linguists like to cite, of the kind *I saw the man with a telescope*, are, almost without exception, invented examples, hardly likely to occur in actual discourse. There is, however, one context in which ambiguities abound, and this is newspaper headlines (in English, at least). The urge to compress a headline into as few words as possible can lead to distortions with respect to statistical probabilities of occurrence.

Perhaps the most famous of garden path sentences is the following, due to Bever (1970):

(8)   The horse raced past the barn fell.

One's initial interpretation is that the horse did the racing, past the barn. This reading is frustrated when we encounter the word *fell*. This forces us to backtrack and reanalyse *The horse raced past the barn* as a nominal, more specifically, as a nominal containing a reduced relative: The horse (which was) raced past the barn.

The availability of the two readings rests on the ambiguity of the word-form *raced*. This could be the past tense form of the verb *race* or it could be the past participle. Manual inspection of fifty examples of *raced* randomly selected from the BNC showed that forty-five (= 90%) were past tense forms.[18] It is therefore not surprising that this is the interpretation which listeners initially select.

As a matter of fact, the notion of past participle itself hides a further ambiguity, namely between a past participle *stricto sensu* (that is, a participle used in the formation of past tenses, as in *has raced, had raced*) and a passive participle, used in passive forms such as *was raced, will be raced*. The ambiguity is systematic; there are no verbs in English which differentiate the two forms. Part of speech tags do not recognize the distinction, both forms being classified as 'past participles'. The distinction is, however, relevant to the case in hand, since we are dealing not only with a past tense vs. reduced relative reading of *the horse raced*, but also with different valencies of the verb *race* and with different semantic roles of *the horse*, namely as the subject of an intransitive verb (the entity which 'races') and the 'causee' of a transitive (the entity which someone 'races', or which 'is raced' by someone). Inspection of the five participial instances of *raced* in the sample referred to above showed that only two occurred in passive constructions. Not only, then, is the participial use of *raced* rather infrequent; even more infrequent is the use of the verb in passive configurations.

All these factors conspire against a listener even entertaining the possibility of a reduced relative interpretation of *the horse raced*. Sentence (8) is rightly famous for the processing difficulties which it presents.

For some verbs in English, the past tense form is phonologically distinct from the past (and passive) participle. *Sing, speak*, and *drink* are examples (*sang* vs. *sung, spoke* vs. *spoken, drank* vs. *drunk*). For most verbs, however, the two forms are identical. This ambiguity has provided a rich source of experimental material. Consider the following two sentences:

---

[18] Once again (see footnote 16), BNC taggings prove unreliable, with many past tense examples of *raced* being incorrectly tagged as past participles.

(9)   a. The woman sent the flowers was pleased.
      b. The woman awarded the prize was pleased.

Both sentences are ambiguous until the word *was* is encountered (McClelland, St John, and Taraban 1989). The reader, having now been primed on example (8), will have no difficulty coming up with the correct interpretations. As a matter of fact, when presented to naïve subjects, both sentences turn out to be considerably easier to process than (8), with (9b) being easier than (9a). Semantic plausibility cannot be the explanation for this difference. There are no reasons for supposing that a woman is more likely to send flowers or to award a prize than she is to be sent flowers or to be awarded a prize. Frequency data, however, suggest that a listener may be differently biased in the two cases. Table 7.7 is based on a random sample of fifty occurrences of the word-forms *sent* and *awarded* extracted from the BNC. (For the sake of comparison, data for the word-form *raced* are included.) As we see, the odds in favour of *awarded* being a passive participle are rather high, almost as high as the chances of *raced* being a past tense. *Sent*, on the other hand, seems to be more evenly split between a passive and a non-passive interpretation.

TABLE 7.7. **Syntactic category of verb forms, based on fifty random examples extracted from the BNC.**

Verb form	as past tense	as past participle	as passive participle
raced	45	3	2
sent	19	4	27
awarded	4	2	44

The ambiguity of the word sequences *the woman sent* and *the woman awarded* is not only a matter of the status of the verbal form. Also at issue is the semantic role of the nominal: on one interpretation the woman is the Agent, on the other she is the Recipient. Table 7.8 shows the semantic role of nominals in construction with *sent* and *raced*. The Recipient role is extremely rare in this configuration, an explanation,

TABLE 7.8. **Semantic role of nominals in the configurations [NP sent] and [NP awarded], based on fifty random examples extracted from the BNC.**

Verb form	NP as Agent	NP as Patient	NP as Recipient
sent	33	17	0
awarded	20	29	1

no doubt, for why the reduced relative is unlikely to be a listener's first parsing option in any of the sentences.

The effects illustrated above are independent of considerations of semantic plausibility. Trueswell (1996), on the basis of corpus data, distinguished between 'high-PP' (= past participle) verbs and 'low-PP' verbs. The distinction concerns the frequency with which the *-ed* form of the verb is used as a participle as opposed to a past tense form.

low-PP: entertain, help, hunt, lift, love, request, scratch, search, want, watch

high-PP: accept, accuse, adopt, consider, describe, expect, propose, record, release, select

Consider, in this light, the following fragments:

(10)   a. The manager entertained...
       b. The woman scratched...

(11)   a. The witness accused...
       b. The mailman expected...

The fragments in (10) contain low-PP verbs; accordingly, these are likely to be interpreted as NP V sequences. Those in (11), however, are also open to reduced relative clause interpretation. Here are some possible continuations of these fragments:

(12)   a. The manager entertained by the comedian left in high spirits.
       b. The woman scratched by the cat was seriously hurt. (low-PP)

(13)   a. The witness accused by the investigator had no real alibi.
       b. The mailman expected by the doctor arrived much too late. (high-PP)

In (12), the continuation conflicts with the low-PP status of the verb forms, whereas in (13) the high-PP status of the verb form is confirmed. It turns out that the sentences in (12) are more difficult to process than those in (13).

In the above examples, both interpretations of the *-ed* forms are semantically plausible. Consider, now, the following:

(14)   a. The bricks lifted by the crane were deposited on the roof.
       b. The alternatives considered by the committee had some limitations.

It would make no sense to suppose that the bricks did the lifting or that the alternatives did the considering. *Lift*, however, is a low-PP verb while *consider* is a high-PP verb. Is this fact likely to slow down the interpretation of (14a)? Trueswell (1996) reports that it does. Irrespective of the semantics of the sentence, the word-form *lifted* is biased towards an interpretation as a past tense form.

To conclude this section I return to the alternative complementation patterns of verbs such as *confirm* and *believe*, mentioned earlier in this chapter. Recall that a verb such as *believe* is biased towards a clausal complement vis-à-vis a nominal complement, while other verbs, such as *confirm*, are biased towards an NP complement. Trueswell, Tanenhaus, and Kello (1993) showed that non-preferred complements slowed down the comprehension process (see also Wilson and Garnsey 2008; Zeschel 2008). Gahl and Garnsey (2004) extended from this finding by showing that these biases are able to influence speech production. Subjects read aloud sentences where the verb is followed by its preferred or non-preferred complement. It was found that when a verb is followed by its non-preferred complement (*believe* + NP; *confirm* + clause), speaking rate is slower and there is less chance that the final t/d of the verb is deleted. It is as if speakers pay more attention to their speech when they are uttering non-preferred sequences, while preferred sequences can be articulated with less care. Interestingly, the effects reported by Gahl and Garnsey do not concern the frequency of words as such, nor the frequency of word combinations. It is not the frequency of the word string *believed the interviewer* that affects a speaker's behaviour, but the probability that *the interviewer* will be the direct object vs. the subject of an embedded clause. The conclusion must be, once again, that speakers of a language have a remarkably accurate knowledge of the relative frequencies of the structures in question in association with specific verbs.

Productivity

In addition to the psycholinguistic evidence that speakers know the relative frequency of elements in their language, there is also language-internal evidence for speakers' implicit knowledge. We have already referred to the phenomenon of drift (p. 131), whereby a frequently used form may acquire a certain degree of autonomy vis-à-vis the parts from which it is constructed (and the schema to which it conforms). It may become associated with a distinctive semantics or with special conditions of use, or it may undergo various phonological processes, such as elision, assimilation, and reduction.

Another manifestation of frequency, though in this case the relation is less direct, has to do with productivity. While speakers may mentally register the expressions that they encounter—a major thesis of this book—they are not restricted to verbatim repetitions of encountered usage. They are able to generalize over the expressions that they encounter and to create new expressions in conformity with these generalizations.[19] A generalization—or, in Cognitive Grammar terms, a schema—is productive to the extent that it is able to sanction new instances, over and above the

---

[19] They are also able to innovate vis-à-vis the generalizations that they have abstracted, as will be discussed in Chs. 11 and 12.

instances on whose basis it was abstracted. A schema is unproductive if the set of instances which it sanctions is to all intents and purposes closed.

Productivity is not a direct function of frequency of occurrence. One of the most frequent words in English is the indefinite article *a*. Before a vowel-initial word the article appears as *an*, with an epenthetic 'n'. The occurrence of the epenthetic 'n' is, perforce, rather common. The frequency of the phenomenon has not caused speakers to insert a linking 'n' elsewhere in the language. Forms such as *the* [n] *apple* are unthinkable. What renders epenthetic 'n' unproductive is, precisely, the highly entrenched status of the idiosyncratic form of the indefinite article.[20]

As argued by Bybee (1995), Baayen and Lieber (1991), and Baayen and Renouf (1996), the entrenchment of instances is likely to militate against the productivity of a schema. What is likely to enhance schema productivity is, on the contrary, an array of instances, many of which are of low frequency and not subject to semantic or phonological drift. Symptomatic of this state of affairs, with respect to word formation processes, are the occurrences of hapaxes (that is, word-forms attested only once in a corpus), or, in the case of syntax, novel word combinations.[21] Unproductive schemas, on the other hand, are associated with a fixed number of instances, which recur as a corpus increases in size.

Productivity is a matter of degree and has been studied mainly in relation to patterns for word formation. Consider, for example, three processes for the creation of nouns, involving the suffixes *-th* [θ], *-ity*, and *-ness*. The first is associated with a half dozen or so nouns (*depth, length, width, strength*, and a few more). Note that these nouns involve a change in vowel quality vis-à-vis the base adjective; the relation between the noun and the adjective is therefore not fully transparent. Indeed, for some nouns in *-th*, such as *wealth* and *health*, the base forms (*weal, hale*) are no longer extant. Not surprisingly, the suffix is almost completely unproductive (the recent innovation *coolth* notwithstanding: see Rosenbach 2007). The second suffix, *-ity*, is also relatively unproductive, in spite of the large though stable number of nouns which are formed in this way. The most productive of the three suffixes is, of course, *-ness*. If, in the present context, I were to speak of the 'productiveness' of the suffix, the usage would probably not strike the reader as outrageous. The suffix can be—and is—attached to just about any adjective, even if a conventionalized alternative is available.

---

[20] In older forms of English, epenthetic 'n' occurred more widely, as when possessive *my* and *thy* preceded a vowel-commencing word. Relics of this usage still persist: witness the somewhat jocular *mine host* (with twelve attestations in the BNC, though none in the COCA) as well as archaicizing uses of *mine eyes, thine enemies*, and the like, often with allusions to Shakespeare or the King James bible.

[21] The same goes for words and their collocations. Compare the words *unmitigated* and *foregone* in attributive (i.e. prenominal) position. The latter is virtually restricted to the collocation *a foregone conclusion*. The productivity of *foregone*, in this environment, is close to zero. While *unmitigated disaster* is also a common collocation, the attributive use of *unmitigated* is moderately productive, in that the word is able to modify, if only infrequently, a wide and potentially open-ended set of nouns.

Clausner and Croft (1997) insightfully applied this account of morphological productivity to the study of metaphors. A conceptual metaphor such as THE VALIDITY OF AN ARGUMENT IS THE STRUCTURAL INTEGRITY OF A BUILDING can sanction an open-ended set of metaphorical expressions. We can 'strengthen the foundations' of a building/ argument; we can say of both kinds of entity that it has a 'solid base', that it is 'shaky', or that it can easily be 'knocked down' or 'demolished'. While the metaphorical basis of *spill the beans* is also transparent, the underlying metaphor is not at all productive. We cannot generate new expressions based on the notion that revealing confidential information is scattering the contents of a container. Idiom variability might also be seen in this light. The lexical variation associated with the frighten idiom (pp. 77ff) testifies to its productivity, while the lexical rigidity of *pull someone's leg* shows the idiom to be unproductive.

In contrast to word formation processes—which, by common consent, display varying degrees of productivity—syntax is often thought of as the domain of fully productive processes. Some syntactic schemas are indeed highly productive. Consider, for example, the schema for a transitive clause [NP V NP] or for a prepositional phrase [P NP]. It is not just the fact that we encounter a large number of different instances of these schemas. Equally important is the fact that the instances are not, in general, very well entrenched. Moreover, we are continuously being confronted with new instances. Even syntactic schemas which might not occur very frequently might still be productive. The *way*-construction (p. 136) is a case in point. A wide range of verbs is attested in the construction (e.g. *She danced her way to fame and fortune*: Goldberg 2006: 100; see also Goldberg 1995) in association with a great variety of prepositional phrases. Nevertheless, even highly productive syntactic schemas may be associated with idiosyncratic restrictions, as extensively discussed in Chapters 2 and 3. We noted that a number of 'transfer' verbs fail to occur in the ditransitive construction (p. 28) while some transitive verbs do not readily passivize (p. 478). In fact, there is probably no such thing as a fully productive schema, unconstrained by idiosyncratic restrictions on its instances.

Subjective estimates of frequency

In this chapter I have reviewed converging evidence that frequency information is an important aspect of a speaker's linguistic knowledge. To round off the discussion, let us consider the direct evidence for speakers' knowledge. Do speakers have reliable intuitions about the relative incidence of elements of their language, as measured against corpus-based data?

There are a number of ways to tap into frequency intuitions. One strategy is to ask subjects to judge the relative frequency of two or more items (near synonyms, for example). Another is to ask subjects to rank a set of items for their relative frequency or to assess their frequency on 5- or 7-point scale. One of the earliest studies (Tryk

1968) attempted to obtain numerical estimates of a word's occurrence in a person's linguistic experience. Tryk presented subjects (undergraduate psychology students) with a list of words and asked them to estimate the frequency with which the words are used by 'the average American'. The instructions were as follows:

Your task is to estimate how often the average American uses each of the following words in his [*sic*] conversation. Imagine how often he might speak a given word during any convenient time period. For example, if he uses the word X about five times per day, then write in the space next to the word X, ' 5 : : day.' If he uses the word Y about once every two years, write for the word Y, '1 : : 2 years,' etc., for each word. If you think he would *never* use a word, write 'never' in the space. Be as accurate as you can, but work rapidly.   (Tryk 1968: 172)

Alongside this estimate of 'public' frequency, subjects were also asked for 'private estimations', concerning how often they would use a word during a certain time interval.

Tryk's results, based on 100 nouns, mostly monosyllables and ranging from rare to very common, showed that the two procedures correlated closely; they also accorded with objective corpus-based measures. Indeed, Tryk went so far as to claim that the subjective estimates might in some circumstances be superior to corpus-based data:

The results indicate that the subjective estimation-procedure may provide quite adequate data when an investigator has need to measure frequencies of words (or phonemes, morphemes, phrases, etc.) not adequately sampled by the word counts. The method may be particularly valuable when the word counts are suspected of misrepresenting the probable frequency of a set of words such as those of special significance in a regional or subcultural dialect, those taken from a foreign language, or obscenities.   (Tryk 1968: 176)

Frequency judgements have been investigated under more controlled conditions. Hintzman (1969) presented subjects with a word list consisting of 320 items. Some of the words on the list occurred only once, others occurred two, four, six and ten times. Subsequently, subjects were asked to judge the frequency with which words had been presented. Their frequency estimates were a logarithmic function of actual frequency, that is to say, the frequency of the more frequent words tended to be underestimated vis-à-vis that of the less frequent words.

Half a century of research has confirmed that speakers' subjective judgements do indeed correspond, by and large, to objective measures of frequency, as established from corpora, or, in more recent research, Internet searches (Balota, Pilotti, and Cortese 2001; Carroll 1971; Shapiro 1969). Even non-native speakers have a pretty good idea about the relative frequency of words in the target language (Schmitt and Dunham 1999).

There are, to be sure, a number of methodological issues associated with this kind of research (Alderson 2007; McGee 2008). As noted, there are different ways in which frequency estimates can be elicited. A further question concerns the possible confusion, for subjects, between frequency and familiarity and between their estimate of their own use and that of others. An important question, also, concerns the data against which subjective estimates are to be evaluated. Earlier studies had to rely on the Thorndike and Lorge (1944) word count, first compiled in 1921 as a resource for school teachers and subsequently updated to reflect a written corpus of about 18 million words. Even for more recent word counts, based on large electronic corpora, there is no guarantee that corpus data will match the linguistic experience of an individual subject, and indeed it has been reported that the estimates of more educated, well-read subjects tend to correlate more closely with corpus-based results (Balota, Pilotti, and Cortese 2001).

A particular point of interest are cases of gross discrepancies between speakers' subjective estimates and corpus-based data, discrepancies which would be difficult to account for in terms of the unreliability of the corpus, the peculiar linguistic history of a subject, or the nature of the experimental task. We have already referred to Popiel and McRae's (1988) study (p. 75), in which subjects massively over-reported the frequency of idioms such as *kick the bucket* and *spill the beans*; these were assessed at 5.9 and 5.75 respectively on a seven-point scale ranging from 1 (= never encountered) to 7 (= encountered everyday). On the other hand, estimates of some words appear to be under-reported. Alderson (2007: 399) gives the example of the verb *draw*.

Some possible causes of these discrepancies are addressed by McGee (2008). He refers to Tversky and Kahneman (1973), who argue that a person judges the frequency of an event in terms of the ease of generating an exemplar of the event; frequency, in other words, tends to be confounded with availability. It is plausible, therefore, that subjects overestimate the frequency of idioms precisely because it is relatively easy to generate a situation in which the idiom might be used. Indeed, the more contentful and semantically coherent an expression, the more available it is likely to be and the easier it will be to imagine a context in which it might be used. Under-reporting of the frequency of a word such as *draw*, on the other hand, may be due to the fact that the phraseological uses of the word (*draw a conclusion, draw to a close, draw up a plan*) may have been overlooked, with subjects generating examples pertaining only to the 'lexical' meaning, having to do with making marks on paper with a pencil. Sinclair (1991: 113) made a similar point, noting that a common verb like *take* tends not to elicit the word's typical collocations, such as *take a look*. These observations link up with findings reported in Chapter 6, concerning the entrenchment of frequently used expressions (pp. 130–1). The very fact that an expression is in frequent use tends to obscure its internal structure.

In conclusion

Frequency effects are pervasive throughout the grammar. No matter which element of language structure we choose to study, we find that some exponents occur more frequently than others. For the most part, the skewed frequencies cannot be explained in terms of the vicissitudes of the external world or in terms of speakers' referential intentions. For one thing, non-meaning-bearing elements of a language, such as the vowels and consonants, are subject to frequency effects which are just as robust as those associated with words and word combinations.

In this chapter I have documented a number of examples of skewed frequencies. The main burden of the chapter, however, has been to argue that frequency effects are not simply a matter of language-as-used, but are an intrinsic aspect of a person's language knowledge. Speakers know the relative frequencies of the various elements which make up their language. Frequency influences performance on all manner of linguistic tasks, not the least of which is the comprehension of potentially ambiguous sentences. Frequency is also implicated, albeit indirectly, in the productive application of schemas to new instances. It is as if, in the course of a lifetime's exposure, speakers have been keeping a mental tally of the number of times they have encountered the words, the sounds, and the constructions of their language.

8

Skewed frequencies as a design feature of language

The ubiquity and pervasiveness of skewed frequencies raises some basic questions for linguistic theory. Why should the various elements of a language—the phonemes, the consonant clusters, the words and word combinations, and all the rest—be associated with distinct frequency distributions, distributions which in most cases are independent of the semantic intentions of speakers and which are remarkably stable across comparable text samples? Note that at this point we are not asking why a particular word, such as *mishap*, should be less frequent than another word, such as *accident*, or why the DRESS vowel of English is more frequent than the TRAP vowel, or why *sent* and *awarded* differ in their occurrence as past tense forms or as past and passive participles. We are asking why such skewings should exist at all and why they should be so robust.

In this chapter I consider three approaches to this question. (The approaches are not mutually exclusive.) First, we can consider skewed frequencies to be an emergent property of any language-like system. On this view, the mere use of the system will give rise to, and perpetuate, frequency effects. No predictions can be made as to which elements will emerge as more frequent, only that *some* elements will end up more frequent than others and that the frequency distributions will be strengthened through further usage.

A second approach—markedness theory—does make predictions. Markedness theory deals mostly in binary contrasts, maintaining that the unmarked member of a contrast will be more frequent, both within a single language and across languages. (As we shall see, markedness is also claimed to correlate with a number of other properties of the items in question.) Given its focus on binary contrasts, the theory is relevant only to those areas of a language which are amenable to a description in such terms. In addition to problems inherent in the theory itself, the theory has little to say about the relative frequencies of items which do not participate in any obvious way in markedness relations.

A third approach sees frequency effects in relation to learnability. A requirement of any language is that it must be learnable by new generations of speakers. Language learning proceeds, most of the time, without explicit instruction. Learners must therefore be able to infer the properties of a language on the basis of exposure. I will defend the hypothesis that a crucial factor in the learnability of language is, precisely, the skewed frequencies of its various elements. A language each of whose elements occurred with equal frequency would be impossible to learn and could therefore not be transmitted to future generations of speakers. It is in this sense that we can regard skewed frequencies as a design feature of human language(s).

Skewed frequencies as an emergent property of language

It is difficult to even imagine a language without frequency effects. In such a language, every sound, syllable, word, and construction would have an equal probability of occurring. While such a language might be maximally efficient (in the sense that all the elements of a subsystem are 'put to work' to an equal degree) it would be a less than optimal tool for communication. This is because the language would lack REDUNDANCY.[1] The redundancy of natural languages makes it possible for hearers and readers (provided that they are proficient in the language in question) to anticipate the future choices that a speaker or writer is going to make. They are also able to guess, often with considerable accuracy, the identity of elements which have been missed through inattention or obscured by background noise. Without redundancy, any error in encoding, transmission, or reception would be fatal to comprehension.

Two aspects of human languages contribute to redundancy. One is the skewed frequency of basic units, such as the vowels and the consonants, or, in the written language, the letters. As every Scrabble player knows, the letters Q and X are 'worth more' than E and R, due to their lower overall frequency in the written language. A second contributing factor is TRANSITIONAL PROBABILITIES between the basic elements. Given the occurrence of the letter Q, the identity of the next letter—U—can be predicted with almost total certainty, independently of the overall frequency of U in the writing system. Similarly, to take an example from Chapter 7, the occurrence of the word *unmitigated* greatly increases the chances that the following word will be *disaster*, rather than any other word in the language. Transitional probabilities have to do with the fact that the occurrence of one element tends to correlate, either positively or negatively, with the occurrence of other elements in its near or

---

[1] For redundancy (and its converse, information content), see Shannon and Weaver (1963 [1949]: 7–16). The information H in a system is given by:

$$H = \Sigma p_i \log_2 p_i$$

where p_i is the probability of occurrence of each term in the system. H will range between 1 (maximum information, where each term is equiprobable) to vanishingly small, as probabilities become increasingly skewed.

immediate vicinity. Indeed, as was pointed out in Chapter 7, it is not only the basic elements of a language—the sounds and the words—which exhibit skewed frequencies; of equal, if not greater importance are the skewed frequencies of combinations of words and sounds, and the degree of attraction between words and the constructions in which they are liable to occur.[2]

Apart from the fact that a language without skewed frequencies would be a far from optimal instrument for communication, the notion is incoherent from another point of view. This is because the very act of using the language would skew the probabilities in favour of the items being used. Imagine a language in which each syllable type had an equal probability of occurrence. If an utterance commences with a certain syllable, this fact alone raises the probability of occurrence of this syllable vis-à-vis all others in the language. Any future choices in the language will therefore not be choices amongst an array of equiprobable items. Continued use of the language would reinforce these disparities. Tambovtsev and Martindale consider the matter from the perspective of phoneme frequencies:

We could assume a very unlikely stream of speech in which each of the phonemes has been used once. The next phoneme would be chosen at random with each having a probability of $1/n$, where n is the number of available phonemes. The next phoneme would be chosen at random from the set of phonemes, one of which now had a probability of $2/n$ of being chosen. After a few recursions, some phonemes ... will be very common and some very uncommon.

(Tambovtsev and Martindale 2007: 9)

These considerations reinforce a point made in Chapter 1, concerning the dialectic relation between language as used (E-language) and language as represented in the mind (I-language). A speaker's use of a particular option is the product of her I-language, itself a distillation of her experience of the E-language. The listener, likewise, will be inclined to parse an incoming signal in accordance with the probabilities and expectations generated by his I-language. The communicative event will modify, if only minimally, the I-language of both speaker and hearer, by increasing the probability of the selected form.

Consider in this light some aspects of the comprehension process, discussed in Chapter 7. In principle there is no reason why the *-ed* forms of certain verbs should be biased towards the past tense, the past participle, or the passive participle. Yet such biases exist and they appear to be known to language users who draw on this

---

[2] The redundancy of language is exploited in the so-called CLOZE PROCEDURE. Here, every nth word (typically, every seventh word) of a text is replaced by a blank and subjects are required to guess the identity of the deleted items. Cloze procedure was developed to estimate the readability of a text; the higher the closure rate, the more readable the text (Wilson Taylor 1953). The procedure was subsequently employed as a means for estimating the proficiency of foreign and second language learners (Oller 1979). A variant of the standard cloze test, the so-called C-test, requires the second half of every second word to be restored. The C-test is claimed to have higher validity as a test of language proficiency (Klein-Braley 1997).

knowledge in their parsing of incoming speech. For this reason, *the woman awarded* ... is more likely to be given a passive interpretation than *the woman sent* ..., while a passive interpretation of *the horse raced* ... would hardly ever be entertained. A person who wished to speak about a horse which had been raced would be inclined to use the full relative clause, being aware of the problems that would be caused by the use of a reduced relative. In this way, the behaviour of both speaker and hearer entrenches the frequency biases already existing in the E-language (and, perforce, in their respective I-languages). There are, of course, circumstances in which a statistically less preferred form might be used. If such were not the case the less preferred forms would simply disappear from the language. We might suppose, however, that contextual information is able to prime the listener for the less expected option. When heard out of the blue, *time* would almost certainly be taken to be a noun. However, the context *I want to* ... would obviously activate the verbal sense of the word, as would a preceding imperative (*Take out your stopwatch and time* ...). If such special uses were to become more common, the frequency profile of the element in question would change; the rare form might end up being not so rare after all. A number of scholars have suggested that precisely this kind of process underlies language change. A well-known example concerns the consolidation of English as a V-O language, that is, as a language in which the direct object follows the verb, in contrast to earlier stages of the language in which the object preceded the verb (Lightfoot 1979).

Markedness

Markedness theory is based on the observation that whenever a set of choices exists one option often counts as the default; it is the option that is selected unless one of the others is specifically indicated. Markedness serves to promote the redundancy of the system in that the unmarked choice, being more predictable, conveys less information (in Shannon and Weaver's sense) than the marked choice(s). Markedness generally operates over binary choices, that is, choices between one of two alternatives. In many, though by no means all cases, the choice can be seen in terms of the presence or absence of a particular feature, whereby the marked choice consists in the addition of a feature to the unmarked option.

As an example, consider the status of a vowel as oral or nasal. In principle, a vowel could be either. It turns out, however, that most vowels in most languages are oral; only very few languages have nasal vowels which contrast with oral vowels and in these languages the nasal vowels are fewer in number than the oral vowels and occur less frequently in running text. According to most accounts of the language, French has twelve oral vowels and four nasal vowels, a ratio of 3:1. Token frequencies are even more skewed. Greenberg (1966: 18) reports that the ratio of oral to nasal vowels in the first thousand vowels in Stendhal's *Le rouge et le noir* is 4.71:1.

Markedness theory can be brought to bear on stop consonant frequencies reported in Chapter 7 (p. 163). Given their higher overall frequency, alveolars would be regarded as unmarked vis-à-vis labials and velars, voiceless stops as unmarked vis-à-vis voiced stops, while the voiced and voiceless stops taken together are unmarked vis-à-vis nasal stops. These relations are not peculiar to English. Greenberg (1966) and Zipf (1935) report similar data from a number of languages.

There are many subsystems in a language which can be analysed in terms of markedness. Singular can be regarded as unmarked vis-à-vis plural, affirmative polarity as unmarked vis-à-vis negative, active voice as unmarked vis-à-vis passive. Three-way contrasts might also be handled in this way; for example, the singular–dual–plural contrast found in some languages can be analysed as singular (unmarked) vs. non-singular and plural (unmarked) vs. dual. A well-known example of markedness concerns complementary opposites, such as *long–short, wide–narrow, high–low*. The dimension itself is designated by the positive item; we speak of the length, width, and height of a thing, rather than its shortness, narrowness, or lowness. We enquire how long something is, even though the thing itself might be quite short. We say of a narrow gap that it is only a millimetre wide, not a millimetre narrow. Not surprisingly, the positive terms turn out to have a higher text frequency than the corresponding negative terms.

Greenberg (1966) pointed to a number of accompaniments of markedness, in addition to frequency of occurrence. These include:

- *Syncretism.* This has to do with the fact that contrasts which are operative in the unmarked option may be absent in the marked option. In German, singular nouns (in the nominative case) take one of the three definite determiners, *der, die*, or *das*, according to their gender, while plural nouns, whatever their gender, take the determiner *die*. This is in line with the view that plural is marked vis-à-vis singular.
- *Phonological substance.* It is often the case that the marked option contains more phonological material than the unmarked form. In many languages, for example, plurals are formed by adding material to the singulars.[3]
- *Irregularities.* Unmarked categories tend to be associated with a greater degree of irregularity than marked forms. Consider, for example, the verbal paradigms in Romance languages. The irregular verbs typically display a greater degree of

---

[3] There are, of course, many examples where this does not hold. Singular and plural might be signalled by different morphemes, of the same length, as in Italian. Cases where the singular form is longer than the plural are not unknown, though they are comparatively rare. An example is the Māori singular demonstratives *teenei/teenaa* 'this/that' vs. plural *eenei/eenaa* 'these/those'. Welsh also has a few examples, e.g. singular *pysgodyn* 'fish', *coeden* 'tree', and *aderyn* 'bird', whose plurals are, respectively, *pysgod, coed*, and *ader*.

irregularity in the present indicative (the unmarked option) than in any other tense or mood.

- *Neutralization*. This is where a potential contrast is, as it were, put in abeyance. In such circumstances, the unmarked form will be used to cover both options. In compound nouns, such as *bird-watcher* or *home-owner*, the first element lacks the plural inflection, irrespective of how many birds or how many homes are involved, in accordance with the unmarked status of the singular. The word *day* can contrast with *night*; the word may also be used to refer to a 24-hour period, thus neutralizing the day–night contrast (Coseriu 1977). Even so, markedness reversals do occur. You would probably count your length of stay in a hotel as so many nights rather than as so many days. It used to be the case in English that the masculine pronoun *he* was used when the sex of the referent was unknown or irrelevant, confirming the unmarked status of masculine vis-à-vis feminine. Nowadays, speakers are careful to state both options in the awkward locution *he or she*; alternatively, they use the plural form *they* (though with singular meaning) as an unmarked pronoun. This usage would imply that plural was unmarked vis-à-vis singular, thus contradicting quite a lot of indications that singular is the unmarked option.

A number of linguistic theories explicitly incorporate notions of markedness. Markedness, for example, plays a crucial role in Halliday's systemic-functional grammar (Halliday 1991).[4] The notion is especially associated with phonological theories. In so-called underspecification theory (Archangeli 1988; Stoel-Gammon and Stemberger 1994) it is proposed that the underlying representation of a segment needs to be specified only for the marked values of its features, the unmarked values being predictable by rule. Thus, assuming that [alveolar] is the unmarked value for consonant place of articulation, alveolars do not need to be specified as such, in contrast to labials and velars, which do need to be specified. If one were to assume further that [stop] is the unmarked value for a consonant, and, moreover, that [–voice] is the unmarked value for word-final consonants, the final segment of a word such as *bit* needs to be specified only as [consonant], all the other features being supplied by markedness rules.[5]

The explanatory and predictive power of markedness theory has not gone un-challenged. Lass (1975) has been particularly scathing, claiming that the notion is

---

[4] Halliday distinguishes between those contrasts where each option is equally likely to occur (the choice of present vs. past tense being one of his examples) and contrasts where one option is unmarked (affirmative vs. negative polarity). He hypothesizes that the frequency ratio of unmarked to marked will approximate to 10:1 and cites some evidence in support.

[5] It will be observed that underspecification theory represents yet another variation on the theme of the predictable vs. the idiosyncratic (see pp. 34–5). It is based on the distinction between those aspects of a language which can be derived by rule and which therefore do not have to be stated and those which have to be specifically listed.

essentially tautological, the term 'unmarked' being used for whatever option happens to be the more frequent. Haspelmath (2006: 63) also concludes that the contrast between marked and unmarked may capture little more than "the sense of everyday words like uncommon/common, abnormal/normal, unusual/usual, unexpected/expected". Indeed, markedness accounts often have a *post hoc* quality to them. Consider again the case of oral vs. nasal vowels. In terms of markedness theory, nasalization is a feature which is added to the articulation of a vowel. However, there is no a priori reason, it seems to me, for regarding nasal vowels as inherently more complex, or containing more features, than oral vowels; we declare [+nasal] to be an added feature because that is how the markedness relation plays out.[6] The theory also comes under pressure from exceptions and markedness reversals. We have already noted some examples. The use of *they* as a gender-neutral (singular) pronoun conflicts with considerable evidence that points to plurals being marked vis-à-vis singulars. In such cases, we might want to set up local markedness relations, which override more general relations operative in a language. Once we go down this track, the notion of markedness becomes vacuous. We declare an option to be unmarked simply because it is more frequent. It amounts to little more than the claim that "whatever is more likely to happen is more likely to happen" (Lass 1997: 330).

Categorization

The thesis that I would like to propose in this chapter is that skewed frequencies promote the learnability of language. I address this issue by first considering some aspects of categorization. Hopefully, the relevance of this discussion will soon become apparent.

I take my cue from Labov, who stated that a central issue in linguistic theory is categorization (Labov 1973: 342). Every time we describe a scene using language we have to categorize its various elements and the relations between them. We have to decide whether to refer to the thing in front of us as 'a cup', 'a vase', 'a bowl', 'a receptacle', or indeed, quite simply, as 'a thing'. When describing the location of an entity vis-à-vis a landmark we need to categorize the spatial relation as an 'in' relation, an 'on' relation, an 'at' relation, or whatever it may be. Importantly, language itself is also a system of categories. Sounds must be categorized as instances of phonemes, sequences of sounds as instances of words, word sequences as instances of constructions, and so on (Taylor 2003*b*).

---

[6] The reason why nasal vowels are relatively infrequent and are less numerous than their oral counterparts may have nothing to do with feature complexity but with the manner in which the sounds are perceived. By reason of their formant structure, nasal vowels are less distinct, perceptually, than the corresponding oral vowels (Johnson 1997: 159). On the role of perceptual contrast in the structure of phoneme inventories, see Liljencrants and Lindblom (1972).

A central topic in categorization research has been how to define a category. (For a review, see Murphy 2002.) Additional questions concern the way in which categories are acquired, what their internal structure is, and what constitutes a 'good', or 'viable' category.

On the CLASSICAL APPROACH to categorization, a category is defined in terms of a set of features, each of which is necessary and which together are sufficient. The classical approach captures the intuition that all members of a category have to have something in common; otherwise, why place the things in the same category? Thus, 'bachelor' may be defined as the conjunction of the features [+human], [+adult], [+male], and [−married]. As many scholars have argued, this approach is problematic, not least because it fails to predict the well-documented fact that some members of a category may be considered to be better, or more representative members than others.[7]

It was in response to the shortcomings of the classical theory that Rosch developed her theory of PROTOTYPE CATEGORIES. The theory went through several stages of development (Taylor 2008). On the basis of her research on colour, Rosch initially proposed that a category could be defined in terms of a single best example and that things belonged to a category to the extent that they resembled the prototype (Rosch 1975). For more complex notions, such as 'fruit' or 'furniture', a more sophisticated theory was needed. For these kinds of categories, Rosch proposed that the prototype need not be constituted by any particular instance; rather, prototypicality was defined in terms of features which could differentiate the category from neighbouring categories (Rosch and Mervis 1975). The approach entailed that features could be weighted according to how well they cued category membership, whereby the category prototype maximizes the diagnostic value of its features. In her later work, Rosch was to emphasize the cultural embeddedness of categories and their role in speakers' practices and beliefs (Rosch 1978; see also Murphy and Medin 1985). She insisted, for example, that features are not objectively given, the same for all observers: features are those similarities amongst entities that speakers perceive to be relevant to their concerns.

Parallel to Rosch's work, a number of researchers explored the possibility of an EXEMPLAR THEORY of categories. On this approach, a category is simply a collection of remembered instances (Medin and Schaffer 1978; Smith and Medin 1981). A person's 'bird' category is constituted by a memory store of all the things that have been called 'birds'. Likewise, an English speaker's representation of the KIT vowel consists in memory traces of the acoustic properties of previously encountered instances (Pierrehumbert 2001, 2002). New instances are categorized in virtue of their resemblance to already encountered exemplars, while the statistical centre of the category emerges

---

[7] The bachelor example is discussed in more detail in Chapter 10 (p. 238).

as the category prototype. In its pure form, exemplar theory denies that people make generalizations at all over encountered instances. Computer simulations have shown that exemplar models are able to replicate many of the experimental findings on human categorization, including a range of prototype effects (Hintzman 1986; Kruschke 1992). Mixed theories might also be entertained. Instances which closely resemble each other coalesce into a schematic representation which captures their commonality and filters out the idiosyncratic detail (Ross and Makin 1999).

A major deficit of the classical model is that it says nothing about which categories are likely to be useful to language users. It is easy to invent a category defined by a combination of ad hoc features. We can invent a category defined by the features [green], [weighs over 20kg], and [made in 1980]. Although perfectly well-formed in terms of the classical theory, it seems fair to say that such a category would never be named by a word in any human language. One reason for this is that such a category fails to fit in with broader systems of knowledge and belief.

We can also consider the matter from a functional perspective. As Rosch and others have emphasized, the function of a category is to minimize uncertainty and thereby to facilitate our interaction with the environment. On observing only one or two features of an entity, a person may make a reasonable inference concerning what kind of thing it is. Having done this, he may then be able to infer further properties of the thing. If it looks like a tiger, chances are that it is one, and you would be well advised not to approach it. The classical theory does not permit this kind of inferential reasoning. The only way to determine whether entity e is a member of category C is to check off e for all the features which define C. Thereafter, nothing further can be said about e.

As the tiger example shows, there are two stages of the inferencing process. On the one hand, the presence of a feature may strongly suggest that an entity is a member of a certain category; this is the CUE VALIDITY of the feature. On the other hand, the knowledge that an entity is a member of a certain category may allow inferences to be made about the features of the entity; let us refer to this as CATEGORY VALIDITY (Murphy 2002: 215).

> *Cue validity.* A feature has high cue validity to the extent that possession of the feature makes it possible to predict membership in a category. The cue validity of feature f with respect to category C is the probability of C given f, i.e. $p(C \mid f)$. For example, if a creature is able to fly, what is the probability that the creature is a bird? Quite high, obviously, though not 100 per cent; you may be dealing with a butterfly, a bat, or an aeroplane. On the other hand, having a liver has virtually zero cue validity for the bird category. Although all birds do indeed have a liver, so too do countless other creatures. It is the features with the highest cue validity which are most heavily weighted in a characterization of the category prototype.

Category validity. This has to do with the probability that a member of category C will exhibit feature *f*, i.e. $p(f \mid C)$. Suppose we learn that something is a bird. What is the probability that it will fly? The probability is quite high, though not 100 per cent, since some birds are flightless. On the other hand, to take up a previous example, the probability that the creature will have a liver is 100 per cent.

It is the interaction of cue and category validity which makes it possible for categories to be cognitively useful. If we observe that a creature waddles like a duck, we may reasonably infer that it is a duck (cue validity). If it is a duck, we may again reasonably infer that it will quack, and will taste nice when cooked in orange sauce (category validity). We also see why an invented category like the one proposed earlier, defined by the features [green], [weighs over 20kg], and [made in 1980], would be cognitively useless. Each of the proposed features lacks cue validity for the category in question. The fact that something might have been made in 1980 is a very poor cue to membership in the category since there are countless other things, not in the category, that were made in 1980; likewise for the two other features. The category would also lack category validity. Once membership in the category has been determined no further properties can be predicted of the entity; this is because possession of the three named features would not correlate with the possession (or indeed the absence) of any other feature. The category would be virtually useless.

The usefulness of a category is thus dependent on features being correlated, either positively or negatively. According to Rosch,

the perceived world is not an unstructured total set of equiprobable co-occurring attributes. Rather, the material objects of the world are perceived to possess...high correlational structure.... [C]ombinations of what we perceive as the attributes of real objects do not occur uniformly.   (Rosch 1978: 29)

It is the fact that things which build nests in trees also tend to be things which have beaks and lay eggs which promotes the emergence of the category 'bird'. If these features were randomly distributed over the things which populate the world there would be no basis for forming the category in the first place. In brief, it is the skewed distribution of features over entities which makes the emergence of categories possible.

It will be noted that Rosch, in the above-cited passage, was careful to refer, not to the correlation of attributes in the world, but to the correlation of attributes that we *perceive* in the world. The nuance introduces a subjective and cultural dimension to the categories that we appeal to in interacting with the world. Whether or not a particular attribute is relevant, or indeed how the attribute is to be characterized, may be dependent on the needs and cultural values of a community of speakers. If such were not the case, we should expect that the categorization of the world would be identical for all humans and that the categories would change only if the world was to change. One of most important of the cultural influences on categorization is, of course, language itself. In perceiving the correlation of attributes in the world a person is guided by the categories that are conventionalized in their language.

For English speakers, the category 'chair' has a certain inevitability. It might, to be sure, be difficult to formulate a classical definition, one which encompasses all and only the things we might want to call chairs. (The definition would need to be broad enough to include deckchairs, beanbag chairs, dentists' chairs, and even electric chairs. It would also need to exclude car seats and aeroplane seats; as their names suggest, these entities are 'seats', not 'chairs'.) More compelling is an account which maximizes the cue validity of features which differentiate chairs from other kinds of entities, such as tables, beds, sofas, cupboards, stools, and seats. Features with high cue validity might include 'intended for sitting on', 'intended for one person', and 'possessing a rigid back'. On this account, beanbag chairs and deckchairs would, rightly, have a somewhat marginal status in the category. Even so, it comes as a surprise to English speakers to learn that there is no simple German translation of English *chair*. German has two words, *Stuhl* and *Sessel* (Gipper 1959; Geeraerts 2010: 66–8). *Sessel* corresponds, roughly, to English 'armchair'. But whereas in English an armchair is a kind of chair, a 'Sessel' is not a kind of 'Stuhl' (or vice versa); the words refer to contrasting categories.

Categorization may not seem to be very relevant to the topic of skewed frequencies in a language. To see how it might be relevant, let us change the terms of the discussion. Consider, as one kind of category, a syntactic construction, whose features, or properties, are the words which make up the construction. The category, then, is the construction; the words which occur in it are its features. Applying the notions of cue and category validity to this situation, we can consider the extent to which a word cues a construction and, conversely, the extent to which a construction cues a word.

> *Cue validity of words vis-à-vis constructions.* Given an occurrence of word *w*, what is the probability that *w* features in construction *C*?

> *Category validity of constructions vis-à-vis their component words.* Given an occurrence of construction *C*, what is the probability that word *w* features in *C*?

Some words are able to cue, with a very high degree of probability, the constructions in which they occur. This is true, almost by definition, of so-called cranberry words (p. 71). The word *cahoots* is virtually restricted to occurring in the phrase *in cohoots (with)*, *intents* cues the phrase *to all intents (and purposes)*, while *dint* occurs almost exclusively in the complex preposition *by dint of*.[8] On the other hand, an

---

[8] Of the seventy-three instances of *dint* in the BNC, sixty-seven occur in the complex preposition. Of the six remaining examples, one is a dialectal rendering of *didn't* while four are an alternative to the word *dent* (*she made a little dint in the ground*). Only one (*with dint of great effort*) exemplifies a variation on the phrase *by dint of*.

occurrence of the configurations [in * with] and [by * of] are not very likely to cue an occurrence of the words *cahoots* and *dint*, since very many words can occur in these environments and most of them have a much higher probability of occurrence than the cranberry words. Data we have previously discussed can be seen in this light, also. *Whereabouts* (as a noun) strongly cues a possessive construction, whether prenominal (*his whereabouts*) or postnominal (*the whereabouts of the suspect*) (p. 58); the same goes for *lap* (in the body region sense) (p. 51). Once again, an occurrence of either the pre- or postnominal possessive construction is not likely to cue the words *whereabouts* or *lap*; there are countless other candidates for the possessee slot of these constructions.

Taking the perspective of category validity, we find that some constructions are highly predictive of the words which occur in them. An example already mentioned is the [WAITING TO HAPPEN] construction (see p. 141). This construction strongly cues the words *accident* and *disaster*. The words *disaster* and *accident*, on the other hand, are by no means limited to occurring in this environment; they have very low cue validity vis-à-vis the construction.

An interesting case of category validity—though he does not describe it in such terms—is discussed by Verhagen (2005). At issue is the phenomenon of long-distance *wh*-extraction. An initial question word, such as *who* or *what*, may correspond to a direct object constituent in the same clause, as in *Who did you meet?*, *What do you want?* Here, the *wh*-word has been 'extracted' from its postverbal position (compare: *You met who?*, *You want what?*). Extraction from within the same clause is very frequent. Not so common is extraction across a clause boundary from a subordinate clause, as in *Who did you say that you met?* (compare: *You said that you met who?*).

For reasons that we need not go into here, long-distance *wh*-extraction has played an important role in syntactic and especially Chomskyan theories. (For a discussion of some of the issues, see Culicover 2009: Chapter 9). The phenomenon has also attracted the attention of more functionally minded linguists. This is because the acceptability of long-distance extraction is known to vary considerably. The following examples are based on Deane (1992: 41–2):

(1)   a. Which guild do you think we should join?
    b. Which guild did he say we should join?
    c. Which guild will they suggest that we join?
    d. Which guild did he make the suggestion that we join?
    e. Which guild did he retract the suggestion that we join?
    f. Which guild did he photocopy the suggestion that we join?

The examples have been arranged in approximate order of decreasing acceptability. Most people would accept (a) without question while (f) would probably be rejected outright, with intermediate judgements for the remaining examples. Various explanations for this variation have been offered, concerning the semantic content of the material intervening between the *wh*-word and its extraction site and the distribution of information over the sentence (Deane 1991; Goldberg 2006: Chapter 7).

Verhagen approached this matter on the basis of corpus data, in both English and Dutch. In a small, 720,000 word Dutch corpus, he found only six examples of long distance *wh*-extraction and only eleven in the 1 million word Brown corpus of English. Remarkably, all six Dutch examples had *denken* 'think' as the main verb, which in all cases occurred with a second person singular subject (*je* or *u*).[9] Ten of the English examples also had *think* as their main verb and nine had *you* as their subject.[10] A larger Dutch corpus confirmed the preference of *denken* as main verb (34 out of 43 examples), also of second person subjects (36 examples). In brief, the extraction construction very strongly cues the main verb *think/denken*, in association with a second person subject.

The examples we have discussed so far exhibit a notable asymmetry of cue and category validity. A word such as *whereabouts* strongly cues the possessive constructions it occurs in; possessive constructions, however, are hardly predictive at all of the word *whereabouts*. Conversely, the long-distance *wh*-extraction construction strongly cues the verb *think/denken*; the verb, however, is likely to occur in many different environments and is therefore useless as a predictor of the construction. It may be no accident that the cases discussed have a somewhat marginal status in the language. *Whereabouts* is not a frequently used noun, and long-distance extraction is also rather rare. More typical, we might suppose, of the language at large are cases where cue and category validity are more in balance; the construction 'mildly' predicts its constituents and the words 'mildly' predict the construction.

Take, for the example, the configuration [a(n) X of NP] (Renouf and Sinclair 1991). There are over a quarter of a million instances (260,135, to be precise) of this configuration in the BNC and there are very many items which can occupy the X slot. Table 8.1 lists the ten most common words in this environment as well as the overall frequency of these words in the corpus. The table also includes a few words which are less frequent in the construction.

The most frequent exponent of the construction (*a number of*) accounts for 5.8% of all instances. The five most frequent exponents account for 18.4%, while the ten most frequent make up 26% of all instances. Moreover, the words that occur in the construction tend to show a strong attraction to it. There are, to be sure, some exceptions: over 90% of all tokens of *group* occur outside the construction.

---

[9] An example from the Eindhoven corpus: *Wat denk je dat ie zei?* 'What do you think he said? (lit: What think you that he said?).

[10] An example from the Brown corpus: *What do you think you are doing?*

TABLE 8.1. **Words which occur in the [a __ of NP] environment.**

Words occurring in the environment [a __ of NP]	N^1: Number of tokens in the [a __ of NP] environment	N^2: Overall frequency in the BNC	N^1 as % of N^2
number	15,160	48,876	31.02
lot	14,647	23,953	61.15
couple	7,071	11,917	59.34
series	5,996	14,245	42.09
bit	5,039	13,234	38.08
matter	4,405	16,375	26.90
variety	4,287	8,656	49.53
member	3,983	17,425	22.86
group	3,544	41,053	8.63
range	3,363	19,432	17.31
handful	966	1,351	71.50
bunch	550	1,169	47.05
clump	80	204	39.22
swarm	44	83	53.01
spoonful	33	114	28.95

For the others, however, we note a remarkable preference for the construction. The major uses of *lot* and *couple* are in the construction. The attraction of words to the construction is not restricted to high-frequency items. Relatively infrequent nouns like *handful, bunch*, and *swarm* strongly favour the [a __ of NP] environment.

The interaction of words and constructions has also been studied by Goldberg (2006). Goldberg focused on three argument structure constructions:

- The intransitive motion construction: [V PP], e.g. *go into the room.*
- The caused motion construction: [V NP PP], e.g. *put the book on the shelf.*
- The transfer construction: [V NP NP], e.g. *give Chris a book.*

She found that in the language addressed to child learners all three constructions were used with a wide range of verbs. However, in each case, the 'lion's share' was taken by just one verb. Thus, of the thirty-nine different verbs used in the intransitive motion construction, one verb—*go*—accounted for 39 per cent of all instances of the construction. Of the fourty-three different verbs used in the caused motion construction, one verb—*put*—accounted for 38 per cent of all instances, while of the thirteen different verbs used in the transfer construction, one verb—*give*—accounted for 20 per cent of all instances (Goldberg 2006: 76).[11] Conversely, for the verbs *put* and *give*, the lion's share of their tokens was in the respective constructions (p. 109).[12] Thus, of the 114 occurrences of *put* in the corpus, ninety-nine were in the caused motion construction, while of the fourteen occurrences of *give*, eleven were in the transfer construction. In these cases, then, we see that the verb strongly cues the construction, while the construction is typically associated with the verb.

Both cue and category validity—the fact that certain verbs, such as *put* and *give*, strongly cue the caused motion and the transfer constructions, while the constructions themselves strongly cue the respective verbs—underline the status of certain instances of the constructions as the construction prototypes. Goldberg hypothesizes that this state of affairs is crucial to the learnability of the constructions, in both their semantic and formal aspects. In the first place, the preferred verbs appear to encapsulate the meanings of the respective constructions, a fact which is likely to facilitate the learning of the constructions' schematic meanings. Second, the very fact that the constructions appear with a preferred verb raises the learner's awareness of the constructions and thereby establishes them as syntactic entities in the learner's mental grammar, while the occurrence, albeit less frequently, of other verbs points the learner to the possibility of productively extending the constructions beyond the encountered instances. The hypothesized role of skewed frequencies was tested experimentally on the learning of a novel construction in an artificial language (Goldberg 2006: 79–83). The construction was presented sixteen times, with five different verbs. On one condition, the frequency of the verbs was fairly evenly balanced (three verbs occurred four times, two verbs each occurred twice). On the other condition, one of the verbs was presented eight times, the other four verbs were presented twice. Subjects, both adults and children, learned the construction and its associated semantics more efficiently in the skewed condition.

As Rosch pointed out, in the passage cited earlier, the world does not present itself to us as "an unstructured total set of equiprobable co-occurring attributes" (Rosch 1978: 29). It is the "correlational structure" of the world—the fact that attributes are not randomly distributed over the things that we encounter—which underlies the viability and indeed the very *raison d'être* of the categories that we construct, learn, and operate with. Language, too, does not present itself to us as 'an unstructured set of equiprobable elements', whether the elements be sound segments, syllable types, words, or constructions. The elements that we perceive in a language do not occur uniformly and they are not distributed randomly over the speech that we encounter.

---

[11] Goldberg (2006: 76) notes the Zipfian distribution of the verbs in the constructions, with, for each construction, a single item accounting for a large percentage of the tokens and a range of other options occurring comparatively rarely. Zipf, of course, did not address the frequency of words in specific environments. The existence of Zipfian distributions in these environments is therefore all the more remarkable.

[12] Data for *go* are not reported.

It is the 'correlational structure' of language which makes possible the emergence of linguistic categories, thus ensuring both the viability of the language as a system of communication as well as its learnability.

Skewed frequency as a design feature of language

In a series of publications, summarized in Hockett and Altmann (1968), Charles Hockett proposed a number of DESIGN FEATURES of human language. The notion of design feature is intended to capture what is unique to human language(s) in comparison with other communication systems, whether human or animal. Initially, Hockett proposed seven features; this was subsequently increased to thirteen, then to sixteen. Perhaps the best-known of the features is 'duality of patterning'. One level of patterning has to do with the arrangement of a smallish and fixed number of meaningless elements (phonemes); the second level concerns the arrangement of a large and extendible number of meaningful units (words and morphemes), which are themselves built up from the meaningless phonemes. Duality of patterning makes it possible for the users of a communication system to construct a virtually open-ended set of messages out of a small and finite set of basic elements (the phonemes). A communication system which did not exhibit this feature would be qualitatively different from any human language. For one thing, the number of meaningful messages would be restrained by the number of distinct forms that the user could learn and discriminate. Arguably, children do pass through such a stage. However, once the number of these form–meaning gestalts reaches a certain critical size, some internal analysis becomes necessary. The system comes to exhibit what Abler (1989) called a "particulate structure". Words come to be analysed into their component parts, correspondences across different words are recognized, and the parts become available for use in other words (Taylor 2002: 81).

Another of Hockett's design features is 'learnability'. By this is meant the fact that "a speaker of a language can learn another language" (Hockett and Altmann 1968: 64). I suggest that a more radical understanding of this feature is needed. A language must be learnable, not only by individuals who already know a language and who are thus familiar with the general structure of human languages, but also by infants who have no prior knowledge of human language and its workings. I have argued in this chapter than one aspect of human languages that is necessary for their learnability is the skewed distribution of their various elements.

In conclusion

In a sense, the conclusion that we have reached is paradoxical. The elements of a language—the vowels and the consonants, the words and the morphemes, the conjugations and declensions, the idioms and the constructions—have to be learned by each generation of speakers. One might suppose that learning will be a function of frequency of input, with more frequent items being learned more quickly and more easily than less frequent items. Items with a very low frequency of occurrence might not even be learned at all; they will, in other words, simply drop out of the language. Over time, and over generations of learners, frequency distributions will become less and less skewed until, eventually, the language will reach a stage in which all of its elements, at each level of description, will have an equal frequency of occurrence. No language exhibits this tendency towards the levelling of frequencies.

The skewed frequencies which characterize every level of language description are not an accidental property of language; they arise inevitably from the requirement that language is learned anew by each generation of speakers. Paradoxical as it may seem, skewed frequencies are a prerequisite for the learning of the full range of frequency distributions, from the more common to the extremely rare.

9

Learning from input

In Chapter 8 I proposed a functional explanation of the skewed frequencies which are to be found everywhere in a language. The explanation concerns the requirement on any human language that it be learnable by each generation of speakers. A language in which each element (in a particular subsystem) occurred with equal frequency could not exist, because it could not be learned by new generations of speakers.

In the first part of this chapter I examine in more detail the role of skewed frequencies in the acquisition process. The discussion begins with phonological acquisition; more precisely, the process whereby the infant learner comes to categorize the multiplicity of sounds that she hears into a smallish number of linguistically relevant units. The example of phonological acquisition is particularly instructive, not only because phonological categories are inherently meaningless (the acquisition process therefore cannot be driven by semantic intentions) but also because, in the initial stages at least, when an infant has not yet acquired any meaningful words, it is unrealistic to suppose that the process can be bootstrapped by reference to preexisting lexical–semantic categories. A crucial determinant of learning is, rather, the skewed distribution of the sounds that the child, in a given linguistic environment, is likely to hear.

The plausibility of this account rests on the assumption that learners, and language users more generally, are able to notice and to record all manner of features of the utterances that they are exposed to. The second half of this chapter considers some evidence that this is indeed the case. I will go further, and suggest that the noticing and recording of input language contributes to, and indeed may even be constitutive of, the learning process.

Phoneme acquisition

In this section I address the role of skewed frequencies in the acquisition of the sound system of a language. Let us begin by considering how language might present itself to the new-born infant.[1]

---

[1] This section develops ideas first presented in Taylor (2006c).

We might suppose that initially the infant perceives only a continuous blur of sound, without structure and with few distinguishing features, marked only by variations in pitch and loudness and by modulations of gross acoustic quality. Learning the sound system of the language would be a matter of learning to make progressively finer perceptual distinctions in the acoustic blur. Vowels need to be distinguished from consonants, then, for the consonants, stops need to be recognized as different from sonorants. The stops then undergo further differentiation, according to voicing, aspiration, place of articulation, and so on, until the full inventory of the distinctive sounds of the ambient language has been acquired. After all, speech production appears to follow this route. Children start out by making indistinct syllable-like utterances. They need time to learn the various sounds which are able to occur in the syllable frame. They need time to master the articulations of [ta] vs. [da], and even more time to produce clear instances of [sa] vs. [fa] vs. [θa].

The study of infant perception has shown that this is not how phonological acquisition proceeds. Using a variety of ingenious experimental techniques,[2] researchers have shown that infants up to the age of around six months are exquisitely sensitive to all manner of acoustic contrasts. Of course, infants are not able to make the difference between [ta] and [da], but it seems that they are perfectly able to hear the difference. In fact, they are able to hear contrasts which are exploited in languages other than the one(s) they are exposed to (Aslin, Jusczyk, and Pisoni 1998; Aslin, Pisoni, Hennessy, and Perey 1981; Eimas, Siqueland, Jusczyk, and Vigorito 1971; Jusczyk 1997; Kuhl, 1987).

The ability to hear differences between speech sounds is doubtless a great boon for the incipient language learner; in itself, however, this ability is not enough. A person able to perceive all manner of acoustic-phonetic differences would be rather like the fictitious Funes of Borges's (1998 [1942]) story. In *Funes el memorioso* ('Funes the Memorious'), Borges tells of a man who was able to notice every detail of the reality he experienced but who as consequence was unable to generalize and form abstractions:

He was, let us not forget, almost incapable of general, platonic ideas. It was not only difficult for him to understand that the generic term *dog* embraced so many specimens of differing sizes and different forms; he was disturbed by the fact that a dog at three-fourteen (seen in profile) should have the same name as the dog at three-fifteen (seen from the front). His own face in the mirror, his own hands, surprised him on every occasion. Swift writes that the emperor of Lilliput could discern the movement of the minute hand; Funes could continuously make out

---

[2] These include the sucking paradigm and the head-turning paradigm (see Kuhl 1994 for details). With respect to the sucking paradigm, the infant sucks on an electronically monitored dummy. The assumption is that a change in the child's environment will stimulate the child's attention, causing an increase in the sucking rate. At first, the child is exposed to a series of identical stimuli—consonant–vowel syllables, for example. Once the child has habituated to the sounds and the sucking rate stabilizes, a new syllable is presented. An increase in the sucking rate is taken as evidence that the child has noticed a difference.

the tranquil advances of corruption, of caries, of fatigue. He noted the progress of death, of moisture. He was the solitary and lucid spectator of a multiform world which was instantaneously and almost intolerably exact....

Without effort, he had learned English, French, Portuguese, Latin. I suspect, nevertheless, that he was not very capable of thought. To think is to forget a difference, to generalize, to abstract. In the overly replete world of Funes there were nothing but details, almost contiguous details.   (Borges 1998 [1942]: 103–4)

In order to acquire the phonology of a language, it is not enough to be able to hear the difference between two utterances; it is also necessary for categories of acoustic events to be recognized in the kaleidoscope of auditory impressions. Some chunks of the acoustic signal need to be regarded, in the phonological system that is being acquired, as being 'the same' as other chunks.

How do these sound categories emerge? How does the child come to appreciate that a certain range of vowel qualities counts as instances of the KIT vowel, while other vowel qualities count as instances of the FLEECE or DRESS vowels? (Bear in mind that the very same range of vowel qualities might be categorized differently in other languages, and indeed in different accents of English.) Or, to take a different example, how does the child learner come to know that a certain range of plosive sounds at the beginning of an utterance counts as instances of /k/ whereas others count as instances of /g/? Again, different languages may draw the boundary between k-like and g-like sounds differently. Some languages make a three-way distinction between voiceless aspirated /k^h/, voiceless unaspirated /k/, and voiced /g/. For mature English speakers, this three-way contrast is notoriously difficult to make and to hear. Yet, as noted above, newborn infants, whatever the ambient language, are able to make the perceptual discriminations.

The task might appear to be no different, in principle, to that of learning semantic categories, such as those designated by the words of a language. The child encounters a range of creatures, of different sizes, shapes, colours, behaviours, and temperaments. Some of these are referred to as 'dogs', others are called 'cats', others are called 'cows' and 'ducks'. (The situation is complicated by the fact that a creature might also be called 'a pet', 'an animal', or 'Buster'.) The problem facing the child is to work out which creatures belong to these various categories. This is what Brown (1958) called 'The Original Word Game', the game of linking up words and things. In the case of the animal names, the solution to the game is largely driven by gross perceptual differences between the different types. Even so, the solution is not fully given by the world as it is. Even for natural kinds, languages differ in the categorizations which they make. English distinguishes between snails and slugs; German does not (both are called *Schnecken*). English distinguishes between mice and rats; in Italian, one word, *topo*, covers both. Even for natural kinds, the semantic categories are not simply 'there in the world'; the categories need to be learned on the basis of linguistic experience. When we move beyond natural kinds, differences between languages become even more numerous. As we have previously noted (p. 189), Germans learn to differentiate between two kinds of chair: *Sessel* and *Stühle*; Russians come to regard dark blue (*siniy*) and light blue (*goluboy*) as two different colours, not as shades of the same colour; Koreans and Japanese learn that putting on a hat and putting on a shoe are different kinds of action (Choi and Bowerman 1991). For English speakers, eating (food) and smoking (cigarettes) are different activities; in Māori, the same verb, *kai*, can be used of both.

In spite of the apparent parallels, the learning of phonological categories differs in a crucial respect from the learning of semantic categories. In order to appreciate that the word *dog* can refer to animals which differ one from another in various ways, the child must first be assured that the multifarious ways in which the word *dog* is pronounced all count as instances of the same word. One can imagine that a learner might explore the hypothesis that variations in the duration of the vowel, or whether the final consonant is released or not, might correlate with meaning differences, concerning, for example, big dogs vs. small dogs, brown dogs vs. spotted dogs, well-behaved dogs vs. yapping dogs. Children, presumably, do not systematically explore these possible correlations between pronunciation and meaning. One reason why they do not do this could be that the phonological categories have already been established (or at least have already been seeded). The child already knows that released and unreleased stops (in a given language) count as the same, and that variations in duration and acoustic quality (within certain limits) of a vowel have no bearing on its status within the sound system of the language.

How does this knowledge emerge? I consider three possibilities, before turning to the role of the statistical properties of the input.

(i) One possibility is that the sound categories emerge on the back of the semantic distinctions which they symbolize. For example, a child may notice that one set of pronunciations refers to coats while another set of slightly different pronunciations refers to goats. The need to make the conceptual distinction would trigger awareness of the corresponding phonological distinction, namely, between /k/ and /g/. The learner will be sensitized to the boundary between the two sound categories and learn to ignore differences within the categories. Some such mechanism of phoneme acquisition has been invoked by Heitner (2004) and by Werker and Tees (1984).[3]

The argument rests on the notion of the MINIMAL PAIR. According to this notion, *coat* and *goat* are identical in their phonological representations, apart from the initial segment. Since *coat* and *goat* are different words, with different meanings, the initial segments must belong to different sound categories, namely /k/ and /g/. While the existence of a minimal pair might be cited as evidence that two segments

---

[3] See, however, Werker (2003) for a more nuanced view of the matter.

belong to different phonemes, sound categories are not derivative from minimal pairs nor can sound categories be defined with reference to minimal pairs.[4] In English, there are scarcely any minimal pairs contrasting [ʃ] and [ʒ] or [θ] and [ð], yet we would still want to regard these pairs of sounds as belonging to different categories. Moreover, the existence of minimal pairs will largely be a function of the size of a person's lexicon. For young children, with very small vocabularies, minimal pairs, for any pair of candidate sounds, are vanishingly rare. Caselli *et al.* (1995) list the first fifty words produced and understood by both English- and Italian-speaking children. The English lists contain no minimal pairs at all while the Italian lists contain only the pair *nonna* 'granny' and *nanna* 'sleep'. Even more telling is the fact that by the age of one, children are already well on their way to perceiving the ambient language phonemically, that is, they are categorizing ambient speech sounds in line with the phonological structure of the language they are acquiring. At this stage, children have scarcely learned any words of their language at all, so cannot be relying on lexical contrasts.

(ii) An alternative account of phonological acquisition proposes that all members of sound category share a common defining feature, or features. A vowel would count as an instance of the /ɛ/ phoneme, or a consonant would count as an instance of the /p/ phoneme, in virtue of some invariant acoustic property, unique to these categories. Indeed, Bloomfield (1933: 79) had surmised that each phoneme of a language was associated with a set of "gross acoustic features", which recurred in the sound wave in a "relatively constant shape" in successive utterances. Learning the sound system of language would be matter of learning to respond to those "distinctive features" (Halle 1954) which define the relevant categories.

The invention of the spectrograph in the 1940s (Potter, Kopp, and Green 1947) and subsequent research on acoustic phonetics revealed the illusory nature of these supposed invariants. The spectrograph made it possible, for the first time in human history, to inspect a visual representation of the acoustic structure of the speech signal and much work went into the search for those invariants which might be associated with the units which we hear in the stream of speech. Researchers soon became aware of the difficulties of this enterprise. Failing to find invariant acoustic features corresponding to perceived phonemes, particularly with regards to the different kinds of stop consonants, Liberman and his colleagues (Liberman, Cooper, Shankweiler, and Studdert-Kennedy 1967) developed their motor theory of speech

---

[4] The point was made by Daniel Jones: "An important point to notice is that the phoneme is essentially a phonetic conception [i.e. a phonetic category: JRT]. The fact that certain sounds are used in a language for distinguishing the meanings of words doesn't enter into the definition of a phoneme. It would indeed be possible to group the sounds of a language into phonemes without knowing the meaning of any words" (Jones 1929, quoted in Bloch 1948: 6). We may also note that Chomsky (1964: 82–95) raised a number of serious arguments against the very notion of the minimal pair.

perception, seeking to locate invariance, not in the signal itself, but in the motor commands which gave rise to the acoustic signal. Later versions of the theory located invariance, not in the motor commands themselves, but in a speaker's "intended phonetic gestures" (Liberman and Mattingly 1985: 2). The 'intended gestures' presumably correspond to the 'intended phonemes', thus bringing us back to the initial question of how these intended phonemes emerge in the language development of the individual.

(iii) A further possibility is that sound categories are based in properties of auditory perception and in facts of articulation. There would be parallels here with the acquisition of some semantic categories, such as the colours. It has been estimated that the human eye can discriminate 7.5 million just noticeable colour differences (Brown and Lenneberg 1954). Acquiring the colour categories of a language is a matter of reducing this multitude of visual impressions to a small, manageable number of categories, those named by the colour terms of a language. While there is no unique solution to the colour categorization problem—languages differ in the number of their colour categories and the boundaries of a term in one language might not coincide with the boundary of a seemingly equivalent term in another language—languages do not differ arbitrarily in the ways in which they carve up the colour space. Berlin and Kay (1969) proposed that languages around the world build their colour categories around a small set of focal colours; these are colours which the human visual system is specifically attuned to respond to, such as red and green, blue and yellow, in the first instance, and admixtures of these, such as orange and purple (Kay and McDaniel 1978). Even so, language-specific categorizations still have to be learned; recall the example of Russian, which makes a distinction between two kinds of blue.[5]

With respect to phonological categories, some major distinctions may well be based on properties of human perception and articulation. There are good reasons why languages should have a high front i-type vowel, a high back u-type vowel, and a low a-type vowel. These vowels exhibit a maximum degree of perceptual contrast (Liljencrants and Lindblom 1972). Moreover, according to Stevens (1972), relatively large differences in the articulation of these vowels give rise to relatively small differences in acoustic quality. While it may well be the case that all languages do have these kinds of vowels in their phoneme inventories, the vowels of one language

---

[5] The universality of focal colours as the basis for colour categorization has, however, been challenged. Davidoff (2001) contends that colour categories are learned on the back of linguistic labels and that it is the use of the labels in naming exemplars that triggers the acquisition of the categories. According to Davidoff, "it is only by the application of colour labels that categorization can begin, and thus the conceptual colour-naming train get going" (p. 386). In this respect, the learning of colours would in principle be no different from the learning of other semantic categories.

by no means match those of other languages. One need only compare the vowels in English *see*, *too*, and *coo* with those in French *si*, *tout*, and *coup*.

The innate properties of the human perceptual system have also been invoked with respect to voice onset time, or VOT (Liberman, Delattre, and Cooper 1958; Lisker 1978). VOT is the duration, usually measured in milliseconds, between the release of a stop closure and the onset of voicing, as indicated by the presence of periodicity in the wave form. A positive VOT value, e.g. +50, indicates that voicing sets in after the release; a negative value, e.g. –50, indicates that voicing commences before the release. VOT is known to be a crucial feature distinguishing voiced, voiceless, and voiceless aspirated stops. English /pɑ/, for example, is characterized by VOT values in excess of about 25 ms. VOT values below 25 ms cause the syllable to be heard as /bɑ/. Listeners are, however, relatively insensitive to differences within the two categories, that is, for VOT values on either side of the critical value.

It has been established that prelinguistic infants are highly sensitive to differences along the VOT continuum (Eimas *et al.* 1971).[6] Some scholars, including Eimas, have suggested that this fact alone may be sufficient to trigger the formation of the respective categories. There would, therefore, be grounds to claim that the categorization of stop consonants in terms of their voicing is driven by innate properties of the human perceptual mechanism. Complicating the situation, however, is the fact that different languages exploit the VOT dimension in different ways. To the extent that VOT defines language-specific categories, these categories must be learned from experience. But even within a single language, it may be inappropriate to refer to *the* VOT values which differentiate the different categories of stops. VOT depends on many factors, such as the place of articulation of the stop (VOT values for bilabials are, on the whole, shorter than for velars: Lisker and Abramson 1964), the prosodic properties of the syllable (i.e. whether stressed, foot-initial, or unstressed), the overall speech rate, and whether in utterance-initial or utterance-medial position. These variations in VOT are subtle and numerous and are not able to be captured in even the narrowest of phonetic transcriptions. Native proficiency in a language, however, requires that the speaker–hearer has learned this multitude of specific facts about the stops in the language (Pierrehumbert 2003).

Statistical learning

I now turn to an alternative account of phonological acquisition, based on the statistical properties of the input. Imagine two hypothetical languages in which stop–vowel syllables are characterized by VOT values ranging between, say, –50

---

[6] There is even evidence that other mammals may be sensitive to VOT differences (Kuhl and Miller 1975).

and +50 ms. The one language places a boundary between voiced and voiceless stops at around +5 ms, the other makes a distinction between voiced and voiceless aspirated stops at around +25 ms. Suppose, furthermore, that all VOT values occur with roughly equal frequencies. In order to learn the relevant categories in the two languages, the learner would need to be informed that in the one language VOT-values of +10 and +40 count as the same while in the other language they count as different. This, however, is precisely the kind of information which is unlikely to be available to a young child with only a very limited stock of words. Learning without semantic support would, however, be possible if VOT values were bimodally distributed, clustering, for example, around +5 and +30. Frequency distribution of the stimuli would naturally divide the stimuli into two categories. As it happens, VOT values in natural languages (in a given prosodic position) do indeed tend to be distributed in this way (Lisker and Abramson 1964).

Consider, in this light, some important work reported in Maye and Gerken (2000). The researchers constructed a set of eight CV syllables differing in their VOT values and ranging from a voiced stop, as in English [da], to a voiceless unaspirated stop (of the kind that occurs in English after an initial [s], as in *star.*). The [da]–[ta] contrast is alien to the English sound system and is quite difficult for untrained English listeners to perceive reliably. Subjects were first of all invited simply to listen to the syllables. In one condition the syllables were presented with a monomodal frequency distribution, with 'central' syllables being heard more often than 'peripheral' syllables. In another condition the syllables were presented with a bimodal frequency distribution, with the syllables towards each end of the continuum being presented more often than the central ones (see Figure 9.1). In a second stage of the

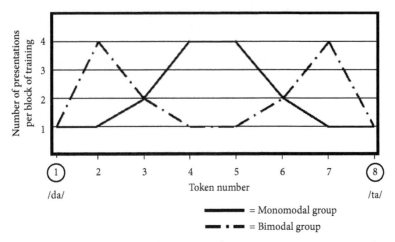

FIGURE **9.1.** Presentation frequency of syllables differing in VOT (From Maye and Gerken 2000: 528; reproduced with permission).

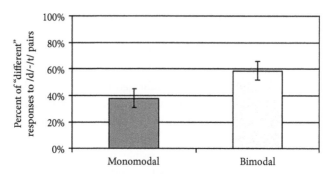

FIGURE 9.2. Categorization of syllables from the ends of the /ta/–/da/ continuum (From Maye and Gerken 2000: 530; reproduced with permission).

experiment the listeners were presented with the syllables at the extremes of the continuum and were asked to judge whether they were the same or different. Listeners who had been exposed to the bimodal distribution responded in a way which suggested that they had constructed two categories of sounds; in other words, they tended to judge the two syllables as different. Those who had been exposed to the monomodal distribution tended to respond that the two syllables were the same (Figure 9.2); these listeners had grouped the stimuli into a single category. In explaining these findings, Maye and Gerken (2000: 530) remark that it is as if listeners "maintain some sort of mental histogram", tracking the frequency of occurrence of acoustic patterns they had encountered.[7]

Subsequent work showed that the same effect obtained with infants (Maye, Werker, and Gerken 2002). Also investigated was the possibility that the newly learned contrast might generalize to other places of articulation. With adult subjects, Maye and Gerken (2001) found no such effect—subjects who had been trained to recognize two categories in the [ta]–[da] continuum failed to transfer this knowledge to the [ka]–[ga] or the [pa]–[ba] continuum. This finding would seem to reinforce the notion that the learning was contingent on the specific stimuli that had been presented. Subsequent work, however, showed that infants were indeed able to make the generalization (Maye and Weiss 2003; Maye, Weiss, and Aslin 2008), suggesting that the infants may have interpreted the categories in terms of a more abstract representation, valid for different places of articulation.[8]

[7] On the role of frequency distributions in speech perception, see also Clayards *et al.* (2008).
[8] Maye and Gerken emphasize that the categories that their subjects learned do not correspond to phonemes, as usually understood:

For linguists, the term applies to categories that include multiple allophones, which appear in different phonological positions. What we are interested in is perhaps more appropriately termed "phonetic categories" or "phonetic equivalence classes;" specifically, sounds which are categorized together in a

In the light of these results, it is entirely plausible that the phonetic categories distinctive to a particular language (such as the aspirated vs. unaspirated stops or the various vowel categories) could be seeded during the first years of life by the statistical properties of the input.[9] Further exposure to the language will, of course, be needed in order to sharpen and refine these categories (Bohn 2000). This process may continue until well into the school years (Hazan and Barrett 2000).

There is now considerable evidence supporting the possibility of learning from the statistical properties of an acoustic input. In an often cited experiment, Saffran, Aslin, and Newport (1996) exposed eight-month-old infants to a random sequence of the nonsense words *tupiro, golabu, bidaku*, and *padoti* (see also Saffran 2001*b*). The only markers of 'word boundaries' were the low transitional probabilities between the abutting syllables. After only two minutes exposure the infants demonstrated greater familiarity with the three-syllable 'words' than with other three-syllable sequences that had not previously been presented:

2 min of exposure to concatenated speech organized into "words" was sufficient for 8-month-old infants to extract information about the sequential statistics of syllables.... Infants succeeded in learning and remembering particular groupings of three-syllable strings—those strings containing higher transitional probabilities surrounded by lower transitional probabilities.

The infants' performance in these studies is particularly impressive given the impoverished nature of the familiarization speech stream, which contained no pauses, intonational patterns, or any other cues that, in normal speech, probabilistically supplement the sequential statistics inherent in the structure of words.   (Saffran *et al.* 1996: 1927–8)

Again using nonsense materials, Gomez and Gerken (1999) showed that one-year-olds were able to extract patterns for the distribution of sets of items—they were, in other words, able to perform a kind of syntactic analysis, recognizing putative word classes and patterns for sequencing word classes. Adults show the same ability (Saffran 2001*a*, 2002). Computer simulations have also demonstrated the power of

---

particular phonological position. However, we point out that the psychological reality of the linguist's "phoneme," comprising multiple allophones, has not been experimentally demonstrated. The categories we account for here could plausibly be the *only* psychological correlate to phoneme categories.

(Maye and Gerken 2000: 532)

On the cognitive status of phonemes, as traditionally understood, see Mompeán (2006), Nathan (2006), and Taylor (2006*c*).

[9] The possibility that distributional properties of the input might drive category formation was also investigated by Kornai (1998) with respect to the vowel formant data reported in Peterson and Barney (1952). Peterson and Barney took measurements of the first three formants of 10 American English vowels produced by 76 talkers (men, women, and children). A cursory glance at a graph plotting the formant data for all the vowel tokens gives the impression of a broad swath of values, with few natural boundaries. Kornai reports, however, that automatic clustering procedures were able to assign the formant values to 10 categories, corresponding closely with the 10 intended vowels.

distributional cues for the emergence of word classes (Redington, Chater, and Finch 1998).

For a further testament to the power of statistical learning, from a different area of linguistic structure, consider the example of the gender systems which characterize many languages of the world. Gender is a property of nouns and shows up in agreement patterns with determiners, adjectives, participles, and sometimes even the finite forms of verbs, as well as in the choice of pronouns. Many gender systems, to be sure, have a semantic base, such as biological sex and animacy. Gender categories may also be cued by the phonological properties of a noun.[10] Even so, the gender of a noun is ultimately a matter of linguistic convention; a speaker is not free to choose this feature of a noun. *Mädchen* 'girl' and *Kind* 'child' are neuter in German, in spite of their meanings; *silence* is masculine in French, in spite of its sounding feminine; while *professeur* is masculine, even when the referent is female.

Essentially, gender is a matter of the distribution of morphemes within the noun phrase and sometimes even beyond, and concerns the co-occurrence of elements in agreement with a given noun. A masculine noun, in French, is one which (by definition) co-occurs (in the singular) with *le, ce, petit*, etc., while a feminine noun, by definition, is one which co-occurs with *la, cette*, and *petite*. It is on the basis of these co-occurrences that children learn the genders of the nouns in their language. In fact, there is evidence that children grasp the notion of grammatical gender even before the notion of biological gender, as shown by the fact that they are able to use gender-specific pronouns—equivalent to *he* and *she*—with reference to inanimate objects earlier and more reliably than with reference to male and female humans (Levy 1983). Experiments with artificial languages (Boroditsky, Schmidt, and Phillips 2003) confirm that subjects are indeed able to pick up on the co-occurrence patterns which typically mark noun gender.

Do listeners notice input features?

To claim that language learners are able to exploit the statistical properties of the input for the acquisition of language-specific categories is to presuppose that they are able to notice, and register, all manner of features in the input. There is a considerable body of evidence that this is indeed the case.

Consider in this connection some well-known findings by Goldinger (1996). A commonly used paradigm in memory research presents subjects with a list of words which they are invited to attend to. Some time later another list is presented and subjects must state, for each word on the new list, whether it already featured on the original list. The variable, in Goldinger's experiment, was the voice with which

---

[10] For German, see Köpcke and Zubin (1984); for French, see Carroll (2005) and Matthews (2010).

the words were spoken. Subjects listened to a list of words spoken by two, six, or ten voices. Subjects were better able to recognize a word as old if, in the second part of the experiment, it was spoken by the same voice as in the initial presentation. The effect was observed after a delay of five minutes, after one day, and—remarkably—even after one week.[11]

Memories of a speaker's voice are also able to influence the way a speaker subsequently pronounces a word. Goldinger and Azuma (2004) had subjects read a list of words. One day later they performed a task which involved identifying these words, each of which was spoken up to twelve times by a single speaker. One week after the initial session the subjects read the list of words again. In order to find out whether the second reading had been influenced by the intervening training session, a group of listeners was asked to judge whether the first or the second reading of each word counted as a better imitation of the training pronunciation. The imitation effect was particularly marked for low-frequency words (defined, in the experiment, as words estimated to occur less than five times per million).

Given the imitation effect, we should expect a person's pronunciation to change over time in response to her changing social contacts and to sound changes under-way in the speech community. Sociolinguists, on the other hand, have tended to assume that a person's accent remains more or less constant throughout adulthood. It is on this basis that comparisons between the pronunciations of persons in different age groups can be interpreted in terms of pronunciation changes over time. There are, of course, practical difficulties in accessing a person's pronunciations over a lifetime; I have no idea what I sounded like when I was in my twenties. The matter has, however, been studied by Harrington, on the basis of Queen Elizabeth's broadcast Christmas messages (see Harrington 2006, and the references cited therein). Harrington found that the Queen's pronunciation has changed over the past half century, away from an ultra-conservative RP, no doubt in response to changes underway in the RP accent. For example, the HAPPY vowel—the vowel that occurs at the end of words such as *happy*, *city*, and *pretty*—shifted from an [ɪ] quality to a tense [i] quality.

These findings are strong evidence against the commonly held view that words are stored in memory in a stripped-down format, not dissimilar to a broad phonemic transcription, which captures only the linguistically relevant contrasts of the language (Chomsky and Halle 1968; Halle 1957). On this view, identifying a word in the stream of speech is a matter of attending only to those features which serve to contrast the phoneme categories of the language. The specific acoustic properties of the segments, as well as more general aspects of the speech signal such as those which pertain to the voice quality of the speaker, are simply disregarded as so much extraneous noise. It

---

[11] Similar findings have been reported for visual presentations. Subjects are better able to recognize a word as old if it is in the same font as on its initial presentation (Jacoby and Hayman 1987).

turns out, however, that listeners not only attend to these 'linguistically irrelevant' aspects of the speech signal, they also register them in memory. The picture that emerges is that a person's knowledge of how a word is pronounced consists, not in a disembodied minimalist representation, but in a cluster of specific memories which document the range of possible pronunciations in considerable phonetic detail (Lachs, McMichael, and Pisoni 2000; Port 2007, 2010). Recognizing a word is a matter of matching the incoming signal in all its phonetic detail with a stored memory trace, while speech production is a matter of reactivating and re-performing one of the traces.

While these conclusions certainly go counter to mainstream accounts of phonology, they should not perhaps be surprising after all. In fact, they resonate with some aspects of everyday experience and are therefore not at all counterintuitive. We are able to recognize speakers by their voices and we are remarkably sensitive to matters of accent and accent-variation (Hay and Drager 2007). These everyday observations would be inexplicable without some mechanism for the storing and accessing of specific memories of heard utterances.

Further evidence that language users register facts about incoming speech comes from recency effects, to which we now turn.

The recency effect

Slipperiest—the superlative form of *slippery*—is not a very common word. Some readers may find it only marginally acceptable, preferring the analytic form, *most slippery*. The word is not recorded in the BNC nor in the *Time* Magazine Corpus (though thirteen instances were found in the COCA). Here is an example of the word from the New Zealand newspaper *The Press* of 10 November 2007:

(1)   They say that sorry is the hardest word. It can also be the slipperiest.

There are, as everyone knows, two ways to create comparatives and superlatives. One is by suffixation of *-er* and *-est*, the other involves the use of *more* and *most*. Example (1) raises the question of which of the two strategies is to be employed. Though seemingly straightforward, the matter is in fact rather complex. A general rule of thumb is that short, one-syllable adjectives take the inflections, whereas long adjectives, of three or more syllables, require the analytic construction. Disyllabic adjectives can go either way, with, possibly, an overall preference for the inflectional option. The length rule, however, cannot always be relied upon. Monosyllabic *apt* and *prone* prefer the analytic construction—*I am {more prone / ?proner} to accidents than you are, There could not be {a more apt / ?an apter} description*—while example (1) shows that trisyllabic *slippery* is not incompatible with the inflectional option. As a matter of fact, a large number of adjectives allow both the inflected and the analytic forms; Hilpert (2008: 414–15) lists 240 adjectives from the BNC which allow both forms in the comparative. The choice between the two constructions would appear to be a purely formal one, with no consequences for the conceptual content that the speaker wishes to express.[12] Even so, the two sets of forms are not in free variation, in the sense that an inflected form can be replaced, willy-nilly, by the analytic form, and vice versa. While many adjectives are compatible with both constructions, most show a strong preference for one over the other. Thus we have *more obscure, more intense,* and *more likely* rather than *obscurer, intenser,* and *likelier.* Other adjectives prefer the inflected form, e.g. *heavier, fuller, vaguer.* For a small number of adjectives, such as *just, pleasant,* and *yellow,* are the odds more evenly balanced.

What, then, determines the choice, in any particular instance? A number of factors have been identified (Mondorf 2003; Hilpert 2008). The length of the adjective, measured in syllables, has perhaps the greatest impact. Others include:

- Stress location. Disyllabic adjectives with final stress tend to prefer the analytic construction: *more sincere, more diffuse*
- Final consonant clusters. Adjectives ending in a consonant cluster tend to prefer the analytic construction: *more apt, more corrupt*
- Predicative vs. attributive use. Predicative position tends to favour the inflected form, while attributive position tends to favour the analytic construction
- A following complement phrase tends to trigger the analytic construction: *more prone to accidents, more worthy of attention.*

These factors constitute tendencies, of varying strengths, which may often be overridden and which may well be in conflict with each other in a given context. None—not even number of syllables of the base adjective—has the status of a categorical rule.

The case of comparatives and superlatives is symptomatic of a more general issue. Many of the things that speakers say could have been said differently, with little or no consequences for conceptual content.[13] You go the window and observe *It's started to rain again.* You could also have said *It's started raining again.* Here are some more examples of the choices available to speakers:

---

[12] Consider, though, the following contrast, where the choice of construction does appear to correlate with two senses of *dear.*

(i) These are dearer (= more expensive) than those.
(ii) You are more dear to me than anyone else.

[13] The study of variation—situations where a speaker has two or more options available to her for the verbalization of her intentions—has, of course, been a major topic of sociolinguistic research over the past half century. The research has, in the main, focused on phonological variants within a speech community, such as the occurrence of post-vocalic 'r' in words such as *fourth* and *floor,* or the pronunciation of the verbal *-ing* inflection as [ɪn] or [ɪŋ]. Relevant to the choice of variant are such factors as the speaker's age, social class, educational level, gender, and ethnicity (Labov 1972). The term SOCIOPHONETICS is sometimes applied to this branch of research (Foulkes and Docherty 2006; Hay and Drager 2007).

- The caused motion vs. the ditransitive construction: *Give a bone to the dog* vs. *Give the dog a bone*
- Particle placement: *Look the word up in the dictionary* vs. *Look up the word in the dictionary*
- Presence vs. omission of complementizer *that*: *I believe that you are mistaken* vs. *I believe you are mistaken*
- Prenominal possessive vs. postnominal *of*-phrase: *the company's director* vs. *the director of the company.*

The variants in question are equally acceptable and differ hardly at all in their conceptual content. As with the comparatives and superlatives, however, there are a number of factors which are likely to affect a speaker's choice. In the case of particle placement, for example, important factors are properties of the postverbal nominal, whether definite or indefinite, animate or inanimate, whether a full noun phrase or a pronoun and, if a full noun phrase, its degree of internal complexity (Gries 2003a, b). In addition, certain verb–particle combinations might be inherently biased towards one or the other of the two constructions. The interpretation of the verb phrase— whether it receives a more literal as opposed to a more metaphorical or idiomatic interpretation—can also play a role.

There is another factor which has been shown to be important in the speaker's choice of one variant over the other. This is the recent use of the form in question. A form, once used, can be contagious (Calude and Miller 2009). Consider once again the example cited at the beginning of this section. I have already commented on the rarity of the word *slipperiest*. In the example sentence the word comes hard on the heels of another superlative form, *hardest*. The rare word has been formed on the same pattern as the earlier word. Imagine that the first sentence of the example had been: *Sorry is one of the most difficult words to say.* Chances are, I think, that this context would have triggered the continuation: *It is also one of the most slippery.*[14]

The RECENCY EFFECT goes under other names, such as SYNTACTIC (or STRUCTURAL) PRIMING (an earlier use activates the structure in question, making it more easily available to the speaker) and syntactic (or structural) PERSISTENCE (a form once used tends to be re-used). A related phenomenon, familiar to sociolinguists, goes under the name of ACCOMMODATION: a speaker tends to 'accommodate' to the usage of her

---

[14] For an example where a recent use inclines the speaker to use the analytic form, consider the following:

(i) Red Desert is at once the most beautiful, the most simple and the most daring film yet made by Italy's masterful Michelangelo Antonioni. (*Time*, 19 February 1965)

The use of *most beautiful* seems to trigger the choice of the less usual *most simple* (79 examples in COCA) over the more common alternative *simplest* (1,949 instances).

interlocutors, for example, by adopting features of their pronunciation (Giles 1973; Giles, Coupland, and Coupland 1991).[15]

An early documentation of the recency effect was provided by Levelt and Kelter (1982). They discovered that the wording of a question was able to influence the form of an answer. The researchers telephoned stores in town and asked when they closed, using one of the following questions:

(2) a. Hoe laat gaat uw winkel dicht?
         'What time does your shop close?'
     b. Om hoe laat gaat uw winkel dicht?
         'At what time does your shop close?'

Question (b) tended to be answered with a preposition (e.g. *om vijf uur* 'at five o'clock'), while question (a) elicited a response without the preposition. A smaller effect was still obtained if distracting material was interposed between the question and answer.[16]

Levelt and Kelter's experiment leaves it unclear whether responses were based on the syntax of the questions or whether it was simply the preposition that was primed. Subsequent research demonstrated the reality of syntactic priming. Bock (1986) found that if a picture is described using, let us say, a passive construction (e.g. *The building manager is being mugged by a gang of teenagers*) or by a ditransitive construction (*The governess makes the princess a pot of tea*), subjects are liable to describe a subsequent picture using the same syntactic form (e.g. *The church is being struck by lightning* or *The man is reading the boy a story*).

The recency effect has also been demonstrated in non-experimental situations, namely, on corpus data (Gries 2005; Szmrecsanyi 2005, 2006). Szmrecsanyi attempted to untangle the many factors which influence the choice of a number of variants, such as *will* vs. *going to* for the expression of future, analytic vs. synthetic

---

[15] To give a personal example: I normally pronounce *data* as [deɪtə]; the predominant pronunciation in New Zealand, however, is [daːtə]. In conversing with students about their data, I have found myself consciously opting for what is for me the non-preferred pronunciation. Conversely, I have observed students hesitate over their use of [daːtə], using instead my pronunciation [deɪtə].

[16] Levelt and Kelter (1982) found the same effect when they questioned subjects about a picture. Thus, question (a) tended to elicit a response with the preposition *op*, whereas (b) elicited a response without the preposition.

(i) a. Op welk instrument speelt Paul?
         'On which instrument does Paul play?'
     b. Welk instrument bespeelt Paul?
         'Which instrument does Paul play?'

It should be noted, however, that these two questions differ also in their argument structure, with (b) making use of the transitive verb *bespeel* in contrast to (a) with intransitive *speel*. The syntax of the question would therefore work against a prepositional response to (b).

comparatives, particle placement, and the choice (available for some verbs) of an infinitival vs. an *-ing* complement (*start to rain* vs. *start raining*). Of the alternations that Szmrecsanyi studied, the comparative turned out to show the largest recency effect. Intriguingly, even a prior use of *more* in a non-comparative context was able to increase the odds in favour of the analytic comparative form.[17]

Recency and micro-learning

What are we to make of the recency effect? One possibility is that it is little more than a purely local, transient phenomenon, relevant only to language production in progress and having no lasting impact on the language system or on the speaker's linguistic knowledge. This appears to be the view of Pickering and his associates (Pickering and Branigan 1998; Branigan, Pickering, Stewart, and McLean 2000; Pickering, Branigan, and McLean 2002). On the other hand, the very fact that a particular form has been used will serve to entrench this form, if only to a minuscule degree, in the mental grammar of a speaker, thus increasing, if only minimally, the availability of the form for future use. Seen in this way, the recency effect contributes to implicit learning. It illustrates, on a micro level, the very process of language learning.

Bock and Griffin (2000; see also Bock, Dell, Chang, and Onishi 2007; Chang, Dell, Bock, and Griffin 2000) endorse the view that the recency effect is a learning mechanism. They reach this conclusion on the grounds that the priming effect can persist over lengthy periods of time and in spite of intervening activities, after which the specific wording of the prime is no longer available for conscious recall. However, in putting forward this view, they draw a curious distinction between learning a language and learning to use a language:

We interpret our results as suggesting that structural priming can arise within a system that is organized for learning how to produce sequences of words, as a consequence of the learning processes themselves. Seen in this light, structural priming is a dynamic vestige of the process of learning to perform language. We call this process *learning to talk*, in the completely literal sense of *talk*. It is not learning language but learning to produce it. In this sense, learning to talk involves learning procedures—cognitive skills—for efficiently formulating and producing

---

[17] The converse of persistence, i.e. the avoidance of repetition, dubbed *horror aequi* 'horror of the same', has also been documented (Rohdenburg 2003). While *It's started raining* is fine, *It's starting raining* would be avoided due to the repetition of the *-ing* suffix (Bolinger 1979). In phonology, the phenomenon goes under the name of DISSIMILATION. For example, there are in English no words commencing in [bw] or [pw]; English, it seems, disallows consonant clusters which share a labial articulation. Unlike persistence effects, avoidance of repetition would appear to be a very local phenomenon, affecting only items in very close proximity. It is also very selective. There is no prohibition against *I'm enjoying reading this novel*, in spite of the repeated *-ing* suffix.

utterances. What structural priming suggests is that these procedures may undergo fine-tuning in every episode of adult language production.   (Bock and Griffin 2000: 188–9)

The distinction appears to be a vestige of the Chomskyan distinction between competence and performance. The underlying assumption appears to be that (mature) speakers of a language know the rules which generate, let us say, ditransitive clauses; this is an aspect of their competence. After the initial learning period, in childhood, competence is assumed to be relatively static throughout the course of a person's life. Learning to use a language, however, is a matter of acquiring a skill. Proficiency in using a language is variable and can be improved by training and practice (or can atrophy through lack of use). The distinction is, I think, a false one. One facet of knowing a language is, precisely, to know the relative frequency of its various elements and the circumstances in which these can be used. It is not just a matter of the frequency of lexical items, but the relative frequency of constructions and the degree of attraction between words and constructions. This knowledge is not static, but is liable to fluctuate in accordance with one's day-by-day linguistic experience. Intriguingly, Szmrecsanyi's (2006) research suggests that the recency effect may be weaker for older speakers. Just as elderly people are (supposedly) reluctant to change their personal habits, so also, it would seem, they are resistant to modifying their linguistic habits in response to the language they hear around them.

Research by Jaeger and Snider (2007) throws further light on the workings of the recency effect. One of their findings is that more unusual structures—structures which are statistically less frequent in the language—have a greater priming effect than more predictable structures. For example, passives are on the whole less frequent than actives. It turns out that the recency effect is larger with passives than it is with actives. Similarly, while many verbs are compatible with both the ditransitive [V NP NP] and the prepositional [V NP PP] construction, a particular verb may be strongly biased towards one of the constructions. *Cost*, for example, is a verb which is typically used in the ditransitive environment (*It cost the industry a lot of money*; *The policy will cost the party a lot of votes*) but only rarely in the prepositional construction (an example from the COCA: *It does cost a lot of money to the movie industry*). Jaeger and Snider found that an unusual (statistically speaking) prepositional construction has a stronger priming effect than a more predictable expression.

The strength of the priming effect for more unusual primes provides yet more evidence that speakers of a language 'know' the relative frequencies of things in their language. The finding also highlights some aspects of the learning process itself. Usual structures, by definition, have been encountered many times before. They have been 'overlearned', such that additional exposure will barely increase their already highly entrenched status. Unusual structures, on the other hand, are likely to be noticed. As Jaeger and Snider put it, they have a 'surprisal' effect. For this reason, their impact on the language system is likely to be greater and the hearer will be more disposed to re-use them. It is along these lines that we can offer a speculative explanation for why some structures and some words can be learned even on the basis of minimal exposure. Precisely because of their unusualness, they have a surprisal effect—they are noticed. As we have previously observed, most English speakers appear to know the expression *kick the bucket*, in spite of the infrequency of the expression (according to corpus data). We might suppose that the very strangeness of the expression is likely to register with anyone who hears it.

It is interesting to note, in this connection, that researchers into second language acquisition have proposed that a learner's disposition to notice new or unusual aspects of encountered language could be a major driver of the acquisition process. According to the NOTICING HYPOTHESIS (Schmidt 1990), successful learners of a second or foreign language are those who notice, in the input, words and structures that they themselves would not have used and who then go on to use these forms in their own production. A matter of some debate is whether noticing needs to be at the level of conscious awareness (Truscott 1998). As originally formulated, the noticing hypothesis supposed that the learner had to be consciously aware of novel aspects of the input. Accordingly, second language acquisition researchers recommended the use of teaching strategies which served to raise the learner's awareness of specific features of the input (Fotos 1993). Research on the recency effect, on the other hand, suggests that priming by unusual structures may well pass below the threshold of consciousness. As Bock and Griffin (2000: 179) observe, speakers can be "wholly oblivious to the features of their speech that are susceptible to structural priming". Certainly, in experimental studies of the recency effect, subjects are not requested specifically to focus their attention on any aspect of the primes, neither is it plausible to suppose that speakers engaging in day-to-day conversation are consciously noticing those features of the ongoing discourse—whether this be the form of comparatives or the placement of particles—which are likely to give rise to recency effects. Indeed, practically *every* feature of the input language—syntactic, lexical, morphological, and phonological—is a candidate for the priming of future production.

For acquisition researchers, the study of priming effects opens a window on the very process of acquisition itself, both in children acquiring their mother tongue (Savage, Lieven, Theakston, and Tomasello 2006) and learners acquiring a foreign or second language. Priming, namely, illustrates 'micro-learning' in progress. Consider, in this context, a study by McDonough and Mackey (2008). The authors monitored the use by second language learners of interrogative forms in relation to forms that had been used in addressing the learners, the research question being the extent to which the learners 'picked up' the syntax of interrogatives from the language to which they had been exposed. Some learners were responsive to priming: that is, they tended to re-use the forms that they had been presented with. It was found that 'high primers'—more specifically, those learners who re-used the syntactic structures of the input and not just its lexical material—went on to achieve better in their subsequent studies:

> [T]he post hoc analysis indicated that those highpriming participants whose questions contained different question words and main verbs developed, whereas the participants who reused the lexical items provided in the scripted interlocutors' questions did not develop. The findings suggest that syntactic priming might be associated with L2 developmental outcomes when participants apply the syntactic structure to a wide variety of question words and main verbs and matrix verbs.   (McDonough and Mackey 2008: 43)

Successful language learners appear to be those who are blessed with "particular aptitudes" which might predispose them to benefit from "the implicit learning processes associated with syntactic priming" (p. 44). In a sense, of course, this observation just replaces one research question with another. If successful language learning is a matter of being able to benefit from priming, what lies behind this particular aptitude?

I recall a former colleague of mine—an otherwise highly proficient second language user of English—who invariably pronounced the word *category* as [kəˈtɛgəriː], with stress on the second syllable, in spite of massive input evidence of the 'correct' pronunciation [ˈkætəgri], with stress on the initial syllable. One wonders why this individual was not able to benefit from the priming process. Why did the pronunciation [ˈkætəgri], when he heard it, fail to have a surprisal effect? Why did he not 'notice' the discrepancy between his own usage and that of his interlocutors? It is not only the production of non-native speakers that is at issue here. Native speakers may also have their idiosyncratic quirks of usage. They may use words in ways which are not sanctioned by common usage or may pronounce words in odd ways, or at least in ways which diverge from the dominant pronunciation in their community. Why does the input which these speakers receive not serve to prime the correct usage?

Jaeger and Snider's (2007) research may be relevant to this question. They found that the recency effect tended to be stronger in cases of SELF-PRIMING, that is, in cases where both prime and target are produced by the same speaker, than in cases where prime and target are spoken by different individuals. A speaker who repeatedly uses an incorrect form is in essence priming himself to use this same form on future occasions. Each time my colleague came out with the form [kəˈtɛgəri] he was strengthening his mental representation of this pronunciation. A not unsurprising finding of Jaeger and Snider's was that repeated use of a certain structure over a stretch of discourse has a stronger priming effect than a single usage.

The recency effect may also be implicated in one of the research methods favoured by many linguists, namely the elicitation of grammaticality judgements. Luka and Barsalou (2005) invited subjects to read a list of sentences. Some of these sentences had been independently judged to be of dubious or marginal acceptability.[18] After a short period devoted to other tasks, subjects were presented with sentences which they were asked to grade for their acceptability. The researchers found that prior exposure to a sentence on the reading task was able to enhance grammaticality judgements when the sentence was subsequently presented for evaluation. The effect also obtained if the target sentences exhibited the same syntactic structure, albeit with a different wording, as the prime. The results suggest that mere exposure to a sentence is sufficient to leave a memory trace in the subject's mental corpus; the sentence, in other words, is assimilated to a person's I-language and becomes, in a sense, part of the mental representation of the language. As will be readily apparent, Luka and Barsalou's findings should be of special interest to syntacticians.[19] A good deal of syntactic theorizing is based on intuitions pertaining to the grammaticality of invented sentences. The methodology is rendered suspect by the fact that the very act of contemplating a sentence, and sub-vocally repeating it to oneself, may enhance a person's assessment of its grammaticality.

In conclusion

In his 1967 textbook *Language and Its Structure*, Langacker asserted that "talking does not consist of parroting sentences that have been heard and memorized". He dismissed that idea that we "go around collecting sentences to hold in memory for

---

[18] The sentences that were deemed to be less than fully grammatical were as follows:

We hate to bake pies anymore.
From the CIA, I assure you that I would never accept a penny.
What Christmas shopping means to me is that I walk my feet to pieces.
I miss having any time to do anything.
Sam recites poems as well as playing the piano.
Sam asked that we leave and he'd give us $10.
We want for most people not to catch on.
It's uncertain he'll arrive until after midnight.
What Mark wanted is to look at your notes.
A heart courageous never breathed scant.
My brother was kept tabs on by the FBI.
Which pope's reign was Copernicus born during?
Who did you hire because he said would work hard?
Go see whether the paper's here and bring it in.
You should hire a manager as efficient as the competition has.
You should absolutely come and visit me.
In China, wine is served in small cups, and in Turkey, coffee.
More physicists became farmers than went to law school, and more philosophers did too.
Lester is a better pianist than Janice and better singer than Edna.
Clinton and Dole both promised Dan Rather not to cause each other any trouble.

[19] The findings may also be relevant to foreign language teachers. Repeated exposure to students' errors may well result in the teacher doubting whether the errors are indeed such. The effect, known as SYNTACTIC SATIATION, was experimentally confirmed by Snyder (2000).

future use in speaking and understanding. Nor do we have to search through our personal linguistic archives ... whenever we want to say something" (p. 22). At this stage in his career, Langacker was still in thrall to generative theories of language, with its assumption that sentence production is a matter of rules operating over items selected from the lexicon.[20] Fast forward twenty years, and Langacker takes a radically different view of linguistic knowledge. In the first volume of his *Foundations of Cognitive Grammar*, he argues that linguistic knowledge is the product of usage:

> Every use of a structure has a positive impact on its degree of entrenchment, whereas extended periods of disuse have a negative impact. With repeated use, a novel structure becomes progressively entrenched, to the point of becoming a unit. (Langacker 1987: 59)

Speaking of the semantic representations associated with words and phrases, he claims that

> there is a nontrivial theoretical sense in which every experience that somehow involves an entity has an impact on our understanding of it (and consequently on the meaning of an expression that designates it), be the effect minor or infinitesimal. Though these impacts seldom have direct practical consequences, collectively and cumulatively they are the determinants of semantic structure. (Langacker 1987: 160)

The effects of usage on linguistic knowledge are life-long:

> Every usage event has some impact (even if very minor) on the structure of the categories it invokes.... Any facet of a category network, once established, is maintained or further entrenched by its continued activation in further usage events. For this reason, changes in patterns of experience and communicative needs can alter the specific configuration of a network even for a mature speaker. (Langacker 1987: 376)

Bybee has also argued that repeated usage strengthens the mental representation of the unit in question. In the following, she speaks of words and their entrenchment in memory. What she says of words, however, will also apply to other elements of linguistic structure. Each time a phrase, collocation, or syntactic construction is processed, its mental representation is strengthened, thus making the relevant structure more readily available for future use.

> If we metaphorically suppose that a word can be written into the [mental] lexicon, then each time a word in processing is mapped onto its lexical representation it is as though the representation was traced over again, etching it with deeper and darker lines each time. Each time a word is heard and produced it leaves a slight trace on the lexicon, it increases its lexical strength. (Bybee 1985: 117)

---

[20] See Chapter 2, p. 21.

The notion that speakers of a language lay down memories of previously heard utterances is, on the face of it, highly counterintuitive and conflicts with findings reported by, amongst others, Sachs (1967, 1974) and Jarvella (1970, 1971). These researchers found that the surface form of a sentence is available for recall for only a very short period of time. Jarvella (1971) reports that when the reading of a text was suddenly interrupted listeners were able to retrieve verbatim only the current clause or sentence, even though they were able to respond with a high degree of accuracy to questions testing comprehension of previously heard material. The implication of this research is that listeners process an incoming message solely for its semantic content. They must, perforce, hold the form of the message in memory while it is being processed. However, once the semantic content has been accessed and committed to memory, the form of the message is discarded and is no longer available for conscious attention.

The existence of recency effects, not to mention their ubiquity, shows that even though listeners may no longer have direct access to the form of previously heard utterances, they are nevertheless registering, albeit unconsciously, all manner of properties of the language that they encounter. Research reviewed in this chapter shows that these memories of encountered language are able to influence future linguistic behaviour; they may even, as I have suggested, be constitutive of language learning itself.

10

Polysemy

Polysemy is commonly defined as the association of two or more related meanings with a single linguistic form.[1] The linguistic forms in question are typically taken to be words, though the notion can also be applied to other meaning-bearing units, such as bound morphemes and syntactic constructions.[2] In this chapter, my main concern will be the polysemy of words.

Though seemingly straightforward, and in spite of its being widely accepted, the definition turns out to be problematic in many respects (Taylor 2003c). There are, to begin with, the difficulties which are likely to arise whenever we try to apply the definition to the analysis of any particular set of data (Taylor 1992a). Do two uses of a word exemplify two different meanings or are they better regarded as instances of one and the same meaning? If the meanings are different are they also related, and if so, how? If the related meanings are associated with different syntactic environments, might there be grounds for claiming that we are dealing with so many different words? A further issue concerns the proposed meaning(s) and how they are to be stated. If different uses are to be brought under a single meaning, it is incumbent on the analyst to specify just what this meaning is. Moreover, any meaning characterization must not only be consistent with all the various uses of the item in question, it must also differentiate the item from each of its near synonyms.

I discuss these issues in more detail later in this chapter. In the meantime, in order to get a taste of what is involved, consider the phrases *the water in the vase* and *the crack in the vase*. Both refer to a relation of containment and on this basis we might suppose that *in* has the same meaning. A moment's reflection, however, shows that the containment relation is subtly different in the two cases. In the first example the water is contained in the hollow internal region of the vase (in its upright position), while in the second example the crack is a fault in the material substance of the vase

---

[1] See, for example, Goddard (1998: 19): "Polysemy designates a situation in which a single word has a set of related meanings"; and Ravin and Leacock (2000: 1), who speak of words having a "multiplicity of meanings". Similar definitions can be cited from many sources.

[2] See, for example, Panther and Thornburg (2001) on the polysemy of the nominalizing *-er* suffix and Goldberg (1995) on the cluster of related meanings of the ditransitive construction. Further examples of non-lexical polysemy may be found in Cuyckens and Zawada (1997).

(irrespective of its position). The contrasting interpretations suggest that we should regard *in* as polysemous. We might argue against this view by pointing out that the different understandings of the *in*-relation follow from what we know about water, vases, and cracks. A crack, by its very nature, is a fault in the material substance of a thing. The meaning of *crack* therefore coerces, or imposes, a particular reading of *in*, suggesting that the preposition has only one meaning. An argument in favour of the polysemy account, on the other hand, could be cases of ambiguity. Consider the phrase *the splinter in my hand*. This could refer to a splinter which is embedded in the material substance of my hand or to a splinter which I am holding in my hand. The ambiguity would appear to derive from the polysemy of *in*. Note, however, that the two readings also involve different understandings of *hand*, as a material object or as an entity that is capable of holding things. We could, to be sure, argue that the interpretation of *hand* is coerced by the reading assigned to *in*. Equally plausible would be an account which locates the ambiguity in different senses of *hand*, each of which coerces a particular reading of *in*.

As we see, arguments can be mustered both for the view that *in* is polysemous and for the view that it has only one meaning (in the expressions under discussion). I doubt very much whether the issue can be settled conclusively one way or the other, in this and in many other cases. This depressing conclusion does not, of course, mean that polysemy is not a useful, or indeed a real phenomenon. It does, however, suggest that it might be futile to approach the topic by attempting to associate each word of the language with a fixed number (one or more) of discrete meanings, meanings which can be characterized independently of the contexts in which a word appears. As I shall argue in this chapter, polysemy is better thought of in terms of the ways in which a linguistic form can be used. Words do not stand for so many discrete chunks of semantic content and speakers certainly do not learn the words of their language by learning these form–meaning associations. Rather, words need to be characterized in terms of their CONTEXTUAL PROFILE, having to do with the kinds of items they collocate with, the constructions they feature in, and the kinds of texts they occur in, in addition to their purely conceptual value and their referential possibilities.

How many meanings?

As the above examples show, a major problem with polysemy, as commonly understood, is that it may not be an easy matter to determine whether a word is polysemous or not, and, if polysemy is suspected, just how many different meanings are to be recognized.

To appreciate the extent of the problem, we need only compare the ways in which words are treated in different dictionaries. For the verb *open*, the *Collins English Dictionary* (1979 edition) distinguishes fourteen different senses, the *Collins Cobuild* (1987) lists twenty-nine, while the *Longman Dictionary of Contemporary English*

(1978) identifies only six. Fillmore and Atkins (2000) demonstrate on the example of the verb *crawl* that the definitions of one dictionary do not always map onto the definitions of other dictionaries. Discrepancies between dictionaries cannot therefore be explained away by appeal to the delicacy of the distinctions that are drawn. Clearly, lexicographers studying a given word are liable to come up with different and even incompatible accounts. Fillmore and Atkins report another interesting finding. They discovered that some uses of *crawl* attested in a corpus could not be reconciled with any of the dictionary entries. According to the dictionaries that they consulted, *crawl* designates a manner of motion which can be predicated only of animate creatures, such as babies, humans on all fours, limbless invertebrates (e.g. snakes), and slow-moving insects (e.g. cockroaches). Fillmore and Atkins (2000: 95), however, found examples of crawling predicated of inanimate entities, such as hands, clouds, fog, steam, and darkness:

(1) a. She felt his hand crawling up her thigh.
     b. Dark heavy clouds were crawling across the sky.
     c. He watched the approaching fog crawling forward.
     d. A cloud of steam crawled slowly upwards from the chimney.
     e. Darkness crawled through the suburbs like a flood of black ink.

The failure of dictionaries to mention these uses could reflect a lack of diligence on the part of the lexicographers. It could also suggest the open-endedness of word use: speakers can, and often do, extend established uses to new situations.

In an attempt to answer the question of 'how many meanings', linguists have proposed a number of polysemy tests (Geeraerts 1993; Taylor 2003b: 104–6). Let us consider just one of these, the AMBIGUITY TEST (Cruse 2000a: 31; Quine 1960: 129). An ambiguous sentence has two or more readings, each with its own truth conditions. Accordingly, the sentence may be true (with respect to a given situation) on one of its readings but not true on the other reading(s). It would not be a contradiction (though it might well be pragmatically bizarre) to assert that there is a pig (= farm animal) in the kitchen and, at the same time, that there is not a pig (= greedy person) in the kitchen. *Pig*, by this test, is polysemous. On the other hand, it would not be possible to assert that Frieda is my aunt (= my mother's sister) and that she is not my aunt (= my father's sister). Although *aunt* can refer to different relations to Ego, the word is unspecified for these distinctions. *Frieda is my aunt* 'fails' the ambiguity test, showing that *aunt* is not polysemous (with respect to the distinction at issue).

Unfortunately, the ambiguity test is of only limited help in identifying polysemy.[3] In the first place, there are some cases where the ambiguity test is known to give unreliable results. One example concerns words which are autohyponomous; these

---

[3] Other polysemy tests fare just as badly. See Geeraerts (1993) and Kilgarriff (1997).

are words which have a more general meaning which includes a more specific meaning (Geeraerts 1993). *Dog* can refer to a member of the canine species or to a male member of the species (contrasting with *bitch*). One might therefore expect that *Lassie is a dog* could be either true or false, depending on which sense of *dog* is implicated. This expectation is not fulfilled; a statement that Lassie is a dog (= canine) but not a dog (= male canine) is a contradiction. *Day* gives the same results. The word can refer either to the period of daylight (in contrast to *night*) or to a twenty-four hour period. It would be nonsensical to say that I stayed there for a day (= the period of daylight) but that I didn't stay there for a day (= a twenty-four hour period).

As its name suggests, the ambiguity test is a test for ambiguity. Even when an expression 'passes' the test, we may still be unsure about the source of the ambiguity. Take our earlier example of the splinter in my hand. The phrase has two interpretations and these appear to be due to two different readings of *in* and *hand*. However, the different readings of these words co-select each other: the two putative readings of *in* and the two putative readings of *hand* are not able to combine to give a phrase which is four-ways ambiguous. For this reason it would be difficult to source the ambiguity in either of the two words. Rather, the ambiguity is a kind of prosody which spreads over the whole phrase.

Consider, as another example of this phenomenon, the sentence *I left the university a short time ago*.[4] This could mean that I walked off the campus an hour or so ago or that I terminated my relation with the institution, by resigning or graduating, a couple of months ago. The motion vs. severing-a-relation interpretation affects the semantic value of just about every item in the sentence. *Leave* can refer either to motion out of a containing space or to the severing of a relation; *the university* can refer to a building or to an institution; *a short time ago* can be a matter of minutes or hours or it could be measured in weeks or months. Even the way in which the subject referent is understood is implicated. On the one reading I could be any member of the public; on the other I am a student or employee.[5]

A further problem with the ambiguity test is that in many cases it may not be possible to construct an appropriate test sentence. The ambiguity test requires that

---

[4] The example is adapted from Bierwisch and Schreuder (1992).

[5] Consider also a sentence which Chomsky has cited in various places: *Flying planes can be dangerous* (see e.g. Chomsky 1964: 42, 1965: 21). Chomsky attributed the ambiguity to the transformational history of the phrase *flying planes*. Alternatively, we could say that the phrase can instantiate two different constructions, each with its own semantic value. It could be an instance of the [Adj N] construction, where the adjective in question is a present participle ('planes which are flying'). It could also be an instance of a V-*ing* nominalization denoting the action of (someone) flying planes. The two readings involve two different values of the word *flying* (present participle vs. *ing*-nominalization) and two different semantic roles of the nominal. On the one hand, flying is a property of things that fly (*fly* is therefore understood as an intransitive verb), while on the nominalization reading flying involves the act of (someone) flying things of a certain kind (*fly* is therefore understood as a transitive verb). In this example, once again, it would be futile to attempt to pin-point the source of the ambiguity in any one element in the phrase.

the various senses of the word under investigation are compatible with the same syntactic and lexical environment. Does *over* have the same sense in *We are over the worst* and *The worst is over*? The ambiguity test is of little help, since the transitive and intransitive uses of *over* cannot be collapsed. Does *turn* have the same meaning in *turn over* and *turn round*? One might be inclined to say that it does; the word designates circular motion around an axis, whether the axis is horizontal or vertical being contributed by the preposition/particle. However, since the two uses of *turn* involve two different collocations, it is not possible to construct a potentially ambiguous sentence which could test for polysemy. Or consider the above-mentioned examples with *crawl*. Does *crawl* have the same meaning when the subject referent is a human on all fours, a legless invertebrate, a cat, or an inanimate entity such as a cloud, fog, or darkness? The meaning of the verb is intimately bound up with the kind of entity of which the activity is predicated, thus rendering the ambiguity test inoperative.

Opening and cutting; lumping and splitting

In their approaches to polysemy, linguists can roughly speaking be categorized as lumpers or splitters.[6] Splitters tend to multiply the number of senses they assign to a word, often on the basis of sometimes minute differences in its referential possibilities. Lumpers are inclined to bring different uses under a single more schematic value, deriving more specific values from pragmatic and contextual factors.[7]

Lakoff is well-known for having favoured a splitting approach:

It is common for a single word to have more than one meaning. In some cases the meanings are unrelated, like the two meanings of *bank*—the place where you put your money and the land along the edge of a river. In such cases, there is not one word, but two. They are called instances of *homonymy*, where two words with totally different meanings are pronounced in the same way. In other cases, the meanings are related, often in such a close and systematic way

---

[6] The terms are used of taxonomists and refer to those who go for broad, general categories, ignoring petty differences, in contrast to those who set up a multitude of categories on the basis of these small differences. The distinction is explained in the following quotation from the *OED*:

Cornhill Magazine, 1894: Modern biologists are divided into the two camps of the splitters and the lumpers. The first are in favour of making a species out of every petty... variety; the second are all for lumping unimportant minor forms into a single species.

[7] One of the most radical of the lumpers is Ruhl (1989), who proposed to bring even all the various uses of the verb *bear* under a single semantic category. Minimal polysemy is also a hallmark of Coseriu's (1977, 2000) structuralist approach. Thus, according to Coseriu (1977: 15), "on doit par principe pour toute forme linguistique supposer... un signifié distinct, et plus précisément un signifié unique et unitaire, valable pour tous les contextes où apparaît la forme" ('one should, as a matter of principle, assume for each linguistic form a distinct signification, more precisely, a single and unitary signification, valid for all the contexts in which the form appears'). In defence of splitting, see Tuggy (2003) and, with special reference to Coseriu, Taylor (1999*a*). A middle course—as little polysemy as possible but as much as necessary—is promoted by Tyler and Evans (2001).

that we don't notice at first that more than one sense exists at all. Take the word *window*, for example. It can refer either to an opening in a wall or to the glass-filled frame in that opening. Or take the word *open*. We open doors and open presents, and though the actions described by the word are very different, we would normally have to think twice before noticing the difference. Or the word *run*. It is very different for Harry to run into the woods and for the road to run into the woods. Again, there is a single verb with two senses so intimately related that we have to think twice before noticing the difference. Such cases are called instances of *polysemy*. They are cases where there is one lexical item with a family of related senses.

(Lakoff 1987: 416)

Lakoff appears to take the view that differences in the referential potential of a word are reason enough to justify a polysemy account. As he points out, opening a book involves different activities from opening a present; these activities are different yet again from opening the curtains, opening your arms, or opening your eyes. Similarly with the word *window*. If you paint a window you paint only the frame, not the glass; if you break a window you break the glass, not the frame; and if you open a window you manoeuvre only the moveable portion, not the fixed part (Lakoff 1987: 417). On the face of it, we are dealing with so many different meanings of the words *open* and *window*.

It will be appreciated that Lakoff's approach, if consistently applied, will result in a massive inflation in the number of meanings that are to be assigned to words, even if we restrict our attention to literal, non-metaphorical uses. In itself, of course, "rampant polysemy" (Cuyckens and Zawada 1997: xvii) need not be a reason for concern. There is no a priori limit on the number of different meanings that can attach to a linguistic form. If the facts demand that a word be associated with a large number of different meanings, then our analysis should reflect these facts. Neither should we be concerned about the storage constraints on polysemy. As Fodor (1975: 150) put it, "computing memory is expensive, but long-term memory is cheap". There is indeed a very powerful argument favouring a multiplicity of meanings. It comes from the compositionality principle (see pp. 40ff). Strict compositionality requires that the meaning of an expression can be fully computed from the meanings of its parts and the manner of their combination. If we wish to be able to compute the meaning of *open the window* we will need to combine a very specific sense of *open* with an equally specific meaning of *window*.

This advantage, however, comes at a cost. Polysemy generates ambiguity. If *open* has *n* different meanings, the understanding of any expression containing this word will require that the hearer selects just that sense that is intended. It gets worse. If *open* has n_1 different meanings and *window* has n_2 different entries in the lexicon, *open the window* will be $n_1 \times n_2$ ways ambiguous. The ambiguity will have to be resolved, presumably at a cost in cognitive processing. Moreover, ambiguity will increase exponentially as ever more (polysemous) words are added to the expression. This result goes counter to the fact that additional context tends to reduce, rather than increase ambiguity. Considerations such as these suggest that we should attempt to limit polysemy as much as possible. In the ideal case, we will want to attribute but a single sense to a word.

Examples similar to Lakoff's were discussed by Searle (1980, 1983). Searle (1983) makes an observation similar to Lakoff's, that opening a door and opening a wound involve different kinds of activities; likewise for cutting the grass and cutting a cake (Searle 1980). As a consequence, different uses of *open* and *cut* are associated with different sets of truth conditions. You would not, for example, cut the cake by running the lawnmower over it, nor would you open the door by making incisions in it with a surgeon's scalpel.

Unlike Lakoff, Searle vigorously rejects the idea that *open* and *cut* are polysemous (at least, in their literal uses; he concedes that *open a restaurant* and *cut classes* might exemplify extended senses of the verbs). He is particularly disturbed by the proliferation of polysemes. If we assume that *open* and *cut* have different meanings according to the type of entities that feature as the direct object we would have to entertain the possibility of an indefinite number of meanings. For Searle, "indefinite polysemy" (1983: 146) would be an absurdity. On the contrary, he contends that *cut*, in *cut the grass* and *cut the cake*, has "the same semantic content", and makes the same semantic contribution to the two expressions.[8]

The lumping approach which Searle adopts is also not without its problems. In the first place, if we deny that a word has different meanings in different contexts, we are obligated to say just what the unitary semantic content of the word actually is. What, in brief, does *cut* actually mean, abstracting away from the specifics of different kinds of cutting activity? Second, we need an account of how the unitary meaning gets elaborated, or modulated, in specific contexts of use. Complicating the matter further is the fact—noted by Searle—that the semantic properties of an expression, such as its truth conditions and its entailments, adhere to the contextualized meaning; they cannot be read off from the unitary meaning.

Some words are no doubt easier to deal with than others. For *window*, we might argue that the unitary meaning refers to our conception of a particular kind of architectural feature. Our concept includes knowledge of the function and usual location of windows, their structure, the materials they are made from, and how we typically interact with them. Any specific use of the word is likely to highlight only some facet of the broader concept (Evans 2006, 2009). Langacker (1984) has discussed the matter under the rubric of the ACTIVE ZONE phenomenon. Typically, when an entity is involved in a predication, only some facet of the entity will be highlighted in the conceptualization.

---

[8] It is worth noting that other languages do in fact differentiate these different kinds of cutting. For Mandarin, see Chen (2007).

In some cases, we might appeal to general processes of meaning extension (or, if one prefers, meaning flexibility). Often, meaning variation is productive, in the sense that it generalizes over lexical items of a certain semantic type (Pustejovsky 1991). A well-known example concerns institution words, such as *museum, school,* and *office* (Bierwisch 1983). We are familiar with the functions and activities of the institutions, their typical locations and layout, the kinds of people they serve, and so on. These words, in actual contexts of use, can refer to the institution as such, the premises which house them, or even the people who work in them.

Open and *cut* are more difficult. (The same, I suspect, goes for many other verbs, especially those in common use.) Searle offers, as an explication of *cut*, the notion of "a physical separation by means of the pressure of some more or less sharp instrument" (1980: 224). He is also quick to point out that *cut the grass* could scarcely be paraphrased as "make a separation of the grass using a more or less sharp instrument". With regards to *open* he is curiously silent, perhaps assuming (mistakenly, I would suggest) that the meaning of the verb, abstracting away from all its various uses, is self-evident.

Searle approached the elaboration of unitary meanings in terms of what he called 'the Background'. The Background is constituted by our general knowledge of how the world functions and how we interact with it. It is variously characterized as "cultural and biological know-how" (1983: 148), "a set of assumptions and practices" (1980: 227), and "a bedrock of mental capacities" (1983: 143). We interpret *open the door* the way we do because we are familiar with the practice of opening doors; we know what they are, what they are for, and how we interact with them. In support, Searle notes that different background assumptions may be suggestive of different practices. Normally, cutting the lawn would involve the use of a lawnmower and would result in a shortening of the individual blades of grass which constitute the lawn. But if you are in the instant lawn business and you ask your assistant to 'cut some lawn' for a customer, you would indeed expect the assistant to slice off some of the lawn, similar to how you would slice off a portion of a cake if asked to cut the cake. If no background assumptions can be activated, an expression might not be able to be interpreted at all. Suppose you are asked to 'cut the sand' or 'open the mountain'. You know what the expressions mean (or so Searle would claim) on the basis of your knowledge of the component words. However, you would have no idea how the requests are supposed to be carried out. This is because, according to Searle, there is no accepted practice of 'cutting sand' or 'opening mountains'.

Searle and Lakoff offer radically different solutions to the polysemy question. Both are problematic, as we have seen. In spite of their differences, however, the two approaches do converge, namely, with respect to the importance which they attach to real-world knowledge of how we interact with different kinds of things. For Lakoff, differences in the kinds of things we do when we open a window and open a present are good enough reason to propose different senses of the verb. Searle, on the other hand, appeals to the Background in order to account for the different practices associated with the different uses of the verb.

To my mind, both Lakoff and Searle succumb to the same error. The error is to assume that *open* and *cut*, viewed as entries in a dictionary, whether paper or mental, are associated with a meaning or, as the case may be, several meanings, and that these meanings are involved in the interpretation of expressions in which the words occur. There is another way to approach the matter. To ask what *cut* and *open* actually mean may be to ask the wrong question. After all, children acquiring English do not learn the verbs in isolation; they learn a range of expressions in which the verbs figure, such as *open the door*, *open your mouth*, *open the book*. They know what these expressions mean because they know the kinds of situations they may be used to refer to.[9] For the language user, the units of knowledge are not the individual verbs *per se*, but the typical collocations of the verbs and the kinds of situations that they can refer to. Indeed, if you ask people to state what *open* means, they will typically describe— sometimes resorting to gesture—a specific use of the verb. The language user may, of course, perceive some commonality between the different uses. On the other hand, they may not. In any case, this kind of metalinguistic insight is not a prerequisite for proficiency in the language. All that is needed of the speaker is that she is familiar with the word combinations and the kinds of situations they refer to.

One might object that this kind of item-based approach limits the creativity of language use. Speakers would be condemned to forever using only those collocations that they have already encountered. It seems, however, that speakers have no qualms about extending established uses to contexts which are not fully sanctioned by existing uses. Recall the earlier examples with *crawl*. To say of an inanimate entity such as fog or darkness that it 'crawls' is to go beyond established usage by attributing to the entities in question the kind of slow, gradual movement which is associated with the verb in other contexts. Children are especially apt to extend words in this way. You open a present to find out what is inside the package, so it seems only natural that you can 'open the television' (= switch it on) in order to find out what is showing. And if you can use *open* to refer to starting up a device like a television, might you not also open the electric light (= switch on) or open the water tap (= turn on)? These uses are indeed characteristic of child language (Bowerman 1978), though they are not sanctioned by adult English. (In many languages, though, the translation equivalent of *open* can indeed be used of electric lights, air conditioning, television sets, and the like.) Learning a word involves learning just which uses are in fact sanctioned in the language community.

---

[9] According to theories of situated and embodied cognition (Barsalou 2008; Yeh and Barsalou 2006; Zwaan 2004), understanding *open the door*, *open your mouth*, and the like, would involve not just familiarity with the kinds of activity that the phrases designate, it would also activate vicarious simulations of the sensori-motor experiences of an agent performing the activities.

It is interesting to reflect on how a mature English speaker would interpret *open the television*, should he encounter such an expression. This is not a typical collocation (there are no examples in the BNC or the COCA). The normal strategy, I suggest, is through analogy. One searches in one's mental corpus for other uses of *open* which appear to be relevant to the case in hand. For example, you open a box by removing the lid and so gain access to its contents. Accordingly, opening the television could involve removing the back panel in order to gain access to its inner workings. Consider, in this light, Searle's examples *open the mountain* and *cut the sand*. Searle claims that the expressions are perfectly meaningful, though lacking an interpretation. Lakoff's account, on the other hand, would require that a hearer accesses just one of the many meanings of the verbs and attempts to integrate it into a sensible combination. Since there are (presumably) no listed senses of *open* and *cut* specifically tailored to these phrases, the expressions would be semantically ill-formed. What people do, I suspect, is try to set up analogies between these expressions and already established uses. Suppose the sand is wet and can be moulded. Cutting the sand might then involve dividing the mound into two or more portions.

Relatedness of meanings

According to our initial definition of polysemy, the different meanings of a polysemous item must be related.

There are several ways in which we might seek to relate the meanings of a word. They may share some common meaning component; it may be possible to bring them under a more schematic characterization; one meaning might be a specialization, or alternatively a generalization, of the other; one meaning might be a metaphorical extension of the other; or the meanings may be related by metonymy, that is, a word which basically refers to one kind of entity comes to be used to refer to an associated entity, within a given domain of experience.[10] In many cases, there is the expectation that one meaning can be identified as basic, from which all others can be derived by one or more of the above processes, sometimes even as a result of a chaining process, whereby meaning B is based on A, C is based on B, and so on.

The notion of a basic or central sense can be interpreted in different and sometimes incompatible ways (Fillmore 1982). It could be the historically oldest sense from which the others have developed in the course of time; it could be the meaning which children acquiring their mother tongue learn first and which then gets extended to other situations, by one or more of the processes mentioned above; or it could be the meaning which in some sense is most salient to speakers of a language. These criteria

---

[10] For a survey of the various kinds of meaning relation that have been proposed, see Geeraerts (2010: 25–41).

do not always deliver the same result. The original sense, from a historical point of point, might no longer be extant, or the most salient sense for adult speakers might not coincide with the first uses learnt by a child. Semanticists (and lexicographers) may work with yet another understanding of a basic sense. Viewing the array of meanings associated with a word or other linguistic form, the analyst selects as basic that meaning from which all others can be most plausibly and most economically derived. Not infrequently, given the subjective evaluations needed to implement this approach, different linguists may come up with different proposals for what is supposed to be the basic sense.

The issue is also clouded by considerations of the psychological reality of proposed polysemy analyses. Although the relatedness of two meanings might be apparent to the analysing linguist, it by no means follows that speakers of a language also perceive the different uses to be related. For the linguist, there might be compelling grounds to regard meaning B as an extension of meaning A; there might even be historical evidence for such a process. For the speaker who has learned to use a word in accordance with the norms of the speech community the two meanings might have equal status. The supposed derived meaning might even be the more salient, the more frequent, or the one that is acquired first. The notion of one meaning being derived from, based on, or an extension of another meaning might not feature at all in the speaker's mental representation of the word and how it is used.[11]

We also need to recognize that relatedness of meaning is a graded notion. The uses of *in* mentioned at the beginning of this chapter are obviously very closely related, so closely related, in fact, that we might be inclined to argue that we are dealing with only one meaning. In other cases the relation is more tenuous, such that it may be doubted whether the meanings are related at all. In fact, relatedness of meaning is ultimately a subjective notion and speakers' intuitions in this regard may vary. As a consequence, it may not always be possible to make a clean distinction between polysemy and HOMONYMY (where unrelated meanings are associated with a single form). Take, as an example, the word *ball*, in the meanings 'spherical object' and 'social event involving dancing'. Some people might see in the circular movement of the dancers or the circular shape of a dance floor a relation to the shape of a sphere; for these speakers, the word might count as polysemous. Or take the case of *port* in the meanings 'harbour' and 'fortified wine'. Some English speakers that I have questioned fail to see any connection. For these speakers, *port* is homonymous. These speakers have two different words, with two different meanings, which happen to share the same phonological form.

---

[11] In this paragraph I am, of course, referring to established uses of a word. If a speaker creatively extends a word, as in the earlier example of *open the television*, the relation between the new usage and the usage on which it is modelled is, presumably, evident, at least to the speaker.

Historical evidence is sometimes brought to bear on the matter. As it turns out, *ball* 'spherical object' derives from Old Norse *böllr*, while *ball* 'social event' is from French *bal* (Ayto 1990). The historical evidence suggests that we are dealing with two different words which, in the modern language, happen to share the same phonological form. *Port*, on the other hand, turns out to be polysemous. Port wine was so called because it was exported through the Portuguese city of Oporto ('the port', in Portuguese), similar to how other kinds of wine—such as burgundy and champagne—are named after their places of origin.

Not everyone is aware of the historical development of the words of their language; for this reason alone judgements as to whether a word is polysemous or homonymous are likely to vary from individual to individual. In terms of a speaker's linguistic ability, however, the distinction may not be of any great importance. Whether a speaker perceives a word to be polysemous or homonymous probably has no consequences at all for their ability to use the word appropriately, in accordance with native speaker norms. Indeed, observing how a speaker uses a word would give us no clue as to how she judges the relatedness of its meanings. A speaker simply needs to learn two sets of uses of the word *port*; whether she perceives them to be related is immaterial.

A single linguistic form?

The idea of polysemy as the association of several related meanings to a single linguistic form is problematic from another perspective, namely, that of the 'single linguistic form' to which the various meanings are supposed to be attached. Many words can be used in a variety of syntactic environments. The question arises whether we are justified in speaking of the same word in such cases. In spite of their shared phonological form, we would presumably not want to regard the noun *drink* (as in *have a drink of water*) as the same word as the verb *drink* (as in *drink a glass of water*). We would be inclined to say that we are dealing with two words, notwithstanding the relatedness of their meanings and their shared phonology (at least with respect to their uninflected, citation forms).

The matter is less clear when we turn to more fine-grained syntactic differences, concerning, for example, whether a noun is used as count or mass or whether a verb is used as transitive or intransitive. As a mass noun, *drink* typically refers to a sub-category of things we can drink, namely, those with alcoholic content (*There was plenty of drink at the party*). Likewise, intransitive uses of the verb may refer specifically to the consumption of alcoholic beverages (*Don't drink and drive*). Students of polysemy have generally ignored such fine-grained syntactic differences, lumping together as the same word uses which exhibit different syntactic behaviours. As a matter of fact, different senses of a polysemous item often tend to be associated with different syntactic (and collocational) behaviours (Gries 2006*b*; Gries and

Divjak 2009; Hoey 2005; Miller and Leacock 2000).[12] As documented by Hoey, *reason* in the sense 'explanation' has a different contextual profile from *reason* in the sense 'mental faculty'. Kishner and Gibbs (1996) identified six different senses of adverbial *just*, each associated with a distinctive syntactic and lexical environment. Thus, deprecatory *just* tends to be used before nouns and verbs (*many books, instead of being carefully thought out, are just assembled by putting one word after another*); specificatory *just* often precedes a prepositional phrase (*It happened just before midnight*), while emphatic *just* typically occurs before adjectives (*the plays are just magnificent*). The findings lead to the conclusion that "people's choice of a sense of *just* is largely determined by the statistical co-occurrence of *just* with particular classes of words in one's life experience with language" (Kishner and Gibbs 1996: 19). If this finding should generalize to other words we will have gone a long way towards explaining why polysemy so rarely interferes with language comprehension. Mostly, it is readily apparent how a word is to be interpreted. Even a small amount of context may be sufficient to identify just which of the various meanings of a word is at issue; according to Choueka and Lusignan (1985, cited in Miller and Leacock 2000: 154), a window of about two words on either side of the item in question may be sufficient. Given this state of affairs, it is a moot point whether the different meanings should indeed be associated with the same word or with so many different words, each with its own contextual profile.

One criterion for recognizing the same word across different contextual environments is the identity of its phonological form. *Drink* as a count noun and *drink* as a mass noun might be regarded as the same word since they are pronounced (and spelled) in the same way. This criterion, however, is open to scrutiny. Quite a few words are associated with alternative phonemic representations and some, even, have more than one spelling. The initial vowel of *economics* can be either [ɪ] or [ə]. In my own speech, *either* can be [iːðə] or [aiðə], *schedule* varies between [skɛʤuːl], [ʃɛʤuːl], [skɛdjuːl], and [ʃɛdjuːl]; *data* is mostly [deitə] but sometimes comes out as [daːtə]. Spelling variations are also not uncommon: <centre> vs. <center>, <realize> vs. <realise>, <skeptic> vs. <sceptic>.

The extent of formal variation is much greater than these few examples would suggest. Just about any word can be pronounced in a wide variety of ways (Johnson 2003, 2004). One obvious source of variation is the geographical provenance of a speaker. The phonetic values of the FLEECE, KIT, DRESS, and TRAP vowels are very different in British, Australian, and New Zealand accents.[13] Language users are

---

[12] As noted earlier, this is one of the reasons why the ambiguity test (as a test for polysemy) is often unworkable. The test, namely, presupposes that the different senses of a word are compatible with the same syntactic and even the same lexical environments.

[13] An illustration of the extent of these differences is the fact that a New Zealand pronunciation of *ten*, heard out of context, might be interpreted by a British speaker as the word *teen*.

exquisitely sensitive to sometimes very subtle differences in phonetic values, being able to 'place' a speaker on the basis of minute phonetic cues (Pierrehumbert 2001, 2002; Hay and Drager 2007). The very fact that we are able to identify a regional accent shows that speakers have noted, and have mentally represented, the phonetic values characteristic of the different accents.

Pronunciation also varies according to speaking rate, the formality of the situation, and the phonetic context in which a word is spoken. In careful speech, *upper* may be pronounced [ʌpə], while in more relaxed speech it may come out as [ʌɸə]. Depending on the context, *red* can be pronounced [rɛd], [rɛb], or [rɛg] (compare *red house, red pen*, and *red car*). The combination *because if* is often heard as [ksɪf], *I don't know* can be rendered as [ãːdⁿo]. One approach to these kinds of variation would be to propose a unique phonological representation for each of the words in question, which is then subject to modification by online processes of assimilation and reduction.[14] Bybee (2001) has shown that the incidence of these processes is heavily dependent on the frequency of occurrence of the relevant items. Assimilation and reduction are therefore not to be regarded as automatic processes, which kick in whenever the appropriate phonological conditions are met. She argues that speakers build up a memory store of the variant pronunciations of a word, in association with the contexts in which it has appeared.

In the examples mentioned above, variant pronunciations and spellings are (probably) not associated with different semantic values.[15] This is not always the case. Consider the alternative spellings <program> and <programme>. American usage overwhelmingly prefers the former spelling, while the latter is favoured in British usage. Both spellings are, however, attested in the BNC. The BNC data suggest that the spelling <program> tends to be restricted to computer-related contexts (*a computer program*), with <programme> being preferred elsewhere (*a television programme*). A similar situation holds for <disk> (*floppy disk*) and <disc> (*the yellow disc of the moon*). A major political party in Australia is the Australian Labor Party. Organizations and activities associated with the ALP are named by the spelling <labor>. Otherwise, the spelling <labour> is often used (*Labour Day, a woman in labour*). Langacker (1987: 398) tells us that he pronounces the verb *route* as [raut]; the noun, however, can be either [raut] or [ruːt]. Labov (1972: 251) reports that one of his informants not only used two pronunciations of *vase* but also made a semantic distinction, explaining that "these small ones are my [veːzɪz] but these big ones are my [vaːzɪz]".

---

[14] The most radical implementation of this approach was the generative model developed in Chomsky and Halle (1968). Their agenda was to propose a unique underlying form from which all the variants of a morpheme could be derived by rule. This view was still defended, some thirty years later, by Halle (1997). For arguments against such a view, see, amongst many others, Bybee (1985) and Port (2007).

[15] See however p. 132 on the special semantic value of reduced pronunciations of *I don't know*.

These examples cast serious doubt on the notion of polysemy as a many-to-one relation of meanings to forms. The existence of formal variation (in both pronunciation and spelling) suggests that in many cases we are dealing with a many-to-many relation. In some cases, even, the very notion of 'a word', as a stable, well-defined unit in the mental grammar, begins to disintegrate.

The story of *over*

Many of the issues raised above can be illustrated on the still ongoing story of *over*. The story began with Claudia Brugman's (1981) eponymous thesis, reworked by Lakoff (1987: Case study 2).[16] The Brugman–Lakoff account—which identified a putative central sense of the preposition and a large number of related senses which radiated out from the central sense like the spokes of a wheel—spawned a veritable cottage industry of *over*-studies; see, for example, Deane (2005), Dewell (1994, 2007), Iwata (2004), Kreitzer (1997), Queller (2001), Taylor (2006*b*), Tyler and Evans (2001), Vandeloise (1990), Van der Gucht, Willems, and De Cuypere (2007), and Zlatev (2003). Translation equivalents in other languages have also been examined: see Bellavia (1996), Dewell (1996), and Meex (1997) on German *über*; Geeraerts (1992) on Dutch *over*; and Taylor (1988) on Italian *su* and *sopra*.

There are many reasons for this fascination with *over*. The range of uses of the word is indeed remarkable. It can designate spatial location (*the lamp hanging over the table*), path of motion (*fly over the Atlantic*), rotation (usually around a horizontal axis and usually though 90° or 180°: *turn over, bend over, fall over*), and covering (*the tablecloth over the table*). Further meanings include dispersal (*all over the world*), excess (*over six feet tall*), transfer (*hand over*), completion (*the party's over*), repetition (*do it over again*), and temporal extent (*over the weekend*). Not to be forgotten is the use of *over* in deictic expressions (*over here, over there*) and in various metaphorical contexts (*have influence over someone*). What is especially interesting is that certain meaning components which seem to be essential to some uses—for example, the requirement that the trajector be higher than the landmark[17] and not in contact with it, as in *the lamp hanging over the table*—are defeated in others. If you nail a board over a hole in ceiling, the board is attached to the ceiling and is located below it. If you put your hands over your face, your hands are on the same level as your face (assuming you are in an upright position) and (probably) touching it.

Remarkable, also, is the syntactic flexibility of the word. In addition to its use as a transitive proposition with an overt complement (*the bridge over the river*), it can be

---

[16] For a succinct account, see also Brugman and Lakoff (1988).

[17] Following Langacker's (1987) usage, TRAJECTOR refers to a figure entity, that is, an entity whose location is being specified, while LANDMARK refers to a ground entity, that is, the entity with respect to which the trajector is located.

used predicatively (*the party's over*) and can participate in a number of phrasal verbs, some of which themselves have more than one use (*hand over, put over, get over, look over, come over*, and so on). It can function as a prefix in verbs (*overdo, overeat, overhear, overlook, oversee*), adjectives (*overenthusiastic, overawed, overreliant*), past participles with an adjectival function (*oversized, oversexed*), and even nouns (*overdose, overkill, overpass*) and adverbials (*overseas, overboard, overhead, overall*). There is also a nominal use (an *over* in cricket). In some of its uses *over* is part of a larger phrase, as in *over and over, over again, over and above*, and *all over*, whose usage patterns are distinct from plain *over*. *Do it over again* refers to repetition, yet *do it over* is not possible in this sense.[18] *He had pimples all over his face* is fine, but *he had pimples over his face* is not. Accounting for these uses (and relating them in a coherent fashion) presents an evident challenge.

A second reason for interest in the word is that it exhibits patterns of polysemy which are found elsewhere in the language; its study therefore sheds light on the regularity and productivity of polysemization processes. English prepositions can be divided into two broad classes depending on the 'plexity' of the trajector entity (Taylor 1993). The two classes exhibit different potentials for semantic extension. Some prepositions, such as *in, on*, and *above*, designate the place of a uniplex trajector with respect to a landmark entity (*water in the vase, books on the table, a sign above the door*). Others, including *across, (a)round, through*, and *along*, require that their trajector occupies a multiplicity of places. The requirement can be realized in different ways. One possibility is that the trajector consists of multiple objects lined up in the appropriate configuration; the trajector, in this case, must be a plural noun: *trees around the lake, houses along the road*. Another possibility is that the trajector is an elongated object, whose parts simultaneously occupy a series of places: *a footpath round the lake, the tunnel through the mountain*. A third is that the trajector is a moving object which occupies a series of places through time: *walk round the lake, drive through the tunnel*. Given that multiplex prepositions can express path of motion, they are crucially involved in the description of motion events (see Chapter 5, p. 103). Indeed, in languages which lack multiplex prepositions it is not possible to 'walk over the bridge'; instead, you have to 'cross the bridge on foot', or some such, expressing the path of motion by means of the verb. The multiplex prepositions, as a group, have another property, namely, they can be used to designate a place construed as the end-point of an imaginary path of the appropriate shape: *a village over the river, a shop round the corner, a house up the hill, the person sitting across the table*. The source of the imaginary path may be explicitly stated: *over the river from here, down the street from the post-office*. Otherwise, the source must be inferred from the context and is typically identified with the speaker's subjective viewpoint.

[18] At least, not in British and British-based varieties, such as New Zealand English. The usage is, however, current in North American English.

Over is unusual in that it belongs to both categories of preposition. *The person living over me* illustrates the uniplex preposition; *the person walking over the bridge* exemplifies its status as a multiplex preposition. The first example is roughly equivalent to *the person living above me*. In the second example, *over* is not equivalent to *above*. *The person walking above the bridge* conjures up an image of someone suspended in midair.

Although general patterns of polysemization can be identified, individual prepositions display idiosyncratic properties. Uniplex prepositions can designate not only a static place relation (*the book is on the table*), they can also designate a place which results from the motion of an entity (*put the book on the table*). *At* is unusual in that it does not participate in this pattern. You can 'wait at the bus stop', but you cannot 'go at the bus stop' (*to* would have to be used). On the other hand, you can 'throw rocks at the police', but the rocks do not end up 'at the police'. After you have driven your car 'into the garage', your car is 'in the garage'. But if you drive your car 'into a tree', your car does not end up 'in the tree' (Jackendoff 2002: 342); likewise, if you 'bump into the wall' you do not end up 'in the wall'. *Towards* typically designates a path of motion, and in this respect must be classified as a multiplex preposition. Yet the end-point use is restricted. You can 'walk towards the back of the room', you can also 'stand towards the back of the room', yet it would be odd to say that you 'live towards the sea' (Taylor 2006b). These quirks of usage show that, in spite of the existence of general patterns of meaning extension, in the last analysis the usage range of each preposition has to be specifically learned.

Over has its fair share of idiosyncratic uses. One of the most remarkable is the fact that a multiplex trajector can be randomly dispersed with respect to the landmark, typically in association with *all: walk all over the city, dirty footmarks all over the floor*. Brugman and Lakoff argued that this usage legitimizes the covering sense of the preposition, exemplified by *the table cloth over the table*; in the limiting case, the random path or the randomly dispersed items completely 'cover' the landmark entity. Interestingly, *(a)round* can also have the random dispersal sense: *people were standing around; go round the guests and introduce yourself.* However, it lacks a covering sense.

A factor which has kept the story going over the decades has been disagreement over how many different meanings we need to associate with the word, how these are to be characterized, how they are related, and which (if any) of these is to be taken as 'basic', or 'central'. Consider *jump over the ditch, fly over the city*, and *climb over the fence*. Do these exemplify three different meanings of *over*, differences which have to do with the shape of the path followed by the trajector (horizontal or arced) and with the presence or absence of contact between trajector and landmark? Or do we want to say that the shape differences are derivable from the semantics of the verbs and real-world knowledge of how these actions are performed vis-à-vis different landmark entities? Brugman and Lakoff favoured the former approach, recognizing multiple meanings of *over* on the basis of small topological differences. Others (Tyler and Evans 2001; Van der Gucht *et al.* 2007) have sought to restrain the number of different meanings, leaving fine-grained differentiation to pragmatic and contextual information.

Regarding the putative central meaning, Brugman opted for 'above and across', as in *The plane flew over the field*. (Brugman therefore saw the preposition as basically multiplex). Tyler and Evans (2001), on the other hand, identify the 'protoscene' associated with the word as the uniplex 'above' relation, as in *The picture is over the mantel, The bee is hovering over the flower*. Dewell (1994) took a different line, arguing that a distinctive feature of the preposition is the notion of an arc-like up–down trajectory. If this approach is taken, then *fly over the city* would need to be accorded a different status from the more basic *climb over the fence*. Deane (2005), yet again, characterized the preposition in terms of a trajector entity which intervenes between a (usually unnamed) observer and the landmark. By moving the axis of the line of vision, Deane is able to relate the 'covering' sense and the 'above' sense.

Decisions on these matters may be dictated by considerations of parsimony, elegance, and simplicity. The central sense, for example, should be that from which all the others can be most easily, or most convincingly, derived. Others have pointed out that decisions in this regard should be driven by considerations of psychological reality. How many different senses do speakers of the language actually operate with and which of these, if any, is most salient in the mental lexicon? As Sandra and Rice (1995) have pointed out, empirical evidence, such as it is, is inconclusive.

The matter has also been researched from the point of view of language acquisition. Rice (2003) found that the acquisition of prepositions rarely follows the pattern predicted by network accounts of polysemy, whereby the most central sense must be acquired first, followed by extensions therefrom. On the contrary,

each child seems to have his or her own starting point within a lexical category—one which may not be conceptually basic—with additional senses appearing in a piecemeal fashion, usually as part of a favorite fixed expression, rather than through stepwise semantic extension driven by processes such as metaphor and schematization.   (Rice 2003: 243–4)

Hallan (2001) found that amongst the earliest uses of *over* by children acquiring English are the verbal complexes *fall over* and *knock over* and the deictic expressions *over there* and *over here*. On just about all accounts of the polysemy of *over*, these uses would have to be regarded as extremely marginal, standing at the end-points of chained relations radiating out from some presumed central sense. Moreover, considered by themselves, *over there* and *fall over* would seem, on any reasonable view of the matter, to have very little in common. We should probably have to say that in the grammar of the child learner, *over* is homonymous, with two unrelated meanings attaching to the same phonological form. Only later, as the child acquires other uses of the word and the intervening links in the chains are filled in, as it were, does the possibility of polysemy arise.

The word itself is acquiring new uses. A recent innovation is illustrated by *I'm over shopping.* This usage can no doubt be related to the end-point focus of *He lives over the hill*; the place referred to by *over the hill* is a place that is located at the end-point of a path which goes 'over the hill'. (The origin of the path is not stated; it would normally be understood to be the place of the speaker or some other imagined location.) The intervening landmark may be understood metaphorically as an obstacle on the path of life, as in *I got over my divorce* and *We are now over the worst. I am over shopping* is, however, subtly different. Shopping is not conceptualized as an obstacle which has been overcome, but as an earlier obsession which has since lost its attraction: 'I used to be a shopaholic, but have now lost interest in it'.

Another recent usage—again, one that is not acknowledged in the voluminous literature on the word—is the reflexive *get over oneself.* (The COCA has twelve examples of the reflexive; none are recorded in the BNC.) The usage might again be regarded as a specialization of the obstacle sense illustrated by *I got over my divorce.* The obstacle in question is the person's self, understood as their habitual way of thinking and acting and which holds them back from making progress. The construction is typically used to admonish a person to 'snap out of' their routine and to think or act in new ways: *She should get over herself, and get a life.*

Another variant of the obstacle sense is exemplified in the following (overheard) example: *Some people are gay; get over it.* The tenor of this example is not so much that the addressee should strive to overcome some obstacle, but that they should accept, as a fact of life, some state of affairs. This nuance is typically associated with the imperative *get over it.*

Another curious innovation, this time concerning the phonological form, is the adoption into English of the German cognate of *over, über.* The German word is probably familiar to English speakers through the nationalistic slogan *Deutschland über alles* (attested only once in the BNC, but six times in COCA).[19] This slogan no doubt lies behind the ironic use of the phrase *uber alles,* written without the umlaut and pronounced [u:bə(r)], as in *Politics uber alles, Europe uber alles,* and *California uber alles. Uber* is also being used as a noun modifier, as in *uber director, uber celebrity,* and *uber model* (examples from the COCA). These uses seem to exploit the notion of excess associated with *over/über* and convey an extreme point on a (metaphorical) scale of celebrity or whatever. Thus, *uber geek* appears to denote a person exhibiting an extreme degree of 'geekishness'. *Uber* can also modify adjectives, in the sense 'very' or 'extremely', as in *uber famous.* Internet searching turned up *uber-cool, uber-macho baseball players,* and *uber-fem gay guys.* It is worth noting,

---

[19] The American corpus also attests to twenty-seven uses of *ubermensch,* mostly with an explicit reference to Nietzsche.

however, that *uber* is not exactly equivalent to *over*. To describe a person as 'over cool' would imply that they were 'cool' to an unacceptable degree. *Uber-cool* in contrast means cool to a very high degree (probably even with positive connotations).

Polysemy and idealized cognitive models of language

How should we define the concept 'bachelor'? A simple answer would be that a bachelor is an unmarried man. The definition gives the category a clear boundary such that if a person fits the definition they are 'in' the category, otherwise they are not. It is well-known, however, that the bachelor concept exhibits prototype effects. Some individuals are better, or more representative examples of the category than others. Take the case of Catholic priests, unmarried men in long-term heterosexual relationships, or gay men (whether in long-term relationships or not). Although these individuals may technically fit the definition, they would not be cited as representative examples of the category; it might even be disputed whether they could be called bachelors at all.

Wierzbicka (1990) suggested that the definition 'unmarried man' should be modified to read 'unmarried man thought of as someone who could marry'. The revised definition goes some way towards accommodating the marginal cases mentioned above. One would not normally think of a Catholic priest as someone who could marry. Wierzbicka's definition, however, begs the question of why it is that someone should be 'thought of' as able or not able to marry. The uncertainties which we experience when applying the word to a priest have simply been pushed down into the definition.

A more fruitful approach was suggested by Fillmore and developed by Lakoff. Fillmore (1982: 34) observed that people are categorized as bachelors "only in the context of a human society in which certain expectations about marriage and marriageable age obtain". For Lakoff (1987: 70), these expectations constitute the IDEALIZED COGNITIVE MODEL, or ICM, against which the word is defined. According to the ICM, all members of society are heterosexual, all people are expected to marry, and there is an age at which people are expected to marry. In terms of the ICM, a bachelor may indeed be defined, quite simply, as a man who is not (or who has not yet) married. Prototype effects arise in cases where the ICM does not fit reality on the ground. After all, the ICM is *idealized*—it oversimplifies social reality, it ignores the special circumstances of certain groups, and might not even correspond to the majority situation. Nevertheless, the ICM encapsulates a commonly held assumption of how society, and individuals, should function (Taylor 2003*b*: 99).

A similar situation arises with the verb *lie*. If asked to say what it means 'to lie', most people respond that lying involves saying something that isn't true. It is easy to think of cases where the definition fails. A person might be genuinely ignorant of the facts; she might be confused or mistaken; she may choose to withhold the truth so as not to hurt the addressee; she might simplify for pedagogical or expository reasons; or she may obfuscate, saying something that is technically true but which implicates an untruth. All of these would not be considered prototypical instances of lying. Coleman and Kay (1981) investigated the matter by embedding a number of statements in little stories and having subjects evaluate the statements for the extent to which they would count as lies. They found that prototypical lying was characterized by three features: the factual incorrectness of a statement, the speaker's belief that the statement is incorrect, and the speaker's intention to deceive the addressee. When two or only one of these features was present, a statement was considered to be a less good example of lying. Coleman and Kay were also able to show that the three features are differentially weighted, the most important being the speaker's belief that a statement was untrue, factual incorrectness being the least important.

Sweetser (1987) reanalysed Coleman and Kay's results, proposing that lying should be understood against an ICM of cooperative verbal communication. In terms of the ICM, knowledge is a public good; imparting knowledge benefits the hearer; speakers wish to benefit the hearer; they do this by making assertions; speakers only assert what they believe to be true; and speakers are committed to the truth of what they assert. In terms of the logic of the ICM, a lie can be defined, quite simply, as the making of a statement which is not true (the definition which people are inclined to proffer). Other aspects of lying—the speaker's belief that the statement is not true and the speaker's intention to harm the hearer—fall out from the ICM.[20] Prototype effects arise because the ICM of information exchange may not apply to the situation at hand. The purpose of small talk is not to impart information but to establish and maintain social relations; the truth of statements about how nicely someone dresses or what lovely children they have is not really at issue. Likewise, the purpose of jokes and tall stories is to entertain; the truth of the tale about the Englishman, the Scotsman, and the Irishman is irrelevant. No one, presumably, would censure the joke teller for lying. The ICM of information exchange simply does not apply to these kinds of situation.

The point of this excursion into the semantics of *bachelor* and *lie* is to raise the possibility of a similar approach to the definition of polysemy (Taylor 2003a). Against the relevant ICMs, a bachelor can be defined, quite simply, as an unmarried man and a lie as an untrue statement. In terms of the ICMs, the definitions are perfectly adequate. The definitions become problematic in cases where the ICMs do not fit the realities of specific situations. Similarly, the definition of polysemy as the association of two or more related meanings to a single phonological form is

---

[20] A point often overlooked in discussions of lying, it seems to me, is that a speaker's motivation may have nothing to do with harming the addressee but with benefiting oneself. One lies in order to save one's own skin, or, in less onerous situations, one's face. The ICM of face-saving is, of course, one facet of cooperative communicative exchanges.

problematic, in ways which we have discussed in this chapter, because the ICM presupposed by the definition fails as an account of how language is structured, how it is mentally represented, and how it is used.

The ICM in question is, of course, the generative model, presented in Chapter 2, along with its entailment of strict compositionality. Recall that the generative model is meant to account for the creativity of language use. Speakers do not learn a list of sentences. It is proposed, instead, that they learn a list of basic elements (prototypically, words) and a set of rules whereby these elements can be combined into larger configurations. The words are specified for their phonological properties (their pronunciation) and their semantic properties (their meaning). By the compositionality principle, the rules of combination make it possible to compute the phonological and semantic properties of any complex expression in the language.

One can imagine an idealized situation in which each item in the lexicon is indeed specified in terms of a unique phonological form and a unique semantic representation. Each word would contribute a fixed chunk of phonological and semantic substance to any expression in which it occurs.[21] Barring the case of idioms, full compositionality would be guaranteed. This ideal situation is the exception, not the rule. Most words are able to make different semantic contributions to the expressions in which they occur. In order to maintain compositionality, it therefore becomes necessary—logically necessary, in terms of the ICM—to associate the words in question with a range of meanings, only one of which is selected in the compositional process. In terms of the ICM, a polysemous word is, quite simply, a word which is listed in the dictionary as having more than one meaning.

The definition becomes problematic to the extent that the ICM against which it is formulated does not fit the ways in which language is used and learned. Much of this book is concerned with pointing out the inadequacies of the generative model, and the problems associated with the standard definition of polysemy are yet another symptom of this situation. We have seen, for example, that contrary to the prescriptions of the model, the words of a given syntactic category are not equally available to slot into a given syntactic configuration; conversely, syntactic configurations tend to select their lexical realizations. Moreover, the idiomatic—that is, phenomena which by common consent lie outside the ambit of the generative model—far from being peripheral to the language system, in fact encroaches into just about every aspect of language. The upshot is that the generative model cannot be regarded as a realistic account of language as it is encountered, nor of language as it is learned and mentally represented. The idea that learning a word involves learning its meanings (along with other aspects, such as its pronunciation and its syntactic category) is grossly inadequate.

---

[21] This is the one form–one meaning relation proposed by some linguists and semioticians as the ideal towards which languages aspire and against which polysemy (one form, many meanings) and synonymy (many forms, one meaning) are regarded as deviations; see Taylor (2003c).

Word meanings

I began this chapter by citing a common definition of polysemy as the association of two or more related meanings with a single phonological form. We have seen that just about each term of the definition can give rise to doubts and uncertainties. How can we determine whether two uses of a word exemplify the same meaning or different meanings? How do we judge whether different meanings are related? By what criteria do we identify a single phonological form? Perhaps the most contentious part of the definition, however, is the notion of the 'meaning', or 'meanings', which attach to a phonological form. It is to meanings that we now turn.

On the opening pages of his *Foundations of Cognitive Grammar*, Langacker (1987: 11–12) endorses the Saussurian view of the linguistic sign as an association of an 'acoustic image' with a 'concept' (Saussure 1964 [1916]). Saussure's linguistic sign corresponds quite closely to the Langackerian symbolic unit (see pp. 121–2). The word *tree*, for example, associates the acoustic image [tri:] with the concept 'tree'. Importantly, for both Saussure and Langacker, the two terms of the relation are mental entities. The word does not link up a particular pronunciation with a particular tree in the yard. To have the tree concept means knowing what a tree is; it means knowing what counts as a tree and being able to recognize a tree when you see one. In other words, the concept is a PRINCIPLE OF CATEGORIZATION (Taylor 2002: 43). The same goes for the phonological side of the linguistic sign. A person who knows the word knows how it can be pronounced and is able to recognize an acoustic event as a valid pronunciation of the word.

A conceptualist approach to words and their meanings suggests one way of approaching the polysemy issue. Polysemy would be at hand whenever a word links up with two (or more) different concepts (Murphy 2002: 406). *Pig* can refer to a farm animal or to a greedy person; *port* can be either a fortified wine or a harbour. Farm animals and greedy people, fortified wine and harbours, are different ontological kinds and for this reason would count as different concepts. By the same token, a university as a campus and a university as an institution are different kinds of things; *university* would therefore be polysemous between a building sense and an institution sense. Pursuing this line, however, leads us straight into the problems discussed earlier in this chapter. How different do two entities have to be in order for us to be confident that they fall under two different concepts? The matter is especially tricky with respect to verbal and other relational concepts. Opening a door is a different kind of activity from opening a wound; are we dealing here with one category of event or two? Water in a vase bears a different kind of relation to the vase than a crack in the vase; does the difference testify to two different concepts of containment? Clearly, a focus on the concepts that words can refer to simply raises the old question of whether different ways of using a word reflect different meanings.

A way out of this situation is to focus on the contextualization of words and their meanings.[22] There are two dimensions of contextualization: the conceptual context of the word's meaning and the linguistic context in which the word is used.

Concepts do not exist as so many isolated chunks of information. Langacker addressed this issue in terms of his notion of DOMAIN. A domain is the knowledge framework against which a word's meaning is understood.[23] *Aunt* is understood against the knowledge of a kinship network; kinship itself is understood against such notions as gender, marriage, family units, procreation, and generation, to name the most salient. Without this background knowledge it would be impossible to have any understanding of the concept of 'aunt'.

Typically, a concept is understood against a multiplicity of domains, or DOMAIN MATRIX; moreover, one domain may itself presuppose more abstract domains, such as notions of life forms, gravitational space, time, motion, shape, and colour. Ultimately, the background knowledge needed to understand a concept can reach into just about every aspect of our cognitive system (Clausner and Croft 1999; Croft 1993). Not all domains, to be sure, are equally salient to a concept. For many people—to take up one of Langacker's (2008: 49) examples—the status of snails as a culinary delicacy is probably somewhat peripheral to their snail concept. Even so, this facet is likely to be activated when a person sees snails on a restaurant menu. The example illustrates the important point that different contexts of use are likely to activate some domains and to cause others to become backgrounded. If we say that a photograph is out of focus, we are activating the notion of a photograph as a visual representation produced by a certain technology; if we say that the photograph is faded, we zoom in on the status of the photograph as paper imprinted with the image; while talk of a torn photograph refers only to the state of the paper (Taylor 2002: 444).

Strictly speaking, an image is a different ontological kind from a piece of paper imprinted with the image. In terms of the categories of things that the word *photograph* can refer to, we should have to say that we are dealing with two different concepts. The two concepts are, however, intimately related in virtue of the domain-based knowledge against which we understand the notion of what photographs are. Rather than saying that the word *photograph* is linked up with two different concepts, we might propose that the word provides access to a region in a conceptual network and that different uses of the word activate different linkages in the network (Evans 2006, 2009). The meaning of the word is therefore not a fixed, permanently stored and neatly circumscribed piece of information, which is slotted into the semantic structure of the expressions in which it is used. The meaning is variable and context-dependent

---

[22] Recall Firth's (1957b [1935]: 7) statement that "the complete meaning of a word is always contextual, and no study of meaning apart from a complete context can be taken seriously".

[23] There are affinities between the Langackerian notions of domain and domain matrix and Searle's notion of Background; see Taylor (1996: 76–8) for some discussion.

(Barsalou 1987; Geeraerts 1993; Hanks 2000; MacDonald, Pearlmutter, and Seidenberg 1994: 679–80; Taylor 2002).

When we are required to cite the meaning of a word—as I did earlier, when I glossed the two meanings of *ball* and *port*—we may be doing one of several things. We may be giving a rough description of the region in conceptual space that the word provides access to or we may be activating a default context which foregrounds the domains typically associated with how the word is used. Alternatively, we might invoke what we perceive to be the most frequent or most characteristic use of the word and account for the word in terms of the highlighted domains. (As noted earlier, when a person is asked to give a definition of a word like *open*, they typically invoke a context of use, such as *open the door*, and describe the actions associated with this kind of event.) To the extent that a word may be associated with more than one contextual profile we are likely to attribute different meanings to it.

The approach sketched in the above paragraphs places a high premium on the linguistic context in which words are used. It was, after all, the linguistic environments of the word *photograph* which triggered the different conceptualizations of the entity. It needs to be remembered, however, that the relation between a word and its context is a two-way street. In the first place, how we interpret a word is dependent on the context in which it used. The linguistic context may modulate the concept by activating some aspects of the domain-based knowledge against which it is characterized. On the other hand, how we use a word is dependent on the contexts in which it has already been encountered. If a word is regularly encountered in a certain context, that particular reading of the word will become entrenched. Our accumulated memories of these contextualized uses constitute what Allwood calls a word's "semantic potential" (Allwood 2003).[24]

In conclusion

Some scholars have openly questioned whether it is legitimate to speak of word meanings at all.[25] Wittgenstein's *Blue Book* (1958: 1) opens with the question: "What is the meaning of a word?" The question is not about the meaning of this word or that word, but of a word, that is, any word; the question concerns the nature of word meanings in general. The question, Wittgenstein notes, is liable to induce in us a kind

---

[24] At the beginning of this section I noted Langacker's sympathetic reference to Saussure's notion of the linguistic sign as the association of a concept with an acoustic image. A focus on a word's contextual profile appears to be inconsistent with this view. The brief overview of Cognitive Grammar in Chapter 6 indicates how this tension can be resolved. Recall the phonological example (p. 123). The sound [ŋ] is specified, not only for its inherent phonetic content, as a velar nasal, but also for its role in syllable constructions. Similarly, with respect to their semantic characterization, we need to be open to the possibility that words are specified, not only for their conceptual content, but also for their role in larger configurations.

[25] See, for example, Kilgarriff's (1997) paper, 'I don't believe in word senses'. For Kilgarriff, word meaning is a matter of word use, the meanings of a word being identified with distinct clusters of citations.

of "mental cramp"; we really have no idea how we should set about answering it or what kind of answer would be acceptable. He proposes to bring the question "down to earth" by operationalizing it, that is, by replacing it with the more practical matter of how we might set about determining the meaning of a word. His answer, as is well-known, is that meaning is to be studied by examining how language is used: to say that a word has a meaning is to say that it has "a use in the language" (p. 69); taking this approach, the 'meaning of a word' would be its use in the language.

Another philosopher who was sceptical about word meanings was John Austin. In an eponymous essay, Austin (1962) maintained that 'the meaning of a word' is a "dangerous nonsense-phrase" (p. 56). Sentences, he claimed, have meanings; words do not. The definitions that we find in dictionaries are, at best, aids to the understanding of sentences. In claiming that only sentences have meaning, Austin was probably equating meaning with truth conditions. A declarative sentence may be true or false, depending on whether it accurately depicts the situation at hand; words do not have this property. In his later work Austin (1980) came to doubt the possibility of a truth-based account of sentence meaning, even with respect to declarative sentences; utterances were to be evaluated in terms of the speech acts which speakers were performing. This shift in Austin's thinking only serves to reinforce the difference between word and sentence meaning. Just as the words in a dictionary cannot have truth values, neither can they have illocutionary force.

Both Wittgenstein and Austin were trying to counteract the mentalist view of words as standing for concepts. It is interesting to note that even scholars who are sympathetic to a conceptualist view also recognize the importance of usage. Goddard (1998), for example, rejects the view of meaning as use (p. 6), insisting instead that word meanings are susceptible to precise and accurate definitions.[26] While the aim of the definitions is to capture the concept that a word designates, the criterion for evaluating a definition is whether it "will predict the appropriate range of use of a word". The definition should be "a reliable guide to how to use the word" (p. 31).

As discussed extensively in this chapter, there are many problems stemming from the notion that words are associated with a fixed number of meanings (one or more), understood as rigid units of conceptual information, which are accessed in the processes of speech production and reception. The alternative view presented here is that knowing a word involves knowing the kinds of contexts in which a word can be used. A word provides access, not only to the conceptual domains against which it is understood, but also to the linguistic contexts in which it has been used, as these have been laid down in the speaker's mental corpus. As Kishner and Gibbs (1996: 19) put it, in the paper cited earlier, the ability to use a word is a function of "one's life experience with language".

---

[26] The definitions are couched in the restricted vocabulary of Wierzbicka's Natural Semantic Metalanguage; see Wierzbicka (1996).

11

Creativity and innovation

As we saw in Chapter 2, the creativity of language use is often put forward as one of the main justifications of the generative model. Many of the sentences that speakers produce are unique creations, not only for the speaker herself and her interlocutors but very likely in the history of the speech community as well. It seems fair to say that the sentence which you are now reading has never been written down or spoken in the exact form in which you now encounter it. It follows, so the argument goes, that knowing a language cannot be equated with knowing a set of sentences. We do not learn sentences, we learn how to make (and understand) sentences. The set of sentences that we can make and understand is not only very large, it is infinitely large. The generative model accounts for this state of affairs by proposing that speakers have learned a finite list of basic elements (prototypically, words) along with a set of rules (the syntax) for combining these elements. Importantly, some of the rules are recursive, that is, they are able to apply to their own outputs. In this way, the finite resources of the lexicon and the syntax are able to generate an infinite set of output sentences.

In this book I have pointed to many problematic aspects of the generative model. What, then, are we to make of the argument from creativity? Is the fact of linguistic creativity a knock-down argument for the correctness of the generative model after all, and for everything that it entails?

One way to tackle the generativists' argument would be to query its premise. Is language use indeed creative, in the sense intended by generativists? While the uniqueness of many sentences that speakers produce may well be an indisputable fact about language use, it may nevertheless be advisable to take a more nuanced view of the matter, one which recognizes the conventional aspects of language use alongside speakers' ability to come up with novel combinations of words. As I shall argue below, the generativists' view of creativity is indeed well-founded. The words and the syntactic configurations of a language do not constitute a finite, enumerable quantity. People do come up with new wordings and new syntactic configurations, as well as with newly coined words.

A second approach requires us to examine more closely the notion of creativity. Generative theory draws a clean line between linguistic creativity and linguistic innovation. Creativity involves the application of the rules of grammar to items selected from the lexicon; creativity therefore remains strictly within the bounds of the language system. Innovation is a matter of going beyond the system. Strictly speaking, therefore, innovation involves the production of ungrammatical sentences. As with so many of the entailments of the generative model, the distinction between creativity and innovation turns out to be problematic (some examples will be discussed later in this chapter), thus raising questions about the theory which requires that such a distinction be made.

Most importantly, however, we need to consider whether there might not be alternative approaches which are able to account for the facts of creativity and innovation. If non-generative theories of language can guarantee creativity, one of the standard arguments in support of generative theories loses its force. What is more, non-generative accounts might be in accord with a more realistic view of innovative language use. One such approach—blending theory—is addressed in Chapter 12.

Creativity

On the face of it, the generativists' view of creativity is unassailable. Take any sentence from this book—or indeed from any book—and search a corpus, even a very large corpus, such as that available on the World Wide Web, for an exact replica. Even very short sentences are likely to draw a blank. Moreover, the uniqueness of each sentence is not simply a matter of the choice of the words. Consider some findings reported by McEnery and Wilson (2001: 180–3). McEnery and Wilson examined three corpora from the point of view of the number of different sentence types that they contained. Sentence types were defined in terms of their constituent analysis (while sentences, presumably, were identified by the occurrence of full stops). One corpus was based on transcripts from the Canadian Hansard. In this corpus, the ratio of sentence types to sentences was 1:1.07. To all intents and purposes, every sentence in the corpus exhibited a unique syntactic structure. Admittedly, the Hansard corpus was rather small (about one million words). McEnery and Wilson's findings, however, do suggest that speakers are not only coming up with new word combinations, they are also creating new sentence structures in the course of their language production.[1]

McEnery and Wilson performed the same kind of analysis on two other corpora. One, made up of fictional texts, delivered very similar results. A third corpus, consisting of IBM instruction manuals, was different. Here, the ratio of sentence

---

[1] Recall, in this connection, Sampson's (2007) findings on the types of noun phrase structures in a corpus (see p. 157). The fact that the frequency of the different noun phrase types exhibits a Zipfian distribution suggests that the number of phrase types may be essentially open-ended.

types to sentences was 1:1.66, indicating that almost 40 per cent of the sentences in the corpus exhibited a structure that was shared by other sentences. The difference may be partly explained by the fact that the sentences in the IBM corpus were on average considerably shorter than those in the other two corpora (average sentence length in the IBM corpus was 10.88 words, compared with 23.79 words in the Hansard corpus and 21.33 words in the literary corpus). As sentences decrease in length the number of syntactic options also decreases, thus raising the probability that any two sentences will share the same structure. McEnery and Wilson, however, put the difference down to the kinds of texts which went into the respective corpora. The Hansard and the literary corpora were unconstrained with respect to their subject matter and linguistic content; practically anything could be the topic of the discourse and the speakers/writers could address the topic in whatever way they chose. The IBM texts, in contrast, dealt with a limited set of topics and did so within narrow stylistic parameters. The IBM texts are therefore likely to be markedly less creative (in the generativist sense) than thematically and stylistically unconstrained texts, with respect to both their lexical material and their syntactic structure.[2]

There are, indeed, some circumstances of language use where the notion of creativity may be scarcely applicable at all. Consider types of texts whose structure and content is very narrowly prescribed, such as the evening weather forecasts on the television, summary reports of share-market movements in the newspapers, and even letters of rejection which employers routinely send out to unsuccessful job applicants. These consist, largely, of stock phrases strung together with only limited lexical variation. Speakers who are required to keep up a constant flow of language—auctioneers, race-callers, or live sports commentators—also tend to rely heavily on preformed routines (Kuiper 1996, 2009). Moreover, quite a lot of everyday chit-chat—standard greetings, small talk about the weather, or the routine exchange of pleasantries—is highly formulaic, consisting largely in the repetition of preformed chunks of language. As Firth observed:

It must be repeated that most of the give-and-take of conversation in our everyday life is stereotyped and very narrowly conditioned by our particular type of culture. It is a sort of roughly prescribed social ritual, in which you generally say what the other fellow expects you, one way or another, to say.   (Firth 1957b [1935]: 31)

---

[2] McEnery and Wilson (2001) also report that the IBM corpus exhibited a different lexical profile from the other two corpora. The one million word IBM corpus contained 7,594 word types, while the one million words of the Hansard corpus contained more than twice as many word types, 18,817. Not only this, but the two corpora showed different patterns of lexical growth. After the first 100,000 words of the IBM corpus had been processed, the number of word types increased only very slowly, suggesting that the corpus had recorded virtually all the word types of this particular genre. If the IBM corpus were to be doubled, or even tripled in size, the number of new words would presumably be very small. The corpus, in other words, came close to reaching LEXICAL CLOSURE. Processing of the Hansard corpus, on the other hand, showed a steady though declining rate of adoption of new words. Doubling or tripling the size of the corpus would fail to result in lexical closure.

Not all of language, of course, falls into the above categories. We would like to think that academic texts, newspaper opinion pieces, 'intelligent' conversation, and other instances of language use where the onus is on originality of content rather than social ritual, rise above the stringing together of fixed expressions and standard clichés. Even these kinds of texts, however, are riddled with ready-made units:

for a great deal of the time anyway, language production consists of piecing together the ready-made units appropriate for a particular situation and...comprehension relies on knowing which of these patterns to predict in these situations.   (Nattinger 1980: 341)

Langacker (1987: 35) offers a "small, random sample" of the conventional expressions—collocations, phraseologies, and idioms of various kinds—which characterize language use:

take it for granted that, hold...responsible for, express an interest in, great idea, tough competitor, have a lot of class, I don't care, kill two birds with one stone, good to see you, mow the lawn, turn the page, let the cat out, have great respect for, ready to go, fair play, I'll do the best I can, answer the phone, never want to see...again.   (Langacker 1987: 35)

Langacker even turns the spotlight onto his own usage, citing the conventional expressions which he had used in an earlier paragraph:

fundamental requirement, empirical science, known facts, other things being equal, as if, theory account for...data, more...rather than less, in actual practice, as such, in the context of, if only, very rudimentary, a matter of interpretation, preliminary analysis, deriving from, a set of, underlying assumptions, and *object of study.*   (p. 35)

Indeed, the use of these and similar expressions is the hallmark of an idiomatic and fluent command of the language (Pawley and Syder 1983; Sinclair 1991). To quote Langacker again:

There are literally thousands of these **conventional expressions** in a given language, and knowing them is essential to speaking it well. This is why a seemingly perfect knowledge of the grammar of a language (in the narrow sense) does not guarantee fluency in it; learning its full complement of conventional expressions is probably by far the largest task involved in mastering it.   (Langacker 1987: 35–6)

The existence of conventional phraseology is not in itself incompatible with creativity in the generativists' sense. There is no contradiction in asserting that sentences are, in general, unique creations, while still maintaining that sentences contain chunks of language (collocations, phraseologies, and the like) which do in fact recur, sometimes with great frequency. While sentences rarely repeat themselves, bits of sentences often do. Words tend to select their neighbours, sometimes with a high degree of probability. Even if the exact lexical material of a sentence (or part of a sentence) is a new creation, the pattern which it exemplifies could be based on a well-entrenched construction, whose specification narrows down the permitted degree of lexical variation.[3] The crucial question, though, concerns the logical link between creativity and the need for a generative model. Can new combinations of words and new syntactic configurations come about through processes other than through the application of rules to a finite lexicon? I shall argue that they can.

Creativity and innovation

When generativists speak of the creativity of language use, they are not using the term 'creativity' in the way that a layperson would understand the word. To illustrate the point, consider how we understand the notion of 'creative accounting'. An accountant is being creative, we would say, if s/he presents a company's results in such a way as to hide the losses and exaggerate the profits. We would certainly not think of creative accounting as simply a matter of adding up a column of numbers. Yet it is precisely this kind of activity which would be described as creative on the generative linguist's use of the word, in that the accountant is applying a set of arithmetical rules to a possibly novel set of data, coming up with a computation which may never before have been performed. The analogy with linguistic activity fails for the reasons which have been amply documented in this book. There is, namely, no set of general rules, analogous to the rules of arithmetic, which are able to generate all and only the acceptable expressions of a language.

Consider, in this context, the status of Sapir's (1921: 82) well-known example sentence *The farmer kills the duckling* or Bloomfield's (1933: 161) *Poor John ran away*. I do not think it likely that Sapir and Bloomfield were citing sentences that they had recorded in the course of their fieldwork on the English language.[4] (Internet searches returned only citations of the sentences; there are no examples of the sentences being used.) Most probably, Sapir and Bloomfield had concocted these sentences on the basis of their intuitions about English syntax. In this respect, their sentences must count as parade examples of linguistic creativity, in the generativists' sense, at work.

Laypersons are hardly likely to call these sentences creative; they are more likely to say that they are banal, trivial, and unimaginative. What the layperson understands by creative language corresponds, in the generativists' lexicon, to linguistic INNOVA-TION. This is when a person coins a new word or expression, comes up with an original metaphor or striking turn of phrase, extends the use of a word or construction in ways not fully sanctioned by usage, adds new nuances to conventional expressions, or gives a new twist to a well-worn cliché. Whereas creativity, in the

---

[3] Erman and Warren (2000) estimate that over 50 per cent of the word tokens in the texts (written and spoken) which they examined are parts of conventional expressions.

[4] The same goes for my own example of *The farmer shot a rabbit* (p. 23).

generativists' sense, is a matter of deploying the existing resources of the language to come up with novel strings of words, innovation involves going beyond the available resources, by inventing new words or by combining words in ways which are not in accord with the rule system or even in ways which are counter to the prevailing rules. Whereas creativity merely exploits the system, innovation flouts the system. If the products of creativity must be regarded, by definition, as grammatical, innovative language is, again by definition, ungrammatical.

The distinction between creativity and innovation, between usage which is "system-observing" and usage which is "system-changing" (Botha 1968: 200), is one which falls out from the generative model. As with so many of the entailments of the model, the distinction turns out to be problematic in a number of respects. Its problematic nature not only suggests that the distinction may not be valid; it also puts in question the model of language on which the distinction is based, namely the generative model itself.

In the first place, the distinction may be difficult to apply in the analysis of a particular set of data; we will look at a couple of examples shortly. Moreover, insisting on the distinction can be an impediment to linguistic analysis, in that it has the potential to close off certain avenues of research, concerning, for example, the status of linguistic variation and the role of innovation in language change. We have encountered a similar state of affairs in other areas of language description. We saw in Chapter 10 that the logic of the generative model requires that each word in the lexicon be associated with a fixed number, one or more, of discrete meanings, only one of which is selected in the compositionality process. It is not only difficult in practice to determine just how many meanings a word has; a focus on word meanings detracts from a study of the context-dependence of word use. Likewise, the logic of the generative model requires that the idiomatic be defined negatively, in terms of expressions which cannot be generated by the rules operating over the lexicon (Chapter 4). By drawing a clean line between the idiomatic and the regular, the generative approach marginalizes the study of constructional idioms, collocations, and the interaction between words and con-structions. Below, I discuss a number of examples where the distinction between creativity and innovation is likely to obscure a proper understanding of the facts.

Language change

For generativists, creativity is a fact of language use. There is, however, another fact about language use, one that is just as incontrovertible as creativity: this concerns the variability of language from speaker to speaker, in both space and time. It is evident to even to the most casual observer that speakers of the 'same' language may exhibit variation in their usage patterns according to their geographical provenance, their social status, their educational background, their age, gender, ethnicity, and so on. (It is also a matter of everyday observation that individual speakers may have their own idiosyncratic quirks of usage, concerning their preference for certain expressions or the way they pronounce certain words.) Equally obvious is the fact that languages change over time; young people speak differently from retirees, while texts from earlier centuries may be well-nigh impenetrable.

The generative model understands creativity within the confines of a static language system; this is the internalized grammar (the I-language) of the "ideal speaker–hearer" who exists in a "completely homogenous speech-community" (Chomsky 1965: 3). Given this approach, language variation can only be conceptualized in terms of different speakers having internalized different grammars. In historical change, one grammar, internalized by one group of speakers, is replaced by another grammar, acquired by the next generation of speakers. The change is necessarily discrete, having to do with such matters as the addition or deletion of a rule, the conditions under which a rule may apply, the addition or deletion of a lexical item, or changes to the specification of a lexical item, as when a word comes to be associated with an additional meaning or with a different subcategorization frame.

A challenge for generative theories, therefore, has been how to reconcile variation and change with the axiom of a fixed language system. The typical strategy involves REANALYSIS (De Smet 2009; Hopper and Traugott 1993; Lightfoot 1979). The account goes roughly as follows. A sentence generated by the rules of the grammar G^1 operating over the lexicon L^1 may also be compatible with the rules of a slightly different grammar G^2 operating over a slightly different lexicon L^2. The productions of speaker S^1 with G^1 (an older member of the speech community, let us say) may be taken, by S^2 (a younger speaker) as evidence for G^2. Reanalysis thus rests on the possibility of syntactic and/or lexical ambiguity. Importantly, the ambiguity is attributed to different analyses being performed by different individuals. If an increasing number of speakers share the analysis of S^2, the language system will have changed, without it being necessary to suppose that any individual speaker has innovatively modified the system. The change will only become apparent to an observer when the output of G^2 is inconsistent with the contents of G^1.

In order to see how we might have language change without innovation, consider the well-known development in semantic value of Middle English *bede* 'prayer' to the Modern English form *bead* 'spherical object on a string' (Hopper and Traugott 1993: 81). The change is likely to be categorized as an example of metonymy. A person who was required to recite a prayer a certain number of times would keep count with the aid of beads on a rosary. *Bedes* thus came to refer, not to the prayers, but to the beads which stood for the prayers. Queller (2003) has argued that this change in semantic value need not be due to innovation by any individual speaker (a point already made by Stern 1931: 168). Observing someone repeating their prayers, a speaker S may declare that the person is telling (= counting)[5] their bedes ('prayers'). A hearer H,

---

[5] The older sense of *tell* (i.e. 'count') is still extant in *bank teller* (who counts your money) and in the expression *tell the time*.

observing that the counting involves beads on a rosary, may interpret the utterance to refer to the counting of the beads. The new semantic value of the word has not come about through innovation on the part of an individual speaker, but through the hearer's interpretation of the speaker's utterance.

The development of the word's meaning is unlikely to be as straightforward as this narrative suggests. Subsequent to the situation sketched out above we can suppose that H might go on to use *bede* in its new semantic value, in ways which S may find puzzling. Likewise, H might observe that S uses the word in ways which are incompatible with his semantic representation. Both S and H will be confronted with uses which they find 'ungrammatical' and will need to adjust their mental lexicons to accommodate these new facts. S, we might suppose, will still regard 'prayer' as the basic meaning of *bede*, with 'bead' as an extension. For H it will be the other way round, the basic meaning of the word being 'bead'.

In the absence of documentary evidence on the time period in question, the scenario sketched out above must remain speculative. In order to better study the process, we need to consider some current examples of change in progress. I consider a couple of examples below.

being busy

We often become aware of incipient language change by uses which strike us as slightly incongruous. When I was teaching in South Africa, a couple of decades ago, a student came up to me with the following remark:

(1)   I can't hand in my essay this morning. It's busy being typed.

The item of interest is the word *busy*. According to my mental grammar at the time, *busy* applied, in the first instance, to a person. The word denotes concentrated activity, leaving the person with no free time to do other things. The word can be used both attributively (*a busy executive*) and predicatively, in which case the activity can be spelled out in a V-*ing* phrase (*I was busy working*).

The notion of activity is foregrounded in some other uses of the word. A 'busy road' is one with lots of traffic, a 'busy afternoon' is one in which lots of things are happening, while to have a 'busy schedule' is to have a schedule full of meetings and the like. The idea of 'lots of things going on' motivates some further uses, such as a 'busy photograph', a 'busy painting', and even 'busy wallpaper' (where there are lots of intricate patterns which confuse the eye). A 'busy essay', to the extent that the expression would make any sense at all, would be an essay which deals with lots of different topics, each tugging for the reader's attention. Completely ruled out, in my mental grammar at the time, would be the idea that an essay could be busy doing something. Even more preposterous would be the idea of an essay being busy having something done to it.

Nevertheless, the interpretation of (1) was clear; [*my essay*] *is busy being typed* was meant as a more wordy version of *my essay is being typed*. A clue as to what is going on is the idea of concentrated activity associated with 'being busy'. This opens up the possibility that *be busy V-ing* can be interpreted in two ways. For a conservative speaker, *busy* characterizes the subject referent, with the V-*ing* constituent stating the activity the person is engaged in. The expression can also be construed as a more wordy version of *be V-ing*. If a person 'is working', they are not available for other matters. To say that they 'are busy working' merely underlines the activity sense of progressive *be V-ing*. Consequently, *be busy V-ing* can be reanalysed as a kind of progressive construction, emphasizing the activity in progress. More conservative speakers become aware of the new value associated with *busy* only when more advanced speakers (such as the student in question) apply the word to non-volitional entities, such as an essay.

The status of *busy* as a marker of progressive aspect was reinforced for me by another episode. I was visiting the Johannesburg zoo, looking at ostrich eggs enclosed in a glass incubator. I heard a voice behind me exclaim:

(2)   Look. That one's busy hatching.

Again, this usage did not conform to my mental grammar. An egg cannot be 'busy', since an egg is not a rational creature which can regulate its own activities. The intent of the speaker, however, was clear. It was to focus on the changes that the egg was undergoing.[6]

The *busy* construction fits in with a broader development. It is as if English speakers are not always content to express an activity in progress through the standard resource of the language, namely the progressive *be V-ing* construction. Other, more wordy expressions are coming into use. Amongst these are *be in the process of* and *be in the middle of* (Koops 2004). Both of these could be used in the

---

[6] According to Lass and Wright (1986: 213), progressive *busy* "is apparently unique to S(outh) Af(rican) E(nglish)". The usage, they argue, may well have been aided by the influence of Afrikaans, where *besig* (cognate with English *busy*) is standardly used to express progressivity: *Ek is besig om te ontspan* 'I am busy relaxing'. Mesthrie (2002) does not dispute Lass and Wright's characterization of the construction as a distinctive South African feature, citing a Cape Town graduate student who declared that s/he 'was busy going crazy'. However, he also points to similar developments in other regional varieties of English. Indeed, data cited later in this section indicate that the phenomenon is by no means geographically restricted. Neither, it would seem, is it a recent innovation, being already foreshadowed in Jane Austen. In the following, 'being busy' is associated, not so much with 'doing things' as with mental activity. (The examples also differ from modern usage with respect to the syntactic environment of the word: *be busy in V-ing*, whereas modern English has *be busy V-ing*.)

(i)   She was so **busy in** admiring those soft blue eyes, in talking and listening, and forming all these schemes in the in-betweens, that the evening flew away at a very unusual rate. (*Emma*)

(ii) Marianne was all the time **busy in** observing the direction of the wind, watching the variations of the sky and imagining an alteration in the air. (*Sense and Sensibility*)

above examples (and both would have conformed to my more conservative mental grammar):

(3)   My essay {is in the process of / is in the middle of} being typed.

(4)   The ostrich egg {is in the process of / is in the middle of} hatching.

Be V-*ing* and its alternatives are not freely interchangeable, suggesting that the expressions are not fully equivalent. A likely account is that each of the more wordy alternatives focuses on some particular facet of progressivity. *Be in the middle of* might be restricted to giving an internal perspective on a temporally circumscribed event, while *be in the process of* would be favoured for situations involving change. It would be bizarre to say that the Earth is in the middle of turning on its axis or that the Sun is in the process of shining. *Busy*, on the other hand, in keeping with its 'basic' sense of activity, might be restricted to situations where things can be seen to be happening. It would surely not be possible to say that someone is busy sleeping or that the Sun is busy shining. Or would it?

BNC examples of *busy* generally preserve the idea of 'active', 'occupied with', 'engrossed in', with an agentive subject and an activity-denoting verb:

(5)   a. On the day of the party her lodger was **busy** tending to the needs of a Mrs Brown whom he felt he had nothing to offer but was obliged to visit anyway.

   b. "Evenin', Mr Oakley," said Mrs Fletcher, who was **busy** knitting in the back row.

   c. Those of you partying will doubtless be too **busy** having a good time to care.

Others emphasize concentrated effort, even in the absence of visible signs of activity (a usage already anticipated in the citations from Austen; see footnote 6):

(6)   a. But she was **busy** watching his feet, waiting for him to do a runner.

   b. At the time, Comdisco was **busy** taking advantage of IBM's 3090-E systems, which would eventually become the foundation of today's ESA architecture base.

   c. But I didn't listen too closely, being **busy** trying to stay upright despite slightly rubbery knees.

   d. One of the troubles about Hollywood, everybody's so **busy** being exclusive and hiding their homes behind mountains of greenstuff, they forget about the unfortunate people who have to locate the said homes sometimes.

   e. "I'm **busy** being interviewed by a journalist," the A&R man snorts dismissively.

Especially interesting is (6e), where the subject referent may indeed be busy with some activity; the activity, however, is described using a passive verb form. The example can be seen as a 'bridge' to the usage in (1). Syntactically, the two are similar.

What differentiates them is that in (1) the expectation that the subject referent is a volitional creature is abandoned.

Internet-sourced examples show an even greater usage range, with progressive *busy* being used in an increasing number of environments, including those which earlier I had supposed to be impossible (*I was busy sleeping, the Sun is busy shining*). We find *busy* being used in association with verbs whose semantics are incompatible with the notion of activity, such as *rest* and *sleep*:

(7) a. pick a day and if I'm not **busy resting, relaxing, or taking it easy**, we can go fishing.
     b. Go away, I'm **busy resting!**
     c. We arrived home just after midnight on the morning of the 24th, but we have been too **busy trying to sleep** to get to the computer.
     d. how was the show? sorry I didnt make it out, I was too **busy sleeping.**
     e. All our councillors are **busy sleeping** right now, perhaps have a snooze and call back in an hour.

Busy is also being used in association with stative verbs, such as *be, seem,* and *like*. While these verbs are not incompatible with the progressive, their use in the *be* V-*ing* construction is somewhat restricted. Their occurrence with progressive *busy* is therefore all the more remarkable.

(8) a. Get used to it or you're going to be **busy being** on the defensive.
     b. Simon is too **busy liking** Kellie. He'll be in tears when she gets voted off.
     c. While very **busy seeming** to care about everyone in his town, he seems to have very little emotion left for his young daughter.
     d. when [the film] is not **busy being** a misogynistic, dull-witted bore, it's tossing out head-scratcher dialogue..., and just plain bad acting.

Progressive *busy* is attested with reference to weather conditions (9) and with passives (10):

(9) a. It has been **busy raining** for three days now, but that doesn't bother us very much for the roads are all gravel.
     b. At this time of year, the days can fade straight from dawn to gloomy dusk without ever seeming to reach daylight, while the sun is **busy shining** down-under.

(10) a. our flyers are **busy being printed** right now so you will receive them very shortly
     b. The restaurant is worth the price you pay but it's not cheap and it is **busy being written up** as the "place to go" in all manner of newspapers and magazines.

Indicative of a trend towards ever more wordy expressions of progressivity are examples where *be busy* V-*ing* is 'stacked' with other resources. In (11) it is combined with progressive *be* V-*ing*, to give *be being busy* V-*ing*, while in (12), it is combined with the *in the middle of* V-*ing* construction:

(11) a. I was **being busy being** a full-time mom, full-time wife, full-time house-cleaner, full-time caretaker.
      b. Eskin was **being busy being** interviewed yesterday.
      c. I guess he is **being busy being** the mogul.

(12) a. She phoned me after returning from New York, **in the middle of being busy** selling tickets.
      b. He realized I was going to make him request it, and not just give it to him, even **in the midst of being busy** talking to the doctor.[7]

What these data show is that progressive *busy* is gradually encroaching on the environments typically associated with progressive *be* V-*ing*. The co-opting of *busy* as a marker of progressivity may well have been triggered by the reanalysis of potentially ambiguous expressions such as *I was busy working*. The reanalysis hypothesis, however, is only one small part of the story. It is not as if all instances of progressive *be* V-*ing* could be replaced, at one fell swoop, by *be busy* V-*ing* (at least, we may suppose, in the usage of those speakers who first undertook the reanalysis). The standard expression of progressivity—*be* V-*ing*—is still being used and the basic usage range of *busy* has not been abandoned. It would be more in keeping with the data to suppose that individual speakers have gradually extended the environments in which progressive *busy* can be used. Perhaps, in the fullness of time, *be busy* V-*ing* will become the standard way of expressing progressivity. A more likely scenario, in the medium term, is that different expressions of progressivity will be competing, with each specializing in the expression of some particular facet of the notion.

explain me

While reanalysis might have played some role in the development of progressive *busy*, other innovations cannot be explained in such terms. Consider the ditransitive uses of *explain*, discussed in Chapter 2 (see pp. 28–32).

(13) a. Can someone **explain me** how PHP interacts with Java?
      b. thank you all for your replies. They've **explained me** what I wanted to know
      c. Then **explain me this**, young pup: why do you want to join the expedition?

---

[7] The examples cited in (12) have *busy* in an adjunct phrase. The examples were sourced in March 2011. At the time of the search, I was not able to find examples of these stacked expressions being used in finite clauses, of the kind *be in the middle/midst of being busy* V-*ing*. I venture the prediction that it is only a matter of time (a couple of years, perhaps) before these usages are attested.

The examples point to the artificiality of the distinction between (system-observing) creativity and (system-changing) innovation. Ditransitive *explain* is certainly not the norm. The usage is, however, attested, albeit sporadically and in informal registers, and often in association with certain constructions, such as the interrogative [Can someone (please) explain me Wh ...]. It is therefore not simply a matter of admitting the ditransitive as one of the subcategorization options for the verb, nor can it be prohibited outright. If *explain* were to be listed in the lexicon as a ditransitive verb, many of the sentences which the syntax generates would have little chance of occurring in a corpus and would probably be rejected by native speakers as ungrammatical. If the ditransitive frame were to be prohibited, the grammar would fail to generate those sentences which native speakers sometimes produce and which mostly do not carry the censure of ungrammaticality.

Suppose that over the next couple of decades, the usage exemplified above becomes more frequent, not only in informal registers such as Internet blogs and casual conversation, but in situations where speakers carefully monitor their usage. At the same time, the ditransitive comes to be used in a wider range of constructional environments. At some hypothetical future time, ditransitive *explain* might come to have equal status with the transitive usage. *Explain me it* would be on a par with *explain it to me*, just as, in present-day English, *show me it* stands as an alternative to *show it to me*. The generative model would be able to capture the changed status of the verb in terms of a change in its lexical specification. What the model would not be able to account for are the intervening stages, where the ditransitive use is sporadic and restricted to certain constructional contexts and to certain registers of use.

While there may be a germ of truth in the reanalysis hypothesis (which tries to square the circle by proposing change without innovation), more detailed analyses show that language change cannot be reduced to reanalysis, neither can language use be accommodated within the terms of a fixed language system. Speakers are continuously 'tweaking' the system, combining familiar elements in novel ways and testing existing resources in new environments. Speakers are being creative in the non-technical, everyday sense of the word, not only in the sense intended by generativists.

Idioms and their usage range: the case of *all over*

We might suppose that the idiomatic is the last place we should look when studying linguistic creativity and innovation. As noted in Chapter 4, idioms are often defined negatively, as expressions which cannot be generated by the syntax operating over the lexicon. The idiomatic thus falls outside the purview of the generative model and its understanding of creativity. 'Idiom creativity' would be an oxymoron.

There are many reasons why this view of the idiomatic is mistaken. Leaving aside the very small number of truly fixed expressions such as *How do you do?* (see p. 75), idioms, of whatever kind, are open to greater or lesser degrees of variation. Even lexically fixed idioms, of the kind *spill the beans*, are compatible with various markers of tense, aspect, and modality, and some may even be available for passivization and other rewordings. Moreover, as we saw in Chapter 4, many idioms are characterized by one or more open slots, which can be filled by items of the appropriate semantic and/or syntactic characteristics. These idioms can be more or less productive, depending on the restrictions imposed on their constituents. Some constructional idioms—such as the [WHAT ABOUT X] construction or the [THAT'LL TEACH YOU TO V] construction—are, in fact, able to sanction an open-ended set of expressions. These idioms are not at all inimical to creativity, in the generativists' sense. We should also bear in mind that most idioms, whatever their nature, are able to feature as parts of larger constructions and can, in turn, accommodate idioms as parts of their own structure. Once again, the idioms turn out to be not inconsistent with the generative notion of creativity.

Not only are idioms able to play their part in linguistic creativity (in the generativists' sense), they can also be the source of innovations in the language. In Chapter 4 we looked at some examples where allusions to idioms can give rise to new idiomatic resources. In this section I examine the ways in which the usage contexts of an idiomatic expression can themselves give rise to new idiomatic resources. The process is illustrated on the example of the expression *all over*.

There are cases in which *over* and *all over* appear to share the same contexts of use.

(14)   a. There's water (all) over the floor.
       b. It's (all) over between you and me.

Example (14a) invokes the covering sense of *over* (see p. 233). *All* functions as a quantifier, indicating that all of the floor is covered by the water. The meaning of *all over* thus appears to be a compositional function of the meanings of the component words. In (14b), on the other hand, *all* appears to have an intensifier function (Rickford, Wasow, Zwicky, and Buchstaller 2007). The relationship is not only 'over' (that is, finished), but 'all over' (that is, finished beyond repair). In both cases the occurrence of *all* is optional.

This account doesn't always work. Consider the following example:

(15)   You'd think the Maori Party would be all over this issue. (New Zealand political blog, 2009)

The meaning is that the Maori Party should be scrutinizing the issue and vigorously criticizing it. The interpretation might be seen as a metaphorical extension of the covering sense of *all over*. Interestingly, though, if *all* is omitted, a quite different interpretation emerges:

(16)   You'd think the Maori Party would be over this issue.

The meaning, here, would be that the Party should be able to put the issue behind them, similar to the way in which *I'm over shopping* (see p. 237) means that I have overcome my shopaholic tendencies. In this example, then, *all over* cannot be interpreted compositionally: the expression has a distinct semantic value (in fact, as we shall see, it has several semantic values), not derivable from the meanings of its parts. *All over*, in other words, is an idiom in its own right.

This may be true even of the covering sense of *all over*. Consider the following BNC examples:

(17) a. Oh, God, I thought, she can see the lipstick **all over** me.
      b. I still weigh 66 kilos and still have a galaxy of spots around my nose and **all over** my chin.

With *all* omitted, (a) would be nonsensical while (b) would be, at best, marginal. The examples suggest that these uses of *all over* differ significantly from those cited at the beginning of this section: *all* does not designate total coverage, nor does the word have an intensifier function. Rather, *all over* designates what Queller (2001: 58) calls "random dispersal", with the further nuance that the presence of the trajector entity—the lipstick or the spots—is unwanted. (As a matter of fact, this account might even apply to example (14a), where the water is an unwanted presence on the floor.) Queller contrasts the following (invented) examples:

(18) a. The tablecloth has got bloodstains all over it.
      b. *The tablecloth has got red squares all over it.

The oddness of (b) derives from the fact that the red squares are a design feature of the tablecloth, not an unwanted blemish.

As the above remarks suggest, *all over* not only must count as a (non-compositional) idiom, the idiom has multiple semantic values. What is more, the contexts in which *all over* occurs themselves give rise to new idiomatic locutions.

Consider, first, the use of *all over* in association with geopolitical entities: *all over the world, all over the country, all over Europe*, and the like. The meaning is reasonably transparent: some entity, or process, is claimed to be pervasive within the designated terrain. *All over the place* (attested 471 times in the BNC) might be seen in this light, with, however, the proviso that the terrain is designated only vaguely. Somewhat less frequent, but with similar semantic values, are the variants *all over the show* and *all over the shop*. What is interesting, however, is that *all over the place* has acquired some specialized uses. Compare:

(19) a. someone's left an old choc-ice on the floor, and it's run **all over the place**.
      b. Yesterday's polls looked much of a muchness—they were not "**all over the place**"—but concealed politically crucial variations.

Whereas (19a) concerns random distribution in the spatial domain, (19b) concerns the way in which a set of data is distributed. If you say that the results from your experiment are 'all over the place', you mean that they lack a coherent pattern or trend. Likewise, a lecturer may say of a student's essay that it is 'all over the place', meaning that it lacks a coherent structure. You may even say that the student himself is 'all over the place'.[8]

All over the place in the random distribution sense has itself given rise to variants, such as *all over the map*. An antipodean variant is *all over the paddock*. The expression seems to have been first popularized with respect to havoc on a rugby field:

(20)   The determined and dogged Irish weren't giving up and had the Aussies running ragged **all over the paddock.** (Internet example)

The expression has extended to other contexts. I recall that during the 2005 general election in New Zealand the news media were commenting that the initial results were 'all over the paddock', that is, they were 'all over the place', or 'all over the map', not showing any consistent trends.

Another idiomatic context is given by the expression *written all over*. The expression accounts for about 1 per cent of all instances of *all over* in the BNC. In some cases, an entity (literally) has something prominently written on it.

(21)   My partner for the event . . . turned up with a bag which had "Save the Whales" **written all over** it.[9]

Otherwise, the expression refers to some salient feature of an entity, which, like a written inscription, can be 'read' (22) and might even ascribed to a particular 'writer' (23).

(22)   a. Glazed, red-rimmed, they stare off into some distant past that has mid-1980s **written all over** it.
        b. And it's got faulty **written all over** the box, you know.

(23)   a. Dave's rhythm work has got his name **written all over** it.
        b. This has Paul **written all over** it.

Particularly productive is the further expansion of the idiom, *written all over one's face*. This use is illustrated by the following (BNC) data:

(24)   a. Though Jackson was the first to congratulate Olympic champion McKoy, the disappointment was **written all over his face.**
        b. As William and Harry boarded the 10.30am BA flight, excitement was **written all over their faces.**

---

[8] These examples are based on Queller (2001).
[9] It needs hardly pointing out that *all* in this example does not have its compositional value. It is not as if all of the bag was covered by the inscription, merely that the inscription was prominently displayed on it.

There are seventeen examples of '{an emotion} written all over one's face' in the BNC.[10] The expression exploits the conceptual metaphor of THE FACE AS INTERFACE. A person's face is where emotions and intentions are made manifest and where they can be 'read' by an observer. This conceptualization is prominent in the following (Googled) examples:

(25) a. He approaches slowly, anxiety **visible all over his face**.
      b. The conductor was sitting with satisfaction **clearly visible all over his face**.
      c. Connor peers at him, disgust **legible all over his face**.
      d. the agony was **prominent all over his face** as was the disappointment.

Speakers have creatively (and sometimes amusingly) played on this metaphorical expression, coming up with the following (Internet-sourced) variants:

(26) a. This is a comic, then, who walks on stage with "please like me" **scrawled all over his face**.
      b. Mr Eun glanced at the half-empty classroom, and then back at me, the usual "kids these-days" look **scribbled all over his face**.
      c. He leant over with compassion **printed all over his face in italic type**.
      d. The man has "rising star" **printed all over his face**.
      e. arrogance **inscribed all over his face**
      f. His love of life was **stamped all over his face**.
      g. The delight is visibly **etched all over his face**.
      h. Simon looked up from his computer screen, irritation **engraved all over his face**.
      i. The Source? Simple. It's Dan Rather's daughter. It was **typed all over his face** when he "defended" the story Friday.
      j. Zainab looked up at her mother, helplessness **portrayed all over her face**.
      k. Contempt was **depicted all over his face**.

The data presented above (for a fuller account, see Taylor 2006*b*) show the progressive expansion of idiomatic phrases based on *all over*. It is not just that *all over* is an idiomatic phrase, with a number of (non-compositional) values. Locutions incorporating *all over* have themselves acquired idiomatic status, and these, in turn, are subject to variation and creative extension. We might even say, borrowing the terminology of the generativists, that idiom coinage is recursive!

---

[10] Queller (2001) proposes that *written all over one's face* is associated with the unintentional expression of an emotion, pointing out that the phrase is more likely to be used of guilt and disappointment, which a person might prefer to keep hidden, than of rage or pleasure, which a person freely expresses. While some examples, such as (24a), support this account, others, such as (24b), do not.

In conclusion

There can be no question about speakers' ability to come up with linguistic expressions which go beyond their previous experience with the language. Speakers' ability in this regard is often cited in support of the generativists' claim that linguistic ability resides in knowledge of a set of rules operating recursively over a finite lexicon. What the generativist account tends to overlook, however, is the fact that speakers' productions can sometimes be more appropriately characterized as linguistic innovation rather than as linguistic creativity. Creativity, as understood by generativists, is a matter of applying pre-established rules to items selected from a pre-established lexicon; innovation is a matter of going beyond the rules and the lexicon and coming up with expressions which strictly speaking would have to be regarded as ungrammatical. The case studies examined in this chapter indicate that innovation is incremental. Speakers introduce what at first appear to be minor variants to preformed expressions, then gradually extend accepted usage patterns to new environments and combine existing resources in novel and unorthodox ways.

In this chapter I have argued that there is no logical link between the facts of creativity (and innovation) and the imperative of a generative model of linguistic knowledge. What is needed, however, is a theoretical model which is able to accommodate manifestations of creativity and innovation and which is able to pass muster as an alternative to the generative approach. In the next chapter I examine one such model, based in Fauconnier's theory of conceptual blending.

12

Blending

The thesis of this book is that knowledge of a language can be conceptualized in terms of the metaphor of the mental corpus. Language is acquired by a strictly 'bottom-up' process, through exposure to usage events, and knowing a language consists, not in knowing a battery of rules, but in accumulated memories of previously encountered utterances and the generalizations which arise from them.

On the face of it, this approach is difficult to square with the incontrovertible facts of creativity and innovation. Certainly, there are some routine situations in which creativity is not at a premium and where speakers are quite happy to paste together pre-learned chunks of language. On the other hand, the construct of the mental corpus does not condemn speakers to repeat for ever chunks of language they have already encountered. Previously encountered expressions, and the schematic constructions which they instantiate, can be the source of new linguistic expressions. Speakers can introduce variations to preformed expressions, they can extend accepted usage patterns, and they can blend existing resources to create hybrid expressions which inherit some aspects of their inputs. It is this latter process—the blending of existing resources in the creation of new and sometimes novel outputs—that is the topic of this chapter.

Fauconnier and Turner (2002) have argued that the creativity of human thought is largely the product of conceptual blending, where features of distinct mental spaces are recruited to form new conceptualizations. My focus in this chapter is the blending of linguistic resources, such as words, morphemes, and constructions, in both their formal and semantic aspects. Blending turns out to be a potent source of new expressions and new constructions and thus offers itself as a serious alternative to the rule-based mechanisms of generative theory.

Blending theory

The theory of CONCEPTUAL BLENDING (Fauconnier 1997; Fauconnier and Turner 1998, 2002) developed out of Fauconnier's theory of MENTAL SPACES (Fauconnier 1994). A mental space consists of a set of elements and the relations holding between them, and is constructed incrementally as discourse proceeds. Roughly speaking, a mental space constitutes the subject matter of a discourse—or, more generally, of conscious attention—at any given moment.

The notion of mental space captures the insight that linguistic utterances are not, strictly speaking, about things and events in the world, but about situations as conceptualized by a speaker. To be sure, the contents of a mental space may be deemed to correspond to things and events in the world. This, however, need not be the case; consider the fictional spaces constructed by novelists and story-tellers. And even when we are supposedly talking about the outside world, the content of our discourse is inevitably subject to selection and filtering by the human mind (Jackendoff 1983).

An important insight of Fauconnier is that mental spaces can be dependent on other spaces and that entities across different mental spaces can be linked by a relation of identity. Suppose someone says *I want to marry a rich man*. On the one hand, there is the 'base space' which has as one of its elements the speaker herself. The expression, however, opens up a secondary mental space, which concerns the speaker's wants. The 'want space' is inhabited by the speaker (linked by a relation of identity to the speaker in the base space) and by the prospective husband. The prospective husband may have a counterpart in the base space ('I want to marry a rich man; I met him at the casino'). The prospective husband may, on the other hand, have no counterpart in the base space; he exists only in the woman's imagination ('I want to marry a rich man; unfortunately, I haven't found one yet').

(The reader may have observed a further layer of complexity in the example just presented. 'Suppose someone says *I want to marry a rich man*', I wrote in the above paragraph. The situation of the woman and her wants is located in a hypothetical space, set up by me, the writer. In this space, populated by me and the text that I am creating, there is no such woman who says *I want to marry a rich man*; she exists only in the hypothetical space.)

As will be appreciated from this very simple example, the notion of mental space has important consequences in linguistic analysis. Wishes and suppositions open up imaginary mental spaces. Counterfactual conditionals set up mental spaces whose elements and relations are contrary to those in the base space. Jokes and stories set up fictional spaces. A number of expressions function as SPACE BUILDERS, that is, as explicit instructions to the hearer to open up the appropriate mental space. Example include *if only, what if, suppose, in my dream, in this film, twenty years ago*, and *once upon a time*.

Blending involves the creation of a new space (the blend) by drawing on elements of two (or more) input spaces. As Fauconnier and Turner emphasize, blending is not just a linguistic-semantic phenomenon; it is a crucial feature of everyday cognition. Consider one of their examples (Fauconnier and Turner 2002: 113). You are looking at a Persian rug in a store in town, wondering how it would look in your lounge at home. On the one hand there is the current situation of you looking at the rug. There is also your mental image of your lounge. The two spaces are different, with very little in common. The one concerns the perceptible here and now, the other is a memory of a different location. The one has the rug in the store, the other has your lounge sans rug. But it is a natural and everyday process to try to imagine the rug in your lounge. In doing this, you are creating a new mental space (the blend) which consists of elements of one mental space (features of your lounge) augmented by a feature of another mental space (the rug).

Blending is ubiquitous in everyday thought. It is, first of all, a creative process, in that the blend need not correspond to any actual or previously imagined situation. Moreover, the process is not compositional, with one space simply being added to, or superimposed on, the other. Integration involves selective activation of elements from the different spaces, whereby discrepancies are overlooked and differences in time and space are compressed. Nor, it must be emphasized, is the outcome of blending predictable from its inputs. There is no unique solution to the 'rug in the lounge' problem.

As presented by Fauconnier and Turner (2002), blending is a quintessential conceptual process, taking as its input two (or more) knowledge structures. Fauconnier and Turner do, however, have a brief discussion of specifically linguistic examples of blending (pp. 35ff.). The inputs, here, are linguistic structures, selected features of which are combined in order to create a new expression whose properties are not a simple compositional function of the inputs. Take the case of compound nouns. In principle, any two nouns can be juxtaposed to form a compound (see pp. 35ff). Compounds resist a compositional interpretation. One cannot interpret *land yacht* (Fauconnier and Turner 2002: 365) by somehow combining the notion of 'land' with the notion of 'yacht'. Rather, we selectively activate some facets of what we know about yachts and integrate these with what we know about land, more specifically, since yachts are a means of transportation, about transportation on land. There are, in fact, at least two ways in which the expression can be interpreted. One interpretation concerns a land-based vehicle which is propelled in the manner of a yacht, that is, by sails. The other focuses on a yacht as a large, luxurious vessel, one, however, that is land-based—a commodious limousine, for example, or a house trailer.

In the land yacht example, blending is still a matter of the blending of semantic structures; structurally, the compound consists simply of the concatenation of the two words. In this chapter, I want to focus specifically on the blending of the formal resources of a language, such as words, morphemes, constructions, and expressions of various sizes, where the output is formally distinct from each of the inputs. The examples illustrate the scope of formal blending and testify to its powerful role in linguistic innovation.

Word blending

Long before Fauconnier and Turner developed their theory, the term 'blending' had been used to describe a process of word formation. Well-known examples of word blends include *motel* (a blend of *motor* and *hotel*), *brunch* (a blend of *breakfast* and *lunch*), and *Oxbridge* (a blend of *Oxford* and *Cambridge*). Typically, word blends are made up from phonological material taken from the initial part of one of the inputs in combination with material from the final part of the other input word. In the case of *motel*, the input sequences are dovetailed: [m[əʊt]ɛl]. Moreover, the blend usually takes its prosodic structure (number of syllables, location of stress) from one, or even from both of the input items.[1]

Blending of the phonological inputs corresponds iconically to the blending of the respective concepts. *Oxbridge* refers to a collective comprising the two oldest British universities and their common ethos in contrast to the so-called 'redbrick' universities. *Brunch*, on the other hand, refers not so much to a combination of breakfast and lunch, but to a late and rather generous breakfast, a breakfast, in other words, with features of a lunch. With *motel*, the input is more in the nature of a compound noun, i.e. *motor hotel*, and is interpreted accordingly.[2]

Blending—in English, at least—is a surprisingly common phenomenon, often employed to name new products, new institutions, and new practices and concepts. A recently observed example is *glamping*, a blend of (presumably) *glamorous* and *camping*, referring to a trend towards vacationing in particularly well-appointed tents. Another blend which appears to be gaining some traction is *bankster*, a blend of *banker* and *gangster*, which encapsulates the public's critical view of the banking industry's role in recent financial turmoils. An example from linguistic theory is the term *collostruction*, a blend of *collocation* and *construction* (see p. 140).

Blending can even give rise to what appear to be new morphological resources. Kemmer (2003) discusses the process on the example of *glitterati*, a blend of *glitter* (with some additional input, perhaps, from other words in *gl-*, such as *glamorous* and *glitzy*) and *literati*, and referring to a glitzy, glamorous social elite. Additional forms such as *chatterati*, *digerati*, *designerati*, and, more recently, *twitterati*, point to the emergence of the suffix *-erati*. Another example is the emergence of *Euro-* as a prefix, possibly on the back of the blends such as *Eurocrat* (< Europe + bureaucrat).

---

[1] For a survey of the mechanisms of word blending—concerning such aspects as the order of the input items and the 'breakpoints' at which the inputs words are segmented—see Kelly (1998).

[2] The possibility of an iconic relation between phonological and semantic blending presupposes that word blends are recognized as such. One requirement of a blend, therefore, is that it must preserve a sufficient amount of the distinctive phonological material of the inputs in order that the inputs can be recovered (Gries 2006a). It would not be possible, for example, to propose *latt* or *lot* as a blend of *land* and *yacht*, since the proposed forms fail to evoke either of their inputs. Neither has *Camford* enjoyed much success as a blend of *Cambridge* and *Oxford*.

Motel, collostruction, glamping, bankster, and *glitterati* are examples of what Algeo (1977: 56) referred to as SYNTAGMATIC BLENDS. The input consists of two words, of different meanings and sometimes of different syntactic classes, which are able to occur in close proximity in the stream of speech. The blend 'telescopes' a larger, multi-word syntagm. Algeo (1977: 57) drew attention to a different kind of blend, the PARADIGMATIC, or ASSOCIATIVE BLEND. The inputs to an associative blend are words of similar meaning, either of which would be appropriate in a given context. Whereas syntagmatic blends tend to be conscious creations, associative blends often result from faulty planning and execution. It is as if two words are available to a speaker to express a certain concept. Instead of choosing one over the other, the speaker starts with one option only to switch in mid-articulation to the other. Along with other kinds of speech errors, associative blends have been intensively studied for the light they shed on the mechanisms of speech production (Fromkin 1973, 1980; Laver 1970; Levelt 1989: Chapter 9; MacKay 1972).

The following is a parade example which has been often cited in the psycholinguistic literature:

(1)   didn't bother me in the sleast … slightest (Boomer and Laver 1968)

Here, the nonce form *(not) in the sleast* blends the roughly synonymous alternatives *not in the least* and *not in the slightest.* Hockett (1961: 52) reports that he once admonished his noisy children with *Don't shell* (< shout + yell) *so loud.* Here are some more examples. The first two are from Garman (1990: 160–1), the others are from Wells (1973: 85); the inputs to the blends are those suggested by the respective authors.

(2)   a. that's torrible (terrible + horrible)
      b. have you ever flivven (flown + driven)
      c. behortment (behaviour + deportment)
      d. shaddy (shabby + shoddy)
      e. frowl (frown + scowl)
      f. refudiating (refusing + repudiating)

Inflectional morphology is not immune to blending. On more than one occasion I have found myself on the point of using *arrove* as the past tense form of *arrive,* particularly when the arriving was done by driving. (I do not, however, recall any instance where I actually used the innovative form.) The blend of *arrive* and the past tense form *drove* was no doubt facilitated by the identical rhymes of *arrive* and *drive,* with the output form blending the semantics of the two verbs. The morphological errors induced by Bybee and Slobin (1982) may be seen in this light (see also Taylor 2002: 317–18). Bybee and Slobin required subjects to produce, as rapidly as possible, the past tense forms of verbs. We can reasonably suppose that each of the forty-four adult subjects in the experiment knew the 'correct' past tense forms. Yet under time pressure and in the experimental situation in which the stimulus words were not embedded in a meaningful context, as many as nine subjects proffered *sat* as the past tense of *(to) seat* (correct form: *seated*), while four volunteered *rose* as the past tense of *raise* (correct form: *raised*). There are phonological and semantic similarities between *sat* and *rose* and the stimulus items. In addition, the elicited forms are legitimate past tense forms, albeit of other verbs, namely *sit* and *rise*; significantly, these are verbs which are semantically close to the input verbs. Further candidates for morphological blending are the plurals in [iːz] discussed elsewhere in this book (see pp. 11 and 134). *Processes* [iːz], intended as the plural of *process*, blends the base noun with a pattern for the creation of 'Greek' plurals, such as *theses* and *hypotheses*.

As mentioned, syntagmatic blending is likely to be the result of a conscious process, whereas associative blends are more likely to be the fortuitous result of planning and execution errors. Although I have no evidence to support this assertion, it is unlikely, I think, that a form like *motel* first emerged as a 'slip of the tongue', due to the co-activation of the two input nouns. Nevertheless, some examples of syntagmatic blending have been reported in the speech error literature.[3] The following are from Fromkin (1973: 256–7):

(3) a. shrimp and egg soufflé → shrig soufflé
     b. rubber overshoes → ruvershoes
     c. late afternoon classes → laternoon classes

On the other hand, some examples of associative blending are (probably) conscious creations. An example is *ginormous*, a blend of *gigantic* and *enormous*.

A question of some interest is whether speech error blends—blends which can be seen as the result of planning and execution failure—might nevertheless gain wider currency and even enter the language as accepted forms. On the face of it, we should not expect that this would be the case. Errors are the product of a unique set of circumstances. They are usually recognized as such and sometimes, as in (1), the speaker is able to correct herself. Possibly, quite a few of these blends may even be suppressed before they are uttered, leaving no trace in the linguistic record; this, for example, is the case with my temptation to use the erroneous form *arrove*. Even so, it is interesting to note that of the blends cited in (2), at least two seem to enjoy some wider currency. A contributor to the online Urban Dictionary[4] defines *frowl* as 'a combination of a frown, scowl, and growl, to be employed when each of these individually just isn't enough'. The verb *refudiate* also seems to have gained some

---

[3] A recently observed example (in which art critics were discussing a portrait): *against the blackground* (= black background).
[4] www.urbandictionary.com/

traction. A Google search (October 2009) returned over a thousand hits for this word.[5]

One possibility is that different individuals, at different times and in different places, independently make the same speech error. This would suggest that some errors are already immanent in the language system; they are, if one will, 'errors waiting to happen'. However, in order for the errors to gain wider currency, we should have to suppose that the errors are perceived, by hearers, as useful additions to the expressive resources of the language. In this way, the new forms are able to propagate themselves throughout the language community (Croft 2000).

Phrasal blending

In planning an utterance a speaker may not only have different lexical items available to her for the expression of her thought; she may also have to choose between alternative phrasal expressions or between different syntactic constructions. Lexical blends, such as Hockett's example *Don't shell so loud*, suggests that occasionally a speaker may fail to make a choice, coming out with a word which combines material from the available options. We can imagine that phrasal blends, where alternative phrasal resources are intertwined, will be no less frequent than lexical blends. Here are some examples of the phenomenon. The first three are from Stemberger (1982); the fourth is from Laver (1970).

(4)   a. Do I have to put on my seatbelt on?
       b. This is getting very difficult to cut this.
       c. That might be easier to control for that.
       d. He behaved as like a fool.

According to Stemberger, (4c) results from the activation of two different syntactic constructions with very similar meaning:

(5)   a. That might be easier to control.
       b. It might be easier to control for that.

---

[5] This passage was written before the media hullabaloo over the use of the verb by the American politician, Sarah Palin. A language guru on the *Daily Telegraph* of 20 July 2010 opined:

Sarah Palin's ongoing struggle with the English language entered a new phase this week, when she called on her Twitter followers to "refudiate" the proposal to build a mosque on the site of the World Trade Center. Mockery followed, and a tweet in which she corrected herself and asked people to "refute" it. Not correct, either. Finally, she put an end to it by saying: "Refudiate, misunderestimate, wee-wee'd up. English is a living language. Shakespeare liked to coin words, too." (Philip Hensher, 'Sarah Palin's struggle with English language'. *Daily Telegraph*, 20 July 2010; www.telegraph.co.uk/news/worldnews/northamerica/usa/sarah-palin/7901926/Sarah-Palins-struggle-with-English-language.html)

Similarly, Laver analysed (4d) in terms of competition between the roughly synonymous *as if/though he were a fool* and *like a fool*.

While examples (4a–c) would undoubtedly count as errors, the status of (4d) as a slip of the tongue might be queried. Although proscribed in normative usage, *as like* is not uncommon as an alternative to comparative *like*, especially in informal registers; some BNC examples are given in (6).

(6) a. we didn't have to do jobs **as like** that in the morning
    b. they treat it **as like** pieces of art
    c. Benguiat took it **as like** a threat

While examples with *as like* may not have the status of planning errors, we cannot exclude the possibility that the form arose through the blending of semantically similar inputs along the lines suggested by Laver. Barlow (2000), for one, has suggested that phrasal blending may be an important driver of language innovation and change. The phenomenon has received relatively little attention, probably because phrasal blends, unlike word blends, are likely to go undetected. Word blends are conspicuous. When you first encounter a word like *glamping* you can hardly fail to notice its novelty and will probably wonder what the new word is likely to mean. Phrasal blends do not have this impact. Phrasal expressions are subject to many more degrees of freedom than words. Quite simply, we expect variability in the internal make-up of phrases with respect to the choice of words, the sanctioning constructions, and the speaker's semantic intent. Moreover, phrasal blends do not, usually, pose a problem of semantic interpretation. Precisely because they are not likely to register as such, phrasal blends have a good chance of establishing themselves as part of the language system.

Consider the following examples taken from the COCA corpus.

(7) a. the prime minister and I talked about it **at some detail**.
    b. the response goes on **in some length**.

The standard phraseologies are *in some detail* and *at some length*. Both are attested many times in both the British (BNC) and the American (COCA) corpora. While not synonymous, the expressions do mutually implicate each other. If you talk about something in detail the expectation is that you also talk about it at length, and vice versa. It is plausible, therefore, that both expressions, and their associated semantics, should be simultaneously activated in the mind of a speaker (cf. Coppock 2010).

Whether the examples in (7) do constitute speech errors is, once again, a moot point. *At some detail* and *in some length* are not attested in the BNC and only one example of each is found in the COCA corpus. The very rarity of the expressions may be indicative of their impromptu status. On the other hand, Internet searches suggest that both expressions (as well as variants such as *at great detail* and *in great length*) may be gaining ground, pointing to the emergence of new phraseological resources.

For another example, consider the following:

(8)   It all **stems back to** the early days. (BNC)

There are only three instances of *stem back to* in the BNC as against almost 1,000 examples of the more usual *stem from*. The innovation probably arose through blending with the roughly synonymous *go back to*. Again, Internet searches suggest that *stem back to* has caught on with quite a number of speakers.

As mentioned above, Barlow (2000) has argued that phrasal blending could be a significant cause of language change. An example which he discusses concerns a change in the subcategorization frame of the verb *claim*. According to Barlow (2000: 327–8), in eighteenth-century English *claim* subcategorized exclusively for an NP object:

(9)   a. 1722: Both sides claimed the victory.
      b. 1776: Heroines of such a cast may claim our admiration.

Assert, on the other hand, took a clausal complement:

(10) a. 1726–31: They confidently asserted that the first inhabitants of their island were fairies.
      b. 1782: He asserts that he not only invented polyphonic music, or counterpoint, but the polyplectrum or spinet.

By the nineteenth century, *claim* was able to take a *that*-complement, indicative of a blending of *claim* with the complementation pattern of the semantically similar verb *assert*.

(11) a. 1850: He claimed that his word should be law.
      b. 1878: Watt claimed that Hornblower . . . was an infringer upon his patents.

Barlow (2000: 327) suggests that quite a few common locutions might have originated as blends. One example that he cites is *thanks very much*. The expression's internal structure is odd. *Thanks* is a noun, *very much* is an adverbial. It is plausible, therefore, to regard the expression as a blend of the syntactically more orthodox expressions *many thanks* and *thank you very much*. Another candidate is *for free*. Once again, the expression is odd, if examined analytically. *For* is a preposition, *free* is an adjective—a somewhat unorthodox syntactic pattern. The phrase, according to Barlow, blends two roughly synonymous expressions. If you get something 'for free', you get it 'for nothing'; it comes to you 'free', that is, gratis.[6]

---

[6] The syntactic oddness of *thanks very much* and *for free* is likely to pass unnoticed, precisely because the expressions are so familiar and hence highly entrenched as multi-word units. See the discussion in Chapter 6, pp. 130–1.

As these examples suggest, candidates for a phrasal blending analysis are expressions whose parts do not properly stack up. Here are several more, selected in order to illustrate the scope of the phenomenon.[7]

keeping an eye out

As with other body part terms, *eye* has many non-literal uses, mostly based in metonymies (Hilpert 2006). The eye, most obviously, is the organ of sight. If you cast your eye over something you inspect it, either literally or metaphorically; if you keep an eye on something you monitor its development; if you have an eye for a bargain you are able to detect (i.e. 'see') its value; if you eye someone up and down you inspect them carefully; and so on. These expressions are reasonably transparent, given general processes of metonymy and metaphor. But to keep an eye *out* for something? The expression is odd, if considered analytically. It is plausibly analysed as a blend of *watch/look out for* and *keep an eye on*.

ever since I can remember

In its temporal uses, *since* refers to the beginning of a period of time in contrast to *for*, which refers to the length of the time period in question. You say that you have been waiting since 10 o'clock but for three hours. *Ever since I can remember*—there are seven instances of the phrase in the BNC and thirty-five in the COCA[8]—violates this quite strict distinction; as a matter of fact, the complement of *since*—namely, *I can remember*—designates neither a period of time nor a point in time. Strictly speaking, therefore, *ever since I can remember* does not stack up. The meaning, though, is clear. The expression can be regarded as a blend of the roughly synonymous *for as long as I can remember* and *since as long ago as I can remember* (Coppock 2006).

---

[7] On a less serious note, consider the case of PERVERBS. The term itself is a blend of *perverse* and *proverb*, and refers to the humorous blending of proverbs. (There are several websites giving collections, e.g. www.nous.org.uk/perverb.html.) A perverb splices the first half of one proverb, or saying, with the second half of another. Their effect, it goes without saying, presupposes that a hearer is able to recover the input expressions (cf. footnote 2); to this extent, perverbs are a further illustration of the practice of alluding to proverbs, addressed in Chapter 4. Some examples:

    (i) A rolling stone catches the worm.
    (ii) The early bird gathers no moss.
    (iii) Make hay while the cat's away.
    (iv) Tomorrow is stranger than fiction.

I particularly like (iii). It rhymes, it makes sense, and it could even be piece of useful wisdom!

[8] A BNC example: *He limps now, and has done ever since I can remember*. Although the expression typically occurs with *ever*, examples without this word are attested:

    (i) I am more uncertain about the real state of our economy than at any time **since I can remember.** (BNC)
    (ii) This spring, for the first time **since I can remember**, there's nothing on my mind. (COCA)

time and (time) again

The expression is used as an adverbial, with the meaning 'repeatedly'. There are two main variants. The 'standard' form, *time and time again*, occurs 174 times in the BNC and 621 times in the COCA. A more emphatic form, *time and time and time again*, is also attested (twice in the BNC, twenty-nine times in the COCA). A 'reduced' form, *time and again*, is common in the COCA (869 examples); curiously, though, there are no instances at all in the BNC.

Viewed analytically, the expression, in all of its variants, is odd. *Time and again* coordinates a noun and an adverbial. With *time and time again* it is not even clear what is being coordinated: should the expression be analysed as [[time] and [time again]] or as [[time and time] again]? A blending analysis suggests itself. The word *time* derives from the adverbial phrase *time after time* while *and again* comes from the roughly synonymous *again and again*.

being as how

Several examples of phrasal blending came to light in the course of a study of causal connectives (Taylor and Pang 2008). Consider the following (Googled) examples:

(12) a. told cousin Sally that my wife was poorly, **being as how** she had a touch of the rheumatics in the hip.
      b. Well, **being as though** I just recently recuperated from the flu, these first few weeks of the semester haven't exactly been the easiest for me.
      c. I submitted his picture, and received no response which isn't surprising, **considering as how** the casting director probably got 500 pictures for that one part, and there were probably forty roles to fill.

The highlighted expressions are certainly not standard connectives and might even be dismissed as errors. All are based, however, on established causal expressions. As a matter of fact, English is particularly rich in this category of connectives. In addition to *since*, *because*, and *as*, English speakers can choose amongst *considering (that)*, *given (that)*, *seeing (that)*, and several more.[9] Common in colloquial speech are other locutions, such as *being as*, *seeing as how*, and *seeing as though*.[10] What seems to be happening in the examples in (12) is that the speakers have blended aspects of these resources in order to come up with novel expressions of causality. Thus, (12c) blends the roughly synonymous *considering (that)* and *seeing as how*, (12b) blends *being as* with *seeing as though*, while (12a) is an amalgam of *being as* and *seeing as how*.

---

[9] The connectives, while all expressing the reason for a state of affairs (or the reason why a speaker deems it appropriate to assert a state of affairs), are not strictly synonymous. Subtle differences are discussed in Taylor and Pang (2008).

[10] *Being as* and *seeing as how* are both attested since the nineteenth century. *Seeing as though* would appear to be of more recent origin.

I think that's fair to say

This expression—attested only once in the BNC but as many as twenty-three times in the COCA—has two inputs. One input is a more orthodox use of *fair*, illustrated in the following:

(13) a. I think **it would be fair to say** that South Dakota is a little bit different from New Hampshire.
    b. I think **it would be fair to say** I liked Andy from the start.
    c. **It is fair to say** that this view is controversial.

The other input is the so-called object-to-subject raising construction, illustrated by such well-worn examples as *John is easy to please* and *Good housekeepers are difficult to find* (see Langacker 1991: 449–63 for a discussion; also Bolinger 1961 for the role of blending in such constructions). These contrast with their non-raised counterparts, viz. *To please John is easy* and *It is difficult to find good housekeepers*. *Fair*, however, does not in general pattern like *easy* and *difficult*; witness the impossibility of **To say that is fair*.

That's fair to say has a special context of use. In the examples in (13) the speaker is hedging her commitment to the truth of the embedded proposition, whereas in *that's fair to say* the speaker offers a comment on what has already been proposed, typically by another speaker. Indeed, we might suppose that the innovative construction is motivated by the speaker's desire to place the topic of the sentence—what the sentence is 'about'—in initial position, the topic, in this case, being the content of a previous speaker's utterance, referred to by *that*.[11] The blend may thus reflect an "optimization strategy" (Brenier and Michaelis 2005: 47) rather than faulty planning and execution. Interestingly, a number of other adjectives, not usually associated with object-to-subject raising, can appear in the construction:

(14) a. I think that's safe to say.
    b. that's weird to say at age 38.
    c. why does he think that's OK to say?
    d. that's sad to say.
    e. that sounds terrible to say.

Although not attested in the BNC or the COCA, Internet searches suggest that *true* is also being used in this environment, an example being the following exchange:

(15) A: Probably the [friends] he had were real close, though, I imagine.
    B: Yeah, I think that's true to say. He had a few very close friends.

---

[11] Recall that some supposedly ungrammatical uses of *explain* also seem to be the result of a topicaliza- tion strategy (see p. 31).

the most beautifulest girl in the world

One occasionally encounters forms such as *more easier* and *the most commonest*, where the comparative or superlative grade is expressed twice, by the inflection -*er* or -*est* and by use of *more* or *most*. Presumably, both constructions—the inflectional construction and the analytic construction—are simultaneously activated. In terms of normative usage, double comparatives (and double superlatives) would no doubt be castigated as gross errors. They are by no means infrequent, however, in informal speech at least. Some corpus examples:

(16)   a. it's **more easier** for me
        b. they would probably be into a **more younger** scene
        c. they're much **more better**
        d. mum when I lie down I get **more dizzier**!
(17)   a. he said I'm **the most beautifulest** girl in the world
        b. There are many different makes. Chubb is probably one of **the most commonest.**
        c. I was the saddest and **most miserablest** I've ever been.

An interesting aspect of these examples is that the blending of the inflectional and analytic constructions does not consist in the selection of some aspects of each, but in their combination. The novel comparatives and superlatives simply stack the two resources together. We had occasion to refer to STACKING in Chapter 11, in connection with innovative expressions of progressivity (see p. 256). Examples like the following (repeated from Chapter 11) accumulate different resources for the expression of progressivity.

(18)   a. Eskin was **being busy** being interviewed yesterday.
        b. She phoned me after returning from New York, **in the middle of being busy** selling tickets.

The study of causal connectives (Taylor and Pang 2008) also threw up examples of stacking. Consider the following (I leave it to the reader to unpack the source expressions!):

(19)   a. I have come across this site completely by accident, but **seeing as though as** i'm here i thought i'd say hello and post some of my pics for you to share!
        b. I thought I would go to the party and meet a few people **seeing how as though** I don't know anyone yet.
        c. I need to be giving you encouragement **seeing as how though** you just lost your father.
        d. I haven't been in the best of moods lately **seeing as though how** (almost) everything in my life seems to have gone off track.

Innovations in another corner of English syntax provide a further example of stacking. Common in the speech of many younger people is the use of *like*, more specifically, *be like*, as a QUOTATIVE, that is, as an expression which introduces a direct quotation. (For an early account, see Blyth, Recktenwald, and Wang 1990). Consider the following (Rickford, Wasow, Zwicky, and Buchstaller 2007):

(20)   a. And she's **like**, 'Afraid so'
       b. I kinda teased him, I'm **all** 'wow you must reaaaaaally need attention back there....'
       c. And she's **all like**, 'Well you HAVE to. Are you allergic to them?'

The (c) example stacks the independently attested *be like* and *be all* to create the new quotative *be all like*.

explain me this

The use of *explain* in the ditransitive construction—see (13) of Chapter 11 and the accompanying discussion—can also be seen as the output of a blending process. The example is illustrative of a much more general phenomenon, which we address in more detail in the following section.

The blending of words and constructions

Constructions—at least on one understanding of the term (see p. 125)—are associations of form and meaning. Constructions, therefore, need to be described with respect to both their formal and their semantic properties. Take, for example, the caused motion construction. Formally, it may be represented as [V NP PP]. Semantically, it refers to an event whereby an act, designated by the verb V, causes an entity, designated by the direct object nominal NP, to move (either literally or metaphorically) to, towards, or away from a place, in accordance with the content of the prepositional phrase PP.[12]

It is not the case that any randomly selected verb, noun phrase, or prepositional phrase is able to occur in the construction. In the first place, the items need to be compatible with the semantics of the construction. The verb, for example, needs to designate an act which is capable of causing a thing to change its location. In many cases, the speaker's options in this regard are already preempted by the specifications of the lexical items themselves. One important aspect of knowing a word is, precisely, to know the kinds of constructional environments in which the word is able to occur. Thus, the verb *put* is virtually restricted to occurring in the caused motion

---

[12] The account here ignores the possibility of constructional polysemy. A variant of the construction refers to the avoidance of displacement, e.g. *keep the money in the bank*.

construction. At the same time, the specification of a construction often includes information about the kinds of items which are most likely to occupy its various slots. Although in principle very many verbs are able to occur in the caused motion construction, the construction preferentially selects verbs such as *put* and *bring* (Goldberg 2006: 109). Given these perspectives—the characterization of the construction and the selectional preferences of the verb—expressions such as *Put it here*[13] or *Bring it to me* are unremarkable.

Sometimes, however, the construction takes a verb which is typically associated with a different subcategorization frame and which does not usually entail motion or even causation. Fauconnier (1997: 176) cites the following examples:

(21) a. The psychic will think your husband into another galaxy.
      b. Junior sped the car around the Christmas tree.
      c. Frankenstein choked the life out of Dracula.

Fauconnier analyses these in terms of the blending of the construction's semantics with the semantics of the verb. Interestingly, the blend runs differently in the three cases. In (a), it is the psychic who does the thinking while in (b) it is the car, not Junior, which speeds. In (b) Junior performs some (unnamed) act with respect to the car while in (c) Frankenstein acts, not on the direct object referent, 'the life', but on Dracula. The interpretation of these sentences therefore relies heavily on the hearer being able to construct an appropriate scenario, filling in details in accordance with the schematic semantics of the construction. With respect to (a), for example, the hearer needs to supply the causal link between the thinking and the subsequent event of the husband 'going' (in some unspecified way) into a galaxy. Contrast this with the use of a typical caused-motion verb. If you 'throw the ball over the wall', it is evident, first, what you do, second, how this action affects the ball, third, what happens to the ball, and finally, what the causal link is between your action of throwing and the trajectory of the ball.

Fauconnier (1997: 175–6) claims that the examples in (21) illustrate semantic rather than syntactic innovation, in that they merely exploit a syntactic resource already available in the language. On the other hand, the examples certainly do testify to innovative uses of the verbs in question. Hampe and Schönefeld (2006) address the issue under the rubric of 'creative syntax'. By this expression they refer to the phenomenon whereby a verb comes to be used in a construction typically reserved for other verbs (or verb classes). With respect, once again, to the caused motion construction, they cite the following (attested) examples:

(22) a. We need to encourage children into libraries.
      b. He supported her up the stairs.
      c. She paid herself in at the hotel.

---

[13] I analyse *here* as a prepositional phrase, with the meaning 'to/at this place'.

The last two examples are especially interesting, in that the expressions appear to be modelled on specific (and more conventional) instantiations of the caused motion construction, namely, *help someone up the stairs* and *check oneself in (at a hotel)*. The blends are interpreted accordingly: 'help someone up the stairs by supporting them' (alternatively: 'support someone, and thereby help them up the stairs'), and 'check oneself in by paying' (alternatively: 'pay, and thereby check oneself in').

Consider, now, the ditransitive use of *explain* in the light of the above discussion. Semantically, the ditransitive construction [V NP1 NP2] designates an act which causes the referent of NP1 to come into possession (whether literally or metaphorically) of the referent on NP2.[14] Verbs typically associated with the construction include *give, tell,* and *send*. Giving is an act which, by its very nature, causes someone to come into possession of something, while telling is an act which causes someone to come to know (that is, to have cognitive possession of) some piece of information. *Explain* is not typically associated with the construction, even though its semantics might seem to be compatible with it. If the addressee (that is, the person who comes into possession of the explanation) is to be stated, it is normally in a prepositional phrase. No doubt, the blending of the verb and the ditransitive construction is facilitated by the semantic closeness of *tell* and *explain*; after all, explaining is usually done by telling (or by showing). *Explain me this* is thus open to a blended interpretation: 'Tell me by explaining it'; alternatively: 'Explain it, and in so doing tell me'.

The blending of words and constructions is by no means restricted to verbs and their complementation patterns. Consider the following, from Michaelis (2003):

(23)   a. Give me some pillow!
        b. I am really liking your explanation.

Pillow is a quintessential count noun, yet in (a) the word is used in an environment which imposes, or coerces, a mass interpretation. The 'pillow' concept is blended with the conceptualization associated with the mass noun construction. Similarly, the use of a predominantly stative verb, such as *like*, in a progressive construction imposes a progressive interpretation on the verb. Thus, (23b) may be interpreted to mean that my approval is gradually increasing; the expression refers to an ongoing event rather than to a state.

In conclusion

The examples discussed above might suggest that blending is to be invoked in cases where the syntactic and semantic properties of an expression conflict with more general usage norms. The use of *pillow* as a mass noun, *think* as a caused motion verb,

---

[14] Again, I ignore semantic variants of the construction (Goldberg 1995). In *deny someone access*, NP1 is prevented from coming into possession of NP2.

or *explain* as a ditransitive verb, are certainly unusual, and test the limits of what can be acceptable in the language. On the other hand, the use of *give* in the ditransitive construction, or *put* in the caused motion construction, or *pillow* as a count noun, would be unremarkable. One option, therefore, might be to make a distinction between those uses which are fully regular, in the sense that the specification of a word is fully compatible with, and easily slots into an established construction, and cases of innovation, where there is some tension between the construction and its parts, requiring coercion of 'the semantics of a constituent word.

The crux of the matter, in all of this, is what constitutes the normal, or predominant syntactic environment of a word. In the case of *give* and *put*, the answer is evident. What, though, are we to say about the use of *encourage* as a caused motion verb? As Hampe and Schönefeld document, the usage is not at all uncommon. Neither is it obvious whether nouns such as *lawn* and *ocean* (Taylor 2002: 378) are to be regarded as basically count or mass, with one usage being derivative on the other.

Rather than draw a clean line between the regular and the irregular, it would be more appropriate to recognize a cline of compatibility. In so doing, we will need to give up the distinction between those cases where the use of a word in a construction is a case of blending and cases where it is merely a matter of dovetailing a word and a construction. A more parsimonious account is to regard both as instances of blending. Even such a banal example as *The farmer kills the duckling* will turn out to be the product of blending, concerning, in this case, the blending of the verbal and nominal elements with the formal and semantic properties of the transitive construction. Seen in this light, blending is able to do the work traditionally assigned to generative rules; in other words, it is able to account for creativity, in the generativists' sense. More than this, it is also able to accommodate innovative extensions which go beyond creativity in the narrow sense of the term understood by generative theorists.

13

The mental corpus

What does it mean to know a language? Or, to put it another way, when we say that a person knows a language, what is it, exactly, that they know?

This question, in its various guises, has driven the theory and practice of linguistics for at least half a century. I have framed the discussion of it in terms of Chomsky's distinction between external language (E-language) and internal language (I-language) (Chapter 1). E-language is a matter of what people say (and write); it is the language as we encounter it in our daily interactions with other language users. I-language is the language as it is represented in the minds of its speakers. The relation between E-language and I-language is, I have argued, a dialectic one. E-language (by definition) comprises the linguistic utterances of a community of speakers. As such, it is the output of the I-language of individual speakers. At the same time, the I-language of these speakers can only be acquired through their exposure to E-language. In brief, E-language is as it is because of the properties of the I-language of its speakers. Conversely, the properties of a person's I-language derive from the E-language that they have been exposed to, and continue to be exposed to, on a daily basis. The question of what it means to know a language can therefore be reduced to the task of developing an account of I-language which is able to support the linguistic behaviour of speakers and which can be learned on the basis of exposure to linguistic events.

My strategy in this book has been to study in detail selected (and hopefully representative) aspects of language as used, with an eye on the implications this has for the system of knowledge which both emerges from exposure to usage and which makes the usage possible in the first place.

A recurrent finding has been that the description of a language needs to incorporate a vast amount of specific information about the units which make up the language, such as the sounds, words, collocations, and constructions. Thus, to know a word is not just a matter of knowing its meaning(s) and its pronunciation(s) but of knowing about the contexts in which the word is used. One needs to know, for example, the kinds of words it typically co-occurs with and the syntactic configurations it is likely to feature in. As emphasized in Chapter 3, the allocation of a word to one of the standardly recognized lexical categories, such as noun, verb, or adjective (or even to sub-categories of these, such as count noun, transitive verb, or predicative adjective) is grossly inadequate as a guide to the word's use in the language. The usage range of words such as *fun* and *much* cannot be accounted for by declaring the words to be members of, respectively, the categories (singular) mass noun and quantifier, neither would it be sufficient to regard *many* simply as the plural form of *much*. When examined closely, a word's syntactic distribution may well turn out to be *sui generis*. It might also be misleading to speak of *the* distribution of a word. The matter is particular relevant to the issue of polysemy, in that different senses of a word tend to be associated with different contextual profiles. This is the reason why polysemy— outside of linguists' carefully constructed examples—so rarely gives rise to ambiguity (Chapter 10).

A second theme has been the paramount role of *constructions* in the description of a language. Alongside the major phrase structure configurations, such as transitive clause and ditransitive clause, there exists a host of minor constructions, often centred on the use of specific lexical items. Many examples have been discussed; these include, to name just a few, the [OFF WITH] construction (exemplified by *Off with his head!, Into the car with you all!*; see p. 38), the [(NOT) MUCH OF A N] construction (*I'm not much of a cook, It wasn't much of a meal*; see p. 60), the [WHAT ABOUT X] construction (*What about on Tuesday?, What about if she says no?*; see p. 87), and the [NP ON END] construction (*We waited for hours on end, The quotations go on for pages on end*; see p. 96).

Constructions such as these are sometimes syntactically deviant with respect to more general patterns prevailing in the language. For example, the [OFF WITH] and the [WHAT ABOUT X] constructions sanction sentences which lack a finite verb. Often, the constructions are associated with specific semantic values, not fully in accord with the semantics of their constituents. For example, *It wasn't much of a meal* does not quantify the amount of the meal in question—the expected value of *(not) much (of)*— but rather has to do with the extent to which the entity under discussion can be considered a good, or representative example of the category 'meal'.

Some constructions specify the use of certain lexical items. The [OFF WITH] construction concerns a special use of the word *with*. Typically, a construction contains one or more slots which can be filled with a range of items. What is interesting is that the available items often constitute a unique set, peculiar to the construction in question. Consider the kinds of items which are able to feature in the initial slot of the [OFF WITH] construction. Only prepositions and prepositional phrases—more precisely, directional prepositions and directional prepositional phrases—can occur in this slot. Yet not all items meeting this description are admissible. We cannot have **From the table with it!* The set of available items is virtually unique to the construction and cannot be identified with any independently recognized category.

Similar remarks apply to the [WHAT ABOUT X] construction. A large number of different kinds of phrases can occur in the X position: nominal, prepositional, participial, as well as clausal. The latter include temporal clauses introduced by *when*, *before*, and *after*, and clauses introduced by conditional *if*. Reason clauses (with *since* and *because*), concessives (with *although*), and conditional clauses with *unless*, are, however, not permitted. We cannot have **What about unless she leaves?* Again, the set of items available to fill the construction slot would appear to be unique to this construction.

While knowledge of a construction brings with it knowledge of the kinds of items which are able to feature in it, it is also the case that knowledge of a lexical item comprises knowledge of the kinds of constructions in which it is able to occur. The verb *put* virtually requires an occurrence of the caused motion construction [V NP PP] (p. 193), while nouns such as *lap* and *whereabouts* strongly prefer the environment of a possessive construction, either pre- or postnominal (pp. 51 and 58). Some phrases also have their preferred constructional contexts; see the earlier discussion of *not for nothing* (p. 142). Knowledge of words and knowledge of constructions cannot easily be teased apart. Moreover, both involve knowledge of specific facts.

Some constructions, it is true, might be regarded as fairly peripheral to the language as a whole, on account of their low frequency of occurrence and their special semantic or pragmatic values. One can easily imagine living for months in an English-speaking environment without ever hearing, or having occasion to use, the [OFF WITH] construction. It would be an error, however, to attempt to relegate constructions and their idiosyncratic properties to the periphery of linguistic knowledge. The use of such 'basic' lexical items as the prepositions *to* and *on* is tied up with their use in constructions (pp. 53 and 97). What is more, a characterization of even the most general of constructions, such as the transitive clause, needs to be supplemented by a statement of the kinds of items which are able to feature in it. With respect to the verbal constituent of transitive clauses, one might suppose that the classification of verbs as transitive will do the job. Yet what counts as a transitive verb is determined, ultimately, by the possibility of its occurrence in the transitive construction; it is the construction itself which defines the category. Neither is it the case that the transitive clause construction is homogeneous with respect to its possible instantiations and the semantic values of its nominal constituents, nor does the range of instantiations in one language exactly correspond with those of seemingly equivalent constructions in other languages (p. 144). These, once again, are specific facts about the construction which have to be learned.

The conclusion has to be, I think, that a very great deal, perhaps even the totality, of what occurs in a language can be rightly said to be 'idiomatic'. As noted in Chapter 5, there are two ways to characterize the idiomatic. One has to do with expressions whose properties (phonological, syntactic, or semantic) cannot be derived from more general principles and which therefore have to be learned. (On the other hand, as was suggested in the above paragraph and elsewhere in this book, the supposition that there might exist 'general principles' which are immune to idiomaticity might well be an illusion.) The other way of understanding the idiomatic concerns the appropriate thing to say in a given context. Here, again, specific facts have to be learned. In order to speak English idiomatically, that is, in accord with native speaker norms, one has to know that the appropriate way to enquire into a person's age is to ask 'How old are you?', rather than 'What is your age?', or that when wishing to convey that a person crossed a river by swimming the appropriate thing to say, in English, is not that they 'crossed the river by swimming', but that they 'swam across the river'. Knowing the appropriate thing to say is also a matter of sensitivity to the properties of different registers and text types. Indeed, text types cannot only be characterized in terms of their distinctive linguistic properties, these properties to some extent constitute the text types in question (p. 148).

A third motif of this book concerns the importance of the *frequency of occurrence* of items in a language. One of the most robust of the usage norms of a language is, namely, the relative frequency of sounds and sound combinations, of words and word combinations, of constructional patterns for word and phrasal formation, and of the items which slot into these constructions. Remarkably, the frequencies tend to be fairly stable—at least, for a given register. It is here that the dialectic relation of E- and I-language is especially in evidence. Except perhaps in a tiny minority of cases, the frequency with which an item is used has nothing to do with the frequency of eventualities external to the language itself. The relative frequency of the words *accident* and *mishap*, or of the TRAP and DRESS vowels, or of the complementation patterns of the verbs *believe* and *confirm*—the examples are discussed in Chapter 7— is quintessentially a matter of the usage norms of English. As just mentioned, these frequency distributions do not come about because of factors external to the language. They reflect speakers' knowledge of the relative frequencies and these can only have been learned on the basis of exposure to usage.

As documented especially in Chapter 7, there is abundant evidence that speakers of a language know, at least implicitly, the frequency profile of the things in their language. Speakers' sensitivity to frequency norms shows up as a variable on just about every psycholinguistic task that has been devised. It is also a crucial factor in the interpretation of supposedly ambiguous phrases (pp. 166ff) and even in judgements of acceptability. Recall, in this connection, the example cited at the very beginning of Chapter 1 (p. 2). Speakers feel that *total failure* sounds better than *total success*, mirroring the fact that the former is about four times more frequent in the language than the latter. Neither can frequency be regarded as merely an artefact of language in use. Frequency of previous use leads to increased entrenchment of the mental representation of an item. This in turn has repercussions on its phonological, structural, and semantic properties. Frequencies are just as much in the I-language as they are in the E-language.

The highly specific knowledge which constitutes knowing a language indicates that speakers are exquisitely sensitive to the language that they encounter, noting the uses of words, their collocations and their syntactic environments, the constructions and their special semantics and conditions of use, as well the frequency with which all these occur. It is almost as if speakers have been keeping a record of what they have been exposed to, filing everything away under various headings, cross-referencing it, and activating it in their own linguistic performance.

Emphasis on the particular does not, of course, mean that language knowledge consists of a random list of unrelated facts. The units of linguistic knowledge are linked by a *network of relations* (Chapter 6). One relation is that of a part to a whole. In order for the vast number of words and constructions in a language to be able to be stored in memory, some kind of internal analysis is necessary (p. 194). This is not to say that the whole is simply the sum of its parts; typically, an expression has a semantic and even a phonological value which cannot be computed 'compositionally' from the properties of its parts (p. 42). Nevertheless, internal constituents can be recognized and these, more often than not, can be cross-referenced to constituents occurring in other constructions. This makes possible the segmentation of the speech stream into sounds and words; it also (in association with the schema–instance relation) enables the identification of standardly recognized lexical and phrasal categories. The second relation linking the units of linguistic knowledge is the already mentioned relation between a schema and its instances. It is the schema–instance relation which enables the emergence of generalizations over data. Importantly, the relation is recursive, in that a number of minor generalizations over limited sets of data might themselves fall under a broader generalization which may, in turn, be compatible with an even more general formula. It by no means follows that minor regularities can be predicted from the major generalization. On the contrary, even the most robust generalization is likely to be subject to special conditions and restrictions with respect to the range of its possible instances. 'Rules' typically have 'exceptions', which often fall under 'minor rules'.

As a result of the part–whole and the schema–instance relations, practically everything that occurs in a language is *motivated* to a greater or lesser extent, in the sense that some aspects of any linguistic expression can be linked up with other things that are already known (Taylor 2004*a*). To be sure, an English speaker needs to learn the special use of *on* in relation to calendar days; we have *on Tuesday*, not *in*, *at*, or *over Tuesday*. Nevertheless, the phrasal pattern [on + day of the week] instantiates the more general pattern of a prepositional phrase, as well as the metaphorical use of a spatial preposition in a temporal sense (p. 98). While the specific usage has to be learned, it is not totally encapsulated from other patterns in the language. Similarly, the curious syntax of the correlative construction [THE X-ER THE Y-ER] can be aligned with a number of other bipartite verb-less expressions whose first element states the cause, or precondition, for the second (p. 85). To cite just one more example: the discussion in Chapter 4 showed that the so-called WXDY construction (exemplified by *What's this scratch doing on the table?*) shares a number of syntactic and semantic properties with the more general category of *wh*-questions. The fact that an expression is motivated—that it stands at the hub of a network of relations to other things in the language—facilitates its take-up in memory. Nothing that a speaker needs to learn turns out to be fully 'new', since at least some of the properties of the item can be linked to other things already familiar to the speaker.

The possibility of generalizations over data has a second important function: it provides the basis for speakers to creatively extend their linguistic performance beyond expressions already encountered, by offering a template by which items can be combined in novel ways. Not all generalizations, however, are equally productive. The productivity of a generalization (or schema), that is, its ability to sanction new instances beyond those on which it is based, interacts with the degree of entrenchment (itself a function of frequency of occurrence) of already encountered instances and of the schema itself. The interplay of frequency, entrenchment, and productivity has been mainly studied with respect to derivational morphology: *-ness* is a more productive nominalizing suffix than *-ity* and *-th* (p. 174). The same dynamics apply to other structural configurations. The transitive clause construction [NP V NP] is highly productive; the negation pattern illustrated by *I kid you not* is not at all productive. Although *a foregone conclusion* and *an unmitigated disaster* both have the status of established collocations, the attributive use of *unmitigated* is productive, in that the adjective is able to be combined with a potentially open-ended set of nouns, whereas novel uses of attributive *foregone* are more limited and comparatively rare (p. 174).

While generative linguists make great play of linguistic creativity (the possibility of novel combinations of items in accordance with already established generalizations), it is also opportune to emphasize that speakers are by no means restricted by the generalizations that they (may) have made over the data. A robust finding from our investigation is that speakers are happy to go beyond the generalizations and the instances that they sanction. Speakers, in other words, are prone to *innovate* with respect to previous usage, using words in ways not already sanctioned by previous experience, extending the usage range of idioms and constructions, thereby creating new words, new idioms, and new constructional patterns (Chapter 11). An important mechanism in this regard is the process of blending (Chapter 12), whereby new expressions are able to incorporate selected features of already established units.

Any study into linguistic knowledge brings with it the question of how a person can plausibly *acquire* that knowledge. Our investigations point strongly in the direction of a usage-based, that is, an input-driven, bottom-up, empirical account of acquisition. The supposition that the to-be-acquired categories—and their contents—might be supplied by universal and presumably innate cognitive structures goes counter to the idiomaticity of usage and the need for specific properties to be acquired on the basis of experience. Moreover, the dialectics of E- and I-language lead us to assume that acquisition is a life-long process, the current state of a person's linguistic knowledge being subject to the vicissitudes of encountered usage. The fact that innovation would appear to progress gradually, in small incremental steps, as discussed in Chapter 11, supports this contention. The mechanics of the learning process were addressed in Chapter 9. In this chapter I drew attention, first, to statistical properties of the input language, and how these might 'seed' the emergence of linguistic categories. Another topic of Chapter 9 was the recency effect: a previous use of a linguistic form is likely to increase the odds of this form being used again, thereby increasing its entrenchment in the speaker's mental grammar. I suggested that the recency effect can provide a window into the very process of micro-learning, whereby features of encountered language are able to affect not only a speaker's linguistic performance but also her mental representation of the language.

Such an account entails that language users *take note* of features of the language they encounter, building up a 'mental histogram' of frequency distributions (p. 204) while also paying heed to what are statistically unusual configurations or expressions which are in other ways unexpected (p. 214). What is striking, in this regard, is the sheer size and diversity of the possible targets of a person's attention: the targets include aspects of the phonology, the choice of words and constructions, the statistical dependencies between these, as well as the intended semantics and the relation of the utterance to the situational context. There are reasons to suppose, therefore, that attention is relatively unconstrained by the categories of previous experience. If this were not the case, novel and unusual features of the input would simply be overlooked (or overheard); exposure to the language would simply reinforce the current state of knowledge and close it off to further development. We should also bear in mind the ability of speakers to notice, and to record, features of the input which are probably incidental to their momentary communicative needs. The matter was addressed at the very beginning of this book, in connection with a reader's ability to recall the position on a page of a piece of text (p. 1). Language users are also able to notice, and record, subtle details of accent and voice quality (pp. 206–7). Reviewing the evidence for the episodic memory for speech events, Lachs, McMichael, and Pisoni (2000: 164) conclude that "all experience with speech is encoded and preserved in a detail-rich, complex and multidimensional representation". This citation—note especially the reference to '*all* experience with speech', and the implication that the detail-rich and multidimensional representation applies to the structural, semantic, and discourse-related aspects of speech, as much as to its phonetic properties— encapsulates pretty well my understanding of the mental corpus as the repository of memories of encountered language.

The mental corpus should not be thought of consisting of a tape-recording of heard speech. As Lachs *et al.* state, experience with speech is *encoded* in memory. A clue as to what this might mean is provided by Rens Bod, in his essay on 'exemplar-based syntax' and how exemplars can be the basis for the creation of expressions not found in the input (Bod 2006). Bod emphasized that an exemplar (stored in memory) should not be identified with the token event of which it is a representation: "An exemplar is a categorization, classification or analysis of a token" (p. 293). There are many dimensions along which the raw linguistic event can be categorized, classified, or analysed. It can be analysed into its fragments, primarily words and word-like units, but also combinations of words and the syllables and sounds which make up the words. These elements may in turn be categorized as instances of more schematic categories and cross-referenced to elements derived from other exemplars. The exemplar, we may suppose, is also indexed with respect to features of the communicative situation, such as the identity of the speaker, the speaker's gender and regional provenance, as well as the formality and subject matter of the speech exchange. Importantly, the exemplar will be associated with the presumed semantic intent of the speaker and its pragmatic relevance to the current discourse. Thus, a word encountered in a linguistic exchange will be remembered along numerous dimensions, including, amongst others, (a) its immediate lexical environment, (b) the containing syntactic construction and its semantic–pragmatic value, and (c) its pronunciation, indexed with respect to characteristics of the speaker and the communicative exchange. Multiple representations of identical features of the input will result in a strengthening of their mental representation. The empirical findings reported throughout this book lend support to each of these claims.

References

Aarts, Bas. 1998. Binominal noun phrases in English. *Transactions of the Philological Society*, 96: 117–58.

Aarts, Bas, David Denison, Evelien Keizer, and Gergana Popova (eds). 2004. *Fuzzy Grammar: A Reader*. Oxford: Oxford University Press.

Abler, William. 1989. On the particulate principle of self-diversifying systems. *Journal of Social and Biological Structures*, 12: 1–13.

Aijmer, Karin and Bengt Altenberg. 1991. *English Corpus Linguistics*. London: Longman.

Alario, F.-Xavier, Albert Costa, and Alfonso Caramazza. 2002. Frequency effects in noun phrase production: Implications for models of lexical access. *Language and Cognitive Processes*, 17: 299–319.

Alderson, J. Charles. 2007. Judging the frequency of English words. *Applied Linguistics*, 28: 383–409.

Alegre, Maria and Peter Gordon. 1999. Frequency effects and the representational status of regular inflections. *Journal of Memory and Language*, 40: 41–61.

Algeo, John. 1962. A fun thing. *American Speech*, 37: 158–9.

——1977. Blends, a structural and systemic view. *American Speech*, 52: 47–64.

Allwood, Jens. 2003. Meaning potentials and context: Some consequences for the analysis of variation in meaning. In Cuyckens, Dirven, and Taylor (eds) (2003), 29–65.

Archangeli, Diana. 1988. Aspects of underspecification theory. *Phonology*, 5: 183–207.

Arnon, Inbal and Neal Snider. 2010. More than words: Frequency effects for multi-word phrases. *Journal of Memory and Language*, 62: 67–82.

Aslin, Richard, David Pisoni, Beth Hennessy, and Alan Perey. 1981. Discrimination of voice onset time by human infants: New findings and implications for the effects of early experience. *Child Development*, 52, 1135–45.

Aslin, Richard, Peter Jusczyk, and David Pisoni. 1998. Speech and auditory processing during infancy: Constraints on and precursors to language. In Deanna Kuhn and Robert Siegler (eds), *Handbook of Child Psychology: Cognition, Perception, and Language*, vol. 2, 147–254. New York: Wiley.

Austin, Frances. 1980. A crescent-shaped jewel of an island: Appositive nouns in phrases separated by *of*. *English Studies*, 61: 357–66.

Austin, John. 1962. The meaning of a word. In *Philosophical Papers*, 3rd edn, ed. J. O. Urmson and G. J. Warnock, 55–75. Oxford: Oxford University Press.

——1980. *How To Do Things With Words*. Oxford: Oxford University Press.

Ayto, John. 1990. *Bloomsbury Dictionary of Word Origins*. London: Bloomsbury.

Baayen, Harald and Rochelle Lieber. 1991. Productivity and English derivation: A corpus-based study. *Linguistics*, 29: 801–43.

Baayen, Harald and Antoinette Renouf. 1996. Chronicling the times: Productive lexical innovations in an English newspaper. *Language*, 72: 69–96.

Baker, Mark. 2001. *The Atoms of Language: The Mind's Hidden Rules of Grammar*. Oxford: Oxford University Press.

Balota, David, Maura Pilotti, and Michael Cortese. 2001. Subjective frequency estimates for 2,938 monosyllabic words. *Memory and Cognition*, 29: 639–47.

Bannard, Colin and Danielle Matthews. 2008. Stored word sequences in language learning: The effect of familiarity on children's repetition of four-word combinations. *Psychological Science*, 19: 241–8.

Barlow, Michael. 2000. Usage, blends, and grammar. In Barlow and Kemmer (eds) (2000), 315–45.

Barlow, Michael and Suzanne Kemmer (eds). 2000. *Usage-Based Models of Grammar*. Stanford, CA: CSLI Publications.

Barsalou, Laurence W. 1987. The instability of graded structure: Implications for the nature of concepts. In Ulric Neisser (ed.), *Concepts and Conceptual Development: Ecological and Intellectual Factors in Categorization*, 101–40. Cambridge: Cambridge University Press.

——2008. Grounded cognition. *Annual Review of Psychology*, 59: 617–45.

Bellavia, Elena. 1996. The German *über*. In Pütz and Dirven (eds) (1996), 73–107.

Berg, Thomas. 2000. The position of adjectives on the noun–verb continuum. *English Language and Linguistics*, 4: 269–93.

Bergen, Benjamin and Madelaine Plauché. 2001. Voilà voilà: Extensions of deictic constructions in French. In Alan Cienki, Barbara Luka, and Michael Smith (eds), *Conceptual and Discourse Factors in Linguistic Structure*, 45–61. Stanford, CA: CSLI Publications.

——2005. The convergent evolution of radial constructions: French and English deictics and existentials. *Cognitive Linguistics*, 16: 1–42.

Berlin, Brent and Paul Kay. 1969. *Basic Color Terms: Their Universality and Evolution*. Berkeley: University of California Press.

Bever, Thomas. 1970. *The Cognitive Basis for Linguistic Structures*. New York: Wiley.

Biber, Douglas. 1993. Representativeness in corpus design. *Literary and Linguistic Computing*, 8: 243–57.

——2000. Investigating language use through corpus-based analyses of association patterns. In Barlow and Kemmer (eds) (2000), 287–313.

Biber, Douglas, Susan Conrad, and Randi Reppen. 1998. *Corpus Linguistics: Investigating Language Structure and Use*. Cambridge: Cambridge University Press.

Bierwisch, Manfred. 1983. Semantische und konzeptuelle Repräsentation lexikalischer Einheiten. In Wolfgang Motsch and Rudolf Růžička (eds), *Untersuchungen zur Semantik* (= *Studia Grammatica*, XXII), 61–99. Berlin: Akademie-Verlag.

Bierwisch, Manfred and Robert Schreuder. 1992. From concepts to lexical items. *Cognition*, 42: 23–60.

Black, J. W. 1952. Accompaniments of word intelligibility. *Journal of Speech and Hearing Disorders*, 17: 409–18.

Blair, Irene, Geoffrey Urland, and Jennifer Ma. 2002. Using Internet search engines to estimate word frequency. *Behavior Research Methods, Instruments, and Computers*, 34: 286–90.

Bloch, Bernard. 1948. A set of postulates for phonemic analysis. *Language*, 24, 3–46.

Bloomfield, Leonard. 1933. *Language*. Chicago: University of Chicago Press.

Bloomfield, Leonard. 1957. A set of postulates for the science of language. In Martin Joos (ed.), *Readings in Linguistics 1*, 26–31. Chicago: University of Chicago Press. [First published in *Language*, 2 (1926): 153–64.]

Blyth, Carl, Sigrid Recktenwald, and Jenny Wang. 1990. I'm like, "Say What?!": A new quotative in American oral narrative. *American Speech*, 65: 215–27.

Bock, Kathryn. 1986. Syntactic persistence in language production. *Cognitive Psychology*, 18: 355–87.

Bock, Kathryn, Gary Dell, Franklin Chang, and Kristine Onishi. 2007. Persistent structural priming from language comprehension to language production. *Cognition*, 104: 437–58.

Bock, Kathryn and Zenzi Griffin. 2000. The persistence of structural priming: Transient activation or implicit learning? *Journal of Experimental Psychology: General*, 129: 177–92.

Bod, Rens. 2000. The storage and computation of three-word sentences. Paper presented at Architectures and Mechanism of Language Processing Conference (AMLAP-2000), Leiden, the Netherlands.

——2006. Exemplar-based syntax. How to get productivity from exemplars. *The Linguistic Review*, 23: 291–320.

Bohn, Ocke-Schwen. 2000. Linguistic relativity in speech perception: An overview of the influence of language experience on the perception of speech sounds from infancy to adulthood. In Susanne Niemeyer and René Dirven (eds), *Evidence for Linguistic Relativity*, 1–28. Amsterdam: Benjamins.

Bolinger, Dwight. 1961. Syntactic blends and other matters. *Language*, 37: 366–81.

——1963. It's so fun. *American Speech*, 38: 236–40.

——1968. Judgments of grammaticality. *Lingua*, 21: 34–40.

——1979. The jingle theory of double -*ing*. In D. J. Allerton, Edward Carney, and David Holdcroft (eds), *Function and Context in Linguistic Analysis: A Festschrift for William Haas*, 41–56. Cambridge: Cambridge University Press.

——1987. The remarkable double IS. *English Today*, 9: 39–40.

Boomer, Donald and John Laver. 1968. Slips of the tongue. *British Journal of Disorders of Communication*, 14: 382–91. [Reprinted in Fromkin (ed.) (1973), 120–31.]

Borges, Jorge Luis. 1998. Funes the Memorious. In *Fictions*, ed. and trans. by Anthony Kerrigan, 97–105. London: Calder Publications. [First published, in Spanish, in 1942.]

Boroditsky, Lera, Lauren Schmidt, and Webb Phillips. 2003. Sex, syntax and semantics. In Dedre Gentner and Susan Goldin-Meadow (eds), *Language in Mind: Advances in the Study of Language and Thought*, 61–78. Cambridge, MA: MIT Press.

Botha, Rudolf. 1968. *The Function of the Lexicon in Transformational Generative Grammar*. The Hague: Mouton.

Bowerman, Melissa. 1978. The acquisition of word meaning: An investigation into some current conflicts. In Natalie Waterson and Catherine Snow (eds), *The Development of Communication*, 263–87. New York: Wiley.

Branigan, Holly, Martin Pickering, Andrew Stewart, and Janet McLean. 2000. Syntactic priming in spoken production: Linguistic and temporal interference. *Memory and Cognition*, 28: 1297–302.

Brenier, Jason and Laura Michaelis. 2005. Optimization via syntactic amalgam: Syntax-prosody mismatch and copula doubling. *Corpus Linguistics and Linguistic Theory*, 1: 45–88.

Brooks, P. and Michael Tomasello. 1999. Young children learn to produce passives with nonce verbs. *Developmental Psychology*, 35: 29–44.

Brown, Roger. 1958. *Words and Things*. Glencoe, IL: Free Press.

Brown, Roger and Eric Lenneberg. 1954. A study in language and cognition. *Journal of Abnormal and Social Psychology*, 49: 454–62.

Brugman, Claudia. 1981. Story of *over*. Unpublished MA thesis, University of California, Berkeley. Reproduced by the Indiana University Linguistics Club, Bloomington.

Brugman, Claudia and George Lakoff. 1988. Cognitive topology and lexical networks. In Steven L. Small, Garrison W. Cottrell, and Michael K. Tanenhaus (eds), *Lexical Ambiguity Resolution: Perspectives from Psycholinguistics, Neuropsychology, and Artificial intelligence*, 477–508. San Mateo, CA: Morgan Kaufmann. [Reprinted in Dirk Geeraerts (ed.) (2006), *Cognitive Linguistics: Basic Readings*, 109–39. Berlin: Mouton de Gruyter.]

Bush, Nathan. 2001. Frequency effects and word-boundary palatalization in English. In Bybee and Hopper (eds) (2001), 255–80.

Bybee, Joan. 1985. *Morphology: A Study of the Relation between Meaning and Form*. Amsterdam: Benjamins.

——1995. Regular morphology and the lexicon. *Language and Cognitive Processes*, 10: 425–55. [Reprinted in Bybee (2007), 167–93.]

——2001. *Phonology and Language Use*. Cambridge: Cambridge University Press.

——2007. *Frequency of Use and the Organization of Language*. Oxford: Oxford University Press.

Bybee, Joan and Paul Hopper (eds). 2001. *Frequency and the Emergence of Linguistic Structure*. Amsterdam: Benjamins.

Bybee, Joan and Carol Lynn Moder. 1983. Morphological classes as natural categories. *Language*, 59, 251–70. [Reprinted in Bybee (2007), 127–47.]

Bybee, Joan and Joanne Scheibman. 1999. The effect of usage on degrees of constituency: The reduction of *don't* in American English. *Linguistics*, 37: 575–96. [Reprinted in Bybee (2007), 294–335.]

Bybee, Joan and Dan Slobin. 1982. Rules and schemas in the development and use of the English past tense. *Language*, 58: 265–89. [Reprinted in Bybee (2007), 101–26.]

Bybee, Joan and Sandra Thompson. 1997. Three frequency effects in syntax. *Berkeley Linguistics Society* 23: 65–85. [Reprinted in Bybee (2007), 269–78.]

Calude, Andreea and Steven Miller. 2009. Are clefts contagious in conversation? *English Language and Linguistics*, 13: 127–32.

Cappelle, Bert. 2005. The particularity of particles, or why they are not just 'intransitive prepositions'. In Hubert Cuyckens, Walter De Mulder, and Tanja Mortelmens (eds), *Adpositions of Movement* (= *Belgian Journal of Linguistics*, 18), 29–57. Amsterdam: Benjamins.

Carroll, John B. 1971. Measurement properties of subjective magnitude estimates of word frequency. *Journal of Verbal Learning and Verbal Behavior*, 10: 722–9.

Carroll, John M., Thomas G. Bever, and Chava R. Pollack. 1981. The non-uniqueness of linguistic intuitions. *Language*, 57: 368–83.

Carroll, Suzanne E. 2005. Input and SLA: Adults' sensitivity to different sorts of cues to French gender. *Language Learning*, 55: 79–138.

Caselli, Maria, Elizabeth Bates, Paola Casadio, Judi Fenson, Larry Fenson, Lisa Sanderl, and Judy Weir. 1995. A cross-linguistic study of early lexical development. *Cognitive Development*, 10: 159–99.

Chang, Franklin, Gary Dell, Kathryn Bock, and Zenzi Griffin. 2000. Structural priming as implicit learning: Comparison of models of sentence production. *Journal of Psycholinguistic Research*, 29: 217–29.

Chen, Jidong. 2007. 'He cut-break the rope': Encoding and categorizing cutting and breaking events in Mandarin. *Cognitive Linguistics*, 18: 273–85.

Chomsky, Noam. 1957. *Syntactic Structures*. The Hague: Mouton.

——1964. *Current Issues in Linguistic Theory*. The Hague: Mouton.

——1965. *Aspects of the Theory of Syntax*. Cambridge, MA: MIT Press.

——1980. *Rules and Representations*. Oxford: Basil Blackwell.

——1981. *Lectures on Government and Binding*. Dordrecht: Foris.

——1986. *Knowledge of Language: Its Nature, Origin, and Use*. New York: Praeger.

——1995. *The Minimalist Program*. Cambridge, MA: MIT Press.

Chomsky, Noam and Morris Halle. 1968. *The Sound Pattern of English*. New York: Harper & Row.

Choueka, Yaacov and Serge Lusignan. 1985. Disambiguation by short contexts. *Computers and the Humanities*, 19: 147–57.

Clausner, Timothy and William Croft. 1997. Productivity and schematicity in metaphors. *Cognitive Science*, 21: 247–82.

——1999. Domains and image schemas. *Cognitive Linguistics*, 10: 1–31.

Clayards, Meghan, Michael Tanenhaus, Richard Aslin, and Robert Jacobs. 2008. Perception of speech reflects optimal use of probabilistic speech cues. *Cognition*, 108: 804–9.

Coleman, Linda and Paul Kay. 1981. Prototype semantics: the English word "lie". *Language*, 57: 26–44.

Connine, Cynthia and Debra Titone. 1996. Phoneme monitoring. *Language and Cognitive Processes*, 11: 635–45.

Coppock, Elizabeth. 2006. Alignment in syntactic blending. In Carson T. Schütze and Victor S. Ferreira (eds), *The State of the Art in Speech Error Research* (= *MIT Working Papers in Linguistics*, 53), 239–55. Cambridge, MA: MIT Press.

——2010. Parallel grammatical encoding in sentence production: Evidence from syntactic blends. *Language and Cognitive Processes*, 25: 38–49.

Coseriu, Eugenio. 1977. L'étude fonctionnelle du vocabulaire: Précis de lexématique. *Cahiers de lexicologie*, 29: 5–23.

——2000. Structural semantics and 'cognitive' semantics. *Logos and Language*, 1: 19–42.

Croft, William. 1991. *Syntactic Categories and Grammatical Relations: The Cognitive Organization of Information*. Chicago: University of Chicago Press.

——1993. The role of domains in the interpretation of metaphors and metonymies. *Cognitive Linguistics*, 4: 335–70.

——2000. *Explaining Language Change: An Evolutionary Approach*. London: Longman.

——2001. *Radical Construction Grammar: Syntactic Theory in Typological Perspective*. Oxford: Oxford University Press.

——2007. Construction grammar. In Geeraerts and Cuyckens (eds) (2007), 463–508.

Cruse, D. A. 2000*a*. Aspects of the microstructure of word meanings. In Ravin and Leacock (eds) (2000), 30–51.

——2000*b*. The lexicon. In Mark Aronoff and Janie Rees-Miller (eds), *The Handbook of Linguistics*, 238–64. Oxford: Blackwell.

Culicover, Peter. 1970. One more can of beer. *Linguistic Inquiry*, 1: 366–9.

——1997. *Principles and Parameters: An Introduction to Syntactic Theory*. Oxford: Oxford University Press.

——1999. *Syntactic Nuts: Hard Cases, Syntactic Theory, and Language Acquisition*. Oxford: Oxford University Press.

——2004. Review of Huddleston and Pullum (2002). *Language*, 80: 127–41.

——2009. *Natural Language Syntax*. Oxford: Oxford University Press.

Culicover, Peter and Ray Jackendoff. 1997. Semantic subordination despite syntactic coordination. *Linguistic Inquiry*, 28: 195–217.

——1999. The view from the periphery: The English correlative conditional. *Linguistic Inquiry*, 30: 543–71.

Cuyckens, Hubert, René Dirven, and John R. Taylor (eds). 2003. *Cognitive Approaches to Lexical Semantics*. Berlin: Mouton de Gruyter.

Cuyckens, Hubert and Britta Zawada (eds). 1997. *Polysemy in Cognitive Linguistics*. Amsterdam: Benjamins.

Dąbrowska, Ewa. 2004. Rules or schemas? Evidence from Polish. *Language and Cognitive Processes*, 19: 225–71.

Davidoff, Jules. 2001. Language and perceptual categorization. *Trends in Cognitive Sciences*, 5: 382–7.

Davidse, Kristin, Lieselotte Brems, and Liesbeth de Smet. 2008. Type noun uses in the English NP: A case of right to left layering. *International Journal of Corpus Linguistics*, 13: 139–68.

Davies, Mark. 2004–. BYU-BNC: The British National Corpus. Available online at http://corpus.byu.edu/bnc.

——2007–. TIME Magazine Corpus (100 million words, 1920s–2000s). Available online at http://corpus.byu.edu/time.

——2008–. The Corpus of Contemporary American English (COCA): 385 million words, 1990–present. Available online at www.americancorpus.org.

De Smet, Hendrik. 2009. Analysing reanalysis. *Lingua*, 119: 1728–55.

Deane, Paul. 1991. Limits to attention: A cognitive theory of island phenomena. *Cognitive Linguistics*, 2: 1–63.

——1992. *Grammar in Mind and Brain: Explorations in Cognitive Syntax*. Berlin: Mouton de Gruyter.

——2005. Multimodal spatial representation: On the semantic unity of *over*. In Beate Hampe (ed.), *From Perception to Meaning: Image Schemas in Cognitive Linguistics*, 235–82. Berlin: Mouton de Gruyter.

Denison, David. 2001. Gradience and linguistic change. In Laurel J. Brinton (ed.), *Historical Linguistics 1999. Selected Papers from the 14th International Conference on Historical Linguistics*, 119–44. Amsterdam: Benjamins.

Dewell, Robert. 1994. *Over* again: Image–schema transformations in semantic analysis. *Cognitive Linguistics*, 5: 351–80.

Dewell, Robert. 1996. The separability of German 'über': A cognitive approach. In Pütz and Dirven (eds) (1996), 109–33.

——2007. Moving OVER: The role of systematic semantic processes in defining individual lexemes. *Annual Review of Cognitive Linguistics*, 5: 271–88.

Di Sciullo, Anna Maria and Edwin Williams. 1987. *On the Definition of Word*. Cambridge, MA: MIT Press.

Diessel, Holger. 2007. Frequency effects in language acquisition, language use, and diachronic change. *New Ideas in Psychology*, 25: 108–27.

Duffley, Patrick. 2006. *The English Gerund-Participle: A Comparison with the Infinitive*. New York: Peter Lang.

Egan, Thomas. 2006. Did John really promise Mary to leave? *Constructions*, 2/2006. urn:nbn: de:0009-4-6716 [available at: www.constructions-online.de].

——2008. *Non-Finite Complementation: A Usage-Based Study of Infinitive and -ing Clauses in English*. New York: Rodopi.

Eimas, Peter, Eina Siqueland, Peter Jusczyk, and James Vigorito. 1971. Speech perception in infants. *Science*, New Series, 171 (3968): 303–6.

Ellis, Nick. 2002. Frequency effects in language processing: A review with implications for theories of implicit and explicit language acquisition. *Studies in Second Language Acquisition*, 24: 143–88.

Ellis, Nick, Rita Simpson-Vlach, and Carson Maynard. 2008. Formulaic language in native and second language speakers: Psycholinguistics, corpus linguistics, and TESOL. *TESOL Quarterly*, 42: 375–96.

Erman, Britt and Beatrice Warren. 2000. The idiom principle and the open choice principle. *Text*, 20: 29–62.

Eu, Jinseung. 2008. Testing search engine frequencies: Patterns of inconsistency. *Corpus Linguistics and Linguistic Theory*, 4: 177–207.

Evans, Vyvyan. 2006. Lexical concepts, cognitive models and meaning construction. *Cognitive Linguistics*, 17: 491–534.

——2009. *How Words Mean: Lexical Concepts, Cognitive Models, and Meaning Construction*. Oxford: Oxford University Press.

Fauconnier, Gilles. 1994. *Mental Spaces: Aspects of Meaning Construction in Natural Languages*. Cambridge: Cambridge University Press.

——1997. *Mappings in Thought and Language*. Cambridge: Cambridge University Press.

Fauconnier, Gilles and Mark Turner. 1998. Conceptual integration networks. *Cognitive Science*, 22: 133–87.

——2002. *The Way We Think: Conceptual Blending and the Mind's Hidden Complexities*. New York: Basic Books.

Fillmore, Charles. 1982. Towards a descriptive framework for spatial deixis. In R. J. Jarvella and W. Klein (eds), *Speech, Place, and Action: Studies in Deixis and Related Topics*, 31–59. London: John Wiley.

——1986. Pragmatically controlled zero anaphora. *Proceedings of the Berkeley Linguistics Society*, 12: 95–107.

Fillmore, Charles and B. T. S Atkins. 2000. Describing polysemy: The case of 'crawl'. In Ravin and Leacock (eds) (2000), 91–110.

Fillmore, Charles, Paul Kay, and Mary Catherine O'Connor. 1988. Regularity and idiomaticity in grammatical constructions: The case of *let alone*. *Language*, 64: 501–38.

Firth, John Rupert. 1957a. Modes of meaning. In *Papers in Linguistics 1934–1951*, 190–215. Oxford: Oxford University Press. [First published 1951, *Essays and Studies*, The English Association.]

——1957b. The technique of semantics. In *Papers in Linguistics 1934–1951*, 7–33. Oxford: Oxford University Press. [First published 1935, *Transactions of the Philological Society*.]

——1968. A synopsis of linguistic theory 1930–55. In F. R. Palmer (ed.), *Selected Papers of J. R. Firth 1952–59*, 168–205. London: Longmans. [First published 1957, in *Studies in Linguistic Analysis* (special volume of the Philological Society), 1–30. Oxford.]

Fodor, Jerry. 1975. *The Language of Thought*. Hassocks, Sussex: Harvester Press.

Foss, Donald and David Swinney. 1973. On the psychological reality of the phoneme: Perception, identification, and consciousness. *Journal of Verbal Learning and Verbal Behavior*, 12: 246–57.

Foster, Pauline. 2001. Rules and routines: A consideration of their role in the task-based language production of native and non-native speakers. In Martin Bygate, Peter Skehan, and Merrill Swain (eds), *Researching Pedagogic Tasks: Second Language Learning, Teaching and Testing*, 75–94. London: Longman.

Fotos, Sandra S. 1993. Consciousness raising and noticing through focus on form: Grammar task performance versus formal instruction. *Applied Linguistics*, 14: 385–407.

Foulkes, Paul and Gerard Docherty. 2006. The social life of phonetics and phonology. *Journal of Phonetics*, 34: 409–38.

Fromkin, Victoria (ed.). 1973. *Speech Errors as Linguistic Evidence*. The Hague: Mouton.

——(ed.). 1980. *Errors in Linguistic Performance: Slips of the Tongue, Ear, Pen, and Hand*. New York: Academic Press.

Fromkin, Victoria, Robert Rodman, Nina Hyams, Peter Collins, and Mengistu Amberber. 2005. *An Introduction to Language*, 5th edn. Sydney: Thomson. [First edn: 1988.]

Fry, Dennis. 1947. The frequency of occurrence of speech sounds in Southern English. *Archives Néerlandaises de Phonétique Expérimentale*, 20: 103–6.

Gahl, Susanne. 2008. *Time* and *thyme* are not homophones: The effect of lemma frequency on word durations in spontaneous speech. *Language*, 84: 474–96.

Gahl, Susanne and Susan M. Garnsey. 2004. Knowledge of grammar, knowledge of usage: Syntactic probabilities affect pronunciation variation. *Language*, 80: 748–75.

Garman, Michael. 1990. *Psycholinguistics*. Cambridge: Cambridge University Press.

Garnsey, Susan M., Neal Pearlmutter, Elizabeth Myers, and Melanie Lotocky. 1997. The contributions of verb bias and plausibility to the comprehension of temporarily ambiguous sentences. *Journal of Memory and Language*, 37: 58–93.

Geeraerts, Dirk. 1992. The semantic structure of Dutch *over*. *Leuvense Bijdragen*, 81: 205–30.

——1993. Vagueness's puzzles, polysemy's vagaries. *Cognitive Linguistics*, 4: 223–72.

——2010. *Theories of Lexical Semantics*. Oxford: Oxford University Press.

Geeraerts, Dirk and Hubert Cuyckens (eds). 2007. *The Oxford Handbook of Cognitive Linguistics*. Oxford: Oxford University Press.

Gehweiler, Elke, Iris Höser, and Undine Kramer. 2007. Types of changes in idioms: Some surprising results of corpus research. In Christine Fellbaum (ed.), *Idioms and Collocations: Corpus-based Linguistics and Lexicographic Studies*, 109–37. London: Continuum.

Gibbs, Raymond. 1992. What do idioms really mean? *Journal of Memory and Language*, 31: 485–506.

——1994. *The Poetics of Mind: Figurative Thought, Language, and Understanding*. Cambridge: Cambridge University Press.

——2007. Idioms and formulaic language. In Geeraerts and Cuyckens (eds) (2007), 697–725.

Gibbs, Raymond and Jennifer O'Brian. 1990. Idioms and mental imagery: The metaphorical motivation for idiomatic meaning. *Cognition*, 36: 35–68.

Giles, Howard. 1973. Accent mobility: A model and some data. *Anthropological Linguistics*, 15: 87–105.

Giles, Howard, Nikolas Coupland, and Justine Coupland. 1991. Accommodation theory: Communication, context, and consequence. In Howard Giles, Justine Coupland, and Nikolas Coupland (eds), *Contexts of Accommodation: Developments in Applied Linguistics*, 1–68. Cambridge: Cambridge University Press.

Gipper, Helmut. 1959. Sessel oder Stuhl? Ein Beitrag zur Bestimmung von Wortinhalten im Bereich der Sachkultur. In Helmut Gipper (ed.), *Sprache, Schlüssel zur Welt: Festschrift für Leo Weisgerber*, 271–92. Düsseldorf: Schwann.

Givón, Talmy. 1984. *Syntax: A Functional–Typological Introduction*, vol. 1. Amsterdam: Benjamins.

Gleitman, Lila. 1990. The structural sources of word meanings. *Language Acquisition*, 1: 3–55.

Goddard, Cliff. 1998. *Semantic Analysis: A Practical Introduction*. Oxford: Oxford University Press.

Goldberg, Adele. 1995. *Constructions: A Construction Grammar Approach to Argument Structure*. Chicago: Chicago University Press.

——2006. *Constructions at Work: The Nature of Generalization in Language*. Oxford: Oxford University Press.

Goldberg, Adele and Farrell Ackerman. 2001. The pragmatics of obligatory adjuncts. *Language*, 77: 798–814.

Goldinger, Stephen. 1996. Words and voices: Episodic traces in spoken word identification and recognition memory. *Journal of Experimental Psychology: Learning, Memory, and Cognition*, 22: 1166–83.

Goldinger, Stephen and Tamiko Azuma. 2004. Episodic memory reflected in printed word naming. *Psychonomic Bulletin and Review*, 11: 716–22.

Gomez, Rebecca and LouAnn Gerken. 1999. Artificial grammar learning by 1-year-olds leads to specific and abstract knowledge. *Cognition*, 70: 109–35.

Granger, Sylviane. 1998. Prefabricated patterns in advanced EFL writing: Collocations and formulae. In A. P. Cowie (ed.), *Phraseology: Theory, Analysis, and Applications*, 145–60. Oxford: Oxford University Press.

Grant, Lynne. 2005. Frequency of 'core idioms' in the British National Corpus (BNC). *International Journal of Corpus Linguistics*, 10: 429–51.

Greenbaum, Sidney. 1976. Contextual influences on acceptability judgments. *International Journal of Psycholinguistics*, 6: 5–11.

Greenberg, Joseph H. 1966. *Language Universals*. The Hague: Mouton.

Gries, Stefan Th. 2003a. *Multifactorial Analysis in Corpus Linguistics: A Study of Particle Placement*. London: Continuum.

——2003b. Towards a corpus-based identification of prototypal instances of constructions. *Annual Review of Cognitive Linguistics*, 1: 1–27.

——2005. Syntactic priming: A corpus-based approach. *Journal of Psycholinguistic Research*, 34: 365–99.

——2006a. Cognitive determinants of subtractive word formation: A corpus-based perspective. *Cognitive Linguistics*, 17: 535–58.

——2006b. Corpus-based methods and cognitive semantics: The many senses of *to run*. In Gries and Stefanowitsch (eds) (2006), 57–99.

——2008. Dispersions and adjusted frequencies in corpora. *International Journal of Corpus Linguistics*, 13: 403–37.

Gries, Stefan Th. and Dagmar Divjak. 2009. Behavioral profiles: A corpus-based approach to cognitive semantic study. In V. Evans and S. Pourcel (eds), *New Directions in Cognitive Linguistics*, 57–76. Amsterdam: Benjamins.

Gries, Stefan Th., Beate Hampe, and Doris Schönefeld. 2005. Converging evidence: Bringing together experimental and corpus data on the association of verbs and constructions. *Cognitive Linguistics*, 16: 635–76.

Gries, Stefan Th. and Anatol Stefanowitsch. 2004. Extending collostructional analysis. A corpus-based perspective on 'alternations'. *International Journal of Corpus Linguistics*, 9: 97–129.

——(eds). 2006. *Corpora in Cognitive Linguistics: Corpus-based Approaches to Syntax and Lexis*. Berlin: Mouton de Gruyter.

Gries, Stefan Th. and Stefanie Wulff. 2005. Do foreign language learners also have constructions? Evidence from priming, sorting, and corpora. *Annual Review of Cognitive Linguistics*, 3: 182–200.

Gross, Maurice. 1979. On the failure of generative grammar. *Language*, 55: 859–85.

——1984. Lexicon-grammar and the syntactic analysis of French. *Proceedings of the 10th International Conference on Computational Linguistics and 22nd Annual Meeting on Association for Computational Linguistics*, 275–82. Morristown, NJ: Association for Computational Linguistics (available at http://acl.ldc.upenn.edu/P/P84/P84-1058.pdf).

Ha, Le Quan, Philip Hanna, Ji Ming, and F. J. Smith. 2009. Extending Zipf's law to *n*-grams for large corpora. *Artificial Intelligence Review*, 32: 101–13.

Hallan, Naomi. 2001. Paths to prepositions? A corpus-based study of the acquisition of a lexico-grammatical category. In Bybee and Hopper (eds) (2001), 91–120.

Halle, Morris. 1954. The strategy of phonemics. *Word*, 10: 197–209.

——1997. Some consequences of the representation of words in memory. *Lingua*, 100: 91–100.

Halliday, M. A. K. 1985. *An Introduction to Functional Grammar*. London: Edward Arnold.

——1991. Corpus studies and probabilistic grammar. In Aijmer and Altenberg (eds) (1991), 30–43. [Reprinted in M. A. K. Halliday, *Computational and Quantitative Studies* (2005), 63–75. London: Continuum.]

Hampe, Beate and Doris Schönefeld. 2006. Syntactic leaps or lexical variation? More on "creative syntax". In Gries and Stefanowitsch (eds) (2006), 127–57.

Hanks, Patrick. 2000. Do word meanings exist? *Computers and the Humanities*, 34: 205–15.

Harrington, Jonathon. 2006. An acoustic analysis of 'happy-tensing' in the Queen's Christmas broadcasts. *Journal of Phonetics*, 34: 439–57.

Hart, Betty and Todd Risley. 1995. *Meaningful Differences in the Everyday Experience of Young American Children*. Baltimore: Brookes.

Haspelmath, Martin. 2006. Against markedness (and what to replace it with). *Journal of Linguistics*, 42: 25–70.

Hawkins, John. 1994. *A Performance Theory of Order and Constituency*. Cambridge: Cambridge University Press.

——2004. *Efficiency and Complexity in Grammars*. Oxford: Oxford University Press.

Hay, Jennifer and Katie Drager. 2007. Sociophonetics. *Annual Review of Anthropology*, 36: 89–103.

Hayward, Malcolm. 1994. Genre recognition of history and fiction. *Poetics*, 22: 409–21.

Hazan, Valerie and Sarah Barrett. 2000. The development of phonemic categorization in children aged 6–12. *Journal of Phonetics*, 28: 377–96.

Heitner, Reese. 2004. The cyclical ontogeny of ontology: An integrated developmental account of object and speech categorization. *Philosophical Psychology*, 17: 45–57.

Hickey, Thomas J. 1995/2005. *History of Twentieth-Century Philosophy of Science*, book *v* (available at: www.philsci.com).

Hilpert, Martin. 2006. Keeping an eye on the data: Metonymies and their patterns. In Anatol Stefanowitsch and Stefan Gries (eds), *Corpus-Based Approaches to Metaphor and Metonymy*, 123–51. Berlin: Mouton de Gruyter.

——2008. The English comparative: Language structure and language use. *English Language and Linguistics*, 12: 395–417.

Hintzman, Douglas L. 1969. Apparent frequency as a function of frequency and the spacing of repetitions. *Journal of Experimental Psychology*, 80: 139–45.

——1986. "Schema abstraction" in a multiple-trace memory model. *Psychological Review*, 93: 411–28.

Hirschbühler, Paul. 1975. On the source of lefthand NPs in French. *Linguistic Inquiry*, 6: 155–65.

Hockett, Charles. 1955. *A Manual of Phonology*. Baltimore: Waverly Press.

——1961. Linguistic elements and their relations. *Language*, 37: 29–53.

Hockett, Charles and Stuart Altmann. 1968. A note on design features. In Thomas A. Sebeok (ed.), *Animal Communication: Techniques of Study and Results of Research*, 61–72. Bloomington: Indiana University Press.

Hoey, Michael. 2005. *Lexical Priming: A New Theory of Words and Language*. London: Routledge.

Hopper, Paul. 1991. On some principles of grammaticalization. In Elizabeth Traugott and Bernd Heine (eds), *Approaches to Grammaticalization*, 17–35. Amsterdam: Benjamins.

Hopper, Paul and Elizabeth Traugott. 1993. *Grammaticalization*. Cambridge: Cambridge University Press.

Howes, Davis and Richard Solomon. 1951. Visual duration threshold as a function of word-probability. *Journal of Experimental Psychology*, 41: 401–10.

Huddleston, Rodney and Geoffrey Pullum. 2002. *The Cambridge Grammar of the English Language*. Cambridge: Cambridge University Press.

Hudson, Richard. 1990. Review of Langacker (1987). *Lingua*, 81: 272–84.

——1994. About 37% of word-tokens are nouns. *Language*, 70: 331–9.

——2007. *Language Networks: The New Word Grammar*. Oxford: Oxford University Press.

Hundt, Marianne, Nadja Nesselhauf, and Carolin Biewer (eds). 2007. *Corpus Linguistics and the Web*. Amsterdam: Radopi.

Hunston, Susan. 2003. Lexis, wordform and complementation pattern. *Functions of Language*, 10: 31–59.

——2007. Semantic prosody revisited. *International Journal of Corpus Linguistics*, 12: 249–68.

Ingram, David. 1989. *First Language Acquisition: Method, Description and Explanation*. Cambridge: Cambridge University Press.

Inkpen, Diana and Graeme Hirst. 2005. Building and using a lexical knowledge-base of near-synonym differences. *Computational Linguistics*, 32: 1–40.

Iwata, Seizi. 2004. *Over*-prefixation: A lexical constructional approach. *English Language and Linguistics*, 8: 239–92.

Jackendoff, Ray. 1983. *Semantics and Cognition*. Cambridge, MA: MIT Press.

——1996. Conceptual semantics and cognitive semantics. *Cognitive Linguistics*, 7: 93–129.

——1997. Twistin' the night away. *Language*, 73: 534–59. [Reprinted in Jackendoff (2010), 250–77.]

——2002. *Foundations of Language: Brain, Meaning, Grammar, Evolution*. Oxford: Oxford University Press.

——2010. *Meaning and the Lexicon: The Parallel Architecture 1975-2010*. Oxford: Oxford University Press.

Jacoby, Larry and C. A. G. Hayman. 1987. Specific visual transfer in word identification. *Journal of Experimental Psychology: Learning, Memory, and Cognition*, 13: 456–63.

Jaeger, Florian and Neal Snider. 2007. Implicit learning and syntactic persistence: Surprisal and cumulativity. In L. Wolter and J. Thorson (eds), *University of Rochester Working Papers in the Language Sciences*, 3: 26–44.

Janda, Richard D. 1990. Frequency, markedness, and morphological change. On predicting the spread of noun-plural -*s* in Modern High German and West Germanic. In Yongkyoon No and Mark Libucha (eds), *ESCOL '90* (= *Proceedings of the 7th Eastern States Conference on Linguistics*), 136–53. Ohio State University.

Jarvella, Robert J. 1970. Effects of syntax on running memory span for connected discourse. *Psychonomic Science*, 19: 235–6.

——1971. Syntactic processing of connected speech. *Journal of Verbal Learning and Verbal Behavior*, 10: 409–16.

Johansson, Stig and Knut Hofland. 1989. *Frequency Analysis of English Vocabulary and Grammar: Based on the LOB Corpus*. Oxford: Clarendon Press.

Johnson, Keith. 1997. *Acoustic and Auditory Phonetics*. Oxford: Blackwell.

——2003. Massive reduction in conversational American English. *Proceedings of the Workshop on Spontaneous Speech: Data and Analysis*, Tokyo (available at: http://citeseerx.ist.psu.edu/viewdoc/download?doi=10.1.1.142.5012&rep=rep1&type=pdf).

——2004. Aligning phonetic transcriptions with their citation forms. *ARLO* (= Acoustic Research Letters Online), 5 (2): 19–24 (available at: http://buckeyecorpus.osu.edu/pubs/DTW_aligning.pdf).

Jones, Daniel. 1929. Definition of a phoneme. *Le Maitre Phonétique*, 43–4.

Jusczyk, Peter W. 1997. *The Discovery of Spoken Language*. Cambridge, MA: MIT Press.

Kaeding, Friedrich Wilhelm. 1898. *Häufigkeitswörterbuch der deutschen Sprache*. Steglitz bei Berlin: Private publisher.

Kay, Paul and Charles Fillmore. 1999. Grammatical constructions and linguistic generalizations: The *What's X doing Y* construction. *Language*, 75: 1–34.

Kay, Paul and Chad K. McDaniel. 1978. The linguistic significance of the meanings of basic color terms. *Language*, 54: 610–46.

Keller, Frank and Maria Lapata. 2003. Using the Web to obtain frequencies for unseen bigrams. *Computational Linguistics*, 29: 459–84.

Keller, Frank, Maria Lapata, and Olga Ourioupina. 2002. Using the Web to overcome data sparseness. In Jan Hajič and Yuji Matsmoto (eds), *Proceedings of the Conference of Empirical Methods in Natural Language Processing*, 230–7. Philadelphia.

Kelly, Michael. 1992. Using sound to solve syntactic problems: The role of phonology in grammatical category assignments. *Psychological Review*, 99: 349–64.

——1998. To "brunch" or to "brench": Some aspects of blend structure. *Linguistics*, 36: 579–90.

Kemmer, Suzanne. 2003. Schemas and lexical blends. In Hubert Cuyckens, Thomas Berg, René Dirven, and Klaus-Uwe Panther (eds), *Motivation in Language*, 69–97. Amsterdam: Benjamins.

Kessler, Brett and Rebecca Treiman. 1997. Syllable structure and the distribution of phonemes in English syllables. *Journal of Memory and Language*, 37: 295–311.

Keysar, Boaz and Bridget Martin Bly. 1999. Swimming against the current: Do idioms reflect conceptual structure? *Journal of Pragmatics*, 31: 1559–78.

Kilgarriff, Adam. 1997. I don't believe in word senses. *Computers and the Humanities*, 31: 91–113.

Kilgarriff, Adam and Gregory Grefenstette. 2003. Introduction to the special issue on the Web as corpus. *Computational Linguistics*, 29: 333–47.

Kishner, Jeffrey and Raymond Gibbs. 1996. How "just" gets its meanings: Polysemy and context in psychological semantics. *Language and Speech*, 39: 19–36.

Kisseberth, Charles. 1970. On the functional unity of phonological rules. *Linguistic Inquiry*, 1: 291–306.

Klein-Braley, Christine. 1997. C-tests in the context of reduced redundancy testing: An appraisal. *Language Testing*, 14: 47–84.

Koops, Christian. 2004. Emergent aspect constructions in present-day English. In Günter Radden and Klaus-Uwe Panther (eds), *Studies in Linguistic Motivation*, 121–54. Berlin: Mouton de Gruyter.

Köpcke, Klaus-Michael. 1998. The acquisition of plural marking in English and German revisited: Schemata versus rules. *Journal of Child Language*, 25: 293–319.

Köpcke, Klaus-Michael and David Zubin. 1984. Sechs Prinzipien für die Genuszuweisung im Deutschen: Ein Beitrag zur natürlichen Klassifikation. *Linguistische Berichte*, 93: 26–50.

Kornai, András. 1998. Analytic models in phonology. In J. Durand and B. Laks (eds). *The Organization of Phonology*, 395–418. Oxford: Oxford University Press.

——2002. How many words are there? *Glossometrics*, 4: 61–86.

Kreitzer, Anatol. 1997. Multiple levels of schematization: A study in the conceptualization of space. *Cognitive Linguistics*, 8: 291–325.

Krug, Manfred. 2003. Frequency as a determinant in grammatical variation and change. In Rohdenburg and Mondorf (eds) (2003), 7–67.

Kruschke, John K. 1992. ALCOVE: An exemplar-based connectionist model of category learning. *Psychological Review*, 99: 22–44.

Kuhl, Patricia. 1987. Perception of speech and sound in early infancy. In P. Salapatek and L. Cohen (eds), *Handbook of Infant Perception*, vol. 2, 273–382. New York: Academic Press.

——1994. Speech perception. In Fred D. Minifie (ed.), *Introduction to Communication Sciences and Disorders*, 77–148. San Diego: Singular Publishing.

Kuhl, Patricia and James D. Miller. 1975. Speech perception by the chinchilla: Voiced–voiceless distinction in alveolar plosive consonants. *Science*, 190 (4209): 69–72.

Kuiper, Koenraad. 1996. *Smooth Talkers: The Linguistic Performance of Auctioneers and Sportscasters*. Hillsdale, NJ: Lawrence Erlbaum.

——2009. *Formulaic Genres*. London: Palgrave Macmillan.

Labov, William. 1972. *Sociolinguistic Patterns*. Oxford: Blackwell.

——1973. The boundaries of words and their meanings. In C.-J. Bailey and R. W. Shuy (eds), *New Ways of Analyzing Variation in English*, 340–72. Washington, DC: Georgetown University Press. [Reprinted in Aarts *et al.* (eds) (2004), 67–89.]

——1996. When intuitions fail. In L. McNair, K. Singer, L. Dolbrin, and M. Aucon (eds), *Papers from the Parasession on Theory and Data in Linguistics 32*, 77–106. Chicago: Chicago Linguistic Society.

Lachs, Lorin, Kipp McMichael, and David Pisoni. 2000. Speech perception and implicit memory: Evidence for detailed episodic encoding of phonetic events. *Research on Spoken Language Processing, Progress Report No. 24*, 149–67. Indiana University.

Lakoff, George. 1987. *Women, Fire, and Dangerous Things: What Categories Reveal about the Mind*. Chicago: Chicago University Press.

Lakoff, George and Mark Johnson. 1980. *Metaphors We Live By*. Chicago: University of Chicago Press.

Lakoff, George and Rafael Núñez. 2000. *Where Mathematics Comes From: How the Embodied Mind Brings Mathematics Into Being*. New York: Basic Books.

Lambrecht, Knud, 1990. "What, me worry?" – 'Mad Magazine sentences' revisited. *Proceedings of the Berkeley Linguistics Society*, 16: 215–28.

Langacker, Ronald W. 1967. *Language and Its Structure*. New York: Harcourt, Brace & World.

——1984. Active zones. *Proceedings of the Berkeley Linguistics Society*, 10: 172–88. [Reprinted in Langacker (2002) *Concept, Image, and Symbol: The Cognitive Basis of Grammar*, 189–201. Berlin: Mouton de Gruyter.]

——1987. *Foundations of Cognitive Grammar, Vol. 1: Theoretical Prerequisites*. Stanford: Stanford University Press.

——1991. *Foundations of Cognitive Grammar, Vol. 2: Descriptive Application*. Stanford: Stanford University Press.

——2005. Construction grammars: Cognitive, radical, and less so. In Francisco J. Ruiz de Mendoza Ibáñez and M. Sandra Peña Cervel (eds), *Cognitive Linguistics: Internal Dynamics and Interdisciplinary Interaction*, 101–59. Berlin: Mouton de Gruyter.

——2008. *Cognitive Grammar: A Basic Introduction*. Oxford: Oxford University Press.

Lapata, Maria, Frank Keller, and Sabine Schulte im Walde. 2001. Verb frame frequency as a predictor of verb bias. *Journal of Psycholinguistic Research*, 30: 419–35.

Lapata, Maria, Scott McDonald, and Frank Keller. 1999. Determinants of adjective–noun plausibility. *Proceedings of EACL '99* (available at: www.aclweb.org/anthology/E/E99/E99-1005.pdf).

Lass, Roger. 1975. How intrinsic is content? Markedness, sound change, and 'family universals'. In G. Pullum and D. Goyvaerts (eds), *Essays on the Sound Pattern of English*, 475–504. Ghent: Story-Scientia.

——1997. *Historical Linguistics and Language Change*. Cambridge: Cambridge University Press.

Lass, Roger and Susan Wright. 1986. Endogeny vs. contact: 'Afrikaans influence' on South African English. *English World-Wide*, 7: 201–23.

Laver, John. 1970. The production of speech. In John Lyons (ed.), *New Horizons in Linguistics*, 53–75. Harmondsworth: Penguin.

Leech, Geoffrey. 2007. New resources, or just better old ones? The Holy Grail of representativeness. In Hundt, Nesselhauf, and Biewer (eds) (2007), 133–49.

Leech, Geoffrey and Jan Svartvik. 1975. *A Communicative Grammar of English*. London: Longman.

Lemmens, Maarten. 2006. More on objectless transitives and ergativization patterns in English. *Constructions* 6/2006. urn:nbn:de: 0009-4-6802 (available at: www.constructions-online.de).

Levelt, Willem. 1989. *Speaking: From Intention to Articulation*. Cambridge, MA: MIT Press.

Levelt, Willem and Stephanie Kelter. 1982. Surface form and memory in question answering. *Cognitive Psychology*, 14: 78–106.

Levin, Beth. 1993. *English Verb Classes and Alternations: A Preliminary Investigation*. Chicago: University of Chicago Press.

Levy, Yonata. 1983. It's frogs all the way down. *Cognition*, 15: 75–93.

Liberman, Alvin and Ignatius Mattingly. 1985. The motor theory of speech perception revised. *Cognition*, 21: 1–36.

Liberman, Alvin M., Franklin S. Cooper, Donald P. Shankweiler, and Michael Studdert-Kennedy. 1967. Perception of the speech code. *Psychological Review*, 74: 431–61.

Liberman, Alvin, Pierre Delattre, and Franklin S. Cooper. 1958. Some cues for the distinction between voiced and voiceless stops in initial position. *Language and Speech*, 1: 153–66.

Lieven, Elena, Heike Behrens, Jennifer Speares, and Michael Tomasello. 2003. Early syntactic creativity: A usage-based approach. *Journal of Child Language*, 30: 333–70.

Lightfoot, David. 1979. *Principles of Diachronic Syntax*. Cambridge: Cambridge University Press.

Liljencrants, Johan and Björn Lindblom. 1972. Numerical simulation of vowel quality systems: The role of perceptual contrast. *Language*, 48: 839–62.

Lindner, Susan, 1981. A lexico-semantic analysis of English verb particle constructions with OUT and UP. Unpublished PhD dissertation, University of California, San Diego.

Lisker, Leigh. 1978. In qualified defense of VOT. *Language and Speech*, 21: 375–83.

Lisker, Leigh and Arthur S. Abramson. 1964. A cross-linguistic study of voicing in initial stops. *Word*, 20: 384–442.

Liu, Lianyuan and Yifan Ma. 1986. Mandarin tonal distribution and tonal frequency. *Yuwen Jianshe*, 3: 21–3.

Louw, Bill. 1993. Irony in the text or insincerity in the writer? The diagnostic potential of semantic prosodies. In Mona Baker, Gill Francis, and Elena Tognini-Bonelli (eds), *Text and Technology: In Honour of John Sinclair*, 157–76. Amsterdam: Benjamins.

Lovelace, Eugene A. and Stephen D. Southall. 1983. Memory for words in prose and their locations on the page. *Memory and Cognition*, 11: 429–34.

Luka, Barbara and Lawrence Barsalou. 2005. Structural facilitation: Mere exposure effects for grammatical acceptability as evidence for syntactic priming in comprehension. *Journal of Memory and Language*, 52: 436–59.

MacDonald, Maryellen. 1993. The interaction of lexical and syntactic ambiguity. *Journal of Memory and Language*, 32: 692–715.

MacDonald, Maryellen, Neal Pearlmutter, and Mark Seidenberg. 1994. Lexical nature of syntactic ambiguity resolution. *Psychological Review*, 101: 676–703.

MacKay, Donald. 1972. The structure of words and syllables: Evidence from errors in speech. *Cognitive Psychology*, 3: 21–227.

Massam, Diane. 1999. *Thing is* constructions: The thing is, is what's the right analysis? *English Language and Linguistics*, 3: 335–52.

Matthews, Clive. 2010. On the nature of phonological cues in the acquisition of French gender categories: Evidence from instance-based learning. *Lingua*, 120: 879–900.

Maye, Jessica and LouAnn Gerken. 2000. Learning phonemes without minimal pairs. *Proceedings of the 24th Annual Boston University Conference on Language Development*, 522–33. Somerville, MA: Cascadilla Press.

——2001. Learning phonemes: How far can the input take us? *Proceedings of the 25th Annual Boston University Conference on Language Development*, 480–90. Somerville, MA: Cascadilla Press.

Maye, Jessica and Daniel Weiss. 2003. Statistical cues facilitate infants' discrimination of difficult phonetic contrasts. *Proceedings of the 27th Annual Boston University Conference on Language Development*, 508–18. Somerville, MA: Cascadilla Press.

Maye, Jessica, Daniel L. Weiss, and Richard N. Aslin. 2008. Statistical phonetic learning in infants: Facilitation and feature generalization. *Developmental Science*, 11: 122–34.

Maye, Jessica, Janet F. Werker, and LouAnn Gerken. 2002. Infant sensitivity to distributional information can affect phonetic discrimination. *Cognition*, 82: B101–B111.

McClelland, James, Mark St John, and Roman Taraban. 1989. Sentence comprehension: A parallel distributed approach. *Language and Cognitive Processes*, 4: 1287–355.

McDonald, Scott and Richard Shillcock. 2001. Rethinking the word frequency effect: The neglected role of distributional information in lexical processing. *Language and Speech*, 44: 295–323.

McDonough, Kim and Alison Mackey. 2008. Syntactic priming and ESL question development. *Studies in Second Language Acquisition*, 30: 31–47.

McEnery, Tony and Andrew Wilson. 2001. *Corpus Linguistics: An Introduction*. Edinburgh: Edinburgh University Press.

McGee, Iain. 2008. Word frequency estimates revisited: A response to Alderson (2007). *Applied Linguistics*, 29: 509–14.

Medin, Douglas L. and Marguerite M. Schaffer. 1978. Context theory of classification learning. *Psychological Review*, 85: 207–38.

Meex, Birgitta. 1997. The spatial and non-spatial senses of the German preposition *über*. In Cuyckens and Zawada (eds) (1997), 1–36.

Mesthrie, Rajend. 2002. Endogeny versus contact revisited: Aspectual *busy* in South African English. *Language Sciences*, 24: 345–58.

Michaelis, Laura. 2003. Word meaning, sentence meaning, and syntactic meaning. In Cuyckens, Dirven, and Taylor (eds) (2003), 163–209.

Miller, George and Claudia Leacock. 2000. Lexical representations for sentence processing. In Ravin and Leacock (eds) (2000), 152–60.

Mompeán, José. 2006. The phoneme as a basic-level category: Experimental evidence from English. *International Journal of English Studies*, 6: 141–72.

Monaghan, Padraic, Nick Chater, and Morton Christiansen. 2005. The differential role of phonological and distributional cues in grammatical categorisation. *Cognition*, 96: 143–82.

Mondorf, Britta. 2003. Support for more-support. In Rohdenburg and Mondorf (eds) (2003), 251–304.

Moon, Rosamund. 1998. *Fixed Expressions and Idioms in English: A Corpus-Based Approach*. Oxford: Oxford University Press.

Morton, John. 1969. Interaction of information in word recognition. *Psychological Review*, 76: 165–78.

Murphy, Gregory. 2002. *The Big Book of Concepts*. Cambridge, MA: MIT Press.

Murphy, Gregory and Douglas Medin. 1985. The role of theories in conceptual coherence. *Psychological Review*, 92: 289–316.

Nathan, Geoffrey. 2006. Is the phoneme usage-based? – Some issues. *International Journal of English Studies*, 6: 173–94.

Nattinger, James R. 1980. A lexical phrase grammar for ESL. *TESOL Quarterly*, 14: 337–44.

Nerlich, Brigitte, Zazie Todd, Vimala Herman, and David D. Clarke (eds). 2003. *Polysemy: Flexible Patterns of Meaning in Mind and Language*. Berlin: Mouton de Gruyter.

Nesselhauf, Nadja. 2003. The use of collocations by advanced learners of English and some implications for teaching. *Applied Linguistics*, 24: 223–42.

Newman, John and Sally Rice. 2006. Transitivity schemas of English EAT and DRINK in the BNC. In Gries and Stefanowitsch (eds) (2006), 225–60.

Newmeyer, Frederick. 2003. Grammar is grammar and usage is usage. *Language*, 79: 682–707.

Nordquist, Dawn. 2004. Comparing elicited data and corpora. In Michel Achard and Suzanne Kemmer (eds), *Language, Culture and Mind*, 211–23. Stanford, CA: CSLI Publications.

Notess, Greg. 2002. Search engine statistics: Database total size estimates (available at: www.searchengineshowdown.com/statistics/sizeest.shtml).

Nunberg, Geoffrey, Ivan Sag, and Thomas Wasow. 1994. Idioms. *Language*, 70: 491–538.

O'Hara, Kenton, Abigail Sellen, and Richard Bentley. 1999. Supporting memory for spatial location while reading from small displays. In *Proceedings of CHI '98, Conference on Human Factors in Computing Systems*, Los Angeles, CA (available at: www.ict.csiro.au/staff/kenton.ohara/papers/incidentalmemory_CHI.pdf).

Oldfield, R. C. and A. Wingfield. 1965. Response latencies in naming objects. *Quarterly Journal of Experimental Psychology*, 17: 273–81.

Oller, John W. 1979. *Language Tests at School*. London: Longman.

Paardekooper, Petrus Cornelis. 1956. Een schat van een kind. *De Nieuwe Taalgids*, 49: 93–9.

Panther, Klaus-Uwe and Linda Thornburg. 2001. A conceptual analysis of English -er Nominals. In Pütz, Niemeier, and Dirven (eds) (2001), 149–200.

Partington, Alan. 1998. *Patterns and Meanings: Using Corpora for English Language Research and Teaching*. Amsterdam: Benjamins.

——2004. "Utterly content in each other's company": Semantic prosody and semantic preference. *International Journal of Corpus Linguistics*, 9: 131–56.

Paul, Hermann. 1886. *Prinzipien der Sprachgeschichte*, Halle, trans. H. A. Strong. London: Longmans Green, 1891.

Pawley, Andrew. 1985. On speech formulas and linguistic competence. *Lenguas Modernas*, 12: 84–104.

Pawley, Andrew and Frances Syder. 1983. Two puzzles for linguistic theory: Nativelike selection and nativelike fluency. In J. C. Richards and R. W. Schmidt (eds), *Language and Communication*, 191–225. London: Longman.

Peterson, Gordon and Harold Barney. 1952. Control methods used in a study of the vowels. *Journal of the Acoustical Society of America*, 24: 175–84.

Pickering, Martin and Holly Branigan. 1998. The representation of verbs: Evidence from syntactic priming in language production. *Journal of Memory and Language*, 39: 633–51.

Pickering, Martin, Holly Branigan, and Janet McLean. 2002. Constituent structure is formulated in one stage. *Journal of Memory and Language*, 46: 585–605.

Pierrehumbert, Janet. 2001. Exemplar dynamics: Word frequency, lenition and contrast. In Bybee and Hopper (eds) (2001), 137–57.

——2002. Word-specific phonetics. In Carlos Gussenhoven and Natasha Warner (eds), *Laboratory Phonology 7*, 101–39. Berlin: Mouton de Gruyter.

——2003. Phonetic diversity, statistical learning, and acquisition of phonology. *Language and Speech*, 46: 115–54.

Pine, Julien and Elena Lieven. 1997. Slot and frame patterns and the development of the determiner category. *Applied Psycholinguistics*, 18: 123–38.

Pinker, Steven. 1994a. *The Language Instinct: How the Mind Creates Language*. New York: William Morrow.

——1994b. How could a child use verb syntax to learn verb semantics? *Lingua*, 92: 377–410.

——1999. *Words and Rules: The Ingredients of Language*. New York: Basic Books.

Pollack, Irwin, Herbert Rubenstein, and Louis Decker. 1959. Intelligibility of known and unknown message sets. *Journal of the Acoustical Society of America*, 31: 273–9.

Popiel, Stephen J. and Ken McRae. 1988. The figurative and literal senses of idioms; or, all idioms are not used equally. *Journal of Psycholinguistic Research*, 17: 475–87.

Port, Robert. 2007. How are words stored in memory? Beyond phones and phonemes. *New Ideas in Psychology*, 25: 143–70.

——2010. Rich memory and distributed phonology. *Language Sciences*, 32: 43–55.

Potter, Ralph K., George A. Kopp, and Harriet C. Green. 1947. *Visible Speech*. New York: Van Nostrand.

Pullum, Geoffrey. 2007. Ungrammaticality, rarity, and corpus use. *Corpus Linguistics and Linguistic Theory*, 3: 33–47.

Pullum, Geoffrey and Barbara Scholz. 2002. Empirical assessment of stimulus poverty arguments. *The Linguistic Review*, 19: 9–50.

Pustejovsky, James. 1991. The generative lexicon. *Computational Linguistics*, 17: 409–41.

Pustet, Regina. 2004. Zipf and his heirs. *Language Sciences*, 26: 1–25.

Pütz, Martin and René Dirven (eds). 1996. *The Construal of Space in Language and Thought*. Berlin: Mouton de Gruyter.

Pütz, Martin, Suzanne Niemeier, and René Dirven (eds). 2001. *Applied Cognitive Linguistics*, vol. 2. Berlin: Mouton de Gruyter.

Queller, Kurt. 2001. A usage-based approach to modeling and teaching the phrasal lexicon. In Pütz, Niemeier, and Dirven (eds) (2001), 55–83.

——2003. Metonymic sense shift: Its origins in hearers' abductive construal of usage in context. In Cuyckens, Dirven, and Taylor (eds) (2003), 211–41.

Quine, Willard V. O. 1960. *Word and Object*. Cambridge, MA: MIT Press.

Radford, Andrew. 1988. *Transformational Grammar: A First Course*. Cambridge: Cambridge University Press.

Ravin, Yael and Claudia Leacock (eds). 2000. *Polysemy: Theoretical and Computational Approaches*. Oxford: Oxford University Press.

Redington, Martin, Nick Chater, and Steven Finch. 1998. Distributional information: A powerful cue for acquiring syntactic categories. *Cognitive Science*, 22: 425–69.

Renouf, Antoinette and Jayeeta Banerjee. 2007. Lexical repulsion between sense-related pairs. *International Journal of Corpus Linguistics*, 12: 415–43.

Renouf, Antoinette and John Sinclair. 1991. Collocational frameworks in English. In Aijmer and Altenberg (eds) (1991), 128–43.

Rice, Sally. 2003. Growth of a lexical network: Nine English prepositions in acquisition. In Cuyckens, Dirven, and Taylor (eds) (2003), 243–80.

Rickford, John, Thomas Wasow, Arnold Zwicky, and Isabelle Buchstaller. 2007. Intensive and quotative *all*: Something old, something new. *American Speech*, 82: 3–31.

Robinson, Peter and Nick Ellis. 2008a. Conclusion: Cognitive linguistics, second language acquisition and L2 instruction—Issues for research. In Robinson and Ellis (eds) (2008), 489–545.

——(eds). 2008b. *Handbook of Cognitive Linguistics and Second Language Acquisition*. London: Routledge.

Rohdenburg, Günter. 2003. Cognitive complexity and horror aequi as factors determining the use of interrogative clause linkers in English. In Rohdenburg and Mondorf (eds) (2003), 205–50.

Rohdenburg, Günter and Britta Mondorf (eds). 2003. *Determinants of Grammatical Variation in English*. Berlin: Mouton de Gruyter.

Rosch, Eleanor. 1975. Cognitive representations of semantic categories. *Journal of Experimental Psychology: General*, 104: 192–233.

——1978. Principles of categorization. In E. Rosch and B. Lloyd (eds), *Cognition and Categorization*, 27–48. Hillsdale, NJ: Lawrence Erlbaum. [Reprinted in Aarts *et al.* (eds) (2004), 91–108.]

Rosch, Eleanor and Carolyn Mervis. 1975. Family resemblances: Studies in the internal structure of categories. *Cognitive Psychology*, 7: 575–605.

Rosenbach, Annette. 2007. Exploring constructions in the web: A case study. In Hundt, Nesselhauf, and Biewer (eds) (2007), 167–89.

Ross, Brian H. and Valarie S. Makin. 1999. Prototype versus exemplar models. In R. J. Steinberg (ed.), *The Nature of Cognition*, 205–41. Cambridge, MA: MIT Press.

Rothkopf, Ernst Z. 1971. Incidental memory for location of information in text. *Journal of Verbal Learning and Verbal Behavior*, 10: 608–13.

Rudzka-Ostyn, Brygida. 2003. *Word Power: Phrasal Verbs and Compounds: A Cognitive Approach*. Berlin: Mouton de Gruyter.

Ruhl, Charles. 1989. *On Monosemy: A Study in Linguistic Semantics*. Albany, NY: State University of New York Press.

Ruwet, Nicolas. 1982. Grammaire des insultes. In *Grammaire des insultes et autres études*, 239–314. Paris: Éditions du Seuil.

——1991. On the use and abuse of idioms in syntactic argumentation. In *Syntax and Human Experience*, ed. and trans. John Goldsmith, 171–251. Chicago: University of Chicago Press.

Sachs, Jacqueline. 1967. Recognition memory for syntactic and semantic aspects of connected discourse. *Perception and Psychophysics*, 2: 437–42.

——1974. Memory in reading and listening to discourse. *Memory and Cognition*, 2: 95–100.

Saffran, Jenny R. 2001a. The use of predictive dependencies in language learning. *Journal of Memory and Language*, 44: 493–515.

——2001b. Words in a sea of sounds: The output of infant statistical leaning. *Cognition*, 81: 149–69.

——2002. Constraints on statistical language learning. *Journal of Memory and Language*, 47: 172–96.

Saffran, Jenny R., Richard N. Aslin, and Elissa L. Newport. 1996. Statistical learning by 8-month-old infants. *Science*, New series, 274 (5294): 1926–8.

Sampson, Geoffrey. 1999. *Educating Eve*. London: Cassell.

——2007. Grammar without grammaticality. *Corpus Linguistics and Linguistic Theory*, 3: 1–32.

Sandra, Dominiek and Sally Rice. 1995. Network analyses of prepositional meaning: Mirroring whose mind—the linguist's or the language user's? *Cognitive Linguistics*, 6: 89–130.

Sapir, Edward. 1921. *Language: An Introduction to the Study of Speech*. New York: Harcourt, Brace & World.

Saussure, Ferdinand de. 1964. *Cours de linguistique générale*. Paris: Payot. [First published 1916. Trans. R. Harris, as *Course in General Linguistics*. London: Duckworth (1983).]

Savage, Ceri, Elena Lieven, Anna Theakston, and Michael Tomasello. 2006. Structural priming as implicit learning in language acquisition: The persistence of lexical and structural priming in 4-year-olds. *Language Learning and Development*, 2: 27–49.

Savin, Harris B. 1963. Word frequency effect and errors in the perception of speech. *Journal of the Acoustical Society of America*, 35: 200–6.

Savin, Harris B. and Thomas G. Bever. 1970. The nonperceptual reality of the phoneme. *Journal of Verbal Learning and Verbal Behavior*, 9: 295–302.

Schacter, Daniel L. 1987. Implicit memory: History and current status. *Journal of Experimental Psychology: Learning, Memory, and Cognition*, 13: 501–18.

Schmidt, Richard. 1990. The role of consciousness in second language learning. *Applied Linguistics*, 11: 129–58.

Schmitt, Norbert and Bruce Dunham. 1999. Exploring native and non-native intuitions of word frequency. *Second Language Research*, 15: 389–411.

Scholz, Barbara and Geoffrey Pullum. 2002. Searching for arguments to support linguistic nativism. *The Linguistic Review*, 19: 185–223.

Schütze, Carson. 1996. *The Empirical Base of Linguistics: Grammaticality Judgments and Linguistic Methodology*. Chicago: University of Chicago Press.

Searle, John. 1980. The background of meaning. In John Searle, Ferenc Kiefer, and Manfred Bierwisch (eds), *Speech Act Theory and Pragmatics*, 221–32. Dordrecht: Reidel.

——1983. *Intentionality*. Cambridge: Cambridge University Press.

Segui, J., U. Frauenfelder, and J. Mehler. 1981. Phoneme monitoring, syllable monitoring and lexical access. *British Journal of Psychology*, 72: 471–7.

Sereno, Joan and Allard Jongman. 1990. Phonological and form class relations in the lexicon. *Journal of Psycholinguistic Research*, 19: 387–404.

——1997. Processing of English inflectional morphology. *Memory and Cognition*, 25: 427–37.

Shannon, Claude and Warren Weaver. 1963. *The Mathematical Theory of Communication*. Urbana IL: University of Illinois Press. [First published 1949.]

Shapiro, Bernard J. 1969. The subjective estimation of relative word frequency. *Journal of Verbal Learning and Verbal Behavior*, 8: 248–51.

Sichel, Herbert. 1975. On a distribution law for word frequencies. *Journal of the American Statistical Association*, 70: 542–7.

Sinclair, John. 1991. *Corpus, Concordance, Collocation*. Oxford: Oxford University Press.

——2004. *Trust the Text: Language, Corpus and Discourse*. London: Routledge.

Slobin, Dan. 2006. What makes manner of motion salient? Explorations in linguistic typology, discourse, and cognition. In Maya Hickmann and Stéphane Robert (eds), *Space in Languages: Linguistic Systems and Cognitive Categories*, 59–81. Amsterdam: Benjamins.

Smith, Edward E. and Douglas L. Medin. 1981. *Categories and Concepts*. Cambridge, MA: Harvard University Press.

Smith, Michael. 2009. The semantics of complementation in English: A cognitive semantic account of two English complement constructions. *Language Sciences*, 31: 360–88.

Snyder, William. 2000. An experimental investigation of syntactic satiation effects. *Linguistic Inquiry*, 31: 575–82.

Sosa, Anna Vogel and James MacFarlane. 2002. Evidence for frequency-based constituents in the mental lexicon: Collocations involving *of*. *Brain and Language*, 83: 227–36.

Stefanowitsch, Anatol. 2005. New York, Dayton (Ohio), and the raw frequency fallacy. *Corpus Linguistics and Linguistic Theory*, 1: 295–301.

——2007. Linguistics beyond grammaticality. *Corpus Linguistics and Linguistic Theory*, 3: 57–71.

Stefanowitsch, Anatol and Stefan Th. Gries. 2003. Collostructions: Investigating the interaction of words and constructions. *International Journal of Corpus Linguistics*, 8: 209–43.

Stemberger, Joseph Paul. 1982. Syntactic errors in speech. *Journal of Psycholinguistic Research*, 11: 313–45.

Stern, Gustaf. 1931. *Meaning and Change of Meaning*. Bloomington: Indiana University Press.

Stevens, Kenneth N. 1972. The quantal nature of speech: Evidence from articulatory–acoustic data. In Edward E. David and Peter B. Denes (eds), *Human Communication: A Unified View*, 51–66. New York: McGraw-Hill.

Stoel-Gammon, Carol and Joseph Paul Stemberger. 1994. Consonant harmony and phonological underspecification in child speech. In Mehmet Yavaş (ed.), *First and Second Language Phonology*, 63–80. San Diego: Singular Publishing.

Stubbs, Michael. 1995. Corpus evidence for norms of lexical collocation. In Guy Cook and Barbara Seidlhofer (eds), *Principle and Practice in Applied Linguistics*, 245–56. Oxford: Oxford University Press.

——2009. The search for units of meaning: Sinclair on empirical semantics. *Applied Linguistics*, 30: 115–37.

Sweetser, Eve. 1987. The definition of 'lie': An examination of folk models underlying a semantic prototype. In Dorothy Holland and Naomi Quinn (eds), *Cultural Models in Language and Thought*, 43–66. Cambridge: Cambridge University Press.

Szmrecsanyi, Benedikt. 2005. Language users as creatures of habit: A corpus-based analysis of persistence in spoken English. *Corpus Linguistics and Linguistic Theory*, 1: 111–50.

——2006. *Morphosyntactic Persistence in Spoken English: A Corpus Study*. Berlin: Mouton de Gruyter.

Taatgen, Niels. 2001. Extending the past-tense debate: A model of the German plural. In J. D. Moore and K. Stenning (eds), *Proceedings of the Twenty-third Annual Conference of the Cognitive Science Society*, 1018–23. Mahweh, NJ: Erlbaum.

Talmy, Leonard. 1985. Lexicalization patterns: Semantic structure in lexical items. In T. Shopen (ed.), *Language Typology and Lexical Description, vol. 3: Grammatical Categories and the Lexicon*, 57–149. Cambridge: Cambridge University Press.

Tambovtsev, Yuri and Colin Martindale. 2007. Phoneme frequencies follow a Yule distribution. *SKASE Journal of Theoretical Linguistics*, 4 (2) (available at: www.skase.sk/Volumes/JTL09/pdf_doc/1.pdf).

Tao, Hongyin. 2003. A usage-based approach to argument structure. *International Journal of Corpus Linguistics*, 8: 75–95.

Taylor, John R. 1988. Contrasting prepositional categories: English and Italian. In Brygida Rudzka-Ostyn (ed.), *Topics in Cognitive Linguistics*, 299–326. Amsterdam: Benjamins.

——1992a. How many meanings does a word have? *SPIL* (= Stellenbosch Papers in Linguistics), 25: 133–63.

——1992b. Old problems: Adjectives in Cognitive Grammar. *Cognitive Linguistics*, 3: 1–46.

——1993. Prepositions: Patterns of polysemization and strategies of disambiguation. In Cornelia Zelinksky-Wibbelt (ed.), *The Semantics of Prepositions*, 151–75. Berlin: Mouton de Gruyter.

——1994. The two-level approach to meaning. *Linguistische Berichte*, 149: 3–26.

——1996. *Possessives in English: An Exploration in Cognitive Grammar*. Oxford: Oxford University Press.

——1997. Double object constructions in Zulu. In John Newman (ed.), *The Linguistics of Giving*, 67–96. Amsterdam: Benjamins.

——1998. Syntactic constructions as prototype categories. In Michael Tomasello (ed.), *The New Psychology of Language*, 177–202. Mahwah, NJ: Lawrence Erlbaum.

——1999a. Cognitive semantics and structural semantics. In Andreas Blank and Peter Koch (eds), *Historical Semantics and Cognition*, 17–48. Berlin: Mouton de Gruyter.

——1999b. Review of Culicover (1999). *Cognitive Linguistics*, 10: 251–61.

Taylor, John R. 2002. *Cognitive Grammar*. Oxford: Oxford University Press.

——2003*a*. Cognitive models of polysemy. In Nerlich *et al.* (eds) (2003), 31–47.

——2003*b*. *Linguistic Categorization*, 3rd edn. Oxford: Oxford University Press. [First edition: 1989.]

——2003*c*. Polysemy's paradoxes. *Language Sciences*, 25: 637–55.

——2004*a*. The ecology of constructions. In Günter Radden and Klaus-Uwe Panther (eds), *Studies in Linguistic Motivation*, 49–73. Berlin: Mouton de Gruyter.

——2004*b*. Why construction grammar is radical. *Annual Review of Cognitive Linguistics*, 2: 321–48.

——Motivation. In *JCLA 6* (= Proceedings of the Sixth Annual Meeting of the Japanese Cognitive Linguistics Association), 486–502.

——2006*b*. Polysemy and the lexicon. In Gitte Kristiansen, Michel Achard, René Dirven, and Francisco Ruiz de Mendoza Ibáñez (eds), *Cognitive Linguistics: Current Applications and Future Perspectives*, 51–80. Berlin: Mouton de Gruyter.

——2006*c*. Where do phonemes come from? A view from the bottom. *International Journal of English Studies*, 6: 19–54.

——2007. Cognitive linguistics and autonomous linguistics. In Geeraerts and Cuyckens (eds) (2007), 566–88.

——2008. Prototypes in cognitive linguistics. In Robinson and Ellis (2008), 39–65.

——2010. Language in the mind. In Sabine De Knop, Frank Boers, and Teun De Ryker (eds), *Fostering Language Teaching Efficiency through Cognitive Linguistics*, 29–58. Berlin: Mouton de Gruyter.

Taylor, John R. and Kam-yiu Pang. 2008. Seeing as though. *English Language and Linguistics*, 12: 1–37.

Taylor, Wilson L. 1953. Cloze procedure: A new tool for measuring readability. *Journalism Quarterly*, 30: 415–33.

Thorndike, Edward L. and Irving Lorge. 1944. *The Teacher's Word Book of 30,000 Words*. New York: Columbia University Press.

Tomasello, Michael. 2003. *Constructing a Language: A Usage-Based Theory of Language Acquisition*. Cambridge, MA: Harvard University Press.

——2006. Construction grammar for kids. *Constructions*, 1/2006. urn:nbn:de:0009-4-6893 (available at: www.constructions-online.de).

Tomasello, Michael and Daniel Stahl. 2004. Sampling children's spontaneous speech: How much is enough? *Journal of Child Language*, 31: 101–21.

Trueswell, John. 1996. The role of lexical frequency in syntactic ambiguity resolution. *Journal of Memory and Language*, 35: 566–85.

Trueswell, John, Michael K. Tannenhaus, and Cristopher Kello. 1993. Verb specific constraints in sentence processing: Separating effects of lexical preference from garden-paths. *Journal of Experimental Psychology: Leaning, Memory, and Cognition*, 19: 528–53.

Truscott, John. 1998. Noticing in second language acquisition: A critical review. *Second Language Acquisition*, 14: 103–35.

Tryk, H. Edward. 1968. Subjective scaling of word frequency. *American Journal of Psychology*, 81: 170–7.

Tuggy, David. 1996. The thing is is that people talk that way: The question is is Why? In Eugene Casad (ed.), *Cognitive Linguistics in the Redwoods*, 713–52. Berlin: Mouton de Gruyter.

——2003. The Nawatl verb *kīsa*: A case study in polysemy. In Cuyckens, Dirven, and Taylor (eds) (2003), 323–62.

Tversky, Amos and Daniel Kahneman. 1973. Availability: A heuristic for judging frequency and probability. *Cognitive Psychology*, 5: 207–32.

Tyler, Andrea and Vyvyan Evans. 2001. Reconsidering prepositional polysemy networks: The case of over. *Language*, 77: 724–65. [Reprinted as 'The case of over'. In Nerlich *et al.* (eds) (2003), 99–159.]

Van der Gucht, Fieke, Klaas Willems, and Ludovic De Cuypere. 2007. The iconicity of embodied meaning: Polysemy of spatial prepositions in the cognitive framework. *Language Sciences*, 29: 733–54.

Vandeloise, Claude. 1990. Representation, prototypes, and centrality. In Savas Tsohatzidis (ed.), *Meanings and Prototypes*, 403–37. London: Routledge.

Verhagen, Arie. 2005. *Constructions of Intersubjectivity: Discourse, Syntax, and Cognition*. Oxford: Oxford University Press.

Vervaeke, John and John M. Kennedy. 1996. Metaphors in language and thought: Falsification and multiple meanings. *Metaphor and Symbolic Activity*, 11: 273–84.

Wells, John. 1982. *Accents of English*, vol. I. Cambridge: Cambridge University Press.

Wells, Rulon. 1957. Immediate constituents. In Martin Joos (ed.), *Readings in Linguistics 1*, 186–207. Chicago: University of Chicago Press. [First published in *Language*, 23 (1947): 81–117.]

——1973. Predicting slips of the tongue. In Fromkin (ed.) (1973), 82–7.

Werker, Janet F. 2003. The acquisition of language specific phonetic categories in infancy. *Proceedings of the 15th International Congress of Phonetic Sciences*, 21–6. Adelaide: Causal Productions.

Werker, Janet F. and Richard C. Tees. 1984. Cross-language speech perception: Evidence for perceptual reorganization during the first year of life. *Infant Behavior and Development*, 7: 49–63.

Wheeler, Cathy J. and Donald A. Schumsky. 1980. The morpheme boundaries of some English derivational suffixes. *Glossa*, 14: 3–34.

Wierzbicka, Anna. 1988a. Oats and wheat: Mass nouns, iconicity, and human categorization. In Wierzbicka (1988c), 499–560.

——1988b. The semantics of English complementation in a cross-linguistic perspective. In Wierzbicka (1988c), 23–168.

——1988c. *The Semantics of Grammar*. Amsterdam: Benjamins.

——1990. 'Prototypes save': On the uses and abuses of the notion of 'prototype' in linguistics and related fields. In Savas Tsohatzidis (ed.), *Meanings and Prototypes: Studies in Linguistic Categorization*, 347–67. London: Routledge.

——1991. *Cross-Cultural Pragmatics: The Semantics of Human Interaction*. Berlin: Mouton de Gruyter.

——1996. *Semantics: Primes and Universals*. Oxford: Oxford University Press.

Wilson, Michael P. and Susan M. Garnsey. 2008. Making simple sentences hard: Verb bias effects in simple direct object sentences. *Journal of Memory and Language*, 60: 368–92.

Wischer, Ilse. 2000. Grammaticalization versus lexicalization: 'Methinks' there is some confusion. In Olga Fischer, Anette Rosenbach, and Dieter Stein (eds), *Pathways of Change: Grammaticalization in English*, 355–70. Amsterdam: Benjamins.

Wittgenstein, Ludwig. 1958. *The Blue and Brown Books*. Oxford: Blackwell.

Yeh, Wenchi and Lawrence Barsalou. 2006. The situated nature of concepts. *American Journal of Psychology*, 119: 349–84.

Zeschel, Arne. 2008. Lexical chunking effects in syntactic processing. *Cognitive Linguistics*, 19: 427–46.

Zipf, George K. 1935. *The Psycho-Biology of Language: An Introduction to Dynamic Philology*. Houghton Mifflin.

Zlatev, Jordan. 2003. Polysemy or generality? Mu. In Cuyckens, Dirven, and Taylor (eds) (2003), 447–94.

Zwaan, Rolf. 2004. The immersed experiencer: Toward an embodied theory of language comprehension. In B. H. Ross (ed.), *The Psychology of Learning and Motivation*, 35–62. New York: Academic Press.

Subject index

Index of names